Designing History in East Asian Textbooks

Identity politics and transnational aspirations

This book analyses the efforts throughout East Asia to deploy education for purposes of political socialisation and, in particular, in order to shape notions of identity. The chapters also examine the trend of 'common textbook initiatives', which have recently emerged in East Asia with the aim of helping to defuse tensions arguably fuelled by existing practices of mutual (mis)-representation. These are analysed in relation to the East Asian political context and compared with previous and ongoing endeavours in other parts of the world, particularly Europe, which have been keenly observed by East Asian practitioners. Written by a group of international education experts, chapters discuss the enduring focus on the role of curricula in inculcating homogenous visions of the national self and, indeed, homogenised visions of significant 'others'.

Including contributions from scholars and curriculum developers involved personally in the writing of national and multinational history textbooks, this book will be of interest to students and scholars of Asian education, Asian history and comparative education studies.

Gotelind Müller is Professor of Chinese studies, University of Heidelberg, Germany.

Routledge Studies in Education and Society in Asia
Edited by Edward Vickers
Institute of Education, University of London, UK

This series focuses on analyses of educational practices and structures in Asia in their broader social, cultural, political and economic context. The volumes further our understanding of why education systems have developed in particular ways and examine to what extent and why education in Asia is distinctive.

Designing History in East Asian Textbooks
Identity politics and transnational aspirations
Edited by Gotelind Müller

Designing History in East Asian Textbooks
Identity politics and transnational aspirations

**Edited by
Gotelind Müller**

LONDON AND NEW YORK

First published 2011
by Routledge
2 Park Square, Milton Park, Abingdon, Oxon OX14 4RN

Simultaneously published in the USA and Canada
by Routledge
711 Third Avenue, New York, NY10017

*Routledge is an imprint of the Taylor & Francis Group,
an informa business*

© 2011 Editorial selection and matter Gotelind Müller;
individual chapters, the contributors.

First issued in paperback 2013

The right of Gotelind Müller to be identified as editor of this
work has been asserted by her in accordance with the Copyright,
Designs and Patent Act 1988.

Typeset in Times New Roman by
Florence Production Ltd, Stoodleigh, Devon

All rights reserved. No part of this book may be reprinted or
reproduced or utilised in any form or by any electronic,
mechanical, or other means, now known or hereafter
invented, including photocopying and recording, or in any
information storage or retrieval system, without permission in
writing from the publishers.

British Library Cataloguing in Publication Data
A catalogue record for this book is available
from the British Library

Library of Congress Cataloging in Publication Data
  Designing history in East Asian textbooks: identity politics and
transnational aspirations/edited by Gotelind Müller.
     p. cm. – (Routledge studies in education and society in Asia ; 1)
  Includes bibliographical references and index.
  1. East Asia – History – Textbooks. 2. East Asia – History – Study
and teaching – China. 3. East Asia – History – Study and teaching
– Japan. 4. East Asia – History – Study and teaching – Taiwan.
5. East Asia – History – Study and teaching – Korea (South)
6. Education and state – East Asia. 7. Education and state – China.
8. Education and state – Japan. 9. Education and state – Taiwan.
10. Education and state – Korea (South)   I. Müller, Gotelind.
DS510.7.D47 2011
950.071–dc22   2010033501

ISBN 978–0–415–60252–5 (hbk)
ISBN 978–0–415–85558–7 (pbk)

Publication of this volume was generously funded by the Deutsche Forschungsgemeinschaft (German Research Foundation) within the Cluster of Excellence 270/1 'Asia and Europe in a Global Context' at the University of Heidelberg.

Permissions have been granted by the journal *Kaifang Shidai* (Chapter 1), the National Taiwan History Museum and the National Institute of Compilation and Translation (Chapter 5), and Nanam Press (Chapter 10).

Contents

Notes on contributors ix
Acknowledgements xiii

Introduction 1
GOTELIND MÜLLER

PART I
Contesting East Asia, identities and education:
historical contingencies 7

1 The predicament of compiling textbooks on the history of East Asia 9
   SUN GE

2 Teaching 'the others' history' in Chinese schools: the state, cultural asymmetries and shifting images of Europe (from 1900 to today) 32
   GOTELIND MÜLLER

3 The construction of 'self' and Western and Asian 'others' in contemporary Japanese civics and ethics textbooks 60
   KLAUS VOLLMER

4 Learning to love the motherland: 'National Education' in post-retrocession Hong Kong 85
   EDWARD VICKERS

5 Telling histories of an island nation: the academics and politics of history textbooks in contemporary Taiwan 117
   LUNG-CHIH CHANG

PART II
History writing in school textbooks: practical considerations   135

6   New curriculum reform and history textbook compilation in contemporary China   137
LI FAN

7   The 'others' in Chinese history textbooks: a focus on the relationship between China and Japan   147
SU ZHILIANG

8   Rewriting history in a textbook in contemporary Japan   163
MIYAKE AKIMASA

PART III
Self-assertion, revisionism and historical reconciliation: conflicts and perspectives   181

9   The 'Tokyo Trial view of history' and its revision in contemporary Japan/East Asia   183
STEFFI RICHTER

10   Historical conflict and dialogue between Korea and Japan: a focus on Japanese history textbooks   207
CHUNG JAE-JEONG

11   Historical reconciliation between Germany and Poland as seen from a Japanese perspective: the thoughts of a Japanese historian and their development   229
KAWATE KEIICHI

12   Mediating textbook conflicts   245
FALK PINGEL

Concluding remarks   277
GOTELIND MÜLLER

Index   283

Notes on contributors

Lung-chih Chang, assistant research fellow and the chairperson of the cultural history research group of the Institute of Taiwan History, Academia Sinica, Taiwan. His research interests include the social and cultural history of Taiwan, comparative colonialism in East Asia and contemporary Taiwanese historiography. His major publications include *Ethnicity and rural Taiwan* (in Chinese, National Taiwan University Press, 1991) and 'From island frontier to imperial colony' (Ph.D. dissertation, Harvard University, 2003). His most recent project is a monograph on Japanese colonial knowledge formation and cultural politics in early twentieth-century Taiwan.

Chung Jae-jeong, Ph.D., professor of history and dean of the College of Humanities at the University of Seoul. His special interest is in the history of Korean–Japanese relations. He currently serves as president of the Northeast Asian History Foundation. He has been a coordinator of the Korean historians' group discussing historical issues with Japanese historians and has headed an earlier joint Korean–Japanese committee set up to discuss historical reconciliation. Among the books he has authored are: *Japanese colonial control over Korean railroads and the Korean people's response (1892–1945)* (published in Korean and in Japanese); *A new history of nineteenth and twentieth-century Korea* (in Japanese); *The teaching of Japanese history in Korea* (in Japanese); *The teaching of Korean history in Japan* (in Korean); *The history of Korean–Japanese relations as seen from Kyoto* (in Korean).

Kawate Keiichi, professor of European modern history at Tokyo Gakugei University. His main field of research is German modern history. Recent publications include: '*"Foruku" to seinen – mainoriti mondai to doitsu seinen undō* ['*Volk*' and German youth – the Germans as an ethnic minority and the German youth movement]', in Tamura Eiko and Hoshino Haruhiko (eds), *Weimarer Republik als ein Leuchtstrahl* (Kyoto: Shōwadō, 2007, 117–59); *"Mainoriti mondai to Foruku no shisō* [The Germans as an ethnic minority and the idea of 'Volk']", in I. Sadayoshi and M. Hirata (eds), *Kindai Yōroppa o Yomitoku* [*Deciphering modern Europe*] (Kyoto: Mineruva shobō, 2008, 289–325); "*20 seiki Doitsu ni okeru 'Sedai' no* *mondai* ['Generation' in Germany of the twentieth century]", in *Rekishi hyōron* (*Journal of Historical Science*), 698, (2008/6): 2–13.

Li Fan, professor of history and vice president of the History School at Beijing Normal University, China. His main field of research is modern Chinese history and Chinese history textbooks and curricula. He has published extensively and has received various university and national awards. His major publications include *Liu Shipei and the academic study of China and the West* (Beijing: Beijing Normal University Press, 2003, in Chinese), *Chinese academic study: between classics and modernity* (Seoul: New Star Press, 2004, in Chinese) and *Studies in the works of Qing-period academic history of Zhang Taiyan, Liu Shipei and Liang Qichao* (Beijing: Commercial Press, 2006, in Chinese). He has recently authored a high school textbook on modern Chinese history.

Miyake Akimasa, professor of history at Chiba University. His main research field is modern Japanese history. His present project is on the transformation of labour relations in post-war Japan. Publications include: (editor) *Rekishi no naka no genzai [Past and present] Tenbō Nihon rekishi,* vol. 23 (Tokyo: Tōkyōdo Shuppan, 2004); *Sekai no ugoki no naka de yomu Nihon no rekishi kyōkasho mondai* [*Reading the issue of Japanese history textbooks within the context of global trends*] (Tokyo: Nashinokisha, 2002); (co-editor) *Rekishi no naka no sabetsu* [*Discrimination in history*] (Tokyo: Nihon keizai hyōronsha, 2001); *Reddo pāji to wa nani ka* [*The red purge: Japanese labor relations under the occupation*] (Tokyo: Otsuki shoten, 1994); (co-editor) *Nihonshi A* [*Japanese high school textbook of Japanese history*] (Tokyo: Tōkyō shoseki, 1994–2009).

Gotelind Müller-Saini, professor of Chinese studies, University of Heidelberg; vice dean of the faculty of philosophy. Her main research interests are modern Chinese history and history of ideas, and Sino–Japanese cultural exchange. She has authored several books, including her published Ph.D. thesis on Buddhism and modernity in early twentieth-century China (in German) and her published habilitation monograph on China, Kropotkin and anarchism (in German). Her most recent monograph is: *Representing history in Chinese media: the TV drama 'Zou Xiang Gonghe' (Towards the republic)* (Berlin: LIT, 2007). Her scholarly articles include discussions of Chinese history textbook design and the formation of Chinese historical consciousness.

Falk Pingel, Ph.D., was for many years the deputy director of the Georg Eckert Institute for International Textbook Research in Braunschweig, Germany. In 2003–4, he was the first director of the OSCE's education department in Sarajevo, Bosnia and Herzegovina. He also taught contemporary history, as well as theory and didactics of history at Bielefeld University and served as guest lecturer abroad, in particular in Israel, Southeastern Europe and at the East China Normal University in Shanghai. He has conducted comparative textbook projects, among others, in Israel–Palestine, East Asia, South Africa and the Balkans. He is a consultant on issues of textbook and curriculum research and revision to international organisations such as UNESCO and the Council of Europe. Among his publications are: *UNESCO guidebook on international textbook research and textbook revision,* 2nd, revised and extended edition (Braunschweig, Paris: Georg Eckert Institute/UNESCO, 2009); (editor) *Contested past, disputed present. Curricula and teaching in Israeli and Palestinian schools* (Hannover: Verlag Hahnsche Buchhandlung, 2003); *The European home: representations of twentieth-century Europe in history textbooks* (Strasbourg: Council of Europe, 2000).

Steffi Richter, professor of Japanese studies at the East Asian Institute, University of Leipzig. Her fields of research include history writing in Japan/East Asia, as well as cultural studies (consumption culture and modern identities) and the intellectual history of modern Japan. She is co-editor of the series *Leipziger Ostasien-Studien* (former *Mitteldeutsche Studien zu Ostasien*). Her publications include: *Ent-Zweiung. Wissenschaftliches Denken in Japan zwischen Tradition und Moderne* (1994); *Japan Lesebuch III: Intelli* (1996); *Cultural studies in Japan* (2001) (co-edited and co-authored); *Vergangenheit im Gesellschaftskonflikt* (2003) (co-edited and co-authored); *Reading Manga: local and global perceptions of Japanese comics* (2006) (co-edited and co-authored); *J-Culture. Japan-Lesebuch IV* (2008) (co-edited and co-authored); *Contested views of a common past. Revisions of history in contemporary East Asia* (2008, as a result of the Volkswagen Foundation-funded project 'Self-determination, image of "self" and "other": Reconstructing identities and revising history in East Asia since the 1980s') (edited and co-authored).

Su Zhiliang, professor at Shanghai Normal University, is head of the school of humanities, Shanghai Normal University; deputy director of the Urban Culture Research Center at Shanghai Normal University (Chinese Ministry of Education Research Base); editor of Shanghai secondary school history textbooks; vice president of the Historical Society of Shanghai; deputy director of the Research Center of Modern Shanghai Society; and council member of the Chinese Historical Society. He has published more than twenty books in Chinese, including *History of drugs in China*; *A brief history of China*; and *Research on comfort women*. He has edited five sets of Shanghai secondary school history textbooks.

Sun Ge, professor at the Institute of Literature, Chinese Academy of Social Sciences, Ph.D. in Political Science. She has been part of a joint Sino–Japanese group of scholars set up in the 1990s, investigating the possibilities of a common 'East Asian' identity formation. Her main research areas are: the comparative intellectual history of China and Japan and the history of Japanese political thought. Recent projects deal with the formation of subjectivity in post-war Japan and the problem of conceptualising modernity in Japanese intellectual circles. Her main publications in Chinese include: *The space of a segmented subject – the dilemma in framing Asia* (Jiangxi Education Press, 2002); *The paradox of Takeuchi Yoshimi* (Beijing University Press, 2005); *The position of Literature* (Shandong Education Press, 2009). Her main publications in Japanese include: *Standing at the crossroads of history* (Nihon Keizai Hyōronsha, 2008); *Post-East-Asia* (co-editor) (Sakuhinsha, 2006); *The problem named Takeuchi Yoshimi* (Iwanami Shoten, 2005); *The dilemma in framing Asia* (Iwanami Shoten, 2002).

Edward Vickers, reader in education at the Institute of Education, University of London. His research focuses broadly on education and related social issues in Chinese societies (the mainland, Taiwan and Hong Kong), but he has a particular interest in the relationship between schooling and political socialisation, and in the role of museums as vehicles for state projects of identity formation. He is the author of *In search of an identity: the politics of history as a school subject in Hong Kong, 1960s-2005* (Routledge, 2002, 2nd edition CERC, 2005), and the co-editor of *History education and national identity in East Asia* and *Education as a political tool in Asia* (Routledge, 2009). His writings on education, cultural policy and the politics of identity in Taiwan include 'Re-writing museums in Taiwan', in the volume *Re-writing culture in Taiwan* (Routledge, 2009). He is currently working on a book entitled *Education and society in post-Mao China* (to be published by Routledge in 2011), and an article on 'patriotic education', museums and tourism in Tibet, Xinjiang and Inner Mongolia. He is the general editor for the book series 'Routledge Studies in Education and Society in Asia'.

Klaus Vollmer, professor and chair of Japanese studies, Japan Center, University of Munich, holds an MA and a Ph.D. (1993) in Japanese studies from Hamburg University. He has been a post-doctoral research fellow at Osaka City University (1993–4) and grant student of the Deutsche Forschungsgemeinschaft (DFG). His post-doctoral thesis focused on prohibitions of killing and meat-eating in pre-modern Japan (Habilitation, 1997). In 2002 he was a Numata-fellow for studies in Japanese Buddhism. His fields of research and teaching include a broad range of issues in the cultural and social history of Japan (both pre-modern and modern), in particular, self-images, representations and interpretations of Japanese culture and society, the history of discrimination and outcaste status in Japan and representations of history and historiography in neo-nationalist discourse. English-language publications related to his chapter in this volume include: 'Images of Japanese society in the *New civics textbook:* neo-nationalist antidotes for demographic challenges and social change', in *Japanstudien. Jahrbuch des Deutschen Instituts für Japanstudien*, vol. 19 (2007), 221–41.

Acknowledgements

For making this volume possible, I would like to express my huge debt to several institutions and people (apologies to all not named explicitly, but nevertheless included in my heartfelt thanks): without the Cluster of Excellence on 'Asia and Europe in a Global Context' at Heidelberg University, funded by the German Research Foundation (DFG), there would not have been the conference this volume grew out of. Many thanks are due to the extended steering committee that favourably evaluated the project application. I also gratefully acknowledge all the practical help of those people involved in the administration of the cluster at the time, namely Dr Brigitte Merz, Anja Bunnefeld and Anette Kobler. I also thank the IWH (Internationales Wissenschaftsforum Heidelberg) and Dr Ellen Peerenboom for enabling us to hold our conference in a very pleasant atmosphere. When I say 'our' conference here, I not only think of all the participants who are represented in this volume, but, above all, of my colleague in Japanese studies and dear friend Wolfgang Seifert, who helped me prepare the conference but was prevented by his failing health from contributing to this volume and its editing. I feel very sorry for this and want to give him heartfelt, special thanks for his support throughout, with all best wishes for a quick recovery. Many thanks also to Wolfgang's and my research students Xu Miao, Nakada Yuka, Alexander Quaas and Juljan Biontino, who not only shouldered a lot of the organisational work but also, in some cases, time-consuming translations. For spontaneous help with translation work during the conference, I also thank Jan Schmidt and Sarah Lüdecke, and I would like to thank Urs Matthias Zachmann and Thomas Büttner for enriching our conference with their contributions. In preparing the volume, I could not have done it without Subei Wu and, above all, Daniela Schaaf, who patiently got everything in the right format, checked details and translations over months and compiled the index. I would also like to acknowledge Andrea Hacker's help with two chapters. A special thanks go to Ed Vickers for proposing this volume for the series 'Routledge Studies in Education and Society in Asia' and for always being there with needed advice. A word of gratitude is also due to the two anonymous reviewers and their helpful suggestions. Finally, Stephanie Rogers and Ed Needle of Routledge and Charlotte Hiorns and Louise Smith of Florence Production were instrumental in getting the volume to where it is now. Many thanks to them for their very professional handling of the manuscript, their patience and unfailing good humour. I know that this volume would not exist but for all this great support.

Gotelind Müller
Heidelberg, July 2010

Introduction[1]

Gotelind Müller

In East Asia, national history textbooks have become a particularly sensitive topic in recent years. Though history is not the only school subject related to official projects of identity formation, it is often the prime curricular vehicle for official programmes of political socialisation. Thus, discussion of recent East Asian history textbooks frequently centres on attempts by the state to define or shape national 'memory', the related politics of identity and a consequent 'whitewashing' of the historical narrative to produce an image of the nation 'untainted' by any problematic episodes.[2] At the same time, history textbooks and the pedagogical discourses surrounding their design and use reflect the increasingly global flow of concepts and ideals, as evidenced by the extent to which recent East Asian debates over history teaching and curriculum development have been influenced by Western models, particularly as Asian states attempt to borrow elements of Western pedagogical practice seen as promoting 'creativity' or skills of 'critical thinking' crucial to success in the 'global knowledge economy'. Efforts to reconcile Western (frequently European) trends in history education (such as an emphasis on the use of primary sources, the promotion of skills of analysis and the role of history education and joint textbook initiatives in furthering regional unity) with the strongly nationalistic and moralising approaches to history education common throughout East Asia have given rise to growing tensions and contradictions in national agendas for history teaching and related programmes of 'nation-building education'.

This volume brings together analyses by leading Asian and European scholars of state-directed efforts throughout contemporary East Asia to deploy education for purposes of political socialisation – particularly in order to shape notions of identity – with reflections by practitioners in the field of textbook production. A number of chapters discuss the enduring focus in East Asia on the role of curricula for history and related school subjects in inculcating rigid, homogenous and totalist visions of the national 'self', defined in opposition to equally rigid and homogenised visions of significant 'others'. However, several chapters also deal with alternative approaches to textbook design, including the new trend of 'common textbook initiatives', that have recently emerged in East Asia with the aim of helping to defuse tensions arguably fuelled by existing practices of mutual (mis)representation. These trends are analysed in relation to the East Asian political context and compared with previous or ongoing endeavours in other parts of the world, particularly Europe,[3] that have been keenly observed by East Asian practitioners. The present volume largely focuses on this shift, with the aim of offering a new perspective on East Asia's textbook controversies. It also breaks new ground in this field by including contributions from scholars and curriculum developers involved personally in the writing of national and multinational history textbooks. This combination of reflections on practice by individuals in the 'front line' of East Asian curriculum development, with scholarly analysis of textbook issues and related official representations of the past from a variety of disciplinary perspectives (area studies, history, education, political science), bridges the usual gap between practitioners and the academic discourse on their practice. In doing so, this volume offers fresh insights into the history of education's role (through school textbooks and other official media) in political socialisation throughout East Asia and the challenges and tensions that confront current trends and developments in this field.

The volume is divided into three parts: the first, on the historical contingencies that frame contestations of views on East Asia, identity and education, raises a host of questions and problems that the creation of national and regional history poses. This part opens with a theoretical reflection by Sun on the challenges confronting the recent endeavours to come to a common understanding of what a history of 'East Asia' might mean. Sun, herself involved in trinational (Chinese/Korean/Japanese) academic groups convened to explore the possibility of consensus over a broad 'East Asian' historical narrative, discusses the context of these initiatives and the difficulties they face as a result of the various countries' differing historical experiences. Müller, a scholar in Chinese studies who has written on Chinese textbook design, takes up a similar, long-term perspective to evaluate the case of shifting images of 'self' and 'other' in Chinese curricula during the twentieth century, paying special attention to the image of 'Europe' and its possible influence on future conceptions of a regional history in East Asia. Vollmer, a scholar in Japanese studies who has written on Japanese neo-nationalist textbooks, complements this with an analysis, including visual arrangements, of Japanese civics textbooks, arguing for an enlargement of the heretofore exclusive focus on history to include also subjects such as civics as decisive for framing views on 'self' and 'other'. Vickers, a specialist on education and political socialisation in East Asia and former Hong Kong schoolteacher, adopts a similarly broad perspective in his analysis of the special case of Hong Kong identity and the shifts in the latter due to the 1997 retrocession. Here, the asymmetrical defining power relation becomes quite clear, with the moves since the 'handover' to encourage Hong Kong people to adopt a more politicised, state-oriented sense of Chinese identity via 'patriotic' education. Chang, a Taiwanese historian and textbook scholar, parallels these findings with his chapter on Taiwan and its hotly contested identity terrain, focusing on the debate sparked by a particular textbook on Taiwan. He shows how this debate reflects the extent of recent shifts in the identity consensus on the island, which is intimately related to broader changes in society and politics.

The second part follows up on these analyses and zooms in on the ways in which school textbooks design history in practice, covering also many practical problems of curriculum development to implement new educational approaches versus existing institutional structures and admission procedures. The chapter by Li, a noted historian, curriculum developer and author of a history textbook for nationwide use in the People's Republic of China, discusses the practical problems raised by China's textbook production and vetting systems, and issues arising from recent curricula changes connected to experiments with topical (rather than purely chronological) presentation of content, and the encouragement of international comparative perspectives vis-à-vis the traditional 'us' and 'them' divide. Su, a specialist in Sino-Japanese historical relations and regional history, as well as a prolific textbook author, contributes reflections on recent experiments in Shanghai with sets of history textbooks designed specifically for regional use, and explores the highly contested ways in which Japan is framed in Chinese textbooks as an 'other', offering his own solutions for reference. Miyake, a Japanese historian and co-author of a top-selling Japanese history textbook, parallels the Chinese case with an analysis of Japanese textbook production and procedures for having textbooks officially approved for use in schools, focusing on practical attempts to design modern history textbooks by integrating transnational elements, in particular giving 'others' a voice as well, and the challenges this involves for textbook authors.

Finally, in the third part, on self-assertion, revisionism and historical reconciliation, the volume focuses on the question of conflicts raised by national historical perspectives in international as well as intra-regional perceptions, and explores some possible strategies for overcoming such conflicts. Richter, a noted expert on Japanese history textbooks and revisionism, analyses a highly controversial, right-wing Japanese vision of East Asian history and Japan's role therein. She focuses in particular on the portrayal of the Tokyo Trial and convicted war criminals in Japanese right-wing materials, which, besides the notorious textbooks also include films – arguably a far more emotionally appealing medium for redefining the Japanese 'self' vis-à-vis Western (US) and Asian 'others'. Like other authors in this volume, she thus reminds us that analysis of textbooks should be informed by an awareness of the ways in which other media are deployed in attempts to shape views of the national past. Chung, a Korean historian, currently president of the Northeast Asian History Association (noted for its activities to further transnational regional approaches to history) and himself involved in Korean–Japanese textbook commissions, further analyses the phenomenon of right-wing revisionism in the context of recent Korean–Japanese textbook disputes. These have been sparked precisely by revisionist initiatives in Japan, and Chung analyses the background and causes leading to these rifts, and recent attempts at overcoming purely national historical perceptions in binational textbook projects. Kawate, a Japanese specialist in German history, in turn examines endeavours to find solutions for the continuing textbook tensions with comparative reference to the ongoing German–Polish common textbook enterprise, outlining differences from the East Asian case but also possible convergences. Pingel, a high-profile textbook expert and advisor to UNESCO on textbook questions, finally discusses general problems related to textbook disputes and possible strategies for pursuing mediation, drawing comparatively on several cases to generate suggestions for future efforts in this field.

This volume as a whole aims to provide a multifaceted and nuanced analysis of recent shifts in the portrayal of national 'selves' and of European and Asian 'others' in East Asian textbooks and related media, perceiving such portrayals not as culturally determined or rigidly 'fixed', but as the products of historically contingent cultural flows. Such shifts are closely connected to global and regional developments that arguably render conventional history writing more and more problematic. The contributions assembled in this volume integrate philological, historical and in some cases visual analyses of East Asian school textbooks (for history and related subjects) and the content of some other projects of public political socialisation. In focusing on the images of 'self' and 'other' conveyed in such material, the chapters home in on the sorts of issue that are typically the most internationally sensitive, but that – precisely because of their controversial nature – must be central to any efforts to build greater international understanding through school curricula, textbooks and other important media. Thus, in addition to looking back at what has already been done in East Asian textbook production (the focus of most existing scholarship), a number of contributors also ponder how new textbook designs could be envisaged (see, namely, the chapters by Li, Su, Miyake and Pingel). This is made possible by juxtaposing chapters by scholars analysing textbooks in the context of broader projects of political socialisation (those by Müller, Vollmer, Vickers, Chang, Li, Su, Richter, Chung, Kawate and Pingel) with others by authors personally involved in textbook production (Li, Su, Chung and Miyake), as well as contributions from key figures in East Asia's ongoing discussions over how to transcend nationalist histories by constructing 'common' historical narratives (Sun, Su, Miyake and Chung). Being written by authors involved on the ground, these contributions are based on experiences of the difficulties and challenges of textbook production, supplementing the perhaps more detached academic analyses with the perspectives of committed practitioners.

One inspiration for this volume has been the recent tendency to establish cross-national teams for designing history source books and textbooks from a multinational perspective, for use in two or more East Asian countries. Western precedents for such attempts are always lurking in the background (see the chapters by Su, Kawate and Pingel). An important question that arises out of such efforts to write 'new' history textbooks (whether in Europe or

Asia) is how (or whether) it is possible to reconcile conventional perceptions of national identity, rooted as they inevitably are in visions of the history of relations between a national 'self' and foreign 'others', with the project of promoting a genuinely transnational vision of the past (Miyake's chapter offers a concrete example of an endeavour to cope with these tensions). By putting together contributions by East Asian and European experts on East Asian history and education, with important comparative considerations added by an East Asian expert on European history (Kawate) and a European expert on international textbook studies in general (Pingel), we try to explore the ways in which European or Asian 'others' are integrated and represented in national (history) education, and how this could or should be reframed in a transnational perspective. This topic entails various questions: How are 'others' defined and evaluated in terms of historical narrative? How are 'others' integrated in terms of being represented in 'national' history? Who is defined as the most significant 'other' and why? What kinds of 'self' are aimed at, and how do debates over identity reflect social, cultural and political cleavages? And to what extent are aspects of the 'other' stressed as positive 'models' for the 'successful' development of one's own country, especially given the fact that, in some cases, the former enemy (Japan) has now come to be seen primarily as a model of 'Asian' modernity? To what extent are elements of a 'common' East Asian narrative (and 'global' or international perspectives more generally) implicit in the content of current textbooks? And, related to all of these questions, who is involved in the definition process and whose interests does it serve? To what extent does politics, both within individual East Asian states and in their relations with each other, either impede or foster the acceptance of plural readings of the past and their reflection in school curricula and other media directed at young people?

Europe and the US have played and arguably still play an important role in East Asian self-definitions (and vice versa), but in the post-Cold War world Asian neighbours are increasingly important 'others' as well, whether in the form of historical rivals, developmental models or something in between. The question thus entails the shifting representations, not only of the 'total other' (inter-regional) (see the chapters by Müller and Vollmer), but of the 'relative other' as well (intra-regional) (see chapters by Su, Richter and Vollmer). Such changes to perceptions of the identity and characteristics of the most significant 'others' inevitably involve a reconfiguration of the national (or sub-national) 'self' (see chapters by Vickers, Chang and Richter). A consequence of the ruptures caused by contested mutual representations, combined with economic developments that have added to rivalries but that also have reinforced the interdependency of East Asia's major societies (and thus arguably raised the incentive for elites to overcome mutual antagonisms), has been the recent endeavour to design bi- or trinational textbooks: Japanese–Korean and Chinese–Japanese–Korean. This attempts to overcome the traditional limitations of 'national' history education, thereby potentially relativising the importance of singular governments in defining 'history', 'self' and 'other' for their citizens (chapters by Sun, Su, Miyake and Chung). However, these new textbooks have thus far had only limited impact on the teaching of history in East Asia's national educational systems, and the prospects for any greater impact in the future remain to be seen.

Just because of this, comparing the shifting recreations of a 'self' and of 'others' in East Asian history textbooks between 'national', 'regional' or 'global' approaches is, we believe, not only a very salient topic but also helpful to answer the questions raised and to further the prospects of new-style textbooks to be conceptualised in an ever more transnational way.

Note on style: The single chapters are linked by a short editor's introduction (in italics). With Romanisation, we have adopted the current academic systems, except for Taiwan and Hong Kong, where other systems have been in use and names are more familiar in that spelling. In general, East Asian names are given in their original order, with the family name first.

Notes

1 I would like to thank Edward Vickers for his input.
2 Important work on these and related aspects has already been published also in Western languages. To name just a few recent titles: Vickers, E. and Jones, A. (eds) (2005) *History education and national identity in East Asia*, London and New York: Routledge; Saaler, S. (2005) *Politics, memory and public opinion: the history textbook controversy and Japanese society,* Munich: Iudicium; Richter, S. (ed.) (2008) *Contested views of a common past: revisions of history in contemporary East Asia,* Frankfurt and New York: Campus; Lall, M. and Vickers, E. (eds) (2009) *Education as a political tool in Asia*, London and New York: Routledge. More specifically on World War II: Hein, L. and Selden, M. (eds) (2000) *Censoring history. Citizenship and memory in Japan, Germany, and the United States*, Armonk and New York: M.E. Sharpe; Jager, S. and Mitter, R. (eds) (2007) *Ruptured histories: war, memory and the post–Cold War in Asia*, Cambridge, MA: Harvard University Press.
3 The most important, as already realised, case is the German–French joint history textbook *Geschichte/Histoire,* which is compatible with curriculum requirements in both Germany and France. (Up to now, two volumes of the projected total of three are already in use.)

I
Contesting East Asia, identities and education
Historical contingencies

1 The predicament of compiling textbooks on the history of East Asia[1]

Sun Ge

This chapter reflects on the difficulties faced by 'East Asians' themselves in conceptualising 'East Asia'. It discusses various possible visions of the 'East Asian' identity, reasons why consensus over regional identity and history has proved so elusive and how this lack of consensus has influenced recent attempts to devise a common history textbook for Korea, Japan and China. The author considers the political backgrounds to inner-East Asian exchanges on history, focusing on the different historical experiences which frame perceptions in these societies. Particular attention is devoted to analysing Chinese ambivalence regarding the concept of an integrated 'East Asia', and to discussing what conditions would need to be fulfilled in order to bridge the gulf dividing Chinese, Korean and Japanese historical consciousness, and to render consensus over these countries' common history achievable.

Is it possible for East Asia to have common history textbooks?

Actually, 'East Asia' as mentioned here is strictly confined to the region of Northeast Asia. However, this term does not cover all of Northeast Asia, as North Korea and Taiwan are often ignored because of regional politics. We might be aware of the fact that East Asia is used in general as a noun for the designation of mainland China, Japan and South Korea. Therefore, the attempt to compile a common history textbook of these three countries, which emerged several years ago, is undertaken in this region (Dongya 2005).

Compared with these geographic concerns, it is much more difficult to answer the following exigent question, which is frequently posed in the communications between Chinese, Japanese and Korean intellectuals: why does Chinese society lack a consciousness for Asia? Is it related to the Chinese consciousness of a great power? When compiling history textbooks for these three countries, we are confronted with these questions. Would the intellectuals and people of these three countries be able to reach a consensus on historical narrative? If not, what is the crux of the problem? On the face of it, it is about the difference in writing. However, the fundamental reason for their differences should be sought in their different epistemological approaches to history.

Accordingly, in order to fathom the problem of history textbooks, we must begin with discussions on the approaches to history.

The Chinese intellectuals who are engaged in research of international relationships often think that it is more important to focus on dialogues between East and West than to burden oneself with 'narrating East Asia', or that it would be more appropriate to work out other perspectives as called for by the urgency of reality. For instance, dialogues between Chinese, Russian and Indian intellectuals might be more realistic than dialogues within East Asia. The reason is that China, as a country bordering East Asia, South Asia, Western Asia and the seldom-mentioned 'North Asia', is difficult to situate completely within the frame of East Asia. Thus, why do we have to talk about 'East Asia'?

Indeed, tracing the emergence of the East Asia narrative in China, we find that it is not an outgrowth from its epistemic soil of knowledge, but rather is of a transplanted nature. There are two sides to this transplantation: first, the ideology of modernisation since the reform and opening up in China [i.e. since 1978, G.M.] makes it possible for Japan and South Korea (or the 'Four Asian Tigers') to become visible and enter into Chinese social discourse. Furthermore, thanks to the tendency towards economic integration, East Asia, which was far from being a homogeneous entity during the Cold War period, was now seen as one. The aggregate of research on East Asia in Japan and South Korea until now, together with the various funding agencies in these two countries that have made great efforts to promote projects of East Asia research, has exerted a huge influence over the Chinese 'East Asia narrative'.

Second, the framework of American area studies also plays a part. The perspective of an 'Asian-Pacific region' and the framework adopted by the East Asia departments in American universities make East Asia a relatively independent region. We can say that, in order to respond to new international trends, public criticism in China has also begun to take up East Asia as a theme and increasingly has treated it as properly a part of our consciousness all along.

Nevertheless, examining the East Asia narrative closely, we will find that the East Asia view that emerged in China is relatively 'weak'. However, this does not mean that the topic is not popular, nor that there is not enough output from research on East Asia as an 'organic unity'. Rather, it means that the research on East Asia has not reached a corresponding position on the epistemological level in the Chinese academic world. The research (in China) fails to take into consideration all the questions mentioned above as questions that must be confronted, and has hardly made any response to them. At the same time, because East Asia research is basically confined to the empirical level, and the ontological nature of the object of empirical research is seldom interrogated, consequently the positioning of East Asia research within the intellectual realm and on the level of the production of knowledge in China is vague and without the benefit of self-consciousness. In view of this basic situation, we can offer a sketch of the accepted views on East Asia at the present moment.

The view that enjoys the highest currency is the one articulated from the perspective of Confucianism. In a highly abstract way, this view takes China, the Korean peninsula and Japan as a unified whole within the Confucian system of thought, and attempts to prove the universality of the principal abstract Confucian ideas (for instance, 'benevolence' or 'the golden mean') in this region. This approach does not go very far. Even intuitively speaking, it would be hard to maintain that Confucianism operates in the same way throughout the region, because we have to account for the different trajectories under the influence of Confucianism for Japan and China, with one having taken up capitalism, the other socialism. Furthermore, in the face of the forced partition of the Korean peninsula that brought about two different social systems, we find ourselves even more incapable of determining the respective effects of Confucianism on these two different parts. If we regard Confucianism as a product of past historical phases, then the following problem inevitably arises: Confucianism has different historical modalities in different East Asian countries. Even in its heyday, as an ideology, Confucianism could not directly extend throughout all three countries without mediation. In different countries, Confucianism acquired different contents. It is constrained by the historical specificities of the different societies in question, and cannot be abstracted from these conditions and exist in isolation. Since the modern period, the potential functions of Confucianism in different societies in East Asia are at great variance. This has already been proved by many case studies. Therefore, if the Confucian perspective is the initial point from which to observe East Asia, then we have to start with the differences, not the similarities, of Confucianism in these societies, and we need to mobilise our imagination on historical structures rather than rely on intuitive experience. Even if we tried to determine the trajectory of Confucianism in this region by means of a 'transmission approach', we would find it hard to proceed with a view to identifying the progenitors and their successors. Instead, we should be more attentive to the modifications that occurred in the course of transmission, because, in this process, the basic issue is that different politics work on Confucianism to reshape it. Confucianism can never be detached from the political environment in which it is embedded and 'travel' within a vacuum. In enlisting Confucianism as a perspective for the articulation of an 'East Asia narrative', if we continue to adhere to the intuitive view that Confucianism is a self-same identity for the different Asian countries, then this East Asia perspective will be just idle talk, because of the lack of historical and realistic features.

Indeed, strictly speaking, the Confucian perspective is not necessarily the same as the East Asia perspective. Rather, this is the construction of a strained historical narrative afterwards, and cannot be regarded as identical with the logic of history itself. For Confucianism, the frame of East Asia is not a necessary condition, but, for this frame of a historical narrative of East Asia, Confucianism is a necessary adhesive force. Therefore, the function of Confucianism as a contemporaneous perspective is not to learn about the 'history of East Asia' but to argue for the existence of an integrating power running through 'East Asia'. Surveying the contemporaneous narrative of 'Confucianism in East Asia', we can find that the function of this narrative is to eliminate the inner differences in East Asia (basically China, Japan and South Korea) with the help of Confucianism and to build a narrative structure for arguing that there exists a unified relatedness.

The second East Asia perspective is actually influenced by Japan, i.e. 'the perspective of modernisation'. It is a way of thinking pursued by Japan after the Meiji Restoration. In this thinking, East Asia was regarded as a region for the realisation of modernisation so as to surpass and counter the West, and Japanese intellectuals were framed by such a way of thinking in their consideration of an East Asia perspective. Today, in the East Asia narrative in Japan, this way of thinking is still being reproduced, in which China and the Korean peninsula are seen as competing against Japan in their attempts to overtake the West, rather than as allies to counter the West.[2] Who represents East Asia is still the latent question. After the reform and opening-up programme, modernisation became a received ideology in China, making it possible for the Japanese East Asia narrative to be introduced into China. Through narrating 'East Asia', the form of modernisation for East Asia has found an expression and subsequently become common sense: this should be the base for East Asia to become a relatively integrated system. However, as a kind of modernisation perspective, the East Asia narrative involves a directional error: the degree of modernisation in East Asia will be ranged chronologically, i.e. diachronically, while the [synchronous, G.M.] differences in substance in different regions or countries in East Asia are cancelled. An abstractly rendered 'Western mode' as a similarly unified entity is put forth as a given model of modernisation. This modernisation is reduced to only one form, that is: to realise the building of a 'welfare society' through industrialisation and post-industrialisation. Under this perspective, we can see an evolutionary logic in the East Asia narrative: different regions in East Asia, which are in different phases of social development, will eventually arrive at the same goal of modernisation. Therefore, the countries that developed first cannot but regard the situation of those that developed later as reflecting what was once their 'yesterday'. Conversely, those that develop later would look upon their predecessor as reflecting their 'tomorrow'.

There is also a third perspective: the one formed around the traumatic memories of war. Of course, there is a reason why an integral framework for narrating East Asia has come into existence. This is owing to the tragic dimension that cannot be ignored – war memories. Japan attempted to invade mainland China, expanded the war to the countries in Southeast Asia and consolidated colonial domination in the Korean peninsula and in Taiwan. It was a brutal 'adhesive force' in East Asia. Until now, the main region, which moved 'East Asia' to a deeper level of common war memory, has been Northeast Asia. And it needs to be pointed out in particular that the attempt by Japanese progressive forces to investigate responsibilities of the war and correctly carry on the war memory is an element that should not be undervalued. It enabled the war memory of victim countries in East Asia to become an external pressure on social transformation in Japan, and the trauma memory of the victims to receive some response. In recent years, a series of issues, such as school textbooks, visits to Yasukuni Shrine (*Yasukuni jinja* 靖国神社), the legal cases relating to 'comfort women' (*jūgun ianfu* 従軍慰安婦) or to biological warfare and compensation for the victims of chemical weapons after the war have forced Japan to 'internationalise' these problems in order to tackle them properly. The process has brought an unforeseeable gain: the civil societies in East Asia have started to mix together to some extent, and, gradually, a transnational bridge for people in East Asia has been built, which has helped them to a common understanding. This is a very important progress. Nonetheless, we can also observe that this progress is accompanied by a profound interior tension, which implies the objective need for adjusting epistemologies. First, when we talk about the trauma memory of the war, individual memories can only take the form of historical memory when they are integrated in the frame of the nation state. In this case, the national interest will be an absolute premise. So, perspectives that are not problematic in one nation could be problematic when they enter the East Asian frame. Compiling the school textbook entitled *History that opens the future: the modern and contemporary history of three East Asian countries* (Dongya 2005), as a valuable experiment, offers us information on this concern: as to the evaluation of historical issues, the history writers of the three countries, namely Japan, China and South Korea, had to undertake a very difficult coordination to reach a relatively unified narrative. The reason is that 'national interest' is an obstacle that is not easy to get over. The problem is: if the war, as a central issue of modernity, was undertaken by the nation states, and, at the same time, there are differences between 'victim countries' and 'perpetrator countries', between 'victorious countries' and 'defeated countries', then the problem might not be reduced to a homogenous proposal of 'criticising and going beyond the nation state'. Homogenisation will confuse historical details in concrete situations and will objectively exonerate the 'perpetrator countries' from their crimes. But, at the same time, if we do not consider 'criticising and going beyond the nation state' as an accepted perspective, then this will mean that the compiling of history textbooks will be identified with either the interests of the defeated countries or the interests of the victorious countries. We will be confronted with huge epistemological problems, in particular when there is not only one defeated country (and not just one victorious country), and conflicts of interests between them; further, if we tackle war history in a dualistic, totalising way, we may be compelled to avoid complex but crucial differences and use abstract and oversimplified evaluations such as 'pros' or 'cons'. These problems related to principal theories of international politics are already quite complicated in themselves, and, in addition to this complication, the post-war Japanese government was controlled by the Americans and signed a unilateral agreement with Taiwan. Thus post-war remedial work with mainland China was deferred, and it was not until the 1970s that it was set into motion, leaving many remaining problems behind. Under these circumstances, China, as a victim country, faced too many historical complications that discouraged Chinese social discourses from finding perspectives outside the nationalist frame to handle war history. This forms, objectively, a challenge for the East Asian perspective.

In addition, on the problem of dealing with war memory, the intellectuals of these countries are confined to their own national historical developments and social ideologies. Their consciousness of problems and approaches would not become 'East Asian' in one go. This means that intellectuals are still not in a phase in which they could act together and build profound understanding of each other. Actually, intellectuals in East Asia have not come to a common understanding on many major issues. In particular, under present circumstances where the ideology of the Cold War has not been truly overcome, the intellectuals in China, Japan and South Korea, who belonged to different blocs during the Cold War, have not really surpassed the Cold War imagination and reached an ideological common understanding. A typical example is the number of victims during the Nanking Massacre (*Nankin gyakusatsu* 南京虐殺). Although many intellectuals in Japan are unhappy with the way leftist historians do textual researches on the number of victims, for a long period the Japanese Left was motivated to prove the number of victims, not only to counter the argument of the Right (that 'the "Nanking Massacre" is fiction'), but also to allude to the idea that 'China under authoritarianism' lacks freedom of speech and academic autonomy. On the other hand, Chinese public opinion is short of historical analysis and perception of the analytic method employed by the Japanese Left and sometimes simplistically, in a binary way, classifies them as rightist.

As analysed above, the East Asia perspective as war memory is still very much alive. But it lacks some basic elements, which are as follows: a concern for the historical flow from the Japanese war of invasion and World War II, to the constellation of the Cold War. Especially after half a century, the constellation of international political powers since the 1940s has transformed into another structure, which has developed from World War II. Therefore, when we nowadays talk about war history between China and Japan, we should not ignore the development of the international constellation behind it and should not separate the task of investigating responsibilities for the war and the task of considering the historical flow. Otherwise, if decontextualised, the historical logic would not be clear. But if we integrate the history after the war into our historical horizon, we will have to pose the question in a new way: can East Asia (here I take East Asia as Northeast Asia) be simply regarded as a conglomerate of mainland China, Taiwan, South Korea and Japan?

In effect, the objects of the three East Asia perspectives elaborated above are different. The Confucian perspective can cover the regions where Confucianism had its impact. Hence, some regions in Southeast Asia, such as Vietnam and Singapore, should also be included in this perspective. The perspective of modernisation might take South Korea as a representative for the whole Korean peninsula, which implies the absence of North Korea. At the same time, this perspective covers China, Japan and the Korean peninsula only for a short period. When the dynamic balance between the countries is broken, this perspective has to be replaced by the perspective of war. As to the perspective of war memory in historical realms, we cannot treat East Asia in isolation, because the USA and the USSR cannot be excluded from East Asia during this period of history. Moreover, US military bases still operate on the Japanese and South Korean territories up to the present day, and there is only a 'ceasefire' between the northern and southern parts of the Korean peninsula, not a 'complete truce'. As for the relationship between China and Taiwan, its precariousness still has a huge influence on the peace of the whole Asian-Pacific region.

However, when we discuss East Asia, these differences are often ignored, so that an abstract 'East Asian frame' is formed. Furthermore, the Japanese and Korean East Asia narrative implies the 'China–Japan–Korea frame', which strengthens the fixed image of the East Asia narrative and constructs this image as an addition to these three nation states. This abstract quality of the East Asia perspective means that 'East Asia', which was originally so closely fixed to our history, cannot find its place in our spiritual and ideological world, and it cannot arrive at the goal of genuine reconciliation among the nation states through 'common history school textbooks'.

The imbalance within East Asia in modern history

In building an East Asia framework, there is a premise that we cannot deny. That is: East Asia has to be an object that is relatively independent. As a narrative unit, East Asia should be autonomous, or at least it must be possible to integrate it in some logical way. Only by this can an 'East Asian Community' exist as a proposition. Although tension in East Asia is still high, the concept of 'community' expresses a subjective idea: if East Asia cannot be integrated as a whole, how could it qualify for an independently existing category?

One does not need to cite Edward Said (1935–2003) to ascertain that East Asia exists because it was named so by the West. But when we only consider the origin of this proposition, the question is not to the point, because there are two issues involved that require closer examination. First, if East Asia is a counter-proposition to Western Europe, or, say, is 'constructed' as a medium so that Western Europe can establish its self-identity, does this mean that East Asia as a whole is simply an extension of the proposition of a Western Europe? In other words, when we emphasise today the 'Western European origin' of the concept of East Asia, is this to try to break up the concept of a so-called 'non-Western European essentialism' of East Asia, or is this to try to investigate its epistemological feature more profoundly? If it is the former, then it is not worth continuing the discussion of this topic, because as a conclusion it is already established. But, if it is the latter, then the question should be clarified. For East Asians, this conception, then, not only exists in Western European thinking, but also comprises the will of the East Asians to identify themselves. However, because this conception is regarded as a synonym of 'countering modern Western Europe', and because Japan had tried to transform the concept of East Asia into the 'Greater East Asian co-prosperity sphere' (*Dai-Tō-A kyōeiken* 大東亜共栄圏), which was a Japan-centred brutal process full of violence and war, the proposition of an East Asia cannot take the 'Western European concept of the Far East' as centre, because this concept will blur the most gruesome parts of our history.

Second, and vice versa, East Asia also regards Western Europe as an integrated concept. Western Europeans (including the intellectuals in the EU) prefer not to be treated as a whole, but the image of Western Europe held by East Asians is such a whole. The perspective from outside always tends to integrate the object, and the perspective from inside always concentrates more on the differences. In this sense, it is not important where the conception of East Asia comes from. What is relevant is: what kind of self-definition does the historical development of this perspective entail for us?

Before modern times, a concept such as East Asia did not bear any real meaning. As a geo-political category, the existence of East Asia is directly related to the invasion and penetration of the West in modern times. Nonetheless, once this concept is formed, its function is detached from the origin of its formation and acquires a new, individual meaning. It should be noted that the East Asian narrative could hardly be regarded as an organic whole in the historical process. Especially after the tragic historical chapter in which Japan began with 'Asianism' (*Ajiashugi* アジア主義) and ended with the 'Greater East Asian co-prosperity sphere', it is much more difficult to treat East Asia in terms of an integrated narrative. Such an East Asia narrative would imply an essential problem: who represents East Asia? Once, Sun Zhongshan's 孙中山 (Sun Yat-sen; 1866–1925) 'Greater Asianism' clearly attempted to articulate 'the kingly way' he perceived as centred on the state, if not on a civilisatory view. But no matter what kind of political situation Sun Zhongshan was in, and no matter whether China disposed of a real self-awareness as a state, Sun Zhongshan's 'Greater Asianism' was still not a pluralistic narrative of international politics. This inevitably leads to the association with, and criticism of, 'chauvinism'. Korean criticism can help us nowadays to put this narrative in perspective.[3] Actually, the problem is not whether Sun Zhongshan is a Chinese chauvinist, but whether it is possible for us not to postulate a centre in a discourse on East Asia. Because of its utopian nature, Sun Zhongshan's Asianism cannot be put on a par with Japanese Asianism. Japanese Asianism was entrapped by the 'Greater East Asian co-prosperity sphere' and embarrassed the Asia narrative, because its aspect of utopia was not central. It is a tragedy in history that the Asianism Sun Zhongshan envisaged, which rejected military force for moral power, was suppressed by the 'hegemon's way', which is the opposite of Sun's 'kingly way', and vanished in the end. But, if we set aside the content and just look at the approach, then we can see that the 'kingly way' and the 'hegemon's way' are nevertheless similar in their structure. Both of them postulate a centre. And this is why Sun Zhongshan's 'Greater Asianism' was criticised by Korean intellectuals.

After Sun Zhongshan's death, Chinese Asianism did not develop any similarly explicit and creative new narrative. On the contrary, in the later war period and post-war period, the Asia narrative was integrated into other narratives that focused on other matters. Under such circumstances, East Asia as a perspective basically did not have any important function in modern Chinese history. And it was even more difficult on an epistemological level to integrate East Asia as a whole. After World War II, East Asia became a down-sized Cold War: following the Korean War, the 'Iron Curtain' was drawn across the Korean peninsula, and the states on both sides of the 'Iron Curtain' (South Korea, Japan, Taiwan vs. USSR, China, North Korea, Mongolia) were in a situation in which they did not share the same ideology but were socially opposed to, and spiritually isolated from, each other. In this historical process, the basic conditions needed to discuss 'East Asia' and to regard it as a unit were lacking. One of the ideological consequences that the fall of the Berlin Wall brought about is that the [remaining] socialist bloc [in East Asia, G.M.] became relatively tolerant to some ideologies (especially the market economy, which seems to be a non-political ideology) of the capitalist bloc. This broke down the rigid opposition between these two ideologies, and it even seems that the Western ideology of freedom played a dominant role. In this context, the 'East Asian Community' as a new conception (though first as an idea for an economic institution) has now found a base to constitute an integrated narrative. This base is the theory of modernisation and modernity.

Nonetheless, an inevitable problem emerged while the East Asia narrative was making progress in some regions of East Asia: how to treat the real problem of China's weak 'consciousness of East Asia'? Admittedly, the East Asia narrative is not absent in the Chinese social discourse, but it is only in respect of an economic community that the conception 'East Asia' finds its place in the domain of Chinese discourse, ideology and theory. Moreover, East Asia in this perspective does not cover the whole East Asian region. It takes modernisation as its criterion, which involves the problem of 'preferring the rich and despising the poor'. As for other conceptions, such as East Asia as an ideological function, these lack any basis. In other words, although research and discussions about East Asia took and take place all the time, their relationship with the Chinese ideological intellectual world is still not clear. For Chinese intellectuals, the question is still not answered: why do we have to talk about East Asia? However, for intellectuals in the neighbouring countries, this undecided attitude of Chinese intellectuals looks like a kind of 'Sinocentrism'. The shaky concept of the 'dialogue between China and the West' has always targeted Chinese 'Sinocentrism'. Until now, however, although Chinese intellectuals have been trying to carry out an East Asia dialogue, this situation has not radically changed. In fact, whether to pursue a narrative on East Asia in the region does not mean whether the Chinese intellectuals forget their own position, but whether an East Asian consciousness can find a place in Chinese thought. If there is not such a place, then we will have to look into it closely to see whether the problem merely lies in 'Sinocentrism' or whether there are some more basic historical reasons.

Looking back in Chinese history to the time when China became an independent sovereign country and built its subjective narrative, we can see that – before the structure of the Cold War disintegrated – there had been two regional perspectives. The first was the 'Asia and Africa perspective', which the Chinese premier Zhou Enlai 周恩来 (1898–1976) had taken up at the Bandung Conference in 1955, and the subsequent perspective of 'Asia, Africa and Latin America'. (During that time, the Non-Aligned Movement (NAM) flourished, the relationship between China and the USSR broke down, and Mao Zedong changed his 'Leaning to one side' politics. At the beginning of the 1960s, he proposed the strategy of 'striving for an intermediate position' and changed the perspective on 'Asia and Africa' to the 'perspective on Asia, Africa and Latin America'.)[4] The second was the so-called 'Third World' perspective, which had been used since the beginning of the 1970s. It is worth noting that these two perspectives serve the same goals in the Chinese discourse, namely to keep a necessary distance within the American and Soviet constellation caused by the Cold War, and to get rid of the colonial crisis in the fight for sovereignty. As a cushioning zone of the Cold War constellation, the Asian, African and Latin-American national liberation movements and the movements of the 'Third World' fulfilled an international political function. At the same time, this entailed the problem of the definition of the international political concept of a 'Far East'.[5] It is hard to imagine that this history of about half a century could disappear suddenly after the fall of the Berlin Wall. Furthermore, the Cold War structure cannot really cover the whole historical process of 'Asia, Africa, Latin America' and the 'Third World'.

Because this history cannot disappear overnight, it is largely unavoidable that a strong East Asia narrative cannot be formed in the ideological context of Chinese society. Although the reform and opening up policy has brought with itself a strong economic need [for it, G.M.], East Asia as a relatively independent region still needs to prepare a lot to accomplish internal political exchanges and a shared thinking. If we use conceptions such as 'Asia, Africa and Latin America' or 'Third World', we can locate them in some historical periods in the Chinese academic world. But, if we talk about East Asia, there is no clear historical development for it as an independent unit. Nowadays, when we try to clarify the history of modern times, especially the history of the war, East Asia is considered as a narrative unit, but it has still not developed to a degree that it reflects a subject identification. Hence, it is quite limited. At the same time, we can also see another perspective paralleling the one on East Asia, namely the perspective of 'developing countries'. This viewpoint develops the perspective of the 'Third World' and fulfils an important function: on the one hand, it implies the continuum from the Mao Zedong era to today's Chinese society; on the other hand, it limits the function of the East Asia perspective in the ideological construction of China: It requires that, in Chinese contemporary spiritual life, the East Asia narrative gives answers to the questions above, which were covered by the larger historical perspectives cited above that exceeded the East Asia perspective or even made it disappear. This is precisely the reason why the East Asia narrative has not yet found a valid place in today's Chinese academic world.

For Japan, 'East Asia' has always been a sensitive framework. It used to represent the Japanese anti-Western cultural stance. (However, as Okakura Kakuzō 岡倉覚三, alias Okakura Tenshin 岡倉天心, 1863–1913, stated, as a cultural unit, 'Asia' was a much more common framework.) It also used to express its disappointment in neighbouring countries in some specific historical periods in East Asia (as Fukuzawa Yukichi 福沢諭吉, 1835–1901, presented in his article on the *Departure from Asia, Datsu-A ron* 脱亜論 1885). It not only expressed the ambition of Japan to replace China and to be the centre of East Asia or even Asia, but also led to the idea of settling accounts with Japanese militarism. One can say that 'East Asia' or 'Asia' is one of the basic propositions in Japanese intellectual history in modern times. Although the 'Greater East Asian co-prosperity sphere' cast a shadow over the Japanese East Asia narrative, the relationship between Japan and Asia, especially East Asia and, at a higher level, the self-orientation of Japan in East Asia, has always been a key question of subjective identification and an epistemological key point of its intellectual history in modern times. In this respect, we can say that the 'Greater Asianism' (*Dai-Ajiashugi* 大アジア主義), the 'Greater East Asian co-prosperity sphere' and the narrative 'Japan comes back to East Asia' (as an inverse proposition of the ideology of the 'Greater East Asian co-prosperity sphere') are similar in being a modality of historical epistemology: regardless of the motive and goal, East Asia as a narrative unit has its huge limitation in these historical periods. This limit is quite different from the limit that China faces when taking 'Asia, Africa and Latin America', the 'Third World' or 'developing countries' as narrative units. The problem that Japanese intellectual circles are facing is not whether there is an East Asia, but how to handle the relationship between East Asia and Japan. Therefore, the problem does not lie in the existence of the East Asia narrative but in the question how East Asia should be narrated. From the geographical dimension to narrative theories, all became a focus of discussions in Japanese intellectual circles. Basically, however, these questions are not yet significant in China.

I do not have a profound knowledge about East Asia consciousness on the Korean peninsula. Hence, I cannot make any clear judgement. But if, for the moment, we do not trace the issue back to the historical situation of the Korean peninsula before modern times and are only concerned here with South Korea, which was formed after World War II and was consolidated after the Korean

War, it seems that we can at least point out this fact: the rise of East Asian consciousness is directly related to the Korean 'post-war thought'. Although the post-war situation on the Korean peninsula is still not resolved, and the US military bases are still there in South Korea, the democratisation of South Korean society has made the identification with East Asia an exigent question. For South Korean society, identification with the USA or with East Asia is a question related to its subject construction; moreover, South Korea defines its position in East Asia differently from Japan, China or other regions: South Korea has the USA to its east (in fact, the USA is also present within South Korea), China to its west, Japan to its south and Russia to its north. By constructing an East Asia identification in this international political situation, South Korean society and South Korean intellectual circles (of course, these are not to be equated with the South Korean government) are making strategic choices. Moreover, it is a historical fact that the forming of the East Asian 'Iron Curtain' after World War II had the Korean peninsula as its centre, so that the attitude of Korean intellectual circles towards 'East Asia' has a special historical connotation. Therefore, we can imagine that there are certainly deep differences in South Korean intellectual circles about the question of identifying themselves with East Asia or the West (and here the USA and Western Europe would also represent different orientations). These differences are barely understood in Japanese and Chinese intellectual circles. And there is another delicate problem: the attitude of South Korean intellectual circles towards China. In the East Asia narrative in South Korea, China plays a very important role. From the abolition of using Chinese characters over the change of the name of the capital from Han Cheng (Han City) to purely native 'Seoul' to the [contested claims over the ancient state, G.M.] of Koguryŏ, we can clearly see how pressure from China is experienced within Korean society. Being different from the relationship between South Korea and Japan, the attitude of South Korean society towards China is neither pure confrontation nor empathetic understanding. There is even a greater lack of mutual understanding between the Chinese and South Korean societies than between the Japanese and South Korean ones. The root of this lack of understanding is the imbalance between the perspectives of the two sides. This causes Chinese and Korean societies to have quite different attitudes towards the same issues, and hence there are a lot of obstacles to the exchange of thought.

Another region that is often omitted in the perspective of intellectuals from mainland China is Taiwan. The construction of an Asia narrative in Taiwan after World War II was, in fact, a rather difficult task. This was not only because the relationship between Taiwan and the mainland entailed complex identification problems, but also because it used to be a key nodal point during the Cold War in East Asia. The complexity of the relationship between Taiwan and mainland China, the position of Taiwan in the Korean War and the relationship between Taiwan and Japan in the past and the present, all make it difficult for Taiwan to be integrated into East Asia as a whole. It is precisely the regional tension in East Asia that, in turn, has formed ideological problems in Taiwan. Because the intellectual circles in mainland China lack any understanding of these complex issues concerning Taiwan, China only focuses on the issue of reunification or independence in Taiwan. This leaves Taiwan's special position in East Asia to be ignored, and the intellectual circles of mainland China scarcely care about how Taiwan constructs (or why it is difficult for Taiwan to construct) its own East Asia perspective.

What we have discussed above is just one part of the situation in East Asia. According to the above, the East Asia narrative clearly demonstrates an imbalance between some areas of East Asia and implies an internal tension. Actually, in today's East Asia narrative, we ignore the situation of some other parts: the Democratic People's Republic of Korea, the Mongolian People's Republic, Vietnam and other countries in Southeast Asia. These societies will, I am afraid, gradually join the perspective of the East Asia narrative. However, another problem will emerge: the areas that, for various reasons, have not expressed any opinion on an East Asia narrative yet might harbour their own imagination of East Asia. But it might be also quite the opposite: some societies may not need an East Asia narrative. In other words, not all the countries and societies in East Asia will necessarily strive for an East Asia narrative. It depends on the historical development of the respective societies and countries. Even when they strive for an East Asia narrative, the internal logic will be quite different, depending on the different societies that take East Asia as their way of subject identification for their self-construction. Hence, we must face a basic difficulty in our epistemology: if we construct a unified East Asia on a logical level, then this imbalance must be ignored on purpose. If we construct a balanced East Asia perspective from our own imagination, and follow the idea of 'seeking common points while retaining differences', which is based on theory and not on practice, then we might obliterate, to a large extent, the important constraining function of historical differences. This may even result in our inability to face the necessary differences in reality, so that the whole question would be led to the abstract level of: 'Is it possible to integrate East Asia or not?'

The relationship between the history of the Cold War and East Asia

On the epistemological level, it is questionable whether East Asia could be a narrative unit by itself. However, this problem refers back to its logical premise and cannot lead directly to an explanation of history. In fact, whether 'Far East' or 'East Asia', they are both independent objects of history. But their existence is not logically grounded. They do not have as a precondition the elimination of the international political relationships in East Asia. On the contrary, they have the external political powers as a necessary reason for their own development. It is the history of the Cold War that caused this situation.

In the Chinese-speaking world, there is already quite a lot of excellent research about the Cold War, which can be used as a reference to review this phase of history. Hence, I need not describe this period of history.[6] Based on this existing research, I have to first explain the following three points, because they are directly related to the analysis in this chapter.

First, we need to distinguish the real historical process of the Cold War from the Cold War ideology. The former intends the antagonistic blockage strategy of the USA aimed at the USSR after World War II. This reached a peak during the Korean War. But after this, the connotation of the Cold War has been changing during different periods of the international political situation. Further, the opposition of the USA and the USSR, which underpinned the Cold War structure, was not always unalterable. For example, the word 'Iron Curtain', which Churchill used in his lecture in 1964, and the word 'Cold War' sensationalised by the US press in 1947, formed key conceptions of the ideology. But this is a fixed image of the Cold War and is not congruent with the real, dynamic Cold War. Even when the Cold War structure had already disintegrated in reality, the ideology of the Cold War still remained in its relatively independent static form and became more and more reductive and solidified. Because this ideology is simplified as an abstract criticism of the politics of centralisation of state power and regards liberal democratic politics as a myth, it is directly linked to the ideology of neo-liberalism. It needs to be pointed out, in particular, that the ideology of the Cold War was produced by the Western capitalist bloc. As it is an ideological attack on the communist countries, the attitude of the socialist bloc to this conception was rather indifference. At the same time, however, in order to fight against the ideology of the Cold War from the West, the countries of the socialist bloc also produced communist ideologies to simplify and vilify the Western bloc. The war of ideologies is a very important component of the Cold War period. Its extreme oppositional character draws a distinct and simplified profile of the real, complex historical process. It is meaningful in this context that, after the disintegration of the Cold War structure, the Western ideology of the Cold War was globalised in a simple form: it was transformed to a utopian narrative of democracy and liberation, which was accepted by intellectual elites of different social systems.

Second, although the Cold War is regarded as the historical period between Churchill's lecture on the 'Iron Curtain' in 1964 and the fall of the Berlin Wall in 1989, the Cold War during this period was not a homogeneous period. The essence of the Cold War was the economy and trade blockade by the Western capitalist world against the socialist countries, which aimed at containing the USSR. As to countries such as China, which were independent of the control of the USSR, the West took the strategy of 'alliance and struggle'. This makes it difficult to divide the two blocs by the single criterion of social systems. At the same time, there are profound differences in the strategies of the Cold War, not only in the Western bloc, but also among the communist countries, where there are tensions and conflicts. For instance, the differences and even conflicts between China and the USSR at the end of the 1950s caused the relativisation of the Cold War structure, or even an imbalance. But, from the beginning of the 1970s, the establishment of diplomatic relations between the USSR and West Germany and the real contacts between China and the USA all brought essential changes to the contents of the Cold War.

Third, the Cold War cannot cover the whole constellation of the world after World War II. The so-called 'Third World' and the 'Asia, Africa and Latin America' perspectives have all emerged through emphasising the immense areas outside the Cold War structure. During World War II, many Asian countries were not independent or liberated as a nation. The conception of the Cold War by Britain and the USA aimed at the only power that could confront them – the USSR.[7] After World War II, a massive transformation in the constellation of Asia took place. China became a country ruled by the Communist Party. At the same time, with regard to its shaking off control by the USSR and proposing its own prospects of world revolution, China soon kept its distance from the Cold War structure. At the same time, big countries such as India and the countries in Southeast Asia played more and more important roles in international affairs. For example, India's statements at the United Nations during the Korean War and Nehru's attitude at the Bandung Conference in 1955 were important in reducing tensions and keeping world peace. These all reveal the perspective of the Cold War to be just one of numerous perspectives in observing the global constellation after World War II.

Based on the above three points, I now want to discuss the East Asia perspective in the Cold War, especially with a focus on the historical features of the East Asia perspective, and not so much on its ideological function.

In 1972, the Far Eastern Institute of the Soviet Academy of Sciences started a quarterly magazine entitled *Far Eastern Affairs,* which was also translated into English and Japanese (from 1980 onwards there was also a Spanish version). This magazine was published and sold to Japanese universities, until the publication of the Japanese version was stopped in 1990 because of financial problems. (It is said, however, that some universities had always been supplied with complimentary copies of the magazine by the USSR Embassy.) In fact, it is held by many Japanese universities. But, interestingly, none of the universities seems to have a complete collection of this magazine, although it is not a series with a long history. The earliest I could locate is number 2 of volume 3, from June 1974. In fact, the issues of the previous two years are not to be found in the electronic index of the Japanese library system. The rigid writing style and the dogmatic narration make the reading less than exciting. It is therefore quite natural that, according to loan records, the magazine did not receive much attention. Nevertheless, from this incomplete and very dogmatic magazine, we can still obtain some very important information.

The function of *Far Eastern Affairs* obviously went beyond an academic magazine. It not only published the speeches, articles and declarations of the leaders of the Soviet Communist Party, it also used an official tone in the articles, and, hence, it cannot be regarded as strictly academic.[8] Therefore, although it was not the mouthpiece of the Soviet government to the outside, we could consider it as 'the academic attitude' of the USSR government.

In the Japanese version of the Soviet publication, which started in the early 1970s and closed in 1990, we find a consistent perspective of the USSR over these 20 years, namely the portrayal of the USA as the adversary of East Asia. Directed against this strategic enemy, the USSR constructed East Asia and even South Asia as an organic unit. Here, East Asia was not a geographic region in its natural sense, but a net of tensions generated by international political relations. The East Asia narrative was not based on 'striving for the common', with a sense of integration. On the contrary, if there had not been any tensions from inside and pressure from outside, the USSR most likely would not have been able to construct the frame of any East Asia narrative.

If we say that *Far Eastern Affairs* transmitted an ideology of the USSR government about the East Asian region from the 1970s to the 1990s, then it is worth paying close attention to the rapid adjustment of this ideology in this dynamic period of twenty years. The first ten years can be summarised as follows: the social system and the political ideology were taken as the highest criteria to judge reality. Under these criteria, the *Far Eastern Affairs* magazine, which took politics and society as its main research object, and culture as a minor object, insisted on a consistent antagonistic attitude to its biggest enemy in the Cold War – the USA. However, as to countries in East Asia, including Japan, which was rated as an accomplice to the USA in East Asia, its attitude was flexible and adjustable. The adjustment presented itself most vividly after the mid 1980s, and most evidently at the end of the 1980s. What was discussed in the magazine was the possibility of economic cooperation between the USSR and Japan, emphasising that the USSR was the best economic partner for Japan. In the mid 1980s, *Far Eastern Affairs* changed its focus from social systems and political theories to the adjustment of economic construction. Thus, there were more and more articles about economic cooperation in the Far Eastern region. Relatively speaking, the articles about resisting the penetration of the USA and defending the gains of socialism started to be reduced. The most evident change was in the attitude towards China. After 1988, the magazine continued publishing criticisms of China, but the main focus had already shifted. Chinese reforms, including their failings, were regarded as a reform experiment within the socialist bloc, and there was an attempt to share experiences and lessons provided by them. Thus, the relationship between the USSR and China started to ameliorate. These changes clearly related to Gorbachev's rise to power in 1985. The reform that he promoted in the USSR changed the relations between the USSR and other countries in East Asia. Although, on the surface, the ideological discourse had not changed much, the change in frequency of certain jargon and the change of focus implied that the narrative, which had been based on the social system and political theories, shifted to a narrative of economic needs and social life. Especially from 1989 onward, the relationship between the USSR and China clearly improved. Not only was cultural exchange renewed, but also expressions such as 'friendship between the USSR and China', which had been absent from official discourse for a long time, emerged again in this magazine. This means that, synchronous with the diplomatic changes occurring between the USSR and China, the *Far East* had become an important voice for internal reforms of the USSR. Certainly, this reorientation also shows the attempt by the USSR to remain the leader of the socialist bloc. But, at the same time, this subject position facilitated its narrative to offer an interpretation that differed from the Western ideology of the Cold War.[9]

As the position of this magazine after 1991 is not known, some hypotheses must remain speculations. However, regarding the international relationship in East Asia after the 1990s, we may say that the disintegration of the structure of the Cold War and the USSR has not caused the retreat of Russia from East Asia. On the contrary, it has been involved in East Asian issues at a deeper level and, in fact, has become an organic component of East Asia. The 'Six-Party Talks' about the North Korean nuclear issue not only drew North Korea – which had been kept outside the modern East Asia narrative – into the East Asia perspective, but also established Russia's place as a member of East Asia. It should be noted that, in the current, general East Asia perspective of China, Japan and Korea, the North Korean nuclear issue has not been integrated into the East Asian frame. It is regarded more as a contingent international political issue than a modality of the East Asia narrative. This is because the three East Asia perspectives that I talked about at the beginning of this chapter do not cover the historical perspective on the international changes brought about in East Asia by the formation and disintegration of the Cold War. Nevertheless, if we construct another perspective by means of *Far Eastern Affairs*, then not only does the North Korean nuclear issue belong to East Asian issues, but also the Shanghai Cooperation Organisation (SCO) will be part of the East Asia narrative.

Since the rigid ideological articulations have already lost their function of dominating society, today, *Far Eastern Affairs* can hardly be directly seen as part of the historical process itself. However, precisely because of its pure ideological modality, we can easily identify the basic presuppositions of its framework. If East Asia was an important arena of the Cold War for the USSR, then we cannot skip the Cold War when we today talk about whether or not East Asia can be integrated. Not only can the USA, which has its military base in East Asia, not be eliminated from the East Asia narrative – even the former USSR and today's Russia can hardly be eliminated from the East Asia perspective. On the other hand, just because the Cold War was a historical process of confrontation between the USSR and the USA, the roles of some countries in this region are asymmetrical with this structure, and even have an antagonist relationship with it, e.g. China's post-war history. In this respect, we can neither consider the history of East Asia after the war simply as a 'history of confrontation in the Cold War', nor simply apply or copy the confrontational structure symbolised by the USSR and the USA mechanically on to the history of post-war East Asia.

Furthermore, the history of the Cold War handled in the East Asia perspective is different from the history of the Cold War as an object of international relationships. This is because it is related to the historical process before the Cold War, and thus does not constitute an isolated research object by itself. As a chapter of the East Asian history narrative, the real structural relationship between the ideology of the Cold War, the history of the Cold War and the post-Cold War period is closely related to the whole historical process of East Asia. Therefore, the history of the Cold War in research on East Asia should be theoretical and not conjunctural. The focus of study of East Asia should not be on the historical process of the Cold War, but on the structural changes behind it. In this respect, analysis of the process of the Cold War in East Asia after World War II must be related to the three East Asia perspectives mentioned at the beginning of this chapter. By means of the dynamic Cold War perspective, we can discern relatively easily that the already established East Asia narrative is static not dynamic, descriptive not analytical, abstract not historical. Because of the reasons above, the East Asia narrative does not have its theoretical value yet and remains merely on the level of 'regional identity' in an empirical sense. Especially after the Chinese reform and opening-up, the fall of the Berlin Wall and the disintegration of the USSR, the 'China, Japan and South Korea' narrative framework, which takes modernisation as its underlying logic, has been rapidly constructed and strengthened, so that all the other imaginations of East Asia are regarded as derivatives of this framework. This narrative has its own historical reason. But it is problematic to consider it as the premise of the East Asia narrative. When we regard this framework, without deliberation, as the basic construction of the historical process of East Asia, we will be confronted with some problems: the Taiwan issue and the opposition on the Korean peninsula are then basically considered as subsidiary issues under the framework of 'China, Japan and South Korea'. They will not be regarded as a main link in the contemporary history of East Asia. As Southeast Asia's narrative is also based on modernisation, it functions as an extension of the framework of China, Japan and South Korea, and does not relativise this framework to the maximum. On the other hand, the 'China–Japan' dimension is often regarded as the main component of this East Asian frame. If this East Asia perspective is regarded as a relatively established and fixed perspective, then it will be very difficult to bring the complexities of history to the East Asia narrative. Therefore, we will face this dilemma: when we talk about East Asia, are we producing an ideological modality vis-à-vis regions outside East Asia (for instance the EU or USA), or are we confronting the history of this region? If it is the latter, how can we integrate the two world wars and the Cold War into the historical horizon without regarding them only as objects of international relationships?

The post-Cold War period has just begun, but it does not mean the end of the ideology of the Cold War. For example, the discourse of the Western media about China and Russia does not go beyond the imagination of the Cold War period. The Western bloc's economic and military domination of the communist countries continues to penetrate into the economic and financial structures of East Asia by the process of globalising capital during the post-Cold War period, which has caused a series of internal tensions. The function of the ideology of the Cold War in East Asian societies has changed greatly after the antagonistic constellation of the social systems disappeared on the surface: on the one hand, the idealisation of the Western capitalist system has contributed to the fantasy of 'market democratisation' inside communist countries, which are still 'developing countries'. On the other hand, the economic and systemic crises in the Western world have caused thinkers in the 'developed countries' to turn and look for new possibilities and idealise them in transforming the 'developing countries' in East Asia. However, this all is still in the framework of the Cold War perspective, namely: one just sets aside the antagonism of social systems during the Cold War, and now takes the ideology of the 'Western market economic model' as the epistemological premise. In East Asian international relationships, the disintegration of the structure of the Cold War only caused the Cold War ideology to be further internalised, and not the opposite, i.e. East Asia's getting rid of the constellation of the Cold War to form a new international order.

As, on the practical level, the regional integration of East Asia cannot eliminate the involvement of the USA, one will be confronted with a grave epistemological dilemma if one regards East Asia as an entity that can stand by itself. Moreover, while North Korea emerges and Russia enters, East Asia is confronted with the issue of a new reintegration of its framework. In the actual dynamic of the current political situation, it is not only difficult to firmly establish a 'Chinese, Japanese and South Korean' frame in historical realms, but also in reality it is rapidly losing validity.

We have to acknowledge that, be it Japanese Asianism or Chinese Confucianism in their 'pure' form, it is difficult to regard either of them as principles of East Asia today, because they neither represent the basic axis of the social systems nowadays, nor are principles in the epistemological sense. At most, they can represent goodwill in academic conferences. If these thoughts are to be transformed into principles of the East Asia narrative, they need to undergo a complicated transformation process, and must be integrated with heterogeneous elements. And these elements are so-called non-local, 'Western' theories that have been 'domesticated' during the process in modern times.

Today, the proposition of an East–West opposition has long collapsed. The old hypothesis of 'Chinese learning as the fundamental structure, Western learning for practical use' (*zhongxue wei ti, xixue wei yong* 中学为体, 西学为用) (the Japanese parlance is 'Japanese spirit, Western technology' [*wakon yōsai* 和魂洋才]) must be re-scrutinised. Parallel to the acceptance of a modern global consciousness by East Asian society (at first by the elite East Asian intellectuals who produced epistemologies) in a context of European and American military and economic exploitation, the epistemology and political and social process of the inverted formula – 'Western learning as the fundamental structure, Chinese learning for practical use' – had already developed secretly beneath the raging 'nationalist narrative'. When East Asian nationalism was affirmed or negated, it was in fact only putting East Asian materials into a Western European and North American epistemological frame. The accomplice relationship between westernisation and nationalism is like the accomplice relationship between the globalisation of capital and nation states. They appear incomprehensible, yet inevitable. This means that our cognition of the world must be adjusted as well, and that the cognitive modality to go from one extreme to the other should also be removed. In other words, when, in practice, an 'East Asia principle' cannot accomplish the mission of accounting for the history and actual situation of East Asia, it does not mean that we have to abandon all research on possible East Asia principles and simply assert that East Asia as an epistemological perspective does not have its worth. While the 'modern knowledge' produced by the old Western European colonialist nations during the time of colonialism and the 'worldview' of American global strategy more and more reveal their bias, we are confronted with an exigent problem: if we endeavour to turn these epistemological resources, which developed in the advanced regions and have then been forced on to the whole world through violence, into the legacy of human thought, then it is not adequate to regard them straightforwardly as a 'universal narrative' just by relying on existing theoretical frameworks. They must first be 'particularised' and regarded as resources of thought of one region. Only through such a necessary process will the 'West' really belong to all of humanity.

However, the problem is: even if we can set straight the simplistic and reductive value judgements by an open, integrating modality, and even if we have a pluralistic understanding of historical situations, this still does not mean that we have already constructed an East Asian epistemological principle. We may say that, in this regard, we are still at an early phase of self-cognition. The task nowadays is to set things straight, not to construct. Only when we reach some common understanding of the problems to set straight can we avoid being entangled by false questions. This is the aim of a close examination of the East Asia perspective at the epistemological level. Maybe the relevance of the East Asia perspective today is to lead us out of the chaos of knowledge to an epistemological self-awareness. Although we still need other media to reach this self-awareness, the East Asia perspective is irreplaceable because it is determined by a specific historical process. After all, some important historical events can only be synthetically analysed within this specific East Asia perspective. As new historical processes are continually emerging, the East Asia perspective will surely contribute new dimensions of thought and resources of thinking.

Notes

1 An earlier version of this chapter appeared in Chinese as Sun (2009) 'Dongya shijiao de renshilun yiyi' 东亚视角的认识论意义 [The epistemological implications of the different perspectives on East Asia] in the journal *Kaifang shidai* 开放时代 (2009, no. 5 (issue 203)). Permission has been granted by Kaifang Shidai Company.
2 The most interesting work on this approach is Yamamuro (2001). This book presents a lot of materials and focuses on discussing the problem of 'modern anxiety' at the time of transformation in Japan and even Northeast Asia. It considers Northeast Asian countries' response to the challenge of the modern West and sees them as competitors in the contest for dominance in modernisation. In his book, Yamamuro pointed out that Asianism is a transformation of the way of self-cognition after the confrontation of Northeast Asia with the Western world in the seventeenth century. This entailed a series of mutually linked reactions in the realm of thoughts, cultural customs and even political practices. The book offers many good analyses and clues to materials. Especially, it ponders the relation between 'the nation's interest' and ideology and is an important work for understanding the development of Japanese Asianism. But this book ignores the structural heterogeneousness of China, Japan and Korea with regard to Asianism. It also overstresses the modern anxiety of Northeast Asia in the modern transformation phase as an absolute premise of Asianism, so that it simplifies the historical complexity of this ideological subject. Still, this book is a work of high quality and is representative of Japanese opinion about Asianism in modern times.
3 Cf. Bai (1999).
4 Cf. Mao (1994: 508). For the Asian–African perspective, and also the Asian–African–Latin-American perspective, the former is directly related to the Bandung Conference in the 1950s, and the latter to the collapse of the Chinese–Soviet relationship in the 1960s and the needs of the struggle against the USA. The biggest difference between these two perspectives is the attitude towards the USSR. The Asian, African and Latin-American perspective includes the connotation of 'fighting USSR hegemony'; in contrast, the Asian–African perspective does not emphasise this. On 8 December 1956, Mao Zedong gave a lecture named 'Is it correct to lean on one side?' at the forum of provincial representatives of the second congress of the Chinese Industrial and Commercial Union. He emphasised that China could not remain neutral between the USA and the Soviet Union at that international conjuncture and could only take the strategy of leaning on the side of the Soviet Union. Although Mao also used the parlance of the Asia, Africa and Latin-America perspective in the 1950s, it was used in terms of independence. Although the Asia–Africa perspective was not in opposition to the USSR, the Asia, Africa and Latin-America perspective was a product of the beginning of the 1960s. In his later *Theory of three worlds* (1974), Mao explicitly classified the USA and the USSR as the 'First World', the 'developing countries' – including China – as the 'Third World' and Japan – as well as other 'developed countries' – under the 'Second World'.
5 According to Wu Jianmin, Prime Minister Zhou Enlai used the words 'Far East', not 'East Asia', when he gave a speech at the Bandung Conference. When presiding over the meeting of the eight countries' delegations, Zhou Enlai stated: 'The Chinese Government would like to sit down with the US Government to negotiate and discuss how to temper the tense situation in the Far East, especially to temper the tense situation in the Taiwan region' (Wu 2007: 52).
6 Here I just list a few works that I have consulted: Shen (2006), Niu (2006), Yang (2006), Li and Shen (2006), Shen (2003) and Kong (2004).

7 Cf. Fleming (1961) *The Cold War and its origins, 1917–1960*. (Interestingly, the name of the 1966 Japanese translation changed the title into *The history of modern international politics*.) This brilliant work, which profoundly analyses the origin of the Cold War, unveils this problem. In the first part, *Friend and enemy*, Fleming pointed out that, during World War II, Britain and France were more afraid of the USSR than of Germany. Their defence against communism exceeded the resistance against fascism. As they hoped Hitler would reduce and even destroy Soviet power, they obstructed their own chance of an effective anti-fascist battle in Europe. This enabled Hitler to march rapidly on the East European battlefield and push his front forward. The USA began its propaganda against communism after the Russian Revolution in 1917, at the same time that the USA began to purge socialists in Congress. In 1933, after sixteen years, the Roosevelt administration was forced by the oil crisis and the later attack by Hitler to acknowledge the legitimacy of the USSR government. Fleming wrote this book to unveil how the history of the Cold War was born out of the fear of the Western world of communism. At a possible turn of the Cold War constellation at the beginning of the 1960s, by reviewing the history since World War II, he suggested that Western society should take an 'internal understanding' of the communist bloc and end as soon as possible the antagonistic situation caused by prejudice and arrogance.

8 For instance: the speech of Head Secretary Brezhnev about the International Conference of Peace and Security in Asia was published in no. 2, 1975. The announcement of Andropov about the USA was published in no. 4, 1983. Gorbachev's speech at the award-giving ceremony of the Lenin medal was published in no. 2, 1987. Gorbachev's interview with the Chinese magazine *Liaowang* (瞭望) was published in no. 4, 1988. Gorbachev's speech at Krasnoyarsk was published in no. 2, 1989. His speech at the International Conference in Uray (乌拉基尔) was published in no. 3, 1989, etc. Moreover, this magazine also published the Soviet and Indian Joint Declaration (January 1983) and other Soviet diplomatic documents on Asia and Soviet politics concerning East Asia at the 25th, 26th and 27th Soviet Congresses. There are also quite a few interpretations of these governmental documents and related topics.

9 After Gorbachev took power, this magazine began to publish research about China's reform. After 1989, the magazine started a column called 'The road of China's reform' and began to focus on the Chinese reform and research on it continuously. Zotov's article 'The reason and result of the Chinese political crisis' was published in no. 3, 1990. He analysed the 'Tiananmen issue' from economic and social perspectives, and in this he differed from the Western media, who simplified the whole issue as an ideological symbol of 'repression of democracy'. The subject position of this article is worthy of attention: it regards the dilemma of China's reform as representing an experiment of reform in the socialist bloc and consequently does not take an attitude of a mere on-looker. In fact, this subject position ran through all the articles on China's reform published by this magazine.

Bibliography

Bai Y. 白永瑞 (1999) 'Shiji zhi jiao zai si dongya' 世纪之交再思东亚 [Reconsidering East Asia at the turn of the century], *Dushu*, no. 8: Beijing: Shenghuo, dushu, xinzhi sanlian shudian.

'Dongya sanguo de jin-xiandaishi' gongtong bianxie weiyuanhui《东亚三国的近现代史》共同编写委员会 [Common editorial commission of The Modern and Contemporary History of Three East Asian Countries] (ed.) (2005) *Dongya sanguo de jin-xiandaishi*.

Yi shi wei jian; *mianxiang weilai* 东亚三国的近现代史。以史为鉴。面向未来 [*History that opens the future: the modern and contemporary history of three East Asian countries*], Beijing: Shehui kexue wenxian.

Fleming D.F. (1961) *The Cold War and its origins, 1917–1960*, Garden City, NY: Doubleday.

Kong H. 孔寒冰 (2004) *Zhong-Su guanxi ji qi dui Zhongguo shehui fazhan de yingxiang* 中苏关系及其对中国社会发展的影响 [*The China–Soviet relations and their influence on the development of the Chinese society*], Beijing: Zhongguo guoji guangbo.

Li D. 李丹慧 and Shen Z. 沈志华 (2006) *Zhanhou Zhong-Su guanxi ruogan wenti yanjiu* 战后中苏关系若干问题研究 [*Research about several issues between China and the USSR after the war*], Beijing: Renmin.

Mao Z. 毛泽东 (1994) 'Zhongjian didai you liangge' 中间地带有两个 [There are two middle zones], letter from 5 January 1965, in *Mao Zedong waijiao wenxuan* 毛泽东外交文选 [*Selected diplomatic writings of Mao Zedong*], Beijing: Zhongyang wenxian & Shijie zhishi.

Niu J. 牛军 (2006) *Lengzhan shiqi de Mei-Su guanxi* 冷战时期的美苏关系 [*The relationship between the USSR and the USA*], Beijing: Beijing daxue.

Shen Z. 沈志华 (2003) *Mao Zedong, Sidalin yu Chaoxian zhanzheng* 毛泽东, 斯大林与朝鲜战争 [*Mao Zedong, Stalin and the Korean War*], Guangzhou: Guangdong renmin.

—— (ed.) (2006) *Lengzhan shiqi Sulian yu Dong-Ou de guanxi* 冷战时期苏联与东欧的关系 [*The relationship between the Soviet Union and Eastern Europe during the Cold War*], Beijing: Beijing daxue.

Wu J. 吴建民 (2007) *Waijiao anli* 外交案例 [*Diplomatic cases*], Beijing: Zhongguo renmin daxue.

Yamamuro S. 山室信一 (2001) *Shisō kadai toshite no Ajia: kijiku, rensa tōki* 思想課題としてのアジア―基軸·連鎖·投企 [*Asia as a subject of thought – basic axis, link and project*], Tokyo: Iwanami shoten.

Yang K. 杨奎松 (2006) *Lengzhan shiqi de Zhongguo dui wai guanxi* 冷战时期的中国对外关系 [*The diplomatic relations of China during the Cold War*], Beijing: Beijing daxue.

2 Teaching 'the others' history' in Chinese schools

The state, cultural asymmetries and shifting images of Europe (from 1900 to today)

Gotelind Müller

This chapter develops the regional analysis presented in the preceding chapter, focusing specifically on the case of China and its portrayal in school texts of significant foreign 'Others'. It provides a historical overview of how official curriculum developers envisioned the teaching of world history in Chinese schools during the twentieth century. The various shifts in curricula design are analysed as clues to changing agendas of how to frame 'the self' and 'the other' in the normative setting of school education and the cultural asymmetries expressed in these shifts. Special attention is paid to the depiction of Europe. This is taken up in more detail in a second section on current history textbooks, which analyses the various ways in which 'Europe' is framed by Chinese curriculum developers today, and what this might tell us about the official perspective on projects of regional integration in general, and East Asian regionalisation in particular.

Introduction

To become aware of oneself is necessarily intertwined with becoming aware of the other. This truism is well documented for individual identity formation by developmental psychology's empirical studies. In the cultural field, the fact holds true as well, even if the other is arguably less important than in the case of children, who in their earliest phase totally depend on the other for survival. Thus, how strongly the other determines the self of cultural groups varies, but its – at least assumed – existence is nevertheless indispensable for drawing the line between the in- and out-groups and defining what is particular about the in-group. The degree of the other's importance is supposedly already an expression of real or perceived asymmetry: we preoccupy ourselves more with what seems essential (or threatening) to us, and are less inclined to invest in acquiring knowledge on 'others' just for knowledge's sake. The history of schoolbooks confirms this assumption as one way of defining 'self' and 'other' in a normative setting. What textbooks are required to talk about and what they are not, and how they do it, give us some clues on the guiding specific interests and motivations, as well as the conceptions of the 'self', at least on the side of textbook producing/designing agents (though not necessarily on the side of the addressed audience, i.e. the pupils). It also provides insights into which aspects of 'others' are deemed that important that future generations of the cultural–national 'self' should learn about them (be it for emulation or defence).

In the case of China, historically, there was not much official interest in *knowing* about the other, as long as there was no *need* to do so. The notion of China as 'all under heaven' (*tianxia* 天下) is well known enough, mirroring the officially maintained attitude of cultural superiority, even if *Realpolitik* in history sometimes was forced to acknowledge an inverted asymmetry, at least in terms of power relations (e.g. with the Liao, the Jin, the Mongols or the Manchus). Interest in the far-away West/Europe thus was much less developed than the other way round – a fact that has been bemoaned by many reformers and modernisers in China since the mid nineteenth century, when China suddenly appeared to lag behind in a more complex and competitive multi-centred world.

In the course of the nineteenth century, the situation changed, and East Asia was forced to pay more attention to the West/Europe. In China, at first reluctantly, information on the West was gathered and presented to the Chinese reading public.[1] However, only with the establishment of a modern school system did learning about the West/Europe become institutionalised and available to a greater number of Chinese. The school system's outlook owed much to European models, partly mediated via Japan. Besides learning about China's history, curricula now envisioned also the teaching of foreign history, including neighbouring Asian cultures at times, but above all focusing on Europe.

History education, its form and content, was an important place of knowledge production, guided by the state and its interests. It expressed a power asymmetry of the state enforcing its preferred history view via at times quite detailed guidelines, and, during most of the twentieth century, history education and textbook writers hardly managed to escape strict state control. But asymmetry was also at the basis of *what* was to be learned about the West: there was a perceived *need* to learn *from* the West/Europe how to develop (or what to avoid to achieve quick development). The overpowering social Darwinism paradigm thus conditioned much of how (world) history textbooks were framed and designed, what was to be included, and what not. This urge has still not lost its salience. Furthermore, Western (including also Soviet) books on European history often were used as reference when compiling Chinese textbooks.[2] This makes for a remarkably stable pool, for example, in the realm of illustrations.

The status of China vis-à-vis 'the world', however, changed and shifted over the twentieth century, and at the beginning of the twenty-first century China has regained much of what it had lost in status since the nineteenth century. Thus, the current attitude towards Europe, though still being influenced by developments and shifts over the twentieth century, has opened up new lines of interest. This is owing to the objective factor of China being more globalised and integrated into the world as a major player in economics and politics today (cf. China's participation and standing in various international organisations), but it is also owing to subjective factors connected to the objective/outward 'rise' and position/placement in global networks, nurturing a new national(ist) self-appreciation. Thus, asymmetries have shifted on material as well as psychological levels, and one of the consequences is a steady shift from 'victimisation history' to more 'happy history'. Connected to this, there is also a cautious but steady drive towards stronger integration of China also on a regional level.

Images of 'the others' consequently changed and shifted as well, along with shifts of interest by those teaching their history in China. To follow these shifts, this article will outline what the Chinese state wanted to teach about 'the others' history' over the twentieth century, and then look at how Europe in particular is presented today in history schoolbooks and what this may tell us about shifts in asymmetry between China and Europe.

Configuring Europe and the world in Chinese history curricula through the twentieth century: an overview

The earliest textbooks on world history had already come out in China before a national school system was officially established[3] and thus were largely free to design their contents, though in practice they took Western or Japanese textbooks as models.[4] It was only in the very last years of the Manchu Dynasty, in 1909, that the state actively intervened in history education and put out its first brief regulations for the teaching of history, including world history. Here 'foreign history' (*waiguo lishi* 外國歷史) is named as a third topic after 'Chinese history' (*zhongguoshi* 中國史) and the 'history of Asian nations' (*yazhou geguo shi* 亞洲各國史; LSJ 2001b: 9).[5]

However, it was only in the Early Republic that the regulations become more detailed. In 1913, the first to change was terminology: former 'Chinese history' became 'history of our country' (*benguoshi* 本國史), asserting the new national claims after the abdication of the 'foreign' Manchus. 'Asian history' was to be more specifically 'history of [East] Asian nations' (*dongya geguo shi* 東亞各國史),[6] and 'foreign history' became 'Western history' (*xiyangshi* 西洋史), thus narrowing down, at least terminologically, the scope of interest in comparison with the broader outlook of the late Qing (LSJ 2001b: 12).

The early 1920s were unique in that an all-encompassing 'history' class was aimed at, giving up the division between 'us' and 'them'.[7] This move was quite conscious, as the 1923 regulations for junior secondary school (*chuzhong* 初中) demonstrate. The 'conventional' division is to be overcome to present the common advance of mankind – and to overcome traditional dynastic periodisation. It thus helps to integrate and reframe *Chinese* history, above all, by theoretically presenting the whole world in one and the same framework. However, in a short enumeration of topics to be taught under the umbrella of a broad periodisation into 'antiquity' (*shanggu* 上古), 'middle ages' (*zhonggu* 中古), 'early modern' (*jingu* 近古) and 'modern' (*jinshi* 近世), the subchapters retained the division into Chinese and 'others', but for a few chapters on cultural contacts (LSJ 2001b: 14–15). At senior secondary school (*gaozhong* 高中) level, the guidelines of 1923 were even more innovative, including also new approaches to method. Thus, historical material was to be categorised and introduced to pupils also in a theme-oriented fashion, breaking up the purely chronological narrative. For the first time, as well, explicit emphasis was placed on modern times, which were to make up two-thirds of history teaching. These 1923 regulations were surprisingly modern from today's point of view also in the sense that they asked for simultaneous use of various materials, not just one textbook, stipulating also a more investigative type of learning. The teachers were called upon to give only some brief outlines and otherwise to use a question-based, interactive teaching method. This 'modern' outlook can also be detected in small, but telling, content details: the Mongols, for example, are presented in the context of their world empire as a 'centre', spreading out to the west and east during their expansion (LSJ 2001b: 19). This underlines the strong 'internationalist' and 'China-decentred' design of history teaching in the 1920s, which had given up China's traditional claim of representing the centre alone. 'Europe' as a term comes up here for the first time, with the Middle Ages and feudalism. Pupils were to learn about the Renaissance (termed here *fugu* 復古!, putting the accent on the 're' of 're-naissance' and implying a somewhat backward-oriented movement),[8] represented by Italy, and the rise of 'the nation' is specified here more broadly as 'Western' (*xiyang* 西洋), not 'European'. On the other hand, colonisation and economic invasion are associated with 'Western Europe' in the seventeenth/eighteenth century, focusing more precisely on England, Spain and France (i.e. on perceived 'great' nations). But this 'negative' feature is counterbalanced by integration of 'Western European' thought, i.e. humanism, rationalism and romanticism, as well as economic thought during that period (LSJ 2001b: 19). Thus, the pupil is obviously supposed to differentiate between 'the West' and various nations of 'Europe' in most cases, rather than being confronted with a consistent overarching category. 'The West', in turn, is named in connection to a 'middle-class' struggle for democracy, epitomised in the American and French revolutions. East Asian rival Japan, however, is interestingly not characterised as 'Westernised' but 'Europeanised' (*ouhua* 歐化). And it was 'European' powers that struggled among themselves because of economic aggression, in which context their aggression in China is situated, and the latter's fight against it. Thus, one gains the impression that 'the West' (which geographically covered the USA as well, but also appeared as more of a 'civilisation category') is rather mentioned in positive contexts, whereas problematic features are 'European', if not more country-specific.[9] Consequently, in 1923, the regulations talk about World War I as a 'European war' – a figure of speech that continued later in Taiwan[10] – which is interesting in view of the fact that China had at least joined the war, if late, and suffered from it during the Versailles Conference owing to Japanese gains on her territory, the immediate reason for the May Fourth demonstrations. Thus, this naming also reflected this remarkably China-decentred (though clearly anti-imperialist) approach to history in the early 1920s, following the general trend of historiography of the time, which was experimental and free to a degree hardly achieved again in the coming years.[11]

A new curriculum shift came with 1929 when the Nanjing regime of the Nationalist Party (GMD) had been firmly established and had ushered in a phase of much stronger state control, including in education. Now, the issue was to educate citizens for a new national(ist) state. Thus, Chinese history and 'foreign' history (*waiguoshi* 外國史) were again neatly separated, though there was an argument for pointing out connections between them in class where feasible (LSJ 2001b: 21), and this division would basically remain in practice until today.[12] On senior secondary school level, there were even two distinct sets of regulations. 'Foreign history' (the master term, although the term 'world history' (*shijieshi* 世界史) also appeared; LSJ 2001b: 24)[13] was now – and for the first time – explicitly devised as 'Euro-centric' (LSJ 2001b: 22).[14] The aim in studying 'foreign history' was decidedly teleological: to 'understand how the present came about', i.e. to 'understand the present international situation'. A certain revolutionary drive is still discernible here,[15] as it is stressed that it was imperialism and capitalism that brought about oppression of 'weak peoples' and workers (Culp 2007: 234). But, after 'the Great War' (*dazhan* 大戰) (i.e. World War I), these had started to protest. Thus, 'foreign history' should – above all – explain how imperialism came about. However, it is underlined: China does not want to learn imperialism in turn from historical example (LSJ 2001b: 37). Rather, the aim is to help redress this situation of being on the exploited side. On the other hand, Western scientific thought was seen as something to be learnt from the West (LSJ 2001b: 37). Thus, one of the newly introduced features was the topic of technology as a contribution to material culture. In other words, in science, the West/Europe was a model; politically it was not. In sum, though some features were retained from the earlier regulations, such as the focus on modern times in history teaching, there were also telling innovations, most notably the explicit connection of history teaching to 'political training' (LSJ 2001b: 21).

As for textbook use, the 1929 regulations were still rather liberal, especially because new textbooks had to be written first. So, creative ways of adapting existing teaching materials or other readings on foreign history, even including books in foreign languages, were accepted. And, for diversification of content, more 'cultural history' was argued for. In terms of time coverage, the post-World War I revolutionary activities in Europe were newly added, and the post-war situation was taken up in some detail. Furthermore, the guidelines asked for some cross-over and comparative teaching, e.g. building connections between geography and history, or drawing comparisons between the French and the Russian (October) Revolutions. Thus, it is interesting to note that these first GMD textbook regulations of 1929 retained quite some sympathy for innovative teaching in practice and for revolutionary history in teaching content. Also, the stress on historical relativity and on the plurality of voices in history is a strongly 'liberal' feature, suggesting a certain degree of continuity with the early 1920s (LSJ 2001b: 41).

This changed, however, in the early 1930s, when the GMD's efforts to keep its grip on the nation had become more decisive.[16] For junior secondary schools in 1932, the new regulations declared anti-imperialism *and* national pride as primary goals of history education (LSJ 2001b: 43). Following this tendency to promote loyalty on the part of Chinese subjects, there were some remarkable shifts in presentation: China now became 'centred' again. Therefore, for example, the Mongols at the time of their world empire were now called 'the Yuan' 元 (!), thus viewing them as 'Chinese' and, by this, laying *Chinese* claims to the world empire the Mongols once conquered, including China. With Europe, in early modern times the topic of the 'rise' to become 'strong nations' and, in the nineteenth century, the topic of nation-building (taking Italy and Germany as examples) were newly introduced (LSJ 2001b: 46), bespeaking the GMD's primary goal of nation-building at home. Connections between 'our' history and 'foreign' history were now reframed and 'institutionalised' by an obligatory final chapter on the relationship of both histories in general, on a comparison of both, and on the specific Chinese contribution to world history to 'centre' China again in the context of the world (LSJ 2001b: 47–8).

In the 1932 senior secondary school curriculum, 'foreign' history became a rather important topic, even getting an almost equal share with Chinese (*benguo* 本國) history.[17] Here, the 'world's races' (*renzhong* 人種) are introduced explicitly for the first time in the starting section as a new content feature, bespeaking the interest parts of the GMD harboured towards fascism at the time and the widespread interest in 'racial studies'.[18] Thus, in the 1930s, the GMD tried to build up a 'common identity', including the minorities in China, by arguing for 'racial bonds'.[19] (This 'racial' framing has reappeared only very recently and is part of current curricula.)

With the next curricula of 1936, at senior secondary school level Chinese and foreign history finally achieved equal shares, thus nominally marking a peak for education in 'foreign' history (LSJ 2001b: 68). However, the remark that foreign history books 'are lacking' suggests that textbook production according to the guidelines had not really made the envisioned progress (LSJ 2001b: 75). Thus, it seems, there were some discrepancies between the guidelines and teaching practice at the grass-roots level.[20]

During wartime, regulations came out to address the specific situation of an educational system under strained conditions and the need to enforce a clear-cut identity to China to hold together against the enemy. World history per se was obviously not of much interest now. Rather, to unify the country, topics such as ethnic amalgamation in China were of primary importance. Thus, world history now was to be taught only cursorily (one-fifth) in junior secondary school (LSJ 2001b: 77).[21] This consisted of a quick tour of Greece, Rome, Korea, Japan and India, which were to be mentioned as ancient cultures, followed by the religions of Christianity and Islam; feudalism, however, had completely disappeared. Thus, 'Europe' was to crop up only with regard to the Renaissance. The former nation-building examples, though, remained, and the discussion of the axis powers drew world history up to the present (LSJ 2001b: 80). In Chinese history, the nationalist move was even more pronounced, for example relegating Western standard calendar reckoning below the reintroduced Chinese traditional dynastic reign years (LSJ 2001b: 81). In senior secondary school, the 1940 regulations gave foreign history a somewhat higher share (two-fifths), but the content only repeated in more detail the topics already taught in junior secondary school. Just one year later, in 1941, the previous division of junior and senior secondary school was abolished (which meant that content, at least, was not to be repeated at both levels). Now, only in one out of six years was foreign history to be taught (LSJ 2001b: 89). In wartime, obviously, there were more pressing issues than teaching foreign history.

In 1948, finally, the last regulations of the GMD were promulgated. As in the early 1920s, there was a move to integrate 'foreign' and 'own' history, at least in junior secondary school (LSJ 2001b: 97). Thus, invoking again the example of the Mongols, the appellation of 'Yuan' when presenting their world empire was tacitly removed. But this move 'back' to some of the early 1920s positions was only partial, as, at senior secondary school level, the division between 'own' and 'foreign' was retained, and 'foreign' history was to be as brief and cursory as in 1940 (LSJ 2001b: 100). Thus, in the very last months of GDM rule, no substantial overhaul of curricula could be achieved.

After the establishment of the People's Republic of China (PRC), curricula were rewritten. In the first years under communism, history was to be a subject even in elementary school. The mid 1950 elementary history curriculum stipulated the new base line: workers and class struggle are the makers of history. And historical materialism is the way to understand history. China was declared a multi-ethnic nation that contributed to world civilisation. Pupils should therefore, above all, learn self-respect, for example that the Chinese people are 'diligent, courageous and smart' (LSJ 2001b: 104). In the whole curriculum, world history made up only a tiny part, basically in terms of a world revolutionary picture (LSJ 2001b: 105). Avoiding duplication with junior secondary school was one declared reason for this short treatment of foreign history (even though the young PRC did not come out with regulations for the latter quickly). Furthermore, 'world history' (in the PRC, consistently called *shijieshi* 世界史) was to focus on the 'daily growing peace camp' under the Soviet Union's leadership, whereas the US-led imperialist 'invaders' camp' was to be presented as being 'doomed'. (One might remember it was also the time of the beginning of the Korean War and the 'socialist North Korean brother's' advance, adding to the Chinese Communists' (CCP) 'conventional' anti-American propaganda.) The third focus of 'world history' was to be on anti-colonial liberation movements and their necessary success (LSJ 2001b: 107). For the first time in Chinese curricular development, illustrations were explicitly asked for and specified: they should comprise 'plans of revolutionary developments, time charts, statues of outstanding personalities, and photos of historic places' (LSJ 2001b: 108). Thus, even though earlier history textbooks did in fact often provide visual material, only now was its specific importance acknowledged by the state by the perceived need to regulate and actively use it.

It was, however, only in 1956 that curricula for all levels were reworked, thus leaving junior and senior secondary schools until then in a kind of grey operational zone. This general overhaul of curricula started again with elementary history lessons. However, world history was almost absent again at that level. The West appeared only in the context of imperialist aggression against China – but for the 'revolutionary' part of the First International, Marx and Engels, Lenin and the like. In addition, the most recent Bandung Conference of Asian and African states was to be mentioned, showing China's new diplomatic efforts and her willingness to speak to and for the (Third) world (LSJ 2001b: 128).

Interestingly, the 1956 curricula in general went back to the old GMD split between 'us' and 'them'.[22] In both junior and senior secondary schools, separate sets of curricula were devised: one for 'Chinese history', one for 'world history', thus stressing the difference even more than did the GMD. (Obviously, Soviet Union (SU) curricular models were influencing this consistent, clear-cut division.[23]) Now there was some coordination between junior and senior secondary school history teaching, as junior secondary schools were to take on mainly ancient history, while senior secondary schools were to focus on modern times. However, compulsory education was still far off, i.e. only a certain percentage of pupils would actually make it to junior and senior secondary school – a marked difference from the Soviet model influential at the time – and thus world history education would only 'reach' some of the pupils (Jones 2005a: 74). The declared aim of world history education was now to educate for an 'internationalist communist world-view' (LSJ 2001b: 166). Thus, the Chinese Revolution should appear as part of world revolution, as the whole world functions according to class-struggle principles, moving through the five economic stages (primitive society, slave-holder society, feudalism, capitalism, socialism). The pronounced marking of 'European' history as basically 'Western European' in most instances is notable (and might reflect current political camps on both sides of the 'Iron Curtain'). With Italy and the ascent of capitalism, this 'rise' of Europe – in GMD times viewed as a critically important nation-building topic – had to be explained now as owing much to Chinese inventions such as printing (!), thus relativising European (capitalist) 'success' (LSJ 2001b: 169).

Looking at the details of the syllabus, which sketched out textbook contents more minutely than ever before, one notes a certain focus on 'outstanding figures', which contrasts the call for a 'materialist interpretation' of history in the general guidelines with a factual 'great men' view: thus, Cromwell, Peter the Great, Pugachev – the only 'unsuccessful figure' in this list – Louis XIV, Voltaire, Montesquieu and Rousseau are listed for the earliest phase of 'modern' history. The French Revolution appears rather critical in historical judgement here, as teachers were explicitly asked to stress the difference between a capitalist (French) and a proletarian revolution (LSJ 2001b: 187).[24] Napoleon, in turn, was to be characterised as an invader, especially in his attacking Russia. (This clearly reflects a Russian/Soviet influence in Chinese history schoolbooks at the time, as, prior to 1949 as today, Napoleon tends to be presented rather as a 'great man'!) And a first kind of 'canonisation' of the 'great powers' of the late nineteenth century was established by designing separate subchapters for Germany, England, France, Russia, the US and Japan, always adding remarks on their aggression in China in the negative and on their own workers' movements in the positive. Only with Russia was its aggression towards China left out – obviously owing to the current 'friendship' with the SU, which was 'extended' backwards also to the portrayal of tsarist times. Worst of all was, of course, the USA as the 'typical monopolistic capitalist'. The newly introduced topic of the Paris Commune, however, became an important dividing line in periodisation (LSJ 2001b: 170),[25] and teleological narration should – in the eyes of the state – point out the 'necessary' victory of communism. Together with this teleological view, there was a pronounced accent on chronology and 'facts' (LSJ 2001b: 171). Owing to the new 'division of labour' between junior and senior secondary schools, the senior secondary school curriculum for world history of 1956 exclusively dealt with modern times. The 'political' act of the English Revolution of the seventeenth century was to mark the beginning of this 'modern' history, which was to end with the October Revolution, again subdivided into a former and later period by the Paris Commune. This 'political' (Maoist) periodisation would remain until the most recent times in the PRC, when, in the Deng era, the 'economic' (traditional Marxist) periodisation came to the forefront again.

As for the rest of the world, the syllabus gives special treatment to 'awakening Asian countries' in the beginning of the twentieth century. Probably not unconnected to the recent Korean War, Korea was especially highlighted, and in the 1950s there was still stressed a communality with Vietnam (later China's enemy) in struggling against the French. (Notably, the old 'vassal' countries, Korea and Vietnam, head the list of 'awakening Asian countries', which then moves further west over India to Persia and Turkey – indirectly bespeaking a China-centred approach.) The treatment of the SU, in turn, went into some detail also on the New Economic Policy (NEP) and later 'socialist' construction, especially addressing the planned economy and its successes – topics that were to become more sensitive in China in the coming years of dispute about economic policies. When taking up the period of the 1930s, the guidelines stipulated that Japan's aggression was to be linked up in teaching with the coming World War II, notably glossing over Stalin's non-aggression pact with Hitler (which could have shaken the belief in the 'firm resistance' against fascism), whereas the appeasement of the Western countries was denounced as 'helping' the fascists (LSJ 2001b: 192). The SU's central (and 'socialist peace-loving') role is reinforced also by presenting it as being forced into participating in World War II by Hitler's attack, therewith, however, marking a new phase of the war.[26] Consequently, it was the SU's combat that put down fascism, whereas the Allies were not credited at all. For developments after the war, anti-colonialism throughout the world was to be shown advancing, suggesting a unilinear development of the whole world in the direction of socialism (LSJ 2001b: 193).

After this most comprehensive outline of history education in the early PRC in 1956 for all levels, which had not much time left to be put into effect before the Anti-Rightist Movement and the ensuing Great Leap shook up the nation and the education system, in 1957 there was an official intervention in history education to the effect that textbooks were 'too demanding', and thus 'simplification' was called for. Reflecting the ever more difficult relationship with the SU and the Chinese Maoist quest for a particular 'Chinese way', it was decreed that only in natural sciences could SU textbooks be used any longer as a model, whereas other textbooks should reflect more 'Chinese conditions' (LSJ 2001b: 236). New textbooks had been, in fact, produced since 1953,[27] but obviously there was no consensus on modifications in 1957, and so just 'simplification' – which went well with the thrust of the Great Leap – was called for.

The next – and last – curriculum reform before the Cultural Revolution came in 1963. Basically, tendencies already present in the 1956 curriculum were now radicalised. However, owing to the ongoing shifts in Chinese politics and the contemporary socialist education campaign, the guidelines were even more contradictory. On the one hand, a focus on outstanding personalities in history was officially rejected in favour of a reading based on social conditions and historical stages, but, on the other hand, the syllabus, in fact, showed a notable accent on 'great men' (LSJ 2001b: 239)! With secondary education, the accent on 'outstanding people' was even called for explicitly, naming, as a kind of baseline, Qin Shihuangdi (秦始皇帝; 259–10 BC), Han Wudi (漢武帝; 156–87 BC), Tang Taizong (唐太宗; 599–649) and Kangxi (康熙; 1654–1722) for Chinese history; Solon, Charlemagne, Peter the Great and Lincoln for world history. This was explained as going in tandem with the idea to highlight people who had made a 'positive contribution' in history, whereas the 'bad' ones should be talked about only in the second line. (That kind of argumentation already prepared much of what became diffused in the coming years during the Cultural Revolution and its favorite 'theory' of the 'three accentuations', *san tuchu* 三突出.[28]) On the other hand, one of the declared key tasks of history education was to drive home the difference between a capitalist and a socialist revolution (which was to be only underscored by some leading revolutionary figures), and class struggle was to be the most important notion of all.

World history had a one-fourth share in history education, again mostly modern world history (whereas the ratio of ancient to modern Chinese history was balanced). However, an uncertainty in (or rather: the contested state of) historical judgement can be seen in the stipulation that now only the period until 1949 was to be discussed in Chinese and world history, thus avoiding taking sides with later developments (LSJ 2001b: 240). Furthermore, history education should demonstrate to the pupils how the Chinese 'great dynasties' influenced the world and what they received – on the other hand – from outside, thus relating Chinese and world history (LSJ 2001b: 257). Furthermore, the guidelines demanded that Eurocentrism should be broken up by adding more non-European history – thus also moving away from Soviet models. Political struggles of the time are also reflected in the outline's call not to talk too much about 'theory', but to get down to concrete issues,[29] even if 'correct' evaluations were mandatory. The guidelines explicitly warned against taking all history as allegorical hints for today – as was the position of the leftists. And world history also should educate towards friendship with neighbours and beware of chauvinism (LSJ 2001b: 259) – a call that went unheard, judging from hindsight, with regard to all the territorial conflicts in the years to come. But the world history syllabus of 1963 secondary education also self-assuredly pointed out, for example with feudalism, that China made the transition to feudalism 1,000 years earlier than Europe! If the end of feudalism in Europe came with peasant uprisings in the fourteenth to sixteenth centuries and the first manufactures in Italy, then China was for most of ancient history's time much more advanced than all others. And – as a kind of addendum to global ancient history – it obviously 'gave much' to other Asian cultures (LSJ 2001b: 302). The detailed syllabus even argued, in the context of the seafarers (namely Diaz, da Gama, Columbus and Magellan), that this 'classical' Western 'rise' topic was now to be 'enriched' by adding Chinese seafarer Zheng He (鄭和; 1371–1433(?)), stressing again that he was 'earlier' than the Europeans (LSJ 2001b: 312).[30] In the context of the 'Asian peoples' struggle against foreign invasion', the more self-assured Chinese attitude is evident as well in presenting the Taiping 太平 in this context as a major force; and the contribution of Chinese immigrants to Indonesia's struggle against the Dutch is also highlighted (LSJ 2001b: 317). Thus, in this historical vision of 'world' history, the emergent self-complacent Sinocentric attitude is striking – and obviously is to compensate for the 'loss' of the Soviet model. In sum, in Chinese perception, an upgrading of the Chinese 'self' was necessary, leading to a readjustment in cultural asymmetry between the Soviet–European and the Chinese side in history textbooks.

After 1963, there was a longer break in curriculum development, owing to the Cultural Revolution. Even though textbooks on history were also produced in this phase, especially in the last years of the Cultural Revolution, there were no official guidelines, as the Ministry of Education remained closed for years. Thus, the next official regulations came out only after the Cultural

Revolution, in 1978. Here, the transition to a new framework emerges. For the first time, Maoism is explicitly referred to, and recent political struggles are evident: there is a denunciation of 'Liu Shaoqi (劉少奇; 1898–1969), Lin Biao (林彪; 1907–71) and the 'Gang of Four's' idealist history view' and especially of the 'Gang of Four's' distortion of history, which used it only as a weapon for attack (LSJ 2001b: 327), such as speaking about Confucianism versus Legalism when intending 'classes'. Now, classical Marxist history concepts such as the relations of production and the like were reinstated. The still prevailing uneasiness over how to tread on the contested field of education is reflected anew, however, in frequent, cautious insertions of citations of Mao's works, which had almost never been cited earlier in guidelines during Mao's lifetime. Previously, hardly any citations were to be found, and where they were, they were usually from Marx and Engels or Lenin (LSJ 2001b: 328).[31] Looking more closely, however, one realises that Mao's chosen words are skilfully used to defend and shield the transition to what is actually a new framework that differed in content from the earlier 'Maoist' thrust in education. A new note is, for example, struck by China being defined again as multi-ethnic, *without*, however, insisting on the 'central role' of the Han. Typical of the new, post-Cultural Revolution framework was also the new accent on economy in history. In general, world history was to be taught only in the first year of senior secondary school (which was integrated in the newly established 'whole ten-years education system'), and it was stipulated that it had to be taught through to the end of World War II only, whereas the time afterwards was to be merely sketched out, naming the SU – in accordance with 'politically correct' parlance of the time – as representing socialist imperialism, US imperialism, the Cold War and the 'Third World's awakening'. (With Chinese history, however, it was decided that it should be taught until 1957, arguing that this was the year the fifth volume of the official edition of Mao's works came out. Thus, obviously, one still felt safe only under Mao's 'umbrella'.) In textbook styles, there was one new feature introduced: a division into main text and smaller sections for 'self study' signalled a breaking away from the exclusive focus on the teacher's narrative along textbook lines (LSJ 2001b: 330). In addition, a new attention to complementary material such as films etc. is to be noticed (LSJ 2001b: 330), again suggesting a first move towards a greater consideration of soliciting pupils' interest.

All in all, these 1978 guidelines show a first tentative move to break free of Maoist fetters without a complete rupture with the past, hiding the shift behind a carefully constructed Maoist façade, which resulted in the obviously transitional character of the guidelines. The transition went on with the 1980 curriculum, but, in 1986, the new framework fully emerged, and the educational system was overhauled on all levels, thus marking the year as the second decisive moment in the PRC history curriculum development after 1956. Finally, history would now be taught up to the present, i.e. up to the 1980s. (This was very probably owing to the 1981 party resolution on history, which had decided upon historical 'verdicts' also for the more recent period. Thus, an official genre such as textbooks could finally follow up trends that had been spelled out already in academic historiography (LSJ 2001b: 441).[32]) All in all, the tone of the 1986 guidelines was moderate. In post-World War II history, the successes of the capitalist countries were now conceded, and their innovative power was acknowledged. The socialist countries, in turn, were spoken of somewhat vaguely as being 'set upon reform', and the attacks on the SU were notably toned down (LSJ 2001b: 483), reflecting the political détente underway. Structurally, there were some new chapters added, such as the ones on Western science, literature and art, which, however, were marked as 'not relevant' for examination (LSJ 2001b: 487), thus again demonstrating a move towards a more complex design of lessons and textbooks, with obligatory and facultative sections.

Shortly afterwards, in 1988, another important step was taken by new regulations that established finally the new compulsory education system of nine years, with six years of elementary and three years of junior secondary school, as it is still today. Several other new developments can be discerned here: there was a whole new section introduced in the guidelines on 'principles' of structuring content. These stress that the economy has to be the most important aspect, and only on this basis should one discuss politics and culture (an anti-Maoist and Dengist stance). A further principle is 'friendship' with other countries, another historical materialism. Thus, there is clearly a return to 'classical' Marxist positions (LSJ 2001b: 511), which had been the direction of change since the Cultural Revolution but was only now safely engrained enough to be declared explicitly. Chinese history was to be taught in an ancient–modern ratio of 1:1, whereas world history was to remain mainly modern (1:2; LSJ 2001b: 512). Structurally new are the introductory 'guiding questions' taking up general problems such as why and how one should study world history (LSJ 2001b: 533), thus adding a more reflective note to the 'traditional' simple memorising of historical facts.

In 1990, the next curriculum came out, encompassing now both junior and senior secondary schools, but the contents were not significantly altered. Only in 1991 did a new turn become evident in an official comment on history education, based on then-General Secretary Jiang Zemin's (江澤民; 1926–) call for an education 'fitting the national sentiment' (*guoqing* 國情; LSJ 2001b: 607). Here, clearly, the current upheavals in the socialist world were in the background. Language became more aggressive again, for instance interpreting post-World War II history as being nothing else than a continuation of imperialism by other means (LSJ 2001b: 631). History education had, again, become problematic owing to context changes, and thus these years were another little transitional phase before a decision was reached on how to deal with these recent challenges in the world, with the demise of the Soviet Union and Eastern European socialist states[33] adding to inner-Chinese tensions epitomised in the 1989 protests and their crushing. Obviously, established views of 'self' and 'other' had to be readjusted.

Current images of Europe in Chinese history textbooks: an analysis

With the new regulations for junior secondary school history textbooks in 1992, history education started to shift towards readjusting to the current situation (LSJ 2001b: 656–85). On the one hand, owing to worldwide, massive changes in connection with the dissolution of the SU and the recent legitimacy crisis in China in 1989, a new section on 'ideological education' was added to the guidelines for history classes (LSJ 2001b: 678–9). However, also introduced was a more 'modern' stress on 'competence education', thus demonstrating a simultaneously defensive and modernising reaction to cope with the situation (LSJ 2001b: 679). In terms of evaluations of European history, one notable issue is the more and more pronouncedly positive evaluation of the French Revolution (LSJ 2001b: 677), which in the years to come would finally shake off the 'ambivalent' reading of its being a 'capitalist' revolution to being declared, if not hailed as, a 'great revolution' (*da geming* 大革命) in 1994 (LSJ 2001b: 701). The 'ideological' topic of the Paris Commune, though, was downgraded in importance. This is one of the signs of how Chinese historiography tried to bridge the gap to world historiography abroad at the time without forsaking 'revolutionary history' per se.[34] Furthermore, when talking about the most recent period, history classes in the mid 1990s would, for the first time, also take up the issue of European integration – and try to explain the end of the SU to Chinese pupils (LSJ 2001b: 684). In this context, a new reading of the post-Cold War world, with the new political formula of 'one superpower' (i.e. the USA) and the multipolarisation of the world (*duojihua* 多極化), was introduced in the 1996 guidelines (LSJ 2001b: 704). Thus, the discussion of Europe *apart* from the USA also came up in the context of a certain 'counterweight' to the negatively 'hegemonic' United States. The 1996 section on 'ideological education', furthermore, argued that the world has grown competitive, implying that the educational aim of patriotism is also meant to help China remain competitive through the loyalty and dedication of her subjects (and thus not only to bolster the CCP's claim to power, probably to gain wider acceptance for the need of 'ideological education'; LSJ 2001b: 705). The periodisation also manifests a new approach: it is, in a way, much more traditionally Marxist in giving higher priority to economic than political developments – something that is in line with the whole readjustment after the Cultural Revolution, as we have seen, but that only now was firmly entrenched enough to even tackle periodisations. Whereas, in the Mao era, the 'political' English Revolution had usually marked the beginning of 'modern times' (*jindai* 近代), now that place was taken by the 'rise of capitalism' – going well also with the CCP's cautious reappraisal of market economy at the time (LSJ 2001b: 706). The 2000 guidelines add a new perspective only with regard to the fact that the crumbling of communism in Eastern Europe is now explained as a momentary 'low ebb of socialism' and that one should understand the world as being in 'continuous turmoil' (LSJ 2001b: 730), thus making room for no longer having to end with a 'rosy' revolutionary future perspective, as CCP textbooks had been required to do for decades, which had become ever more difficult to sustain in view of realities. Some reason is given also for the 'failure' of Eastern Europe: reforms in the 1970s and 1980s were 'not adequately' undertaken, thus implicitly throwing into profile the 'correct' Dengist course. China's future – a kind of continuous warning – depends on it being made fit for 'international competition', and in this regard the CCP has historically 'proven' to be the most capable agent.

The present guidelines demonstrate some further shifts in designing 'self' and 'other' in history teaching.[35] Now, for the first time, state-authored curricula – notably terminologically downgraded to 'curricula standards' – in the PRC devise an obligatory enumeration of the 'three races' (white, yellow, black) in the very first section of the world history course (LKB 2001a: 21),[36] thus ironically taking up a legacy of the GMD in the 1930s. Even though this might be explained as a (nineteenth-century) Marxist-driven attempt to ground 'history' again in 'materialist' biological factors, it goes well with the new 'racial' recasting of Chinese identity and culture (blending the 'racial' and the cultural 'self') discernible in China mainly since the 1980s and thus, again, proves textbooks to be mirrors of the state's general agenda.[37] Furthermore, it goes well with the perceived global 'competition' for which education has to make Chinese citizens fit. Thus, for example, historical issues such as cultural contacts, which earlier were divided in textbooks into singular sections when considering a specific region (e.g. Arab civilisation, followed by Sino–Arabian cultural contacts; Korean civilisation, followed by Sino–Korean contacts, etc.), were now reorganised into a new comprehensive chapter on global cultural contacts and conflicts, from the Greco–Persian Wars to Marco Polo, thus focusing on the theme of coexistence and rivalry through the ages. In this way, the pupil is also to realise that interaction and integration with the world often entail politically and culturally asymmetrical arrangements, but also constant efforts to readjust them.

As for the framing of 'Europe' and the West, in pre-modern history the term 'Europe' comes up – as in earlier textbooks – as 'Western Europe' only with the Middle Ages and 'feudalism'. In modern, i.e. 'real' world, history (LKB 2001a: 23),[38] in turn, the 'most important European nations' are to be focused upon, as they (and later Japan) made the transition from feudalism to capitalism and only then moved ahead of China. This all remains in the established framework. Notable, however, is that this section on the 'rise' of capitalism switches back in language to a rather emotional and aggressive tone, for instance stating that capitalism 'cruelly exploited' other peoples or that the powers aimed 'madly' at enlarging their colonies (LKB 2001a: 23), which in the – for the rest – rather prosaic style of today's guidelines appears somewhat anachronistic. The 'most important countries' of 'Europe' and America are, however, also credited for initiating the second industrial revolution and for having art, as technology, boom in an 'unprecedented way'

(LKB 2001a: 23). Thus, 'modern' world history is designed to above all 'analyse capitalism's progressing character, brutality, greediness and expansiveness' to make pupils 'realise the great historical importance of the birth of Marxism' and to 'understand the righteousness and reasonableness of the fight of the colonised peoples against capitalist invasion and expansion' (LKB 2001a: 24). In sum, the 'modern' West still appears as highly problematic in these current guidelines.

If one looks to the syllabus details, however, there are slight differences:[39] for example, for the early phase of 'modern' history, not only is capitalism mentioned (in terms of maritime expansion), but also the Renaissance (in terms of an art topic), as a 'counterbalance'. The three major developments of the English Glorious Revolution, American independence and the 'great French Revolution' are to be represented by the 'Bill of Rights', the 'Declaration of Independence' and the 'Declaration of the Rights of Man', thus introducing pupils to crucial texts of Western (liberal!) tradition. And, for the 'personal' part, Washington and Napoleon are chosen as standing for the (great) 'capitalist politicians'. Thus, the stress is much less on the negative aspects, which leaves one with the impression that the general guidelines might be more of a political statement, whereas the syllabus is more interested in the West's 'contributions' to 'world history'. The suggestions for activities also add new features in that, for example, with the Renaissance, the reading whether the 're' was more important or the 'naissance' should be discussed, which makes for an interesting (more complicated) view compared with the formerly simple 'progressive' reading of that topic in the PRC. Napoleon, on the other hand, is even part of 'emotional education' with the suggestion of the film *The Battle of Austerlitz* (*Austerlitz*, German film of 1960), notably shifting him from the earlier somber figure – under Soviet influence, which denounced him for his attack on Russia – to a 'great man' dominating Europe![40]

Only with colonisation, another 'emotional' topic that, however, touched China herself, is the negative image of Europe consistent: the 'brutality' of it has to be demonstrated to the pupil. Thus, the example of Robert Clive, who laid the foundations of British rule in India, is newly introduced, adding to the already established narrative of Britain having been able to become a 'great nation' only thanks to exploitation of its colonies. Again, there is a suggestion to educate emotionally – this time towards sympathy with anti-colonial forces – by a movie on the Indian 'Queen of Jhansi', who attempted to resist the British in the mid nineteenth century (LKB 2001a: 25).[41] In a sense, then, where Napoleon represents the topic of European great power (at home), the 'Queen of Jhansi' points at that power's abuse (abroad).

Furthermore, with a view of how the rest of the world *positively* coped with that European/Western power, a kind of tentative comparative discussion of reform policies is introduced with the Meiji Restoration and Japan's way to 'capitalism' by contrasting it with the (failed) Chinese 1898 reforms (LKB 2001a: 26).[42] Europe, however, is to be looked at also for the development of the workers' movement and communism, i.e. as providing important lessons on how to deal with capitalism critically as well. A major topic is, of course, the world wars, namely World War II. In this context, a slightly new note is provided by suggesting the film *The Defense of Stalingrad*[43] – stressing the Soviet contribution to anti-fascism – together with the film *General Patton*[44] – now also crediting the Allies with this US 'hero'(!) – by which pupils should gain confidence that righteousness will be victorious in the end (LKB 2001a: 30). In this way, the aim of teaching World War II in the context of 'world history' classes – in marked difference from the teaching of it in 'Chinese history' classes, which focuses on the Chinese–Japanese conflict and Japanese wartime atrocities in China – is a view of World War II's global implications, stressing the common (achieved) goal to subdue fascism. As for the post-war period, compared with earlier guidelines, a new feature in the current ones is the integration of biotechnology and Western popular culture (jazz or Hollywood movies) as new topics to be covered by 'world history', making for a more diversified and less exclusively 'political' image of the present West/Europe, thus opening up new lines of interest to pupils.

Now, how do the guidelines translate into textbooks? And what images of Europe in particular emerge? I will take a look at three currently used sets of world history textbooks for junior secondary school based on the national curriculum standards (still in the testing phase), which also provide some regional diversification:[45] the indisputably most widely used People's Education Press (PEP)[46] textbook in current (2008) use, appearing in Beijing, the textbook for the Shanghai region by East China Normal University Press[47] and the one for Sichuan in South-West China, published by Sichuan Education Press. As the most relevant shifts for a 'new' way of configuring 'Europe', China and their contemporary impact are focused on the *current* role of Europe and China in the world,[48] I will consider here specifically the representations of the post-war era in these textbooks.

The PEP textbook takes on the prescribed post-war topic of 'the most important capitalist countries' development and change' by covering 'Western Europe' and Japan in one chapter (after having presented the USA in a separate one), discussing their economic take-off. It states that, in the early 1950s, Western Europe already was beyond its pre-war economic level. Furthermore, the pupil learns about how West Germany and France became the nucleus of the European Community. The textbook also tells in detail what has changed with integration: everyone and every good or capital can move freely, one can take up work and settle or study everywhere. The tendency to come closer to a unified foreign policy is also stressed. The participant countries 'share' their resources and complement each other (which sounds almost communist), and all benefit economically. (The growth of the European Union is up to date to 2007.) There is one passport, one flag and one anthem (Beethoven's *Ode to Joy* – which is very famous in China, though few Europeans might be aware that it is the 'common anthem' of the European Union). The institutional structure of the European Union is presented as well. Thus, the image of the European Union emerges as extremely positive

'The others' history' in Chinese schools 49

and driven by ideals (*Shijie lishi, xia* 2007: 54–6).[49] (The book, however, does not talk about Asian integration, e.g., the ASEAN, as others do.) In the chapter on the present situation, it becomes quite clear that the 'exaltation' of Europe also has some 'anti-US background'. It is pointed out in the introductory section, at length,[50] that the USA were close to a voting debacle in 2000 for elections to the UN Human Rights Committee, which is thought to show that many countries, i.e. including the 'traditional' US allies in Western Europe, are less inclined to accept US 'hegemony' today (*Shijie lishi, xia* 2007: 90). The present 'multi-polar' world, the textbook states, at least includes Europe, Japan, China and Russia, besides the USA, as 'poles' (*Shijie lishi, xia* 2007: 91). And as the guidelines ask for a special treatment of the Kosovo Conflict to denounce US/NATO actions, the blame on the whole conflict is put on the USA exclusively, and the bombing of the Beograd Chinese Embassy is accentuated by a photo of Chinese youths demonstrating against the 'US bombings' (*Shijie lishi, xia* 2007: 92). The USA is to be 'unmasked' for having 'used' the human rights argument to invade a sovereign European country (the Yugoslavian Federation) – which is probably why the aforementioned introductory section had addressed the human rights voting debacle, and the number of warships and airplanes is enumerated to show how the USA forcefully attempted to go against a multipolarisation of the world. Effectively, critical US human rights reports are cited to show America's 'black' side and to make pupils think about US human rights rhetoric even more (*Shijie lishi, xia* 2007: 93). However, the answer to this contested situation should be more worldwide integration, and thus the last chapter deals with globalisation and China's joining the World Trade Organization (WTO), the latter's problematic aspects for China not negating the action, which on balance has been 'the right step'.

The Shanghai textbook is slightly different in tone. On the post-war period, it is more critical, for example also noting the recent (since the late 1980s) trend of a neo-conservative rise around the globe (Wang S. 2006: 89). It does not split the American economic rise from Europe and Japan, as PEP did, and puts the emphasis with European integration on Western Europe's economic necessities and on its being squeezed in between the two superpowers, i.e. it argues for the whole process having been driven by need, not lofty ideals. From the outset, it is described as an activity of 'the Six' (France, Germany, Italy, the Netherlands, Belgium and Luxembourg; Wang, S. 2006: 93). However, only the early developments until 1991 are discussed together in the same chapter. The questions at the end of this chapter, though, explicitly ask whether European integration could be more than a specific case: a model of global significance (Wang S. 2006: 96). Thus, the more 'sceptical' Shanghai textbook is the one to raise the question of China's possible consideration of similar efforts. In the chapter on the liberation movements in Asia, Africa and Latin America, the textbook also takes up the 'rise' of Singapore and South Korea and includes a short discussion of the 'Four Tigers', encompassing 'China's Taiwan' and Hong Kong together with the other two (Singapore and

Korea; Wang S. 2006: 104–5), bespeaking its consideration of 'Asian' contexts and prospects. The part on the WTO, on the other hand, is much more positive than in the PEP textbook, leaving out the latter's reservations and arguing that finally China is part of the world (which might also reflect Shanghai's strong position in international economics; Wang S. 2006: 123). In its treatment of the Gulf, Iraq and Kosovo wars, the Shanghai textbook, however, is even more anti-US than PEP (which, probably, being located in Beijing, close to the government and issuing the most diffused textbooks, would be more cautious also for diplomatic reasons). The USA is furthermore accused of destruction of the environment (and 'Third World countries' of population explosion, the Chinese part in both not directly addressed, however! Wang S. 2006: 124–7). Thus, the Shanghai textbook reflects an awareness of China's being part of international competition and of the need to reconsider the specific advantages of its geopolitical situation to develop its competitive potentials.

The Sichuan textbook, finally, presents still another view: it, again, takes all prospering economies after the war, i.e. the USA, Western Europe and Japan, together as exemplifying the 'golden era' of economic development (Gong 2006: 90). With regard to Europe, West Germany's economic success is particularly highlighted (Gong 2006: 91–2). European integration is also presented, naming above all France and Italy(!), and only in the italics section (not necessary to read) giving more details since 1951. However, the section is very short and no comparison to the rather detailed introduction in PEP. The European Union is mainly seen – like Japan – as a competitor with the USA, 'shaking' the 'hegemony' of the United States (Gong 2006: 95). However, it is precisely the Sichuan book that talks more about 'Asian integration'. Thus, only here does the ASEAN come up (Gong 2006: 108). (The 'Four Little Tigers' enumerated after describing the take-off of South Korea and Singapore notably mean, here, Malaysia, Thailand, the Philippines and Indonesia, bespeaking a stronger interest in Southeast Asia, which – after all – is also geographically close to south-west China (Gong 2006: 108). It means, however, that Taiwan and Hong Kong and their remarkable economic successes in the post-war period do not figure at all!) In the globalisation chapter, international organisations, including the European Union, but also APEC, are cited as examples of growing connectedness (Gong 2006: 121). The story of the European Union is consequently taken up in this context again, focusing on the time since the 1990s. Globalisation, however, is seen as ambivalent to some extent, as with PEP, as it also entails new challenges (Gong 2006: 123). As for the European Union, it is finally taken up a third time in the chapter on multipolarisation. Again, the European Union is evidently presented as a welcome competitor with the USA (Gong 2006: 127), and that the Europeans (like China) often have trade problems with the United States as well is listed (Gong 2006: 128), as is Germany's and France's criticism of the Iraq War. The textbook also addresses the issue of 9/11, but it does so only in terms of a 'positive shock' for the USA, as, after that, the

'The others' history' in Chinese schools 51

United States finally made some moves towards China and Russia (Gong 2006: 130), thus demonstrating that the textbook's interest lies merely in the foreign policy implications of that event. China's joining of the WTO, in turn, is evaluated as very positive (Gong 2006: 133), thus being in line with the basic tenor of the Sichuan textbook, which might be described as 'China's getting back finally to the place it ought to hold in the world'. In a way, where PEP voiced the 'ideals' of an integrated 'rise', with a view to Europe as an implicit 'model other', the Shanghai textbook linked this explicitly to the competitive situation in which China should consider applying a similar strategy, and the Sichuan textbook showed confidence in the success of the latter in terms of an emerging strong, new 'self'.

Taking together these three examples of world history textbooks, one might conclude that there is a notable interest in present-day 'Europe' represented by the European Union, but that this interest is intimately tied up with China's attempt to 'rise' in the context of a 'multipolar' world. Connected to this is the evident ambivalence towards the question of a similar Asian integration. In any case, 'Europe' clearly is framed with a view to outbalancing US 'hegemony' in global politics. Thus, whereas China had felt compelled to learn about (and from) 'Europe's' development earlier, i.e. since the nineteenth century, now cultural, economic and political asymmetries have undergone a substantial shift towards China's dealing with the 'West' at eye level, with the perspective of possibly raising itself to the upper end of a new asymmetry.

Regional integration? Instead of a conclusion

The current PRC world history textbooks show that, not surprisingly, much of the established, classical Marxist view on Western history is still there. Europe's historical image thus remains strongly tied to imperialism and capitalism, but it is noticeable that, at present, these aspects are more downplayed, whereas Europe as a cultural 'model' in the sense of (past) greatness, for example with 'great people' and scientific achievements, comes up again (not dissimilar to the late Qing and Early Republican phase, though the scientific component owes much to later Soviet influence as well). What remains in the wings is the question of regional integration: the European Union is admired, though feelings about whether this will be possible to emulate in (East) Asia are divided. Mostly, regional integration à la the European Union is seen as a political and, above all, economic device. On the cultural foundations of 'Europeanness' as an important background to any sustained regional integration, the textbooks are markedly silent, though it would be easy to take up the thread of China as 'mother culture' in the case of East Asia (cf. key words such as *hanzi wenhuaquan* 漢字文化圈 (cultural sphere of Chinese characters), 'Asian values', Confucianism, Buddhism, etc.). Though it is acknowledged that China played this 'maternal' role towards the rest of East Asia when talking about ancient times, PRC history textbooks hesitate to take it up in the context of possible future developments in the direction of regional integration, as it is a sensitive political issue (and also easily prone to chauvinism).[51] Furthermore, the way World War II is taught – not so much in 'world history' classes but in *Chinese* (modern) *history* classes[52] – remains a constant reminder to the pupils of how difficult a closer connection to Japan would be. As long as there is no agreement on this part of 'common' history, the European Union model will not be a very realistic option. The PRC–Taiwan issue and the two Koreas furthermore complicate any regional integration vision.

In Europe, a crucial issue was the new relationship France and West Germany started after World War II. Without it, the present European Union would not be thinkable. And there was not only economic interest (though it started with economic cooperation), but also the perceived commonness of cultural 'roots' that drew the population favourably into the integration process at first. The European Union, however, has suffered all along from often having been decided above the heads of the citizens.[53] In East Asia, obstacles are much higher. In any case, without building up more trust, which cannot be torpedoed by history education stressing insurmountable differences, a regional integration is hardly possible. Thus, the Japanese–South Korean–PRC common textbook and similar projects are of great significance, even if they still have to be developed and have not yet made it into classes[54] – in marked difference to the German–French textbook, which, however, comes out only after a long history of pronounced German–French friendship.[55] Thus, in the East Asian case, this step already would be probably asking too much. It would need a strong political will, especially in China, if anything in terms of regional integration were to be 'copied' from Europe. In the meantime – as the popular TV series *Daguo jueqi* 大國崛起 (*Rise of the great nations*) and its kind of sequel *Fuxing zhi lu* 復興之路 (*Road to revival*) demonstrate – the point to learn from Europe rather rests in the older visions of 'national greatness'. Probably, only when feeling strong and secure in itself, will China find the vision of regional integration more attractive, but then from a strong position in the world and in the region (whose boundaries might be otherwise defined than simply China, Taiwan, the two Koreas and Japan), so that as 'senior' partner it might treat on its own conditions. Thus, national interest would not have to be sacrificed, and the lost, ancient feeling of 'mother culture' could be revived. Whether, however, the rest of (East) Asia would find such a kind of regional integration attractive remains dubious. Integration in Europe only included democratic (and economically more or less compatible) states and is in itself a basically democratic (though heavily representative) affair. Therefore, the present political outlook of East Asia rather points to the possibility of more economic integration. For a political integration to follow, this would require substantial changes. That even with democratic states this is very difficult bespeaks the present problem of the European Union to get ahead with political integration (cf. the constitution issue). In East Asia, which comprises different political systems, interpretations of the past and designs for the future, this is an even greater challenge.

Notes

1 A good survey is still Xiong (1994).
2 Japanese textbooks were also often used as reference during the earlier twentieth century (see Wong 1986: Ch. 2). These textbooks usually referred to Western/ European history outlines themselves. In China, at first mainly English (US or UK) reference works were used, later Soviet ones.
3 There were, however, first moves to design curricula in 1902 by school edicts for primary and secondary school education. Cf. *Kecheng jiaocai yanjiusuo* 課程教材研究所 [Institute for Curricular Teaching Materials] (comp.) (2001a) *20 shiji Zhongguo zhongxiaoxue kecheng biaozhun, jiaoxue dagang huibian. Kecheng (jiaoxue) jihua juan* 20 世紀中國中小學課程標準, 教學大綱匯編. 課程 (教學) 計畫卷 [*Collected twentieth century curriculum standards and teaching outlines for Chinese secondary and primary school: curriculum (teaching) plans*], Beijing: Renmin jiaoyu. Here, history was also to include foreign history at the secondary school level (see ibid.: 15–16), divided into ancient, medieval and modern. In 1904, this was further specified, stating that education in Chinese history in primary school should stress Chinese identity by the 'great deeds' done by the forefathers (ibid.: 23), even more pronouncedly aiming at national pride in higher elementary (ibid.: 33). Foreign history, in turn, was to be integrated into secondary school, expressly accentuating the 'big countries' and the recent periods (ibid.: 42).
4 For further information on this point see Wong (1986). See also the brief remarks in Hsiung (2004: 38–52, reference on p. 38).
5 All official guidelines for history education during the twentieth century are collected in *Kecheng jiaocai yanjiusuo* 課程教材研究所 [Institute for Curricular Teaching Materials] (comp.) (2001b) *20 shiji Zhongguo zhongxiaoxue kecheng biaozhun, jiaoxue dagang huibian. Lishi juan* 20 世紀中國中小學課程標準, 教學大綱匯編. 歷史卷 [*Collected twentieth century curriculum standards and teaching outlines for Chinese secondary and primary school: history*], Beijing: Renmin jiaoyu (above and in the following cited as LSJ). Before these official history guidelines, some regulations were integrated into the general regulations.
6 As Culp has already noted, *dongya* (東亞) actually comprised in practice also what today would be called Southeast, South and Central Asia (see Culp 2007: 211–45, reference on p. 227, note 50). One may add that this very probably reflected the similarly broad Japanese usage of *tōyōshi* (東洋史) (see Tanaka 1993).
7 See also Jones 2005b: 31–63, reference on p. 58.
8 One can hardly ignore the fact that '*fugu*' at a time so clearly under the spell of the May Fourth Movement was a rather negatively connoted term. This is striking, because, in leading May Fourth publications, the Renaissance (usually termed (*wenyi*) *fuxing* (文藝) 復興!) had a very positive image!
9 One may note that 1923 was a time when China harboured hopes in the US role as a fair arbitrator to help China (and to ward off Japan's ambitions on the mainland), as epitomised in the recent Washington Conference, 1921–2. This may be one further reason for stressing 'Europe' in negative contexts, and talking about 'the West' more broadly in less ambivalent cases.
10 Cf. Chen 1986.
11 For historiography of the time see Tang (1996), Wang, F. (2000) and Schneider (1997).
12 See Jones, who stresses the continuity between GMD and CCP educational politics (Jones 2005a: 65–100, reference on p. 66).
13 The fourfold periodisation into antiquity, middle ages, modern and contemporary was retained, but somewhat shifted, and was more clearly defined: now, antiquity was to be from the Bronze Age to the fifth century AD, the middle ages from the

54 *Gotelind Müller*

fifth to the fifteenth century, modern times from the fifteenth to the end of the nineteenth century, and contemporary times from then on.

14 Interestingly, in this 'shift back' towards a national perspective, World War I, for example, was now renamed a 'world' war, which would be the use until today in mainland China.

15 'Still' refers here to the GMD's break with the Communists in 1927 before establishing itself with the 'Nanking decade' (1928–37). Even though there is also Sun Yat-sen's (Sun Zhongshan's 孙中山; 1866–1925) legacy of anti-imperialism, the latter reflected Sun's disappointment with the Western powers in his later years and some influence of the Soviet Union. For the later GMD, anti-imperialism was more strongly related to Japan's threatening advance on the mainland.

16 One may also note that this was the period of Chiang Kai-shek's (Jiang Zhongzheng 蔣中正; 1887–1975) repeated campaigns against the Communists and against rivals in his own camp.

17 Both were taught three semesters, but 4:3 in hours.

18 Cf. Dikötter (1992).

19 Cf. Leibold (2006: 181–220); see also Müller (2008a: 153–80).

20 Since I know of no statistics on which textbook actually was used where, it is hard to determine how far these state designs translated into social practice, even when considering the various textbooks available at the time. Therefore I limit myself here to the intentions of the state in framing education on 'the others' histories', which can be gleaned from the curricula.

21 The regulations are for junior secondary school and from 1940.

22 See Alisa Jones' argument that the '1949 divide' did not hold much significance for history teaching (Jones 2005a: 66).

23 See G. Wang (1975: 1–24). For the Soviet model in PRC historiography of 'world history' in general, see Martin (1990).

24 In the general outline, at least the 'participation of the masses' was conceded (see LSJ 2001b: 169).

25 See also Dorothea Martin, who notes that, in Western history textbooks, this topic is almost never considered worth an entry (Martin 1990: 67).

26 This, again, marks the presentation as going along 'European/Soviet' lines, as Hitler's attack on the SU was a decisive moment for the European theatre of war, whereas, from a Chinese perspective on World War II, Pearl Harbor would be the more plausible dividing line.

27 This suggests that, even though there were no new guidelines available yet, except for elementary schools, in 1953, obviously new textbook production was taken up already, complying with the same historical principles set out for elementary schools and Marxist historiography in general, always with a view to Soviet model textbooks.

28 These accentuations or 'prominences' are to throw into profile the main hero in contrasting him with evil figures, other good but less perfect figures and by situating him in a corresponding 'positive' setting (see Yang 1998: 111–17).

29 For this kind of debate, see Weigelin-Schwiedrzik (1988).

30 This, by the way, has become a favourite topic again recently, following hobby historian Gavin Menzies' contested publications (since 2002) on Zheng He even being the actual discoverer of the Americas, prior to Columbus! Menzies' thesis received some enthusiastic responses in China.

31 A notable exception is one citation of Khrushchev in the 1956 curriculum (see LSJ 2001b: 187) to the effect that socialism is no longer something in one country but a world phenomenon. (This could be, however, interpreted in various ways: as a simple hailing of socialism; as Khrushchev intending to refer to – and distance

'The others' history' in Chinese schools 55

himself from – Stalin's 'socialism in one country'; or as a Chinese challenge to Moscow's ideological supremacy.)
32 For Chinese scholarship on world history at the time, see Croizier (1990: 151–69), Littrup (1989: 39–64) and E.Q. Wang (2003: 327–52). (Wang and Littrup have published several times on these and connected issues.) See also the general overview of Weigelin-Schwiedrzik (2005: 139–61).
33 How history teaching was affected by these changes in Eastern Europe itself can be gleaned from Zajda and Zajda (2003: 363–84).
34 For the general growing awareness of, and interconnectedness with, foreign historical scholarship since the 1980s, see Xu (2007: 325–50).
35 I focus here on junior secondary school level national regulations (2001, still in effect in early 2009, i.e. aimed at grades seven to nine, with Chinese history taught in grades seven and eight, foreign history in grade nine; each year divided into two textbook volumes) and the 'history' course. There is now also an alternative experimental option of an integrated 'history and society' course at that level, for which two versions of guidelines appeared in 2001. (For a critical discussion of this experiment see the chapter by Li Fan.) Furthermore, some regional regulations exist, but the differences are rather minimal. For senior secondary school level, there are the 2002 regulations for the currently used textbooks on 'history', teaching modern Chinese and modern world history in the first and second year, respectively (and a third optional year on ancient Chinese history); and there are the 2003 guidelines for an experimental textbook series with three volumes for an obligatory integrated 'history' course, covering all Chinese and world history together, in a presentation that differs in approach from volume to volume (i.e. vol. 1: Political history; vol. 2: Socio-economic history; vol. 3: Cultural-intellectual history), after which there is designed a six-volume set for optional courses, again thematically designed and open to pupils' choice as to which aspects they are interested in (i.e. vol. 1: Major reforms in history; vol. 2: Democratic ideas in modern society; vol. 3: War and peace in the twentieth century; vol. 4: Evaluation of Chinese and foreign historical figures; vol. 5: Investigations into historical mysteries; vol. 6: World cultural heritage). However, the differences in the various curricula versions are mainly in arrangement, and contents are described in rather less detail in the other 'curricula standards' versions than in the junior secondary school 'history' guidelines, which thus can be safely taken as representative.
36 *Zhonghua Renmin Gongheguo Jiaoyubu* 中華人民共和國教育部 [Ministry of Education of the People's Republic of China] (comp.) (2001a) *Quanri-zhi yiwu jiaoyu lishi kecheng biaozhun (shiyangao)* 全日制義務教育歷史課程標準 (實驗稿) [History curriculum standard for compulsory education, full-time system, provisional draft], Beijing: Beijing Normal University Press (above and in the following cited as 'LKB').
37 For this contemporary use of 'racial' categories see, e.g., Dikötter (2002: 495–510, especially pp. 504–7); Sautman (2001: 95–124) (see also Sautman 1997: 75–95) and Schmalzer (2004).
38 It is stated that ancient history, though not having lacked in cultural contacts, had not yet reached a global interconnectedness, and so 'real' world history only sets in with the seafarers.
39 As noted above, there are often discrepancies between the general guidelines and the syllabus outlines in the PRC.
40 In the 'history and society' curriculum standards (version 1), he is even the only explicitly named figure in the suggestions for activities (but for Martin Luther King's 'I have a dream'; see *Zhonghua Renmin Gongheguo Jiaoyubu* (2001b: 22)). And in the new senior secondary school curriculum standards, he is named

56 *Gotelind Müller*

as one of the 'great personalities of the period of bourgeois revolution in the West', together with Cromwell and Washington (see *Zhonghua Renmin Gongheguo Jiaoyubu* 2003: 24).

41 *Zhangxi nüwang* 章西女王. This probably refers to the Indian film *The tiger and the flame* (1953). The 'Queen' had been widow of the Raja of Jhansi in Northern India and rebelled against the British annexing the Jhansi territory in the mid nineteenth century.

42 This goes well with the general upgrading of the term 'reform' in Chinese political discourse, counterbalancing earlier 'revolutionary' rhetoric. (The comparison of the Meiji and the Chinese 1898 reforms is even more pronounced at senior secondary school level in the new experimental design of the optional six volumes, of which volume 1 focuses on 'reforms' in history; here, this comparison is a suggested activity in class; see *Zhonghua Renmin Gongheguo Jiaoyubu* (2003: 18).)

43 *Sidalingele baoweizhan* 斯大林格勒保衛戰. This probably means *The great battle of the Volga*, a Soviet film released in 1962.

44 *Badun jiangjun* 巴頓將軍. This probably means the 1970 US film *Patton*.

45 A fourth school textbook that was consulted is the *Zhonghua* 中華 edition, appearing however in Beijing, as does the PEP edition. For an enumeration of available editions, see the chapter by Su Zhiliang.

46 PEP (*Renmin jiaoyu chubanshe* 人民教育出版社) was responsible for textbook production in the PRC since its foundation in the 1950s. Only after the Cultural Revolution was textbook production somewhat pluralised, i.e. some other editions could be produced, though they had to go through a thorough screening before being admitted to be used in schools. However, the lion's share of the textbook market remained with the official PEP.

47 There is also another Shanghai textbook on world history, based, however, not on the national but a Shanghai curriculum, edited by Su Zhiliang. In this Shanghai regional design, world history is taught in grade eight, whereas the textbooks chosen here are all based on the national curriculum standards, which envisage world history for grade nine and thus make comparison easier. (Furthermore, final examinations tend to take the national curriculum as a standard, which creates problems for pupils having used textbooks based on regional curricula. However, the differences in content are rather marginal.)

48 As one may glean from the above overview on curricula designs, in Chinese 'world history' teaching, 'Europe' as a category tended to be merged into the broader category of 'the West' mainly with late nineteenth- and twentieth-century history. Only after the Cold War, was 'Europe' rediscovered as a meaningful category.

49 *Shijie lishi, xia* 世界歷史, 下 [World history, vol. 2] (2007), Beijing: Renmin jiaoyu chubanshe [People's Education Press, above and in the following referred to as 'PEP']. The PEP textbooks still tend to be edited (nominally) collectively.

50 For an interpretation of textual and visual arrangements in Chinese textbooks, see my article: Müller (2008b: 189–206).

51 For possible reasons why there is hesitancy in China to take up the issue of 'East Asianness', see the chapter by Sun Ge.

52 Here, one should stress that images of 'others' are not only transmitted in 'world history' classes but also in classes on Chinese history, as far as they were directly involved with China. In the latter case, obviously, Chinese interests colour the framing of 'others' even more.

53 This is probably one of the reasons why European textbooks are often hesitant to take up the 'idealistic' side of European identity (see Pingel (2002), who finds only German and Italian textbooks to be somewhat more outspoken on the 'ideal'

of Europeanness). Furthermore, the debates surrounding the 'compatibility' of Turkey show how contested older views on 'Europeanness', e.g., pointing to the 'common' Christian faith, have become.
54 See the critical arguments regarding the three countries' textbook of Iwasaki and Narita (2008: 271–83).
55 The German–French senior secondary textbook *Histoire/Geschichte*, of which two volumes have appeared up to now (2006 and 2008), is compatible with both countries' educational system.

Bibliography

Chen S. 陳三井 (1986) *Huagong yu ouzhan* 華工與歐戰 [*Chinese laborers and the European War*], Taipei: Zhongyang yanjiuyuan jindaishi yanjiusuo.
Croizier, R. (1990) 'World history in the People's Republic of China', *Journal of World History*, vol. 1, no. 2: 151–69.
Culp, R.J. (2007) '"Weak and small peoples" in a "Europeanizing world": world history textbooks and Chinese intellectuals' perspectives on global modernity', in T. Hon and R.J. Culp (eds), *The politics of historical production in late Qing and republican China*, Leiden: Brill, 211–45.
Dikötter, F. (1992) *The discourse of race in modern China*, London: Hurst.
—— (2002) 'Race in China', in D.T. Goldberg and J. Solomos (eds), *A companion to racial and ethnic studies*, Malden and Oxford: Blackwell, 495–510.
Gong Q. 龔奇柱 (ed.) (2006; 1st edn 2005) *Shijie lishi, xia* 世界歷史,下 [*World history*, vol. 2], Chengdu: Sichuan jiaoyu.
Hsiung, P. (2004) 'Moving the world according to a shifted "I": world history texts in Republican China and post-war Taiwan', *Berliner China-Hefte*, vol. 26: 38–52.
Iwasaki, M. and Narita, R. (2008) 'Writing history textbooks in East Asia: the possibilities and pitfalls of *History that Opens the Future*', in S. Richter (ed.), *Contested views of a common past. Revisions of history in contemporary East Asia*, Frankfurt am Main and New York: Campus, 271–83.
Jones, A. (2005a) 'Changing the past to serve the present: history education in Mainland China', in E. Vickers and A. Jones (eds), *History education and national identity in East Asia*, London: Routledge, 65–100.
—— (2005b) 'Shared legacies, diverse evolutions: history, education, and the state in East Asia', in E. Vickers and A. Jones (eds), *History education and national identity in East Asia*, London: Routledge, 31–63.
Kecheng jiaocai yanjiusuo 課程教材研究所 [Institute for Curricular Teaching Materials] (comp.) (2001a) 20 shiji Zhongguo zhongxiaoxue kecheng biaozhun, jiaoxue dagang huibian. Kecheng (jiaoxue) jihua juan 20世紀中國中小學課程標準, 教學大綱匯編. 課程(教學)計畫卷 [Collected twentieth century curriculum standards and teaching outlines for Chinese secondary and primary school: curriculum (teaching) plans], Beijing: Renmin jiaoyu.
—— (2001b) 20 shiji Zhongguo zhongxiaoxue kecheng biaozhun, jiaoxue dagang huibian. Lishi juan 20世紀中國中小學課程標準, 教學大綱匯編. 歷史卷 [Collected twentieth century curriculum standards and teaching outlines for Chinese secondary and primary school: history], Beijing: Renmin jiaoyu (above cited as LSJ).
Leibold, J. (2006) 'Competing narratives of racial unity in Republican China', *Modern China*, vol. 32, no. 2: 181–220.
Littrup, L. (1989) 'World history with Chinese characteristics', *Culture & History*, vol. 5: 39–64.

LKB: see Zhonghua Renmin Gongheguo Jiaoyubu (2001a)
LSJ: see Kecheng jiaocai yanjiusuo (2001b)
Martin, D.A.L. (1990) *The making of a Sino-Marxist world view: perceptions and interpretations of world history in the People's Republic of China*, Armonk, NY: M.E. Sharpe.
Müller, G. (2008a) 'Are we "yellow" and who is "us"? China's problems with glocalizing the concept of race (around 1900)', *BJOAF*: 153–80.
—— (2008b) 'Wie sage ich's meinem Kinde? Strategien zur Vermittlung eines normativen Geschichtsbildes in zeitgenössischen chinesischen Schulbüchern' [How to tell my child? Strategies used in current Chinese school textbooks to transmit the normative view on history], in A. Chaniotis *et al*. (eds), *Überzeugungsstrategien* [*Strategies of persuasion*], *Heidelberger Jahrbücher*, 189–206.
Pingel, F. (2002) *The European home: representations of 20th century Europe in history textbooks (reprint)*, Strasbourg: Council of Europe.
Sautman, B. (1997) 'Myths of descent, racial nationalism and ethnic minorities in the People's Republic of China', in F. Dikötter (ed.), *The construction of racial identities in China and Japan: historical and contemporary perspectives*, London: Hurst, 75–95.
—— (2001) 'Peking man and the politics of paleoanthropological nationalism in China', *Journal of Asian Studies*, vol. 60, no. 1: 95–124.
Schmalzer, S. (2004) 'The people's Peking man: popular paleoanthropology in twentieth-century China', unpublished thesis, University of California, San Diego.
Schneider, A. (1997) *Wahrheit und Geschichte: Zwei chinesische Historiker auf der Suche nach einer modernen Identität für China* [*Truth and history: two Chinese historians searching for a modern Chinese identity*], Wiesbaden: Harrassowitz.
Shijie lishi, xia 世界歷史,下 [*World history*, vol. 2] (2007), Beijing: Renmin jiaoyu chubanshe (above cited as 'PEP').
Tanaka, S. (1993) *Japan's Orient: rendering pasts into history*, Berkeley, CA: University of California Press.
Tang, X. (1996) *Global space and the national discourse of modernity: the historical thinking of Liang Qichao*, Stanford, CA: Stanford University Press.
Wang, E.Q. (2003) 'Encountering the world: China and its other(s) in historical narratives, 1949–89', *Journal of World History*, vol. 14, no. 3: 327–52.
Wang, F. (2000) *Fu Su-nian: a life in Chinese history and politics*, New York: Cambridge University Press.
Wang, G. (1975) 'Juxtaposing past and present in China today', *The China Quarterly*, vol. 61: 1–24.
Wang S. 王斯德 (ed.) (2006) *Shijie lishi*, xia 世界歷史,下 [*World history*, vol. 2], Shanghai: Huadong Normal University Press.
Weigelin-Schwiedrzik, S. (1988) 'Shi und Lun: Studien zur Methodologie der Historiographie in der VR China' [Shi and Lun: studies on the methodology of historiography in the PRC], unpublished habilitation thesis, Ruhr University, Bochum.
—— (2005) 'Weltgeschichte und chinesische Geschichte: Die chinesische Historiographie des 20. Jahrhunderts zwischen Universalität und Partikularität' [World history and Chinese history: the Chinese historiography of the twentieth century between universality and particularity], in M. Grandner *et al*. (eds), *Globalisierung und Globalgeschichte* [*Globalisation and global history*], Wien: Mandelbaum, 139–61.

Wong, K.C. (1986) 'Chinese history textbook writing in Late Ch'ing China', unpublished thesis, University of Hong Kong.

Xiong Y. 熊月之 (1994) *Xixue dong jian yu wan Qing shehui* 西學東漸與晚清社會 [*The diffusion of Western knowledge to the East and late Qing society*], Shanghai: Shanghai renmin.

Xu, L. (2007) 'Reconstructing world history in the People's Republic of China since the 1980s', *Journal of World History*, vol. 18, no. 3: 325–50.

Yang, L. (1998) *Chinese fiction of the Cultural Revolution*, Hong Kong: Hong Kong University Press.

Zajda, J. and Zajda, R. (2003) 'The politics of rewriting history: new history textbooks and curriculum materials in Russia', *International Review of Education*, vol. 49, nos. 3–4: 363–84.

Zhonghua Renmin Gongheguo Jiaoyubu 中華人民共和國教育部 [Ministry of Education of the People's Republic of China] (comp.) (2001a) Quanri-zhi yiwu jiaoyu lishi kecheng biaozhun (shiyangao) 全日制義務教育歷史課程標準 (實驗稿) [History curriculum standards for full-time compulsory education (provisional draft)], Beijing: Beijing Normal University Press (above cited as 'LKB').

—— (2001b) Quanri-zhi yiwu jiaoyu lishi yu shehui kecheng biaozhun (I) (shiyangao) 全日制義務教育歷史與社會課程標準 (I) (實驗稿) [History and society I curriculum standards for full-time compulsory education (provisional draft)], Beijing: Beijing Normal University Press.

—— (2003) Putong gaozhong lishi kecheng biaozhun (shiyan) 普通高中歷史課程標準 (實驗) [History curriculum standards for normal senior secondary school (provisional)], Beijing: Renmin jiaoyu.

3 The construction of 'self' and Western and Asian 'others' in contemporary Japanese civics and ethics textbooks

Klaus Vollmer

This chapter complements the Chinese case discussed in the former chapter with the Japanese one. The author argues the case for including 'civics' and 'ethics' textbooks as important media for identity constructions alongside history textbooks. It is noted that the notorious Japanese right-wing history textbook of the Tsukurukai was accompanied by the latter's 'new' civics textbook, which aimed at redefining Japanese identity in terms of projected images of contemporary society, social order, gender relations and the individual. However, it is argued that mainstream textbooks also present an ideologically-skewed image of Japanese society, and its relations with 'others'. In civics textbooks, topics are often presented within a context that implies the idea of 'historical development' and clearly depict images of 'self' and 'other' according to models taken from European or North American history. The chapter addresses the question of how 'others' are constructed and represented in textbook narratives and how 'Japan' is related to various 'others'. It also looks at how a 'common' East Asian narrative is envisaged and to what extent a shift in the representation of the 'total other' (Europe/US) or 'relative other' (East Asia) can be observed.

Introduction

Since the mid 1990s, controversial debates on history and memory have ranked high on the political agenda in East Asia, focusing mainly on issues of twentieth-century history, in particular the Asia–Pacific War in the 1930s and 40s, atrocities and war crimes committed by Japan's Imperial Army in East Asia, the colonisation of Korea and Taiwan and others. Being part of this multifaceted and complex discourse on the entanglement of national histories within the regional context of Northeast Asia, contemporary history textbooks of Japan, Korea and China have become exposed to public view in unprecedented ways. Since the mid 2000s, the creation of history textbooks that aim to transcend the framework of the nation has been eagerly discussed, both as an attempt at experimenting with new forms of transnational historical narrative, and as a highly significant move by actors of civil society in East Asian countries (see Hein and Selden 2000; Kimijima 2000; Richter 2008).[1] Although, in history textbooks in general, starting points for narratives have been memories of victimisation or colonisation, atrocities committed by neighbouring or far-away nations, histories of victory or lessons learnt from defeat and humiliation, discussions also began to focus on more principal issues such as, for example, how history textbooks should be conceived (see Satō, M. et al. 2003; Sakamoto 2003). In this respect, the depiction of 'self' and 'other', which has been a key element determining narrative structures in traditional histories of nations, seems equally fundamental in an age of 'globalised' histories with transnational or regional actors, as Prasenjit Duara has pointed out (Duara 2008: 105). To elaborate, while the narration of incidents of victimisation or atrocities can be an example of a particularly extreme and asymmetrical interaction of 'self' and 'other', this dichotomy, even if barely visible, operates in less controversial discursive fields as well and remaining, in fact, fundamental to the identity-making process in general. Referring to the emergence of new identities as members of a minority group or a particular cultural or regional sphere, for example, Prasenjit Duara emphasises that:

> subject-making itself – that is, the process of creating an agency for historical action and recognition [. . .] – has many similarities to the earlier process of national subject formation, which I have called the *ur*-form of identity politics. This homology of political forms – the identification of the self versus the other – remains a significant factor linking the new identities to nationalism.
>
> (Duara 2008: 105)

It is the aim of this chapter to explore in some detail this process of identity-formation through juxtaposing 'self' and 'others' in Japanese textbooks for junior secondary and senior secondary schools, respectively. In focusing on civics and ethics textbooks, this chapter attempts to broaden our perspective on the issue of identity-formation, which applies well beyond the genre of *history* textbooks. As is well known, at least between the late 1990s and early 2000s, one of the central issues that sparked the debate on textbooks in East Asia was the publication of the highly controversial history textbook of the revisionist group, Japanese Society for History Textbook Reform (*Atarashii rekishi kyōkasho o tsukurukai* 新しい歴史教科書をつくる会, or *Tsukurukai* for short) in Japan (see Höpken and Richter 2003; Saaler 2005: 23–89). For the approach taken in this chapter, it is highly significant, however, that from the outset it was the goal of *Tsukurukai* to produce a social studies or civics textbook for junior secondary school as well. The latter was published in 2001 under the title *Atarashii kōmin kyōkasho* 新しい公民教科書 (*New civics textbook*), and a revised edition that is still in use (albeit in only a very few Japanese schools) appeared in 2005. As I have argued elsewhere (see Vollmer

2007), this project reveals a clear political objective: to shape the attitudes of young Japanese towards state and society. The text is a reminder that neo-nationalist thought is not restricted to the field of historiography but is equally based on projecting images of contemporary society, social order, gender relations and the individual. As I will demonstrate in this chapter, issues of 'history' are not confined to the realm of history textbooks proper but are equally important for the study of society, economics, religion and traditions of thought. It is hardly possible to discuss topics in civics or ethics classes without referring to historical times and places that are naturally imbued with notions of 'self' and 'otherness'. Moreover, in civics textbooks, for example, topics to study are often presented within a context that implies the idea of 'historical development' (e.g. of political systems, of human rights thought, of social issues) that in turn must refer to different stages of societal development in time. These are, again, often related to notions of belonging to 'self' and 'other(s)'.

It is important to recognise that this fundamental observation apparently applies to all textbooks and not only to so-called 'revisionist' or 'neo-nationalist' volumes. Although those Japanese textbooks that present the 'liberal' mainstream might offer a more differentiated image of contested issues and include, at times, a critical perspective that contrasts sharply with the *Tsukurukai* volume's tendencies to vindicate or even whitewash history, they of course construct an equally non-neutral image of society. Thus, implicitly hidden in textbook discourse we often find the modernist notion of 'development' as a seemingly universal and unilinear phenomenon that tends to gloss over consequences that derive from asymmetries of cultural flows. As is the case with Japanese schoolbooks dealing with history, civics and ethics textbooks also clearly depict images of 'self' and 'other', with models of development taken most often from European or North American history. As will be demonstrated in more detail below, this is still a dominant perspective in textbook discourse, although the recent trend to relate more directly to Asian 'others' can also be observed in some Japanese civics and ethics textbooks. Examples from these materials given in this chapter thus reflect a trend that is a major issue of intellectual debate in East Asia and that has also entered discussions about textbooks and curricula (for details, see Richter (2008); for South Korea, see Lee (2008)). So far, however, scholarly research has been largely restricted to the realm of history textbooks only, excluding a wealth of materials contained in volumes designed for the study of other subjects.

In respect to the overall context of this volume, which explores how 'self' and 'others' are recreated in textbook discourse, it is also noteworthy that the topic of how to relate (Japanese) 'self' to (European, Asian or 'international') 'others' is explicitly taken up, for example, in chapters on 'international society' included in textbooks for junior secondary school and senior secondary school, respectively. Civics and ethics textbooks also lend themselves rather naturally to the analysis of cultural flows, as they depict concepts of 'democracy', 'human rights', 'the individual', 'modern society' etc. and often explain their European origin.

This chapter will address the question of how 'others' are constructed and represented in textbook narratives and how 'Japan' is related to various 'others'. As has been already mentioned, I will also look at how a 'common' East Asian narrative might be envisaged and to what extent a shifting of the representation of 'total other' (Europe/USA) or 'relative other' (East Asia) can be observed in contemporary Japanese civics and ethics textbooks. The analysis of 'self' and 'other' in these volumes thus provides a vast area for research from different angles. However, owing to restrictions of space, it will not be possible to give a comprehensive overview. Instead, I will present only some preliminary findings from a close and detailed reading of a small number of examples that represent, in each case, a different mode of juxtaposing 'self' and 'other'. The first example will explore the depiction of human rights thought in textbook narratives for junior secondary school. I will compare mainstream textbook discourse with notions found in the *Tsukurukai* volume on civics. Here, I will examine strategies by which the *Tsukurukai* narrative rejects mainstream discourse and employs different images of 'self' and 'other'. In the second part, I will present examples from civics and ethics textbooks for senior secondary school that seem to suggest some fundamental assumptions on the relation of Japanese 'self' and non-Japanese 'others'. My preliminary findings indicate that mainstream textbook discourse implies a secluded and separated Japanese 'self' and somewhat resembles notions of Japanese 'uniqueness' found in self-representations of Japanese culture popular in the 1970s and 1980s. Although, in this discourse, the criterion of belonging or not belonging to Japan's national culture often seems the most powerful device to order and arrange materials, this narrative might weaken in the future, as alternative representations in textbooks enter the picture. Other than in traditional mainstream arrangements of contents, they put more emphasis on connectedness of 'self' and 'others' by topic and are particularly sensitive to spatial and temporal contexts.

One final note is in order regarding the sources used for research: as is well known, the content of textbooks in Japan is closely regulated by the curriculum guidelines that are periodically reviewed by the Japanese Ministry of Education (*Monbukagakushō* 文部科学省, *Monkashō* 文科省 for short (MEXT)).[2] In light of this rather tight political control of textbook content, one might be tempted to deplore an alleged uniformity of textbook volumes produced by different publishers, but in reality there is quite a wide variety of approaches and treatments of topics that are 'prescribed' by the curriculum guidelines. Moreover, these guidelines can serve as a solid standard of comparison that highlights the differences between textbooks and the emphasis that is put on certain issues in each of them. In contrast to the rather bulky and text-oriented volumes published until the 1980s and 1990s and containing one or two monochrome photographs per double page, since the early 2000s, textbooks in Japan appear as glossy items, with text, illustrations, photographs and other visual materials distributed evenly among their pages. In particular, this rather new visual dimension in textbooks enhances the possibilities to create new meaning and variety in the treatment of certain topics – in contemporary schoolbooks, the selection and representation of visual materials contribute as much to the production of meaning as does the textual narrative.

Universalism versus cultural relativism – narratives of human rights thought in textbooks for junior secondary school

Introduction

In the first example, materials taken from Japanese civics textbooks (*kōmin kyōkasho* 公民教科書) for junior secondary school (*chūgakkō* 中学校) will be presented and analysed. Civics classes (*kōminka* 公民科) belong to courses in 'social studies' (*shakaika* 社会科), comprising classes in geography and history, respectively, besides civics. It might be helpful to recall the overall aim of social studies classes as set down in the MEXT guidelines:

> Taking a broad view [classes in social studies aim at] heightening [the students'] interest towards society and, based on a variety of materials, study [issues] from different perspectives and taking into account their complexity; they aim at deepening the understanding and affection towards the land and the history of our nation and thus cultivate the basic education for the students as citizens (*kōmin* 公民). [Classes in social studies aim to] raise the basis of necessary civic qualities required in students as [future] designers of a peaceful, democratic society and nation living in international society.
>
> (MEXT 2008: 17)

Throughout the guidelines, emphasis is placed on the fact that civics classes should build on information and knowledge taught in geography and history. In particular, civics classes deal with human rights thought, the basics of democracy, freedom, rights and obligations, the relationship of individuals, community and society at large, as well as with issues of economics, the international order and global politics. Civics textbooks currently in use are thus in general divided into four chapters: the first one, dealing with 'living in contemporary society', takes up particularly far-reaching issues and problems pertaining to overall society such as, for example, demographic change, globalisation, development of multicultural society, the impact of media and the Internet on everyday life and so forth. These are grouped together under headlines such as 'Living in contemporary society' (see Nakamura *et al.* 2005) or 'Contemporary society and our everyday life' (see Gomi *et al.* 2006; Satō, K. *et al.* 2006; Yagi *et al.* 2006; Tanimoto *et al.* 2008). This

'Self' and 'others' in Japanese textbooks   65

introductory chapter is followed by three more systematic treatments of politics and the political system in Japan, including, for example, sections on human rights, the constitution, law and the administration of justice. A third chapter deals with the economy, addressing, among others, issues of consumption, mechanisms of market economies, currency and social security. The final chapter in all civics textbooks is dedicated to the study of international or global society: 'Global society and us' (see Gomi *et al.* 2006); 'Contemporary international society' (see Satō K. *et al.* 2006); 'Living as a global citizen' (see Tanimoto *et al.* 2008); and 'Increasing world peace and prosperity of humankind' (see Yagi *et al.* 2006).

In the first example, civics textbooks by four different publishers that represent the mainstream narrative in contemporary civics classes and are used by more than 75 per cent of junior secondary school students will be compared with the *Tsukurukai* volume.[3] These are books published by Tōkyō shoseki (東京書籍; see Gomi *et al.* 2006), Ōsaka shoseki (大阪書籍; see Satō K. *et al.* 2006), Shimizu shoin (清水書院; see Nakamura *et al.* 2005) and Teikoku shoin (帝国書院; see Tanimoto *et al.* 2008), respectively, whose materials will be introduced first and then compared with the textbook commissioned by *Tsukurukai*. From the beginning, the author wishes to emphasise that, for reasons of methodology, in this article he will largely refrain from discussing statements in the *Tsukurukai* textbook within the framework of this group's highly problematic, often chauvinistic ideology in any detail. Instead I will look at the *Tsukurukai* civics textbook as another effort by conservative and right-wing Japanese intellectuals to promote a political agenda that aims at challenging basic assumptions of post-war Japanese mainstream discourse on society, democracy and power (for more details, see Vollmer (2007)). To illustrate this point, I will highlight the differences between the *Tsukurukai* and other publisher's textbooks' discourse, taking the topic of 'human rights' as a case in point. Moreover, the section on fundamental human rights, which also depicts the historical development of human rights thought, can serve here as a typical example how the West functions as model 'other' in Japanese civics textbooks in general. By comparing different textbook narratives, it is obvious that they imply a specific historical timeline, placing Japan in the rather familiar position of a 'late-comer' to modernity and democracy.

'Human rights' and 'human rights thought' as depicted in mainstream civics textbooks

Looking at and analysing the materials on these pages it is obvious that the visual narrative is dominated by a specific set of great Western men who represent different stages of intellectual and social progress: all textbooks depict, for example, the European thinkers John Locke, Baron de Montesquieu and Jean-Jacques Rousseau, and also the famous painting of the French Declaration of Human Rights of 26 August 1789, with its rather blunt allegories referring

66 *Klaus Vollmer*

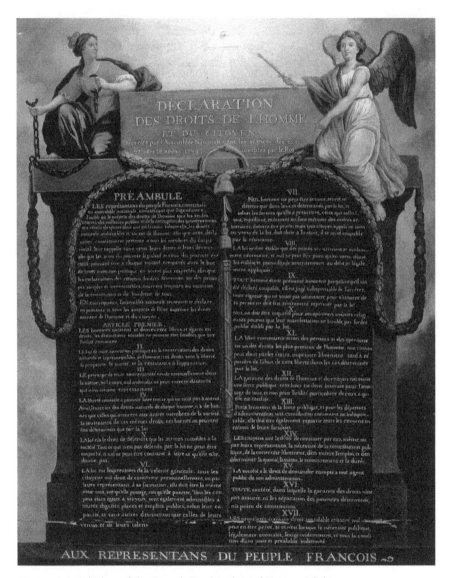

Figure 3.1 Painting of the French Declaration of Human Rights

to the two stone tablets of the Ten Commandments, the light of reason and the broken chains of despotic government (see Gomi *et al.* 2006: 36; Nakamura *et al.* 2005: 38–9; Satō K. *et al.* 2006: 38; Tanimoto *et al.* 2008: 90–1).

Other illustrations refer to the United States Declaration of Independence and then trace the development of constitutions from these declarations of human rights down to the twentieth century (Gomi *et al.* 2006: 36; Nakamura *et al.* 2005: 39; Satō K. *et al.* 2006: 38; Tanimoto *et al.* 2008: 90–1). Although it would be interesting to examine the subtle differences between these four textbook narratives in more detail, the overall message in these volumes quite obviously emphasises a universal historical development starting in the West, i.e. England, the USA and France, which finally spread to Japan in the late nineteenth century and led to the promulgation of the Meiji Constitution.

It is significant that, at this point, the narratives clearly declare the Meiji Constitution as defective, as can be seen in the following section quoted from Tōkyō shoseki's volume, which is used in almost two-thirds of civics classes in Japanese junior secondary schools:

> Human rights thought was brought to Japan from Europe in the Meiji era. It was the constitution of the Great Empire of Japan (Meiji Constitution) of 1889 in which human rights were guaranteed for the first time. However, as a result of the Emperor being the sovereign, human rights were onesidedly seen as 'rights of the imperial subjects' (*shinmin no kenri* 臣民ノ権利) granted by the grace of the Tennō and were limited by law. In actual life in society, too, political movements criticising the government and freedom of speech were suppressed. For the idea of possessing inalienable human rights by birth, that is true human rights thought (*makoto no jinken shisō* 真の人権思想), to be established in Japan we had to wait for the enactment of the constitution of Japan [in 1947].
>
> (Gomi *et al.* 2006: 37)

In this section, the narrative, by its selection of words, stresses the Western model as 'standard ('true human rights thought') and the temporality of the process ['had to wait for' (*matanakereba narimasen deshita* 待たなければなりませんでした)]. The classification of Japan as 'late-comer' vis-à-vis the West is also subtly emphasised by the heading of this section, which takes its symbolism from nature and reads 'The budding of human rights in Japan' (*Nihon no jinken no mebae* 日本の人権の芽ばえ), in contrast to the image of 'maturity' assigned to the West with 'grown-up' human rights thought (Gomi *et al.* 2006: 37).

Albeit in different language, the other civics textbooks develop their narrative along similar lines. At the same time, the unfolding of human rights and human rights thought is depicted as a universal process that finally embraces all humankind and is not tied to any particular culture. Throughout the section, the words 'humans' (*ningen* 人間) or 'humankind' (*jinrui* 人類) prevail. Thus, a paragraph in Tōkyō shoseki's text remarks: 'After the Second World War human rights thought also spread internationally. Today, not only are human rights guaranteed by the constitutions of each country but have become a common idea shared throughout the world' (Gomi *et al.* 2006: 37).

The narrative of Shimizu shoin's textbook uses even more pathetic language when the history of constitutional government based on declarations of human rights is explained. Here again, all references to 'self' and 'other'

◎ロック（1632〜1704年）　◎モンテスキュー（1689〜　◎ルソー（1712〜1778年）
イギリスの思想家。　　　1755年）フランスの思想　フランスの思想家。
主著『統治二論』　　　　家。主著『法の精神』　　主著『社会契約論』

Figure 3.2 Locke, Montesquieu and Rousseau

in terms of different cultures and power relations between them are omitted, and the issue is represented as a natural process unfolding among all humankind:

> The people who gained the country's power by revolution proclaimed human rights like freedom and equality anew as inalienable fundamental rights of humans. Thus it came about that those many rights that mankind had continued to hope for during the long course of history were finally written down. As a principle that people in power and executing government must strictly adhere to, these 'declarations of human rights' were set down as the country's supreme law called constitution, and thus distinguished from other legislation.
>
> (Nakamura *et al.* 2005: 39)

The visual and textual narratives of these textbooks thus stress the universal and unidimensional development of human rights thought, and a very positive tone prevails throughout on these pages. In the volume published by Shimizu shoin, there is an attempt to differentiate this rather homogenous depiction. But the text does not refer, for example, to the culturally rooted differences in the meanings of concepts such as 'freedom' and 'equality', but instead points to the fragility of human rights by introducing an example that is again taken from the historical realm of the Western 'other'. A photograph depicting a family of European Jews being deported, accompanied by a narrative that mentions the Holocaust and World War II, serves as a reminder to be watchful even in peaceful times of democracy and constitutional government, as Adolf Hitler came into power through elections in a democratic system. The Asian 'other' is not at issue on these pages (nor in any of these sections in the four

'Self' and 'others' in Japanese textbooks 69

civics textbooks examined here), and the alleged 'universal' and 'global' outlook means actually to gaze firmly to the West only.[4]

Contrasting views in the Tsukurukai civics textbook: deconstructing mainstream discourse through cultural relativism

A comparison with the materials dealing with fundamental human rights in the *Tsukurukai* volume reveals striking differences, precisely because, at first glance, the reader encounters a set of quite familiar visual materials, such as the depiction of the founding fathers of human rights thought and the French Declaration of Human Rights (Yagi *et al.* 2006: 70–1). But, at the same time, visual and textual narratives take a markedly different turn: other 'others' enter the picture.

The discourse on human rights in the *Tskurukai* textbook differs mainly in two respects: first, the master narrative of a historically linear process of universally unfolding human rights, culminating in their implementation on a global scale in the mid twentieth century, is clearly deconstructed here. Current examples of serious issues of human rights violations are taken to establish a counter-discourse: in this regard, photographs in relatively large format refer to racism based on the ideology of white supremacy prevalent in South Africa until the early 1990s, and the human rights abuse suffered by street children who lost their home and live in utter poverty (most probably depicting a scene in a South Asian country; Yagi *et al.* 2006: 70). Second, the *Tsukurukai* narrative takes particular issue with the alleged 'universal-cum-neutral' character of human rights that is emphasised so highly in the other four civics textbooks analysed before. Another photograph in this section of the textbook introduces this topic by pairing the already mentioned representation of the French Declaration of Human Rights with a scene of women veiled with a *burka* in an Islamic country, probably Afghanistan. That this combination of images serves a particular purpose becomes clear from the caption that is attached to both of them and reads: 'Through the culture and everyday customs of each country, the way of thinking about human rights developed' (Yagi *et al.* 2006: 71). This notion is also stressed heavily in the textual narrative. After the first paragraph explaining the nature of human rights and pointing out that they have become an issue transcending the borders of nations (in this respect somewhat resembling the narrative of mainstream textbooks), a slightly longer section emphasises that 'human rights were born from diverse histories' (*sorezore no rekishi kara umareta jinken* それぞれの歴史から生まれた人権). After referring to their origins in seventeenth- and eighteenth-century Europe, the text continues:

> People rose up against political suppression in a citizens' revolution (*shimin kakumei* 市民革命) and formed the modern nation-state. The American Declaration of Independence and the French Declaration of Human Rights promulgated that 'humans possess the rights of freedom

and equality by birth', thus proclaiming that every person, regardless of race, age, gender and so forth is born with certain inalienable rights. Afterwards this way of thinking spread broadly throughout the world and continued its development, thereby becoming imbued with the history, culture or national character (*kokuminsei* 国民性) of each country. That is the reason why today in the world we find different views and the emergence of various attitudes towards human rights. Views about the value of living humanely themselves are deeply related to a nation's history, tradition, culture as well as religion and law; therefore due consideration is necessary that countries refrain from forcing only their own sense of values or their particular ways upon a neighbouring country.
(Yagi *et al.* 2006: 71)

As already mentioned in the beginning, it is not the aim of this chapter to contextualise in detail statements like these within the framework of the *Tsukurukai* revisionist and at times highly chauvinistic ideology. Nor will I discuss whether this line of reasoning can easily be refuted by a thorough and critical historical analysis. Here, it must suffice to point out the somewhat extreme cultural relativism of the *Tsukurukai* narrative, which implies a concept of human rights that is culturally shaped by many 'others'. In a sense, the hegemonic interpretation of a culturally neutral, allegedly 'universal' concept of human rights, which nevertheless originated in Western Europe at a certain point in time – a fact that thus tends to subtly uphold the notion of the supremacy or at least primacy of the Western 'other' – is rejected.

From this point of view, it is not surprising that the immediately following representation of the Meiji Constitution, which is dismissed as 'defective' in the light of 'true human rights thought' in other civics textbooks, is highly praised here. A whole page is allotted to the depiction of this topic, glorifying, for example, Meiji Japan as 'the first constitutional state in Asia' (this, however, is also mentioned in Tōkyō shoseki's narrative (Gomi *et al.* 2006: 37)), and, in light of international politics of the late nineteenth century, the text stresses the need for Meiji leaders to 'build a strong nation' (Yagi *et al.* 2006: 72). However, at the same time, this textbook mentions the 'Freedom and People's Rights Movement' (*Jiyū minken undō* 自由民権運動) flourishing in the 1870s and 1880s, implying that this movement should be taken as an example of the active discussion and early adaption of human rights thought in Japan. With regard to the relationship of 'self' and 'other' in the textbooks under scrutiny here, it is significant that none of the other civics textbooks under comparison mention the movement in this context. From these findings, we might tentatively conclude that the gaze towards the Western 'other' is so firmly rooted in these narratives that such early attempts at acculturating human rights thought tend to be neglected altogether in mainstream civics textbook discourse. As a result, the image of a passive Japan being 'deficient' and 'late' vis-à-vis the Western 'other' emerges quasi automatically.[5]

Finally, we should note another strategy employed in the *Tsukurukai* civics textbook in order to deconstruct the mainstream discourse on human rights thought. As in the 2005 edition, the volume published in 2001 accentuates that human rights are imbued with different meanings according to differences among cultures and nations:

> There is nothing like absolute rights to freedom or equality that prevail regardless of nation or age. We must not forget that these rights were acquired historically little by little according to each nation's tradition and culture as the result of the efforts of the ancestors.
>
> (Nishibe *et al.* 2001: 31)

Then, an extra column is added in this edition to differentiate the seemingly homogenous human rights discourse of Western 'others' that is a characteristic of mainstream civics textbooks' narratives. The column deals with Edmund Burke, the well-known eighteenth-century Irish–British philosopher and critic of the French Revolution. In the *Tsukurukai* textbook, the conservative thinking of Burke, which tends 'to respect tradition and order of society', is juxtaposed with French thinkers of democracy who – as the narrative has it – 'display a tendency to favour reason and individual rights over tradition and social order'. By introducing the conservative tradition of British democracy, the *Tsukurukai* narrative points to alternative Western 'others' usually omitted from mainstream civics textbook discourse. As has been pointed out, in the *Tsukurukai* textbook there can be discerned a serious attempt to subvert mainstream discourse on human rights by introducing a perspective heavily leaning towards cultural relativism. Although, for this purpose, cultural diversity is emphasised, and multiple 'others' enter the scene, it is still mostly in the realm of the Western 'other' where the ideological battle is fought. To put it bluntly, throughout the civics textbook – and this holds true for the *Tsukurukai* history textbook as well, as scholars have demonstrated (e.g., the Children and Textbooks Japan Network 21 (*Kodomo to kyōkasho zenkoku netto21* 子どもと教科書全国ネット21) 2005: 28–31; Fuwa 2001][6] – Asian 'others' only matter insofar as they can be employed to demonstrate the unique and superior experience of the emergence of the modern Japanese nation state.

Representations of Japanese 'self' and Asian 'others' – examples from Japanese civics and ethics textbooks for senior secondary school

Introduction

In order to sketch the representation of Asian 'others' in contemporary Japanese textbooks, in the second part of my chapter I will turn to examples from civics and ethics textbooks for senior secondary school (*kōtō gakkō* 高等学校) that correspond to the volumes for junior secondary school just examined. Whereas the latter usually appear under the title *Kōmin kyōkasho* 公民教科書, civics textbooks for senior secondary school use the title *Gendai shakai* 現代社会 (*Contemporary society*). The curriculum of civics classes (*kōminka*) in senior secondary school is differently structured from that in junior secondary school and comprises courses in civics proper, ethics and politics and economy, respectively. For each of these sections, different textbooks are provided, entitled *Contemporary society* (*Gendai shakai*), *Ethics* (*Rinri* 倫理) and *Politics and economy* (*Seiji keizai* 政治経済), respectively (MEXT 2005: 9). For this chapter, books on 'contemporary society' and 'ethics' by five publishers (four in the case of ethics textbooks) were examined (Kawai *et al.* 2008; Washida *et al.* 2008; Ikeda *et al.* 2008; Kimura *et al.* 2008; Taniuchi *et al.* 2008; Sasaki *et al.* 2007; Hiragi *et al.* 2008; Yamazaki *et al.* 2008; Hamai *et al.* 2008).

A brief comparative look at the table of contents of some of them reveals that many topics that have been treated in textbooks for junior secondary school are taken up here again. There are, for example, sections on the political system, the constitution and human rights that sometimes even use the same visual materials as textbooks for junior secondary school (Taniuchi *et al.* 2008: 98). As in the latter, these textbooks have an opening chapter on 'various issues of contemporary society' and chapters on democracy, law and the political system, economy and social security, and – again very similar to the volumes designated for use in junior secondary school – a final chapter on 'international society' that often has a title emphasising Japans's role in a global world (e.g. Taniuchi *et al.* 2008; Kawai *et al.* 2008; Yamazaki *et al.* 2008). However, in addition to topics students are already familiar with through studying textbooks for junior secondary school, these civics textbooks introduce some new subjects as well, subjects that pertain to issues of particular interest to young people, such as, for example, adolescence, puberty, development of individual self and so forth. Also, the curriculum guidelines for civics classes in senior secondary school stipulate that an ethical point of view should be added when approaching certain topics that are treated, for example, in sections called 'Searching for a better life' or 'The meaning of youth and self realisation' (MEXT 2005: 10–11). Sections that cover these issues are introduced in narratives for civics classes, but are more thoroughly explored in ethics textbooks. Examples will be introduced in more detail at the end of this chapter, as they provide considerable insight into the configuration of the interaction of 'self' and 'other' as projected by Japanese textbook authors.

It goes without saying that the bulk of textbook narratives under examination refer to the society and culture of Japan, but volumes by all publishers also include visual materials depicting Western or Asian 'others', particularly in chapters on 'international society'. Only a thorough, page-by-page analysis could determine the respective function in relation to Japanese 'self', especially when connected to the textual narrative. As this task has not been accomplished yet, I will only hint at some preliminary conclusions based on just one example. Here, I have excluded those sections that deal explicitly with issues such as 'multicultural society', 'international government' or 'global society', which naturally refer to a multitude of different 'others'. It is thus interesting, for example, to consider chapters on politics that introduce the Japanese political system in some detail but also contain comparative sections about various types of government from a historical perspective. In some of the textbooks that have been examined, this narrative rather closely follows the paragraph on human rights and their history. Again, there are close similarities, but also some differences: most textbooks, for example, refer to Switzerland when introducing the issue of direct democracy, even utilising the same photograph (Yamazaki *et al.* 2008: 99; Kawai *et al.* 2008: 122; for very similar photographs, see Sasaki *et al.* 2007: 125). Whereas two textbooks basically concentrate on the Japanese case only (Ikeda *et al.* 2008: 64–7; Taniuchi *et al.* 2008: 120–3), the other three introduce a section on different political systems. It is interesting to note that Kyōiku shuppan's narrative only refers to the Western 'other' and explains the American and British system in some detail, mentioning also the cases of France, Germany and Italy (Kawai *et al.* 2008: 122–3). In contrast, corresponding narratives in Tōkyō shoseki's (Sasaki *et al.* 2007: 126–7) and Yamakawa shuppan's (Yamazaki *et al.* 2008: 100–1) volumes, respectively, also both describe the political system of the US and the UK, but then allow for the same space to narrate the political system of the PRC. This might be interpreted as just one indication that the 'relative other' has gained some more visibility in contemporary civics textbooks in Japanese senior secondary schools. A thorough investigation taking other topics into consideration as well is necessary to validate these findings.

The depiction of thought and religion in civics textbooks – a Japanese 'self' set apart from all 'others'

As mentioned above, there are sections in civics textbooks for senior secondary schools that are particularly noteworthy, as their layout and structural arrangement of topics seem to indicate some fundamental assumptions about Japanese 'self' and non-Japanese 'other' that are even more fully developed in ethics textbooks, to which I will turn below. As has been suggested in civics textbooks for senior secondary schools, within a chapter on youth in contemporary society, there are paragraphs dedicated to the quest for 'better living' and meaning in life. These cover about ten pages and contain short accounts of religious, philosophical and scientific thinking, respectively, that are more fully developed in ethics textbooks. These accounts thus give a short introduction of how different religions, philosophies and science answer the question of meaning, thereby explaining the basic tenet of each of these modes of thought. Although the universal nature of the quest for meaning is emphasised throughout, the arrangement of textual and visual narratives in all of these civics textbooks tends to construct a division between ways of thinking of the Japanese 'self' on one side and all 'others' on the other (the following examples are taken from Sasaki *et al.*'s (2007: 68–77) and Yamazaki *et al.*'s (2008: 54–61) volumes).

Accordingly, there are subsections dedicated to the question of a 'good life', the narratives of which present the thought of the Greek philosophers Socrates and Plato, the wisdom of Confucius, the teachings of Jesus and of Buddha, i.e. a considerable selection of Western and Asian 'others'; the following subsections on 'scientific thought' and the 'dignity of man', respectively, clearly feature an assembly of assorted Western 'others' only, for example Bacon and Descartes, Kant, Luther, Pascal, Foucault and others. The fourth and fifth subsections of this chapter finally turn to the Japanese 'self', featuring paragraphs on 'how Japanese view things' and 'the reception of foreign culture and traditional thought in Japan'. Whereas, in the former on 'things Japanese', the narrative introduces some 'core values' of Japanese culture and their terminology – e.g. 'purity', 'shame' (*haji* 恥), 'sincerity' (*makoto* 誠) – the latter sketches developments of Japanese Buddhism, Japanese Confucianism and national learning (*Kokugaku* 国学) and mentions representatives of Meiji and twentieth-century intellectual life, e.g. Uchimura Kanzō (内村鑑三; 1861–1930), Natsume Sōseki (夏目漱石; 1867–1916), Nishida Kitarō (西田幾多郎; 1870–1945) and Watsuji Tetsurō (和辻哲郎; 1889–1960).

This basic arrangement is found in all civics textbooks examined here. It is particularly noteworthy that Buddhism and Confucianism are also dealt with in this fashion – subjects that should have the potential to bridge the divide between the narratives on Japanese 'self' and Asian 'other'. As it turns out, however, at least in the case of Japan, this topical relationship is almost always subordinated to the category of 'national culture'. It seems that the category of the culture and history of the Japanese nation defines what distinguishes the 'self' from all 'others'. In the realm of 'others', there appears no such clear distinction according to different national cultures. Instead, considerations regarding the subject that is narrated seem to take precedence over, and relativise, the concern with national cultures and origins. Thus, to give an example from the civics textbook published by Kyōiku shuppan that deals with variations of social thought and theories of society, we find textual and visual narratives refer to Kant, Sartre, Gandhi, Martin Luther King and other mostly Western 'others' who are grouped together here for topical reasons (Kawai *et al.* 2008: 60–1). Why are Japanese thinkers not mentioned here? Is it that there has developed no relevant thought about the individual and society in modern Japan that could be brought to the attention of Japanese senior secondary school students in this section? Or does this arrangement signify that their being Japanese somehow overrides the topical relationship and requires that they be introduced in a separate paragraph emphasising *Japanese* ways of thinking?

Continuity and change in the structural arrangement of ethics textbooks – implications for the depiction of 'self' and 'other'

As mentioned before, the tendency to arrange materials pertaining to religious, philosophical and scientific thought, respectively, in a way that highlights the fundamental division between Japanese 'self' and all 'others' seems even more obvious in many ethics textbooks for senior secondary school use. Although preliminary research suggests that this very much represents contemporary mainstream discourse in textbooks, some indications for change have also to be noted. In my final analysis, the volume published by Tōkyō shoseki serves as an example of the traditional arrangement of topics in ethics textbooks (see Hiragi *et al.* 2008). The book is divided into five chapters, with the second and third chapters being of particular interest here. The second chapter, entitled 'Self-awareness as human beings' (*Ningen toshite no jikaku* 人間としての自覚; Hiragi *et al.* 2008: 21–68), is again divided into three sections, dealing with 'man and philosophy', 'man and religion' and 'man and art'. As has already been observed above in regard to civics textbooks, in this section the basic tenets of Greek and Chinese philosophy, Christianity, Islam and Buddhism are narrated and elaborated on in some detail; the differences between Buddhism and Christianity are even reflected upon in a separate column (Hiragi *et al.* 2008: 65). Again, the textbook presents an assembly of global 'others', with hardly any differentiation as to whether they are Western or Asian 'others'. This distinction, as well as cultural or national differences between them, seem to fade as these 'others' are all set apart from the Japanese 'self' that is dealt with in a separate chapter, entitled 'Self-awareness as Japanese living in international society' (*Kokusai shakai ni ikiru Nihonjin no jikaku* 国際社会に生きる日本人の自覚; Hiragi *et al.* 2008: 69–118). Slightly overstating this observation, one could even argue that these chapter headings are suggesting a difference between 'humans' (*ningen* 人間) as 'others' and 'Japanese' (*Nihonjin* 日本人) as 'self'. Another example from this textbook might further illustrate this point: in the treatment of Buddhism in Tōkyō shoseki's volume, the textual and visual narrative underlines the Indian origin of this religion (Hiragi *et al.* 2008: 58–63). Although a detailed map is inserted that illustrates the eastward spread of Buddhism to Korea and Japan (Hiragi *et al.* 2008: 63), there is not even a cross-reference here directing the student to the section on developments in *Japanese* Buddhism, which is treated under the heading 'Buddhism and the formation of Japanese thought' in another chapter later in the book (Hiragi *et al.* 2008: 77–88).

Against this backdrop, it is interesting that – although it basically follows the same layout of contents – Shimizu shoin's volume has a double page on the reception of Buddhism in East Asia entitled 'The spiritual milieu of East Asia' (*Higashi Ajia no seishin fūdo* 東アジアの精神風土; Kimura *et al.* 2008: 80–1). This essay, illustrated with photographs of Japanese and Korean children, respectively, wearing traditional attire in festivals celebrating Buddha's birthday, is inserted at the end of the section on 'Reception and development of Buddhism' (Kimura *et al.* 2008: 72–81), which is in turn part of the chapter on 'Japanese living in international society' that highly resembles the arrangement of contents in Tōkyō shoseki's and other publisher's ethics textbooks. This paragraph dwells at some length on the issue of an East Asian cultural sphere comprising China, the Korean peninsula and Japan, characterised, for example, by the use of Chinese characters and the influence of Buddhism in each of these countries. The narrative first explains the current fashion to refer to East Asia as a region based on common cultural traits and history and gives a very brief historical sketch that mentions the Silk Road, for example. In the following paragraphs, however, the column stresses the differences in cultural development in China, the Korean peninsula and Japan, respectively, *in spite of* the common reception and adaption of Buddhism, namely the Buddhist scriptures in Chinese. All in all, the tone is rather sceptical, and the narrative urges students to notice considerable gaps in the unfolding of the Buddhist doctrine in each country since ancient times, dwelling at some length, for example, upon different views about keeping the Buddhist precepts in China, Korea and Japan and particularly strong trends towards secularisation that developed rather early in Japanese society. Nevertheless, this example of a narrative exploring the possibilities of 'East Asia' might indicate that there is a growing awareness in publishers that will somehow transcend the still broadly prevailing arrangement of topics that adheres to the strict division of Japanese 'self' and all 'others'.

In this respect, it is significant that there exists already an ethics textbook for senior secondary school that does just this: in Kyōiku shuppan's volume *New Ethics* (*Shin rinri* 新倫理; see Washida *et al.* 2008), the fundamental divide between 'things Japanese' and 'everything else' was largely given up. Here, we find the treatment of religion, philosophy and science in the fifth chapter entitled 'Contemplating man' (*Ningen o mitsumete* 人間を見つめて) (Washida *et al.* 2008: 75–132). The division of subchapters is markedly different, as the contents in this textbook are ordered according to cultural and historical relations that override the concern to mark off the Japanese 'self' from all 'others'. Thus, the depiction of ancient Greek philosophy and developments in ancient and medieval Judaism, Christianity and Islam are presented in the first section: 'The history of ancient and medieval images of man' (*Kodai, chūsei no ningenkan no rekishi* 古代・中世の人間観の歴史; Washida *et al.* 2008: 76–89). The next part gives an outline of 'The history of Eastern images of man' (*Tōyō no ningenkan no rekishi* 東洋の人間観の歴史; Washida *et al.* 2008: 90–107) that, for the first time, incorporates accounts of Japanese Buddhism and Confucianism into the overall narrative on East Asian thought and religion, including the reception and adaption of Western scientific knowledge in eighteenth- and early-nineteenth-century Japan. The following section then introduces foundations of modernity as evolved in Europe since the Renaissance ('Images of modern man', *Kindai no ningenkan* 近代の人間観; Washida *et al.* 2008: 108–25), a narrative that is quite convincingly

Figure 3.3 Representatives of world philosophy, religion and science

connected to the last part of the chapter, which deals with the impact of Western thought in Meiji Japan and the unfolding of modern Japanese thinking ('Japanese thought connected to the world', *Sekai to tsunagaru Nihon no shisō* 世界とつながる日本の思想; Washida *et al.* 2008: 126–32), introducing, among others, the work of Fukuzawa Yukichi (福沢諭吉; 1835–1901), Nakae Chōmin (中江兆民; 1847–1901), Natsume Sōseki (夏目漱石; 1867–1916), Yoshino Sakuzō (吉野作造; 1878–1933), Hiratsuka Raichō (平塚らいてう; 1886–1971), Yanagita Kunio (柳田國男; 1875–1962), Maruyama Masao (丸山真男; 1914–96) and others.

A more detailed analysis would reveal that these are not mere structural changes but that, throughout the volume, the narrative is characterised by a high level of reflection and sensitivity towards the relationship of 'self' and 'other'. In this regard, it is noteworthy, for example, that, in this volume's treatment of Buddhist thought, the visual narrative combines Indian *and* Japanese images (Washida *et al.* 2008: 92), as the relationship by topic is given priority here over the binary opposition of 'foreign culture/Japanese culture', which is usually employed as a device to structure and divide the topic of 'Buddhist thought' into different chapters in other ethics textbooks.[7] To further elaborate on the issue of sensitivity towards 'self' and 'other' in this volume, it is instructive to briefly analyse another example taken from a completely different subject, also covered in ethics textbooks for senior secondary schools.

Often, in the first chapter, issues of development of body and self, adolescence, love and sexuality are addressed. Apart from some historical and scientific background information that usually mentions scholars such as Siegmund Freud and Michel Foucault, key terms of psychoanalysis and their respective relationship, as well as other theories of psychology and human development are also explained. For our purpose, the paragraph on 'love' (*ren'ai* 恋愛) is particularly interesting: the following quote from Yamakawa shuppan's volume represents mainstream ethics textbooks' discourse that can be found in similar phrases in other books as well:

> During adolescence we experience feelings of longing towards the opposite sex. We eagerly await to meet the person we long for and worry about what the other person thinks about us and how to communicate our feelings. However, if loving other people means only pleasure for oneself alone that might look like love but in reality is nothing more than pure narcissism [...] and does not deserve the name 'love'. [...] Only if men and women mutually share feelings of sympathy and happiness towards each other, only then 'true love forms'.
>
> (Hamai *et al.* 2008: 15–16)

After a short paragraph that deals with the development of sexuality and the consequences of sexual intercourse (pregnancy and the possibility of contracting AIDS are mentioned in this respect), the narrative concludes on a similar moralistic tone: 'Only when love towards the opposite sex is an expression of responsibility and sympathy towards the other, then for the first time this feeling rises to the level of true human love' (Hamai *et al.* 2008: 16).

In comparison, the same topic is treated very differently in Kyōiku shuppan's narrative, as can be seen in the following quote:

> The idea of 'love' (*ren'ai*) also originated in modern Europe. The Christian [concept] of 'love' and the medieval worship of noble ladies in chivalry mixed with the idea of the modern self and thus the idea of love as a precious value in human life was born. There also existed the view that true love and sex were in conflict, but on the other hand a sense of value developed that sex accompanied by love was indeed a beautiful thing. And as people held the belief that true love should lead to marriage, the idea that love, sex and marriage are all united together became dominant in modern times.
>
> (Washida *et al.* 2008: 13)

The basic difference between these two narratives is created by the references to historical time and place that are continually mentioned in the phrasing of Kyōiku shuppan's textbook. In addition – and of particular significance for the overall topic discussed in this volume – these are also references to 'self' and 'other'. To elaborate, there is a footnote attached to the first paragraph quoted above explaining that the term 'love' as used today (*ren'ai*) did not exist in premodern Japan but was introduced as a translation from Western sources in the late nineteenth century. Also, the footnote points to predominantly Buddhist connotations of the indigenous vocabulary of love, referring to a more negatively tainted image of love as 'attachment to the senses' (Washida *et al.* 2008: footnote 2). Instead of imposing upon the students a discourse containing moralistic overtones and implicit values, as in Yamakawa shuppan's volume, this narrative explicitly refers to the construed nature of terms such as 'love'. At the same time, the term and its history are contextualised, pointing to 'self' and 'other', which in this case is a dominant Western 'other'.

Conclusions

As has been pointed out in the introduction, the examples taken from civics and ethics textbooks discussed in this chapter provide rich material for the study of the ways that 'self' and 'other' are juxtaposed in these volumes. Moreover, whether explicitly specified or not, the narrative on each topic revealed particular views on history and historical development that also have considerable significance in terms of the relationship constructed between 'self' and 'other'. Although, in recent years, in controversies about history textbooks, contested issues have often evolved from the omission, depiction or interpretation of particular incidents and 'facts', the preceding analysis of civics and ethics textbooks focused more on the overall interpretive framework itself and its underlying assumptions, which might also provide causes for dissent or controversy.

As has been discussed in detail, the approach in the examples from the *Tsukurukai* civics textbook is characterised by cultural relativism that highlights the existence of many different others and acknowledges, for example, claims to different interpretations of human rights based on diverse cultural or historical experiences. Consequently, the 'universal-cum-absolute' character of fundamental human rights is clearly put into perspective. Within the overall agenda of the *Tsukurukai* textbook discourse, this assertion might then be used as a justification to counter 'liberal' assumptions about the relationship of individual, society and nation state. The latter usually advocate a more universal approach towards human rights and thus emphasise their inalienable nature all the more. As has been pointed out, mainstream textbook discourse in its depiction of human rights in fact follows the narrative of universalism that celebrates human rights as an accomplishment of 'all humankind'. At the same time, this view tends to subordinate differences of 'self' and 'other' to the somewhat overwhelming ideas of 'progress' and 'modernity'. Although cultural differences are thus played down or neglected altogether in narratives presented here, they surface again in a different mode: on a linear timescale displayed in civics textbooks, 'self' and 'other' are assigned different positions indicating 'progressiveness' (i.e. 'early' development) and 'backwardness' ('late' development), respectively.

Discussing the structural arrangement of materials in portions of civics and ethics textbooks for senior secondary school, respectively, the strict separation of Japanese 'self' from all 'others' has been emphasised above. Here again, it is noteworthy to highlight the seemingly underlying interpretive framework. The arrangement of contents bears considerable similarity to basic assumptions of self-representations of Japanese culture that were particularly popular during the 1970s and 1980s and became rather (in)famous under the name of *Nihonron* 日本論 ('discourses on Japan'). This voluminous and broad genre has a long history well predating the last quarter of the twentieth century. Some works published as *Nihonron* count as serious comparative studies of culture, whereas many others, however, might be denounced as phantasms of Japanese singularity and superiority. Particularly after 1970, *Nihonron* indeed emphasised the alleged 'uniqueness' of Japanese culture and development that set the nation apart from the West and Asia alike, forming a 'universe' on its own. As *Nihonron* were widely received in Japan as well as in the West and have been analysed in considerable detail by many scholars since the 1990s, there is no need to further elaborate on the genre (Amino 1990; Aoki 1996; Befu 1993; Dale 1990; Mouer and Sugimoto 1990; Sugimoto 1999; Vollmer 2003; Yoshino 1992).

Here, it must suffice to point to the structural arrangement of topics in some textbooks that indicate implications similar to discourses on Japanese 'uniqueness'.

In this respect, it is interesting that basic tenets of *Nihonron* are also explained in some mainstream ethics textbooks in the opening sections of the chapter on 'Self-awareness as Japanese living in international society' (Hiragi *et al.* 2008: 69–112; see above). In Tōkyō shoseki's narrative, which serves as a most striking example in this respect, under the title 'The way Japanese think about things' (*Nihonjin no mono no kangaekata* 日本人のもの の考え方; Hiragi *et al.* 2008: 70–2), the 'spiritual climate of the Japanese' is illustrated by referring to Japan as an 'island' and Japanese society as a 'village', spatial contexts that have allegedly shaped the fundamentals of the Japanese 'self'. Moreover, on these pages, the theories of Watsuji Tetsurō (和辻哲郎; 1889–1960) on the essential relationship between climate, environment and human cultures are introduced and elucidated in some detail. Although Watsuji's work and role in modern Japanese intellectual history are discussed in a separate chapter, later in the book, here textual and visual narratives suggest that students are encouraged to view Japanese culture (and, in fact, culture in general) in terms of classifications supplied by Watsuji and his followers, who had a tremendous impact on certain strands of late-twentieth-century *Nihonron* (see Befu 1993). This impression is reinforced by the narrative itself, which lacks any reflection on the ideological or historical implications of Watsuji's interpretations and also fails to contextualise his ideas in the light of more recent theories of culture. Instead, the student learning about 'the way Japanese think about things' is provided with a set of items that allegedly most strongly characterise Japanese culture and mentality and bear a striking similarity to topics discussed in the most popular *Nihonron*. Among others, these 'characteristics' are marked by the dominance of wet rice cultivation and a receptive and submissive attitude towards nature that, as the narrative has it, sharply contrasts with a more aggressive posture towards the natural environment found, for example, in Arabian or European cultures (according to Watsuji, classified as belonging to 'desert' and 'pasture cultures', respectively). Also, referring to the 'island' character of Japanese culture mentioned above, the text elaborates that society is conceived of as living in a 'village' (*mura* 村), where particular value is attached to 'harmony' (*wa* 和) in communal life deriving from feelings of belonging (Befu 1993: 71–2).

This extensive, *Nihonron*-like treatment of materials regarding the 'core' of the Japanese 'self' generates far-reaching consequences for the imagination of the relationship of 'others' towards this 'self' that, in a sense, cannot evade fundamental separation from the 'other(s)' because of its 'Japaneseness'. In this respect, this narrative clearly corroborates results from my study of the structural arrangement of contents in textbooks presented above. As has been demonstrated, ethics textbooks differing from Tōkyō shoseki's volume's array of topics have appeared in recent years – nevertheless, it is noteworthy that textbooks continue to be submitted and published that still adhere to *Nihonron* ideas of the 1970s and 1980s.

As this chapter builds largely on preliminary research, however, an in-depth analysis is needed to further validate and differentiate these findings. Hopefully, this chapter may at least serve as a stimulus to include subjects other than history in future research on textbook issues in East Asia, in order to explore more fully how textbook narratives construct images of 'self' and 'others'.

Notes

1   In this regard, the publication of a textbook written by representatives from the PRC, Japan and South Korea that was published in 2005 under the title *History that opens the future* (*Mirai o hiraku rekishi* 未来をひらく歴史 (Trilateral Joint History Editorial Committee of Japan, China and South Korea 2005)) is particularly noteworthy. It focuses mainly on the history of modern East Asia and tends to narrate this history in much detail, focusing on perpetration and victimhood. For a critical view, see Iwasaki and Narita (2008).
2   For details on the screening process for history textbooks, see the synopsis and literature in Saaler (2005: 59–68).
3   A detailed list of which publishers' textbooks for use in junior high school were adopted in each district in 2005 is reproduced on the *Tsukurukai* website (see www.tsukurukai.com/18_saitaku_battle/saitaku00_zenkoku_H17.html (accessed 15 September 2009)).
4   With regard to the subtle differences among mainstream textbook discourse mentioned above, it is noteworthy that the volume published by Nihon bunkyō shuppan (日本文教出版; see Itō *et al.* 2008), in its visual narrative on the 'progress of human rights thought', inserts images of Fukuzawa Yukichi (福沢諭吉; 1834–1901) and Nakae Chōmin (中江兆民; 1847–1901) in its timeline (Itō *et al.* 2008: 42–3). Within the timeline, which starts as usual with Locke, Montesquieu and Rousseau in the seventeenth and eighteenth centuries, they are associated with the nineteenth century, along with Abraham Lincoln and a reference to his Gettysburg Address (1863). Both intellectuals of Meiji Japan are characterised in a caption as actors who 'introduced human rights thought in the case of Japan', with short quotations from Fukuzawa's famous *Gakumon no susume* 学問のすゝめ [*An encouragement of learning*] and reference to Nakae Chōmin as translator of Rousseau's *Du contrat social ou principes du droit politique* (*Min'yakuron*

民約論). Thus, this case can serve as an example of how the reference to Japanese 'self' helps to balance asymmetries in the depiction of cultural flows that are rather obvious in the narrative of human rights thought in other mainstream textbooks.
5 Again, this does not apply for Nihon bunkyō shuppan's volume, which also mentions the 'Freedom and People's Rights Movement' in its timeline and gives the year 1874 in which a memorandum was submitted urging the Japanese government to set up a parliament with representatives elected by the people (by Itagaki Taisuke (板垣退助; 1837–1919) and other activists of the movement (Itō *et al.* 2008: 43)).
6 In this respect, see also the elaborate critique directed at Nishio Kanji's (西尾幹二; 1935–) book *Kokumin no rekishi* 国民の歴史 [*History of a people*] (1999), which served as a voluminous blueprint for the *Tsukurukai* history textbook (*'Kyōkasho ni shinjitsu to jiyū o' renrakukai* 2000: 188–204).
7 Figure 3.3 shows a collage of images that depicts some of the figures from the realms of philosophy, religion and science mentioned in detail in the sections before (these people are Prince Shōtoku (聖徳; 574–622, Japan), Mohandas Karamchand ('Mahatma') Gandhi (1869–1948, India), Mother Teresa (1910–97, Albania/India), Natsume Sōseki (1867–1916, Japan), Friedrich Nietzsche (1844–1900, Germany), Hiratsuka Raichō (1886–1971, Japan), Socrates (fifth century BC, Greece), Simone de Beauvoir (1908–86, France), Karl Marx (1818–83, Germany), Confucius (551–479, China)). It is characteristic of this textbook's approach that they appear in a fashion that is clearly intended to transcend divisions of religious and philosophical traditions, nation, culture, gender and age (source: Washida *et al.* 2008: 132).

Bibliography

Amino Y. 網野善彦 (1990) *Nihonron no shiza. Rettō no shakai to kokka* 日本論の視座。列島の社会と国家 [*Perspectives of discourses on Japan. State and society in the Japanese archipelago*], Tokyo: Shōgakukan.

Aoki T. (1996) *Der Japandiskurs im historischen Wandel: Zur Kultur und Identität einer Nation* [*Discourses on Japan in historical transition: culture and identity of a nation*], München: Iudicium.

Befu, H. (1993) 'Nationalism and *Nihonjinron*', in B. Harumi (ed.) *Cultural nationalism in East Asia. Representation and identity*, Berkeley, CA: Institute of East Asian Studies/University of California, 107–35.

Dale, P.N. (1990) *The myth of Japanese uniqueness*, Oxford: Nissan Institute/Routledge.

Duara, P. (2008) 'Historical narratives and trans-nationalism in East Asia', in S. Richter (ed.) *Contested views of a common past. Revisions of history in contemporary East Asia*, Frankfurt am Main and New York: Campus, 99–117.

Fuwa T. 不破哲三 (2001) *Koko ni 'rekishi kyōkasho' mondai no kakushin ga aru* ここに「歴史教科書」問題の核心がある [*This is the core of the problem with 'history textbooks'*], Tokyo: Shin Nihon shuppansha.

Gomi F. 五味文彦 *et al.* (eds) (2006) (Shinpen) *Atarashii shakai, kōmin* (新編) 新しい社会、公民 [(New edition) *New society, civics*], Tokyo: Tōkyō shoseki.

Hamai O. 濱井修 *et al.* (eds) (2008) *Gendai no rinri* 現代の倫理 [*Contemporary ethics*], revised edn, Tokyo: Yamakawa shuppan.

Hein, L. and Selden, M. (eds) (2000) *Censoring history. Citizenship and memory in Japan, Germany, and the United States*, Armonk, NY: M.E. Sharpe.

Hiragi K. 平木幸二郎 et al. (eds) (2008) *Rinri* 倫理 [*Ethics*], Tokyo: Tōkyō shoseki.
Höpken, W. and Richter, S. (eds) (2003) *Vergangenheit im Gesellschaftskonflikt* [*Views on history in Japan*], Köln: Böhlau.
Ikeda Y. 池田幸也 et al. (eds) (2008) *(Kōtō gakkō) Shin gendai shakai* 高等学校新現代社会 [*New contemporary society (senior secondary school)*], Tokyo: Shimizu shoin.
Itō M. 伊東光晴 et al. (eds) (2008) *(Chūgakusei no shakaika) Kōmin. Gendai no shakai* （中学生の社会科）公民。現代の社会 [*(Social studies for junior secondary school students) Civics. Contemporary society*], Tokyo: Nihon bunkyō shuppan.
Iwasaki, M. and Narita, R. (2008) 'Writing history textbooks in East Asia: the possibilities and pitfalls of *History that opens the future*', in S. Richter (ed.) *Contested views of a common past. Revisions of history in contemporary East Asia*, Frankfurt am Main and New York: Campus, 271–83.
Kawai H. 河合秀和 et al. (eds) (2008) *Shin gendai shakai. Chikyū shakai ni ikiru* 新現代社会。地球社会に生きる [*New contemporary society. Living in a global society*], Tokyo: Kyōiku shuppan.
Kimijima, K. (2000) 'The continuing legacy of Japanese colonialism: the Japan–South Korea joint study group on history textbooks', in L. Hein and M. Selden (eds) *Censoring history. Citizenship and memory in Japan, Germany, and the United States*, Armonk, NY: M.E. Sharpe, 203–25.
Kimura K. 木村清孝 et al. (eds) (2008) *Gendai rinri* 現代倫理 [*Contemporary ethics*], revised edn, Tokyo: Shimizu shoin.
Kodomo to kyōkasho zenkoku netto 21 子どもと教科書全国ネット２１ [Children and Textbooks Japan Network 21] (ed.) (2005) *Koko ga mondai 'Tsukurukai' kyōkasho. 'Tsukurukai' shinpan rekishi, kōmin kyōkasho hihan* ここが問題「つくる会」教科書。「つくる会」新版歴史・公民教科書批判 [*These are the problems with textbooks by Tsukurukai. A critique of the new editions of Tsukurukai's history and civics textbooks*], Tokyo: Ōtsuki shoten.
'Kyōkasho ni shinjitsu to jiyū o' renrakukai 「教科書に真実と自由を」連絡会 [Committee for 'Truth and Freedom in Textbooks'] (ed.) (2000) *Tettei hihan 'kokumin no rekishi'* 徹底批判「国民の歴史」[*A thorough critique of History of a Nation*], Tokyo: Ōtsuki shoten.
Lee, E.J. (2008) 'East Asia discourses in contemporary Korea', in S. Richter (ed.) *Contested views of a common past. Revisions of history in contemporary East Asia*, Frankfurt am Main and New York: Campus, 181–201.
MEXT 文部科学省 [Ministry of Education, Culture, Sports, Science and Technology] (2005) *Kōtō gakkō gakushū shidō yōryō kaisetsu. Kōmin hen* 高等学校学習指導要領解説。公民編 [*Commentary on the curriculum guidelines for senior secondary school. Civics part*], Tokyo: Jitsukyōsha.
—— (2008) *Chūgakkō gakushū shidō yōryō kaisetsu. Shakai hen* 中学校学習指導要領解説。社会編 [*Commentary on the curriculum guidelines for junior secondary school. Social studies part*], Ōsaka: Nihon bunkyō shuppan.
Mouer, R. and Sugimoto, Y. (1990) *Images of Japanese society: a study in the social construction of reality*, London: Kegan Paul International.
Nakamura K. 中村研一 et al. (eds) (2005) *(Shin chūgakkō) Kōmin. Nihon no shakai to sekai* （新中学校）公民。日本の社会と世界 [*(New junior secondary school) Civics. Japanese society and the world*], Tokyo: Shimizu shoin.
Nishibe S. 西部邁 et al. (eds) (2001) *(Shihanbon) Atarashii kōmin kyōkasho* (市販本) 新しい公民教科書 [*(Public edition) A new civics textbook*], Tokyo: Fusōsha.

Nishio, K. 西尾幹二 (1999) *Kokumin no rekishi* 国民の歴史 [*The history of a people*], Tokyo: Fusōsha.

Nitchūkan san-goku kyōtsū rekishi kyōzai iinkai 日中韓三国共通歴史教材委員会 [Trilateral Joint History Editorial Committee of Japan, China and South Korea] (ed.) (2005) *Mirai o hiraku rekishi: Higashi Ajia san-goku no kingendaishi* 未来をひらく歴史―東アジア三国の近現代史 [*History that opens the future: the modern and contemporary history of three East Asian countries*], Tokyo: Kōbunken.

Richter, S. (ed.) (2008) *Contested views of a common past. Revisions of history in contemporary East Asia*, Frankfurt am Main and New York: Campus.

Saaler, S. (2005) *Politics, memory and public opinion. The history textbook controversy and Japanese society*, München: Iudicium.

Sakamoto, T. (2003) 'Wie sollten Geschichtsschulbücher geschrieben werden? [How should history textbooks be written?]', in S. Richter and W. Höpken (eds) *Vergangenheit im Gesellschaftskonflikt* [*Views on history in Japan*], Köln: Böhlau, 151–65.

Sasaki T. 佐々木毅 *et al.* (eds) (2007) *Gendai shakai* 現代社会 [*Contemporary society*], Tokyo: Tōkyō shoseki.

Satō K. 左藤幸治 *et al.* (eds) (2006) *(Chūgaku shakai) Kōminteki bun'ya* (中学社会) 公民的分野 [*(Junior secondary school social studies) Civics branch*], Ōsaka: Ōsaka shoseki.

Satō, M. *et al.* (2003) 'Wie Geschichtsschulbücher sein sollten' [How history textbooks should be], in S. Richter and W. Höpken (eds) *Vergangenheit im Gesellschaftskonflikt* [*Views on history in Japan*], Köln: Böhlau, 167–89.

Sugimoto, Y. (1999) 'Making sense of *Nihonjinron*', *Thesis Eleven*, vol. 57: 81–96.

Tanimoto Y. 谷本美彦 *et al.* (eds) (2008) *(Shakaika) Chūgakusei no kōmin. Chikyūmin o mezashite* (社会科) 中学生の公民。地球市民をめざして [*(Social studies) Civics for junior secondary school students. Striving for global citizens*], Tokyo: Teikoku shoin.

Taniuchi T. 谷内達 *et al.* (eds) (2008) *Kōkōsei no shin gendai shakai. Tomo ni ikiru shakai o mezashite* 高校生の新現代社会。共に生きる社会をめざして [*New contemporary society for senior secondary school students. Aiming at a society of living together*], Tokyo: Teikoku shoin.

Vollmer, K. (2003) 'Mißverständnis und Methode: Zur Rezeption der Japandiskurse' [Misunderstandings and methodologies: on the adoption and interpretation of *Nihonron*], *Japanstudien*, vol. 15: 37–68.

—— (2007) 'Images of Japanese society in the *New civics textbook*: neo-nationalist antidotes for demographic challenges and social change', in P. Backhaus (ed.) *Familienangelegenheiten* [*Family affairs*], *Japanstudien*, vol. 19, München: Iudicium, 221–41.

Washida K. 鷲田清一 *et al.* (eds) (2008) *Shin rinri. Jiko o mitsumete* 新倫理。自己を見つめて [*New ethics. Contemplating the self*], Tokyo: Kyōiku shuppan.

Yagi H. 八木秀次 *et al.* (eds) (2006) *(Chūgaku shakai) Atarashii kōmin kyōkasho* (中学社会) 新しい公民教科書 [*(Middle school social studies) New civics textbook*], Tokyo: Fusōsha.

Yamazaki H. 山崎廣明 *et al.* (eds) (2008) *Shinpan: Gendai shakai* 新版―現代社会 [(*New edition*): *Contemporary society*], Tokyo: Yamakawa shuppan.

Yoshino, K. (1992) *Cultural nationalism in contemporary Japan: a sociological enquiry*, London: Routledge.

4 Learning to love the motherland
'National Education' in post-retrocession Hong Kong[1]

Edward Vickers

This chapter takes up the thread of the previous chapter in looking at school textbooks for subjects other than history and examining their role in designing or constructing a political sense of 'self' – this time in the case of Hong Kong. It reviews efforts undertaken so far by Hong Kong's post-colonial regime to (re-)socialise local residents as Chinese patriots, focusing particularly on schooling, but also analysing changes to the broader curriculum. Textbook content is taken as indicative of these curricular changes, while the relationship between textbooks and teaching, and the nature of the textbook publication and vetting processes, are also discussed. The analysis additionally ranges beyond the school gates to consider how the authorities have sought to deploy other vehicles for transmitting patriotic messages, including museums, heritage tourism, events such as the Beijing Olympics and the Chinese Space Programme. The chapter identifies the key messages conveyed through these various channels regarding the nature of 'China', its relationship to Hong Kong's own 'Chineseness' and the definition of the 'patriotic' sentiment that Hong Kong Chinese are expected to share and express following the region's 1997 retrocession.

Introduction

> We must step up civic education so that our youngsters will have a better understanding of China, the Chinese culture [sic] and History ... [We] hope to inculcate in them the passion, and the concern for China, the pride of being Chinese, and a constant readiness to contribute towards the well being of not just Hong Kong but the entire country.
> (Chief Executive C.H. Tung, speech at the gala banquet of the International Forum of Leaders in Higher Education, 4 July 1998, cited in Morris *et al.* 2000: 255)

It is the Government's duty to help everyone, especially our younger generations, to know more about our fast-developing motherland. This year, we mark the 30th anniversary of China's opening up and reform. Next year, we will mark the 60th anniversary of the founding of the People's Republic of China. We will launch a series of activities for this important occasion to enhance young people's understanding of our country. This will help foster a strong sense of national identity in the era of globalisation.

(2nd Chief Executive Donald Tsang, 2008: 27)

Since the return of the territory to Chinese sovereignty in mid 1997, the administration of the new Special Administrative Region (SAR) of Hong Kong has faced numerous political and economic challenges. The political tensions arising from campaigns for greater democratisation and for the preservation of civil liberties (within the terms of the SAR's mini-constitution or 'Basic Law') represent the continuation of struggles begun long before 1997. More sudden and unexpected in its rapidity has been the erosion of Hong Kong's enormous affluence relative to the Chinese mainland and its increasing economic dependence on the latter. The spectre of being superseded as the lynchpin of China's international commercial and financial relations by Shanghai (which had boasted that status prior to 1949) has increasingly come to haunt Hong Kong policymakers. Attempts to bolster the region's comparative advantage over its mainland rivals have meant strengthening and deepening official and commercial ties with the rest of China, while simultaneously celebrating Hong Kong's status as a cosmopolitan metropolis characterised by free speech and the rule of law (in implicit contrast with the mainland). Thus the SAR's first chief executive, C.H. Tung, repeatedly stressed both 'Chinese' pride in the return to the motherland and a determination 'to ensure that Hong Kong's international and cosmopolitan outlook is maintained' (Tung 1998), while proclaiming a 'long-term vision' of 'making Hong Kong not only a major city in China, but also Asia's World City excelling in high value added services' (Tung 2001). In 2001, the report of a commission on strategic development set up by the SAR government encapsulated this aspiration to promote Hong Kong as a global metropolis without offending the People's Republic, suggesting that the region be 'branded' 'Asia's World City, and a major city in China' (see Vickers and Kan 2005).

In the fields of education and cultural policy, the attempt to articulate and popularise a coherent vision of Hong Kong's twenty-first-century role has been complicated by another imperative – that of re-educating local residents as patriotic Chinese citizens. The fact that most Hongkongers have consistently regarded themselves as both Chinese and patriotic is immaterial for the purposes of the new 'National Education' drive, as, for most, this patriotism has long been combined with suspicion of the communist state born of the folk memory of flight from starvation or persecution on the mainland. Local protests against the policies of the national government, particularly the massive local demonstrations against the suppression of the 1989 Student Movement, have reinforced Beijing's conviction that Hong Kong is a potential base for subversion of the communist regime. On the Chinese mainland, a key plank of the regime's response to the Tiananmen crisis was the Patriotic Education Campaign begun in the early 1990s (Vickers 2009). In post-retrocession Hong Kong, official responses to the crystallisation of Hongkongese identity and pressure for democratisation following 1989 have reflected this shift towards an ideology of 'state-centred patriotism' (Zhao 1998). The 1984 dictum of former paramount leader Deng Xiaoping that 'patriots must form the main body of administrators' in post-1997 Hong Kong has been invoked by Beijing's local proxies to signal refusal to countenance full democratisation for the SAR. As Shiu Shin-poor, head of one such proxy, the One Country – Two Systems Research Institute, declared in 2004, 'A stronger sense of national identity has to be the prerequisite for any political reform, otherwise further democratization and universal suffrage will lead to splittism' (*China Daily* 2004). Such statements suggest the strength, in circles close to key local and mainland policymakers, of a view that patriotic re-education is essential to the task of making Hong Kong safe for democracy – in whatever form it ultimately comes.

The purpose of this chapter is to examine official or pseudo-official visions of national and local identity promoted through education and cultural policy, the means by which such visions have been disseminated and the relationship of this project of identity reformation to broader official efforts to reposition Hong Kong economically and politically in the post-1997 era. After surveying the major contours of the political landscape during this period, the chapter will consider some of the ways in which cultural policy has been used by government in attempts to reform identity consciousness among Hong Kong's population – especially local youth. Developments in the museums and heritage sector are briefly discussed, with reference to data from interviews as well as publicly available sources, for the insights they offer into the political pressures that have impinged upon recent attempts to construct a public narrative of the local past. Finally, reforms to the education system and the school curriculum are analysed, with particular reference to the new school subject of 'liberal studies', to assess the balance between the 'local', 'national' and 'global' dimensions of Hong Kong's identity as it is presented to local students in the early twenty-first century.

Political context

Before turning to an analysis of cultural and education policy, it is necessary to consider briefly the broader context within which policymakers have had to operate. Since the Patten governorship (1992–7), Hong Kong's politics have revolved around the manoeuvrings of the two main political blocs already taking shape before 1992: the pan-democrats and the pro-Beijing 'patriots'. The terminology habitually used to describe these two camps is misleading in implying that the pan-democrats are a purely 'localist' grouping. Although they certainly portray themselves as readier than their rivals to put Hong

Kong's interests before those of the mainland regime, a number of the more senior pan-democrat figures continue publicly to define themselves as patriots deeply concerned with political reform on the mainland – an approach Pepper sees as needlessly fuelling communist paranoia regarding Hong Kong's role as a base for 'subversion' (Pepper 2006: 386). However, the compulsion many democrats feel to campaign on mainland-related issues constitutes an assertion of Chinese patriotism that rejects communist attempts to define the terms of Chinese nationhood – and, indeed, issues such as the Sino–Japanese dispute over the sovereignty of the Diaoyutai/Senkakuji islands north of Taiwan have given some local activists occasion to demonstrate the superior fervour and sincerity of their Chinese patriotism (Vickers 2005: 29 and 44).

All elections held since 1997 (or, in fact, since the early 1990s) have seen support for parties advocating the rapid democratisation of Hong Kong hold stable at above 60 per cent (on relatively high voter turnouts), but with no prospect of any spectacular electoral breakthrough. Pepper argues that, following their failure to turn the 2000 elections to Hong Kong's Legislative Council into a referendum on democratisation, demoralisation and decline had set in among local democrats. However, a combination of bureaucratic arrogance, incompetence (particularly over the handling of the SARS outbreak and Asian economic recession) and the 'mainland-style campaign belligerence' of official efforts to enact legislation on 'subversion' (as mandated by the Basic Law's article 23) reinvigorated the reform movement in 2003. That year witnessed mass anti-government demonstrations that, according to Pepper, prompted the central government to assume direct control of the local drive to deny democracy.

Despite assurances regarding self-government for Hong Kong under the 'One Country – Two Systems' principle, there is strong evidence to suggest that Beijing effectively runs a 'shadow government' out of the Central Government Representative Office in the SAR (Cheng 2009), while continuing to work through a number of civil society proxies (the Communist Party remains illegal in Hong Kong). Whether this is a reflection more of concern for the competence of the local authorities than for their political loyalty is a moot point. However, through the Federation of Trade Unions, leftist schools, affiliated media organisations and state-owned companies, Beijing has funded and coordinated the activities of its local supporters, who have become increasingly adept at managing the local media and mastering the 'electoral game' (Pepper 2006: 390). A classic 'for us or against us' drive has been aimed at rallying local 'patriots' (of the pro-Beijing variety), while the central government has unequivocally asserted its sole prerogative regarding when, or whether, Hong Kong democratises at all. As noted above, there have been strong indications since at least 2004 that the timing and manner of democratisation would depend in part on Hong Kong's politicians – and their electorate – demonstrating sufficient 'patriotism'.

While front of stage Hong Kong's two political camps have thus 'fought to a standstill' since 1997 (Pepper 2006: 391), behind the scenes pro-Beijing groups, mainland business interests and the agents of the central government have assumed greater roles in influencing local policy-making. The media remain substantially free, but civil servants are nervous of attracting critical coverage from Beijing's local mouthpieces (and critical attention in Beijing itself), and media outlets are generally conscious of the adverse consequences for advertising revenue that can stem from unguarded criticism of the Chinese authorities. The independence – and indeed continued existence – of the public service broadcaster RTHK has come under attack from pro-Beijing elements who object to the platform it provides to critics of the local and central authorities (Chan and Lee 2007: 53). Prominent thorns in the side of the establishment have also been subjected to criminal violence or the threat of it – as when the journalist and broadcaster Albert Cheng was attacked in 1998 (IFEX 1998), or when a plot to assassinate leading pro-democracy politician Martin Lee and newspaper proprietor Jimmy Lai was foiled in 2009 (Crawford and Leung 2009). Though such attacks remain rare, and do not appear to be officially orchestrated, they reinforce a general sense that airing criticism of the authorities – and especially of the central government – carries risks that, if not actually physical, may well be commercially, financially or professionally ruinous. This helps to account for the prevalence throughout most of the media of the practice of 'self-censorship' – a practice also much in evidence among publishers of school textbooks (see Vickers 2005: 177–80).

However, the carrot has been more important than the stick in reinforcing the local influence of 'patriotic' or pro-Beijing interests. Like other key business leaders, proprietors of many major print and broadcast media outlets have taken up positions on mainland advisory bodies such as the Chinese People's Political Consultative Conference (CPPCC), giving them privileged access to Chinese officials (Chan and Lee 2007: 50). The attractiveness of the rewards for toeing Beijing's line has also increased as the massive growth of China's economy has both swelled the government's coffers and spawned a seemingly endless plethora of enticing investment opportunities. Meanwhile, at the same time as Beijing's capacity for co-opting the local media has grown, impressions of China formed by Hongkongers through everyday interaction with mainlanders or trips across the border have been dramatically transformed. Gone are the days when the mainland was popularly perceived as backward, chaotic and uncivilised compared with modern, orderly and sophisticated Hong Kong. As Chan and Lee note, nowadays,

> even the politically critical newspaper *Apple Daily* (*Pingguo ribao* 蘋果日報) becomes – intentionally or not – the conveyor and promoter of nationalistic sentiments, as illustrated by their coverage of the news on the 2008 Olympic Games in Beijing and the visits of Chinese astronauts to Hong Kong.
>
> (Chan and Lee 2007: 50)

Nevertheless, the continuing concern of both the local and national governments with international perceptions of Hong Kong and China, combined with the free availability within the SAR of international media, limits the capacity of the authorities to control the narrative. The international media can also act as a brake on self-censorship, as cases of blatant self-censoring, if exposed by international coverage, could severely damage the credibility of a local media outlet (Chan and Lee 2007: 52–3).

Given all the cards apparently stacked in its favour, it is thus somewhat paradoxical that the Beijing-appointed SAR government has failed since 1997 to construct a 'governing coalition' as coherent and unified as that maintained by the British prior to the retrocession. Lui and Chiu (2009) argue that this is partly owing to the growing fragmentation of the local business community, itself a result of the decline in relative size and influence of the old British 'hongs' that used to preside over an economy divided into cosy sectoral fiefdoms, and the emergence of competing family-run conglomerates and of local subsidiaries of various mainland corporations (many of them wholly or partly state-owned). However, Scott (2000) attributes the 'disarticulation' of the post-retrocession political system more to the abandonment of the comparatively consensual, conflict-averse and executive- or civil service-led governing style of the pre-1997 years. Whereas the British authorities were conscious of the low legitimacy enjoyed by a 'colonial' administration, the SAR regime – despite possessing no greater popular mandate – has considered itself in possession of stronger legitimacy, and thus of greater capacity to force through controversial measures. At the same time, it has been compelled to deal with far larger economic challenges than the British authorities faced during the latter years of their rule, while confronting demands for further democratisation that it is both unable to meet (owing to Beijing's veto) and unable to sidestep in the manner of successive British governors before the 1990s. The SAR government's attempts to implement an ambitious and controversial reform agenda, while addressing new economic and political challenges, have run up against the constraints of a well-established and relatively independent legal system, the public opposition of popularly elected but powerless politicians in the Legislative Council, criticism in the still-free media and increasingly determined and politicised protests from a maturing local civil society (Loh 2007).

A number of the key features of the political situation outlined above emerged clearly a decade after the retrocession in a 2007 controversy over allegations of interference in the autonomy of the Hong Kong Institute of Education (HKIEd) by the Secretary for Education and Manpower (SEM) and his 'Permanent Secretary' (who was accused of having pressured senior management to sack professors critical of government policy). A subsequent Commission of Inquiry pitted the government and its external appointees on the institute's council against the HKIEd president and vice-president who, in contrast to the council members and government officials, were forced to pay for their own legal representation. However, their legal team was headed by leading democrat (and barrister) Martin Lee Chu-ming, and their cause was supported by a hurriedly organised University Education Concern Group (UECG) consisting of local academics and by the pan-democrat-affiliated Professional Teachers Union. Meanwhile, local media fully reported and hotly debated the proceedings of the inquiry, which ultimately found that the president of the HKIEd had indeed been improperly pressured to curb his staff's criticisms of government policies. This prompted the resignation of Fanny Law Fan Chiu Fan, the former Permanent Secretary for Education, and, two weeks later, following a ministerial reshuffle, the SEM was not re-appointed. Nevertheless, the government, far from accepting the report of its own commission, and probably aware of the indifference with which the international media had regarded this episode, took the unprecedented step of filing an appeal for judicial review of the commission's findings.

On the one hand, this outcome illustrated the integrity of Hong Kong's legal system and its key manifestation, the rule of law, the vitality and maturity of local civil society (in the form of the UECG) and the continuing freedom of the local press, at least when it came to coverage of a domestic political controversy with no obvious mainland ramifications. However, the heavy financial and professional costs borne by Morris and Luk served as a warning to others considering any similar confrontation with officialdom. The affair also illustrated official contempt for, or lack of understanding of, the principle of academic freedom and its ramifications[2] – an impression only reinforced by the application for judicial review of the commission's report (see Adamson and Morris 2010).

Given the government's ambitions to transform Hong Kong into a higher educational 'hub' for East Asia (Coey 2008), officials might have been expected to fear encouraging any international perception that academic freedom was less than entirely respected in the SAR; indeed, the decision to establish the HKIEd Commission of Inquiry may itself be partly attributed to such fears. However, in the event the international media showed virtually no interest in the whole affair – despite the blanket coverage it received locally and the remarkable outcome involving the removal from office of two top government officials (the only substantial article in the overseas press was by the present author (Vickers 2007a)). From this international silence, the authorities could draw the conclusion that, in the eyes of the wider world, Hong Kong was already perceived as just another Chinese city and therefore a place where official interference in academic freedom was not 'news'.[3] But, although lack of international interest in Hong Kong's society and politics might allow the government greater room to clamp down on inconvenient manifestations of autonomy, a widespread perception internationally that Hong Kong is increasingly undifferentiated from its mainland rivals risks undermining the city's attractiveness to investors. This is the paradox that has confronted local officialdom as it has sought to 'renationalise' the region, while continuing to stress its unique advantages as a place in which to live and do business – or to study and conduct academic research.

Cultural policy and China's charm offensive

Official portrayals of Hong Kong's distinctiveness have always tended to express this in utilitarian rather than affective terms, stressing the territory's supreme convenience as a base for commerce and trade, and its incidental charm to passing tourists or visiting businessmen as a place where 'East and West' meet – to go shopping. Until the 1970s, most local inhabitants similarly lacked a strong affective tie to the territory, having arrived there as refugees from China's Civil War in the 1940s, or from the subsequent upheavals of the Maoist period.[4] When local agitation for greater cultural and linguistic recognition gathered momentum in the early 1970s, this was initially expressed primarily as a 'Chinese' movement against British colonialism. However, the emergence during that decade of a generation of young adults for whom Hong Kong was their only home, along with a flourishing of Cantonese-language popular culture, saw the beginnings of a real sense of 'Hongkongese' identity. The British administration's 'Hong Kong is our home' campaign of the late 1970s, which aimed to encourage greater public social responsibility (e.g. refraining from dropping litter) arguably reflected this rising sense of 'Hongkongeseness' more than it stimulated it. The British remained deeply cautious and ambivalent regarding any prospect that a growing sense of Hong Kong identity might spark calls for independence, thus complicating Britain's relationship with China. However, official concerns to maintain the territory's 'depoliticisation' also chimed with the apparent desire of the largely refugee population to leave well behind the fraught political atmosphere of Mao's China.

Ironically, the opening up of China to trade and tourism from the late 1970s, by enabling many Hongkongers to visit their 'motherland' for the first time, initially accentuated a widespread sense of the mainland as an alien, backward and uncivilised place – while correspondingly encouraging a sense of Hong Kong's distinctiveness and superiority vis-à-vis its communist neighbour. The 1982 announcement of China's intention to resume sovereignty over Hong Kong in 1997, the subsequent Sino–British negotiations over the terms of this resumption and the crushing of the 1989 Student Movement on the mainland, gave rise to widespread soul-searching over the nature and value of Hong Kong's distinctiveness, even while many sought the insurance of foreign nationality and/or trimmed their sails to the prevailing political winds from Beijing.

As analysis of the development of the school curriculum for history has shown, officials in the educational bureaucracy were as affected as anyone else by these broader social, cultural and political developments (Vickers 2005). The late 1980s and early 1990s witnessed moves by curriculum developers associated with the official subject committees (within the Hong Kong Examinations Authority and the government's Education Department) to promote the teaching of Hong Kong history, reflecting their sense that Hong Kong's distinctive past and identity deserved greater attention in local classrooms. The sensitivity and suspicion that this aroused among pro-Beijing elements quickly became apparent, as the Beijing-affiliated press claimed that the introduction of local history was part of an insidious plot to dilute the territory's Chinese identity in advance of the retrocession (Vickers 2005: Ch. 6). These accusations foreshadowed those alleging a conspiracy of 'cultural Taiwanese independence' (*wenhua Taidu* 文化台獨) later made by the communist authorities in response to moves on Taiwan to promote the study in local schools of that island's history (Vickers 2007b: 231). However, without the electoral mandate (or American backing) enjoyed by their Taiwanese counterparts, Hong Kong officials, facing the prospect of an ultimate reckoning with Beijing, could not afford to dismiss such pressure. The curriculum was eventually framed so as to place emphasis on the essential 'Chineseness' of Hong Kong's population and its culture and an overwhelmingly positive gloss on the history of Hong Kong–mainland relations (no easy task given the refugee origins of the vast majority of the population).

It was thus apparent well before the retrocession that many in the local pro-Beijing lobby were, at best, deeply uncomfortable with expressions of Hong Kong's distinctiveness that strayed beyond descriptions of its utilitarian advantages as a 'business city' into the more controversial areas of history and culture. Meanwhile, representations of Hong Kong in mainland propaganda have tended to display it in cute, infantile terms reminiscent of depictions of China's minority nationalities, the more to emphasise its willing dependence on the guidance and authority of its mainland Chinese parent. Shortly before the handover, it was announced that a cute cartoon rendering of the Chinese white dolphin (a nearly extinct species) would become Hong Kong's symbolic animal, a mainland official explaining that, like Hong Kong people, the dolphin was 'clever, kind, active and inoffensive' (Lilley 2000). A 1997 propaganda poster shows a delighted baby boy (waving a Hong Kong SAR flag) in the arms of his beaming mother (wearing a red dress), while the faces of various minority nationalities (identified by their distinctive headgear) smile their approval.[5] Opportunities to depict Hong Kong as gratefully dependent on the parental beneficence of Beijing have subsequently increased, as the region's economic and political woes have driven local authorities into closer reliance on the central government. Chiu and Lui cite the Closer Economic Partnership Arrangement (CEPA), announced in June 2003 (just before the 1 July anniversary of the handover, which that year witnessed massive anti-government protests) and designed to symbolise Beijing's determination to help rescue Hong Kong from its economic plight. CEPA, they note, 'was largely intended as a way to help Hong Kong recover from its economic recession and mollify the growing political discontent in 2003, although this motivation was never openly acknowledged' (Lui and Chiu 2009: 146).

Beijing's local charm offensive in fact dates back well before the 1997 handover, having begun with initiatives such as cut-price tours to the mainland organised by the China Travel Service for local teachers and students.[6] Such programmes have been hugely expanded since the retrocession, particularly in 2008, when it was announced that the number of secondary students funded for trips to the mainland every year would be raised from 5,000 to 37,000, to include primary as well as secondary students (Tsang 2008: 27). The premise underlying all such initiatives has been that over a century of 'colonialism', as well as decades of enforced separation from the communist mainland, has left Hongkongers deracinated, ignorant of contemporary China and prejudiced against the Beijing regime. The Hong Kong authorities, acting in tandem with the central government, have taken every opportunity to redress this perceived information deficit, lending maximum publicity to events reflecting glory upon the Chinese nation and its leaders – particularly the Olympics and the National Space Programme – even while carefully eschewing mention of the Communist Party or explicit promotion of the party's ideology. Moreover, this patriotic publicity campaign appears to have been significantly ratcheted up since the demonstrations of July 2003 against government attempts to enact a law against 'subversion' that would have significantly curtailed freedom to criticise Beijing's pursuit of its 'One China Policy'.

Thus, in late 2003, Hong Kong was the first city (after Beijing) visited by China's first astronaut, Yang Liwei, following his historic spaceflight. In 2004, Hong Kong was designated as the first stop on the national victory lap organised for China's medallists after the Athens Olympics. Four years later, the troubled global odyssey of the Olympic torch ended when it touched down on Chinese soil in Hong Kong, where every precaution had been taken over planning the timing and route of the procession to ensure that local protests were stifled or denied coverage.[7] Meanwhile, from 2004, the main terrestrial television stations have been obliged to play the national anthem before their main evening news broadcasts, accompanied by a patriotic video sequence, while, in schools, students have been trained to sing the national anthem (in *Putonghua*) and salute the national flag (Mathews *et al.* 2008: 89).

These initiatives have been pursued under the banner of a broad programme of what in English is officially called 'National Education', but which, in Chinese, is alternatively termed *Guomin Jiaoyu* 國民教育 ('Citizenship Education') or *Guoqing Jiaoyu* 國情教育 (see EDB 2008a). The use of the latter term is significant, as it was coined on the mainland in the early 1990s to describe the educational schemes introduced after 1989 in order to teach the nation's recently misguided youth about the complexities of the 'national situation' (essentially the meaning of *guoqing* 國情; Zhao 1998; Vickers 2009). On the mainland, curricula for teaching students about the *guoqing* have been designed to demonstrate that the daunting nature of the numerous developmental and strategic challenges facing China, as well as the sterling record of the existing regime in overcoming past challenges, mean that continued one-party communist rule is the only wise course for the nation. The 'One Country – Two Systems' principle guiding Hong Kong's post-1997 relationship with the mainland is supposed to uphold the continuing distinction between the systems of governance on either side of the SAR border. However, when it comes to inculcating in young Hongkongers a sense of loyalty towards China as a whole (if not specifically to the party), both the ideology and methods of contemporary 'patriotic education' programmes in the People's Republic have migrated across the frontier.

The implications of the 'National Education' drive for the formal school curriculum are further discussed below. Here, it remains to briefly review some of the extracurricular elements of this programme. Significant national events or anniversaries have been harnessed to the cause of 'National Education' through special lectures (often by invited mainland dignitaries – see EDB 2009a), essay competitions and other activities. Such events include the success of the Shenzhou Five manned space flight in 2003 (EDB 2008a), the 2007 tenth anniversary of the retrocession, the 2008 Beijing Olympics, the thirtieth anniversary of China's 1978 'Reform and Opening', the sixtieth anniversary in 2009 of the founding of the People's Republic of China and the ninetieth anniversary of the May Fourth Movement (EDB 2008b). From 2003, China's October First National Day has been marked by a mainland-style variety show on the theme 'Love my China, celebrate the foundation of the nation' (*Ai Wo Zhonghua He Guoqing* 愛我中華賀國慶), sponsored by official and non-governmental bodies (HKG 2003). The increasingly numerous study tours to mainland China for local students have also featured lectures by luminaries such as former Olympic medallists, members of the National Space Programme and senior officers in the People's Liberation Army (PLA). For example, a July 2004 'National Education' trip to Beijing for local secondary students included a lecture by Yang Liwei, still fresh from his maiden space voyage, and a visit to a military base where students were treated to a combat display and dined in the canteen with senior military personnel. The tour also featured a standard itinerary of patriotically evocative sites – including the flag-raising ceremony on Tiananmen Square, the Yuanmingyuan (the old summer palace razed and looted by a Franco–British army in 1860), Beijing University and the Lugouqiao Museum of the Patriotic War of Resistance against Japan, where students participated in a solemn ceremony to honour the nation's war dead (for one sixth-grade student's journal of this trip, see Gu (2004)). This itinerary has become typical of such trips to Beijing (see EDB 2009a).

In another echo of patriotic education schemes on the mainland, since 2005 the PLA[8] – still indelibly associated by many adult Hongkongers with the Tiananmen crackdown, and whose arrival in the territory in 1997 was anticipated with widespread trepidation – has run an annual 'summer boot camp' for Hong Kong students. Those returning from the first such camp were greeted with a speech by the then Permanent Secretary for Education, Fanny Law:

> Over the past twelve days all classmates have lived together with our elite national military units and this experience will have greatly strengthened your understanding of and identification with the traditions of awe-inspiring military prowess (*weiwu wenming* 威武文明) exemplified by

these sons and brothers of the People. I believe that everyone feels proud of the People's Liberation Army, the defenders of our motherland, and is filled with admiration and respect for the army's spirit of overcoming adversity (*keku jingshen* 克苦精神).

(Law 2005, my translation)

The efforts by the SAR government to boost Hong Kong's flagging economy have involved greater attempts at commercial and infrastructural integration with other cities in Guangdong's Pearl River Delta (Lui and Chiu 2009: Ch. 6). In 2008, it was announced that these economic initiatives were to be paralleled in the educational sphere by attempts to foster in young Hongkongers a sense of belonging to this larger regional entity, encompassing mainland cities as well as Hong Kong. In a programme christened (invoking Olympic imagery) 'Passing the torch' (*xin huo xiang zhuan* 薪火相傳) and given the slogan 'Same Roots – Same Heart' (*tong gen tong xin* 同根同心), groups of students were to be sent on short exchange visits of two or three days to schools in Guangdong Province. The key aim, according to the Education Bureau, was to 'develop in students passion for our country, a sense of national identity and understanding of the close relationship between Hong Kong and the Guangdong Province through exchange and reflection' (EDB 2009b: appendix 1). Reference was also made in the Chinese-language poster promoting the programme to cultivating students' 'hometown sentiment' (*xiangtu qinghuai* 鄉土情懷) – a probable allusion to the fact that most local students can trace their roots back through parents, grandparents or great-grandparents to 'hometowns' in Guangdong. Indeed, the standard travel document for locals travelling to the mainland remains the 'home-going certificate' (*hui xiang zheng* 回鄉證), although most younger Hongkongese retain tenuous ties at best with these Guangdong 'hometowns'. On one level, the 'Passing the torch' scheme thus constitutes an attempt to rekindle the dying embers of a sense of belonging that reaches beyond Hong Kong to the mainland, and at a more personal level than grandiose exhortations to 'love the motherland'.

Much of the energy and resources devoted by the government to cultural policy have thus been channelled into activities that serve the cause of 'National Education' – a cause enthusiastically championed by Beijing's local cheerleaders and conducted with the full collaboration of the National Capital (as demonstrated most notably in the scheduling of visits to Hong Kong by astronauts and Olympic medallists, and by the routing of the Olympic torch through the city). The extent to which this 'National Education' campaign has been driven by directives from Beijing, or by the eagerness of local officials to curry favour in the capital, is unclear. However, as noted above, the buttressing of Hong Kong's global or at least pan-Asian role and identity also remains of great importance to the local authorities, as well as to business interests and the wider population, for whom a sense of their city's 'international' status has long been an important component of its distinctiveness.

Hong Kong's hosting of events such as the 2005 WTO Ministerial Conference and the 2009 Asian Games have offered chances to assert this status, while several of the boondoggles with which the government has tried to boost the post-retrocession economy (particularly the 'Cyberport' initiative, Hong Kong Disneyland and the West Kowloon Cultural District) have been promoted as enhancing the city's reputation for being at the global technological and cultural cutting edge. The international status of the SAR is also, to some extent, institutionalised under the terms of its reunification with China, so that Hong Kong issues its own passports (albeit only to locals of Chinese nationality), retains its own representative offices in major overseas capitals, fields its own teams at sports events such as the Olympics and the World Cup, and boasts a seat at the table at meetings of bodies such as the WTO and World Health Organisation (WHO). Indeed, a Hongkonger – Margaret Chan – was appointed to head the WHO in 2006, having been nominated for this post by the Chinese government.

Nevertheless, Chan's nomination to this post by Beijing reflects the fact that, within the WHO, she represents China, not Hong Kong. Indeed, one textbook for the local school subject of 'liberal studies' (of which more below) features a photograph of Chan in front of the WHO logo, alongside another of the astronaut Yang Liwei greeting a crowd of flag-waving Hong Kong teenagers – in a chapter entitled 'I am Chinese' (*Wo shi Zhongguoren* 我是中國人; Leung 2007: 52). Recognition of the international nature of Hong Kong's economic role spans the 1997 retrocession, having been regarded as uncontroversial by both the British and Chinese authorities. However, Chinese officials made it clear before the handover that any attempt to 'internationalise' the region politically would not be tolerated, viewing the initial proposals to introduce local history into the curriculum for the school subject of history as just one such instance of suspect 'internationalisation' (Vickers 2005: 162). From 1997, local political parties were barred from the sorts of formal tie with overseas political groupings (through bodies such as the Liberal International) that are routine in autonomous democracies, while the top fifteen posts in the administration were reserved for holders of Chinese nationality (barring non-Chinese locals as well as holders of multiple nationality). Local constitutional arrangements have thus been designed expressly to ensure that, while Hong Kong remains 'international' in the commercial and financial sphere, in politics it is locked in orbit around the 'national' centre. Moreover, as local livelihoods have increasingly come to rely upon the proceeds of trade with the mainland, cultural and education policy have been assigned key roles in fostering ties to the Chinese state rooted in patriotic sentiment, rather than simply pragmatic self-interest.

Museums and the portrayal of local and Chinese identities

While the school curriculum has assumed a key role in promoting patriotic sentiment among young Hongkongers, other sectors – especially those falling under the remit of the government's Leisure and Cultural Services Department – have also been drawn into the drive to instil a more state-directed sense of Chinese patriotism. Museums, which in mainland China have been at the forefront of the party's post-1989 Patriotic Education Campaign (see Vickers 2007c), have been foremost among those local institutions that have felt pressure to align themselves with a more explicitly nation-building agenda.

For example, the Hong Kong Museum of History, due to re-open on a new site in 1998, had its opening delayed by three years after pro-Beijing figures on the appointed Provisional Urban Council demanded that several aspects of the planned permanent exhibition, *The Hong Kong Story*, be revised to deliver a more patriotic message (Vickers 2005: 68–75). Meanwhile, curators at the new Hong Kong Museum of Coastal Defence, which opened in 2000, took steps to prevent any similar controversy erupting by revising their original plans for the museum (which was to have been essentially a regimental museum dedicated to the disbanded Hong Kong Volunteer Force), by broadening the exhibition's focus to give it a far more Chinese flavour and by inviting senior officers from the People's Liberation Army Hong Kong Garrison to the official opening ceremony (Ng 2004, interview). The list of temporary exhibitions displayed at the History Museum before and after the retrocession reveals a growing number with China-focused themes. However, with the notable exception of a 1999 display on the rise of modern China (adapted from an exhibition staged at the Museum of Revolutionary History in Beijing to mark the fiftieth anniversary of the People's Republic of China), revolutionary themes and heroes have been largely absent from China-related temporary exhibitions, as have any controversial topics in twentieth-century, and especially post-1949, Chinese history.[9] Coverage of China has tended to focus on remote periods (revealed through archaeological finds); innocuous 'cultural' subjects (e.g. 'Treasures of the Chengde Summer Palace'); 'material culture', urbanism and Chinese modernity (e.g., Shanghai and Hong Kong viewed comparatively); or topics and figures of broad 'nationalist' appeal (e.g. the Great Wall and Admiral Zheng He; Hong Kong Museum of History 2009).

The one modern political personality who has been granted extensive exhibition space is Sun Yat-sen, who featured in temporary exhibitions at the History Museum each year between 2003 and 2006. As leader of the anti-Qing Republican Revolution of 1912 and first president of the Chinese Republic, Sun commands admiration across modern China's political divides and is treated reverentially in both Communist and Kuomintang official histories. In 2007, a Sun Yat-sen Museum opened in a former merchant's mansion (latterly the Mormon Tabernacle) in Hong Kong's Mid-Levels. This arose from a proposal endorsed by the Urban Council at the time of the debates over the permanent exhibition for the new History Museum and was subsequently lobbied for by local 'patriotic' groups, including an association of Chinese history teachers (the *Zhongguo Lishi Jiaoyu Shehui* 中國歷史教育社會). The rationale for establishing this museum involved stressing not what Sun had done for Hong Kong (which was very little), but what Hong Kong had done for Dr Sun (Ting 2004, interview). However, the support given to the museum by both the Hong Kong government (which paid for it) and various mainland museums (which loaned the vast majority of the exhibits) testified to the consonance between this project and the larger nation-building agenda espoused by both the local and national authorities. Indeed, the 2008 report of a government-appointed task group on 'National Education' spotlighted the contribution made by the Sun Yat-sen Museum to the promotion of 'National Education' (TGNE 2008).

It is instructive to contrast the resources thus lavished on memorialising a figure of pan-Chinese rather than local significance with the degree of official regard accorded to popular symbols of a distinctively 'Hongkongese' identity. The government readily acceded to the lobbying for a Sun Yat-sen museum from relatively small but well-connected 'patriotic' groups, but calls for a museum dedicated to the famous Hongkongese actor Bruce Lee (Li Xiaolong) have so far come to nothing (Pun 2009). Moreover, in late 2006, as the Sun Yat-sen Museum was preparing to open, the demolition of the iconic Star Ferry Pier to make way for further reclamation of Hong Kong Harbour went ahead in the teeth of public protests, a petition signed by thousands and a Legislative Council (LegCo) motion calling for more consultation (Veg 2007).

While a general tendency among local officials to prioritise projects with a patriotically Chinese flavour has thus been evident since 1997 (and arguably before that too), what is less clear is the extent to which this has happened at the direct behest of Beijing. When interviewed in 2004, neither the then director of the Hong Kong Museum of History nor the head of the Antiquities and Monuments Office saw the pressures on local museums to take a more patriotic line as part of any coherent or coordinated official programme, despite regular exhortations from then Chief Executive Tung Chee-Hwa concerning the need for Hongkongers to learn more about Chinese history and culture (Ting 2004; Ng 2004). They felt that these pressures arose in a more informal and irregular manner, for example through proposals from 'friends of the chief executive', who might 'ask through [informal] channels for the director of the museum to organise an exhibition' (Ng 2004),[10] or through public posturing from 'sudden patriots' (*turan aiguo* 突然愛國) in the business community (Ting 2004). In other words, there was a perception that, during the initial post-retrocession period, projects with a patriotic tinge were often adopted in response to pressure from old 'leftist' groupings, business leaders keen to establish their pro-Beijing credentials and similarly inclined local officials – without any apparent active central government intervention to steer policy in this direction. However, there seems since 2004 to have been a significant stepping up of efforts by the Hong Kong government to coordinate a broad, state-directed programme of patriotic education – with more vocal and direct support from the authorities in Beijing. This shift coincides with what Pepper argues has been the increased intervention of the central government in local politics following the massive anti-government rallies of 2003 (Pepper 2006).

In 2007, the tenth anniversary of the retrocession and the year before the Beijing Olympics, the Hong Kong government's Commission on Strategic Development established the Task Group on 'National Education' (TGNE). The following year, this produced a report reviewing progress in 'National Education' over the preceding decade or more, looking both at schooling and beyond to teacher training, cultural policy, museums, the activities of the 'National Education Centre' established with EMB funding in 2004 and the range of programmes discussed above (TGNE 2008). The report places 'National Education' in the context of broader official efforts to promote civic education dating back to the 1980s, and represents these official efforts as a response to demands or concerns voiced by various 'community' groups or organisations – though most of those named (such as the Hong Kong Federation of Education Workers) are local 'leftist' groupings aligned with Beijing. The prevalence among local people of an overriding sense of 'Hongkongese' identity is portrayed as a problem demanding official action:

> After years of efforts, results of surveys on the 'public's sense of identity' conducted by the University of Hong Kong and the Chinese University of Hong Kong showed that although the percentage of respondents who identified themselves as 'Chinese' had slightly increased over the past decade since the reunification, it was still lower than that of those who identified themselves as 'Hong Kong People', *reflecting the need for the Government to put in greater efforts in promoting national education.*
> (TGNE 2008: 9; my emphasis)

The text goes on to record how President Hu Jintao 'earnestly advised' local authorities to 'put more emphasis on National Education for the youth in Hong Kong' in his 2007 speech marking the tenth anniversary of the retrocession (TGNE 2008: 10), following this with quotations from speeches by the chief executive and other senior local officials expressing their determination to redouble their efforts in this area. Whether or not it reflects the deepest sentiments of all members of the drafting committee, this report starkly illustrates how, under the post-retrocession constitutional arrangements, local officials feel compelled to account to Beijing for their efforts in the patriotic re-education of the local population. And, as the following section will illustrate, that same pattern of accountability ultimately applies also to curriculum developers and those responsible for approving school textbooks.

'Liberal Studies', schooling and political socialisation since the retrocession

Hong Kong's education system and school curriculum have been subject to a number of significant reforms since 1997 (and in some cases earlier), the cumulative effect of which has been to bring both the structure and ideological content of local schooling far more closely into line with mainland practice.[11] In this connection, it should be noted that the pre-1997 government was not averse to curriculum control – and that it left its post-1997 successor with constitutional powers and administrative structures that could be used to enforce a high degree of conformity with an officially mandated 'line'. These powers had been used in the post-war period to institute a system for mandating school curricula and vetting school textbooks that was designed to exclude from Hong Kong the political turbulence associated with China's Communist–Kuomintang rivalry (which continued to affect the colony after the Kuomintang retreat to Taiwan). Under this new system in the 1950s, the curricula for subjects such as Chinese history were also largely purged of content (i.e. most of China's modern history) deemed liable to excite anti-colonialist sentiment (Vickers *et al.* 2003). However, insofar as these measures served to insulate the territory from mainland-style political radicalism, they enjoyed a large measure of acquiescence, if not active support, from the refugee-dominated local population. In stark contrast to all of East Asia's other 'developmental states' (if it deserves to be included in this category at all), Hong Kong's school curriculum was thus calculated to inoculate the territory against the formation of any political sense of nationhood – even while licensing the inculcation (through subjects such as Chinese literature and Chinese history) of a rather chauvinist sense of cultural 'Chineseness'.

The advent of the long transition to Chinese rule, beginning in the mid 1980s, heralded a gradual abandonment of this studiously depoliticised and stateless conception of citizenship (tellingly, Hongkongers were legally accorded the status of 'residents' or 'permanent residents' rather than 'citizens'). Moves began as early as the 1980s to introduce 'citizenship education' (at this stage as a cross-curricular 'theme' with a strongly cultural focus) into the school curriculum, and already by 1996 this was linked officially to efforts to promote a sense of Chinese 'national identity' among students (Morris *et al.* 2000). These initiatives served a largely symbolic purpose – signalling to Chinese officials that the local authorities were sincere in their desire to prepare the local population for a smooth transition, while also aiming to introduce local teachers and parents to the idea that the inculcation of a sense of Chinese citizenship through the school curriculum was a 'normal' practice not associated with any wholesale communist takeover. However, the relatively tokenistic pre-1997 efforts in this direction have been succeeded since then by a far more sweeping and ambitious programme of patriotic education. Development of the curriculum for history, and especially for the separate subject of Chinese history, has been coloured by a clear expectation in the highest governmental circles that history education should promote a sense of Chinese patriotism – an agenda enthusiastically embraced by many in the Chinese history subject community (no doubt at least partly out of conviction, but perhaps also because of the boost it lends to the status of a subject widely viewed by pupils as excruciatingly dull; Kan *et al.* 2007).

Suggestions made in some pro-Beijing quarters shortly after the retrocession that *Putonghua* 普通話 should rapidly become the default medium of instruction in local schools (as throughout the mainland) have been quietly buried after arousing strident opposition (Adamson and Morris 2010: Ch. 8), but *Putonghua* has become a widely taught school subject. Moreover, after a number of twists and turns in the long-running local debate over medium of instruction policy, which in 1997 (just before the handover) saw the majority of schools required to teach in Cantonese rather than English, the government has progressively backed away from this widely unpopular policy. In 2009, the power to decide medium of instruction was effectively returned to schools, which were permitted to use different languages to teach different subjects (Adamson and Morris 2010: 154). This has seen a number of schools take up the option of teaching subjects such as Chinese language and literature and Chinese history through the medium of *Putonghua* rather than Cantonese, and a shift to the more widespread use of *Putonghua*, with a corresponding decline in the use of Cantonese, is widely viewed as probable. Finally, of potentially major significance for future transfers both of curricular practice and of students and teachers across Hong Kong's border with the mainland is the shift from 2009 to a '3–3–4' structure for secondary and higher education – three years each of junior and senior secondary schooling, followed by four-year undergraduate degrees. This marks the abandonment of the English-style system formerly in place (which had featured three-year degrees preceded by a two-year matriculation course or 'A-level'), bringing Hong Kong's system structurally into line with those of the mainland and of the United States.

As part of this restructuring of the system of schooling, the subject of 'liberal studies' (or, in Chinese, *tongshi jiaoyu* 通識教育, more accurately translated as 'general education' or 'general studies') has been made compulsory at senior secondary level, making it one of only four compulsory subjects (along with Chinese language, English and maths). The rationale for this is presented as meeting a need to broaden the school curriculum, particularly at senior secondary level, giving Hong Kong an education system that meets 'global' or 'international' standards and is fit to prepare students for the 'challenges of the 21st century' (see EDB 2007a: 3). The subject is also given a broad remit in terms of inculcating attitudes and skills associated with active and responsible global, national and local citizenship (EDB 2007b: 1–6). An EDB booklet promoting the subject provides an 'ABC of "liberal studies"':

> Enhancing students' **A**wareness of contemporary issues;
> **B**roadening the knowledge base and expanding the perspectives of students;
> Strengthening students' **C**ritical thinking skills.
>
> (EDB 2007a: 4)

The booklet also notes that 'liberal studies' is not a new subject at senior secondary level, but has been offered as an 'AS level' in the upper forms since 1992. However, this overlooks the fact that the original incarnation of the subject was available only as an option in the sixth and seventh forms (approximately, ages 17–19), was adopted by very few schools and was developed before 'National Education' was as central to the curriculum development agenda as it has become since the retrocession (on the early development of 'liberal studies', see Chan and Morris (1997)).

The focus in the stated aims for 'liberal studies' on critical thinking, broadening students' perspectives and enhancing their awareness of current affairs is linked to the promotion of a pedagogical approach for the subject that is radically different from that to which most local teachers and students are accustomed. The official curricular guidelines envisage teachers creating their own materials for classroom use, devising projects for students to pursue as autonomously as possible, and mediating lively classroom discussions and debate (see EDB 2007a, b).[12] However, little in-service training has been provided to the vast majority of teachers for whom this approach to teaching is alien, leaving them most heavily reliant on the plethora of new 'liberal studies' textbooks that publishers, sensing a new bonanza, have rushed to produce. As noted above, commercially published textbooks are subject not only to the vetting procedures of the Education Bureau's committees, but also to the pressures affecting all businesses with interests and investments in the mainland China market. A brief review of some of the commercially published textbooks for 'liberal studies' in current use at junior level reveals how the priorities of 'National Education' have come to influence the content of the subject – in ways that suggest tensions with the goals outlined in the Education Bureau's own 'ABC of "Liberal Studies"'. For the purposes of this chapter, it has not been possible to analyse textbooks for 'liberal studies' at senior secondary level under the new post-2009 three-year curriculum. However, the subject has been taught at junior secondary level since 2006, with a view to preparing students for the new compulsory senior secondary course, and examination of texts for the junior forms can thus provide some sense of the sort of world-view presented (in Hong Kong's famously text-reliant schooling culture). The focus here will be primarily on the representation in these texts of the local, national and global dimensions of identity.

Significant differences exist between textbooks produced by different publishers, some offering more thoughtful and text-heavy treatment of curricular topics (e.g. Leung 2007), whereas others offer a more text-light and 'safer' approach of the kind many local teachers tend to favour (e.g. LSEB 2006a, b, c). Although local textbooks generally tend to adhere closely to the official curriculum guidelines (a 'safe' approach increasing the likelihood of swift approval and the capture of a large market share), the emphasis on project work in 'liberal studies' also means that the potential range for variation among textbooks is much wider than usual, and that experiences of teaching and learning for this subject may vary more from school to school than is typically the case in Hong Kong.

In a chapter entitled 'I am a Hongkonger' (*Wo shi xianggangren* 我是香港人), in his volume on 'identity', Leung (2007) presents pupils with different generational perspectives on local history through the eyes of two imaginary families. Thus grandfather remembers fleeing from the mainland to Hong Kong in 1941 – though his flight is attributed to Japan's invasion of China rather than the Civil War, which prompted far more migration to Hong Kong later in that decade. None of the family members mentions fleeing to Hong Kong to escape the famines or persecution of the Mao era (especially the Great Leap Forward and the Cultural Revolution) – major causes of post-war migration to the colony. Two individuals in their mid-thirties mention the 1989 Student Movement and the anxieties it aroused in them concerning Hong Kong's future, as well as that of China. However, the second reflects that the events of 4 June made her realise that she was 'linked by flesh and blood with Chinese people' (*he Zhongguoren shi xuepai xiangliande* 和中國人是血脈相連的) and goes on to mention how her more recent business trips to the mainland have 'strengthened her knowledge of and sense of identification with the nation' (*dui guojia de renshi he rentonggan dou jiaqiangle* 對國家的認識和認同感都加強了; Leung 2007: 22).[13] A middle-aged father in his fifties recalls the rapid development of Hong Kong in the 1960s and 1970s, as outbreaks of protest from (Kuomintang-inspired) 'rightists' (1956) and (Red Guard-inspired) 'leftists' (1967) prompted the 'colonial government' to take some interest in the improvement of ordinary people's livelihood (*guanzhu minsheng shiwu* 關注民生事務) and notes how the growth of popular culture (Bruce Lee is pictured) contributed to the emergence of a local sense of identity (Leung 2007: 23). For her part, his wife remembers her role in 'patriotic movements' in the 1970s (the Chinese Language Movement and the Diaoyutai protests). Addressing her children, she reflects that she had been

> worried about your future, because in the 1980s the school curriculum still avoided discussing Chinese politics, and only referred to the appreciation of Chinese culture [an accurate observation, E.V.]. I worried that if you grew up in this sort of environment, you would feel distant from the motherland. Fortunately this situation never arose.
> (Leung 2007: 24)

The children are then featured on the same page expressing fulsome pride in China's strength and prosperity (as evinced by Olympic and astronautical achievements) and desire to further the development of the nation. Leung thus combines the expression of different views or perspectives with the implication that the general trajectory of local identity conforms neatly to the goals of 'National Education'.

This implication becomes even clearer in the subsequent text, as he provides a summary of local history (Leung 2007: 27–8), focusing on threats posed by political turbulence to local stability, and on movements reflecting local patriotism and the sense of 'Chineseness': 'rightist' and 'leftist' violence in the 1950s and 1960s; the 'Hong Kong Festivals' (*xianggangjie* 香港節) instituted by the colonial government in 1969, 1971 and 1973, in response to earlier disturbances, with the aim of restoring stability and building a stronger sense of local 'belonging'; and the Chinese language and 'Protect the Diaoyutai' movements. Students are then invited to reflect on the earlier set of fictional family reflections in the light of this highly selective historical narrative. Three short articles also elaborate on several aspects of post-1997 interaction with the mainland – greater cross-border collaboration in the film industry, increased numbers of Hongkongers travelling to the mainland as tourists or to study *Putonghua*, and the rising intake of mainland students in the local higher education system. 'What influence', students are asked, 'has this daily rise in contacts between the two places [Hong Kong and the mainland] in various spheres had on Hong Kong people's sense of Chinese identity?' (Leung 2007: 29). The answer is provided on the final page of the chapter, where students are informed that:

> before and following the return to Chinese rule (*huigui qianhou* 回歸前後), cultural and economic contacts between the mainland and Hong Kong witnessed a daily strengthening (*rijian jiaqiang* 日間加強); Hong Kong people developed even closer relations with their mainland compatriots (*neidi tongbao* 內地同胞), and gradually strengthened their sense of Chinese identity.
>
> (Leung 2007: 30)

It is inevitable that any discussion of what it means to be a 'Hong Kong person' will have as a major theme the evolving relationship between Hong Kong and mainland China. However, the second part of Leung's chapter entitled 'I am a Hongkonger' (Leung 2007: 31–6) focuses almost entirely on the debate over the appropriateness of playing patriotic songs on the local evening news, the importance of learning one's national anthem, when it should be played, and what effect learning or singing the anthem has on cultivating sentiments of 'patriotism'. This choice of theme is clearly related to a heated local debate dating back to 2004–5 over the playing of a patriotic song, *Xinxi jiaguo* 心繫家國 (roughly translatable as 'Homeland of united hearts'), before the local television news. However, although students are invited to engage critically with this debate (as it relates to the appropriateness or effectiveness of different methods of promoting patriotism), the overall focus of the discussion of Hong Kong identity is thus heavily weighted towards a consideration of the relationship between 'Hongkongeseness' and patriotic Chineseness. The assumption throughout is that Hong Kong identity can only be defined in relation to an active sense of broader Chinese patriotism, and that the strengthening of local patriotic sentiment is an inevitable and welcome consequence of the retrocession.

This assumption becomes more strongly evident and explicit in two chapters entitled 'I am Chinese' (*Wo shi Zhongguoren* 我是中國人), where different views regarding the nature of Hong Kong's 'Chineseness' and the imperative to be 'patriotic' are touched upon. The topic 'Hong Kong people's patriotic spirit' (*xianggangren de aiguo qinghuai* 香港人的愛國情懷) is introduced with a quotation from former paramount leader Deng Xiaoping, declaring that 'a sense of patriotism is extremely important to the development of the country' and that 'patriots are those who respect their own race/nation (*minzu* 民族), earnestly and sincerely support the motherland's recovery of sovereignty over Hong Kong, and do not harm Hong Kong's stability and prosperity' (Leung 2007: 53). Students are not invited to discuss Deng's statement critically, but they are presented with a cartoon of a woman LegCo representative insisting that 'love of country does not mean love of party' (precisely the opposite of the message delivered in mainland textbooks), juxtaposed with another depicting the 'chair of a local political organisation' (*minjian zhengzhi tuanti zhuxi* 民間政治團體主席) asserting that, since the Communist Party represents all Chinese people, patriotic Hongkongers should also 'love the party' (*ai dang* 愛黨; Leung 2007: 54). The text asks students whether they agree with these two contrasting statements. They are then presented with a cartoon of an angry opposition politician berating the Hong Kong authorities for failing to stand up for the rights and interests of Hongkongese investors arrested on the mainland, while alongside a government-supporting party spokesman is depicted mildly observing that Hongkongers are often unable to gain assistance from police when they experience 'accidents' (*yiwai shigu* 意外事故) on the mainland (Leung 2007: 55). He states that helping Hongkongers who get into trouble on the mainland is the responsibility of the mainland police. Students are then asked whether, and why (or why not), the way in which these two politicians express their criticisms of the local and mainland authorities is 'patriotic', and they are invited to discuss how criticism of, or lack of support for, government policy can be expressed 'patriotically'. They are further asked to consider what they should do when they encounter people engaging in 'unpatriotic behaviour' (*bu aiguo de xingwei* 不愛國的行為) and to give examples of Hongkongers behaving in ways they regard as 'patriotic' or 'unpatriotic' (justifying their judgements; examples given earlier in the chapter include burning the national flag). A final question asks them whether they feel it is problematic to judge whether a particular person is or is not patriotic from observing one instance of their behaviour.

The above treatment of Hong Kong identity implicitly embraces a number of assumptions, including that local identity is, and can only be, a sub-set of Chinese identity; that a close relationship between Hong Kong and the mainland is something to be viewed positively and as a source of benefit to local society; that the region's political stability is potentially fragile and requires careful protection; and that the proper conduct of local politics should be infused with a sense of 'patriotism'. There is minimal recognition of the role that mainland influences have played in destabilising local politics in the past (with the Hong Kong reaction to the 1989 post-Tiananmen crackdown represented as symbolic of local people's strengthening patriotic interest in mainland affairs). There is also no consideration of the extent to which a Hong Kong identity might encompass non-Chinese elements – despite the small but significant proportion of non-ethnic-Chinese residents in the region, and the fact that an indeterminate but sizeable minority of ethnically Chinese Hongkongers hold foreign nationality.

The Longman text by Leung does fleetingly acknowledge the presence in Hong Kong of residents who are not ethnically Han Chinese (though not that of ethnic Chinese Hong Kong permanent residents with foreign passports – a very substantial group). In the chapter 'I am Chinese', students are asked to discuss the qualifications for citizenship of various applicants for Chinese nationality – including a Hong Kong permanent resident of British nationality, an overseas Chinese from Indonesia, a Chinese Singaporean, a Brazilian with Chinese parents and a Tibetan (Leung 2007: 41). Students are therefore implicitly challenged to debate the extent to which 'Chineseness' is, or should be, linked to qualities of race or ancestry rather than culture, language or a 'civic' sense of belonging. However, it is significant that this discussion is oriented towards a discussion of what qualifies someone for Chinese nationality, rather than of what makes someone a 'Hong Kong person'. Given the emphasis frequently placed on the region's 'international' status, it might be expected that Hongkongese identity would be represented as rather more inclusive and cosmopolitan than Chinese nationality. However, a reading just of this Longman textbook on identity might well give exactly the opposite impression.

Much of the content of the 'liberal studies' texts that can be construed as contributing to the 'broadening of students' knowledge base' or the enhancement of their 'awareness of contemporary issues' relates to China – an emphasis that chimes with often-expressed official concerns about young people's lack of 'knowledge' and 'awareness' of the motherland. Thus Manhattan Press devotes a whole volume of its junior secondary 'liberal studies' course to 'Chinese culture and modern life'. There is little here that would not already be familiar to students who had studied the subjects of Chinese history or geography, but this book provides a survey of China's history, geography and culture with a distinctly patriotic gloss. The ancient origins of Chinese civilisation are highlighted (and compared with other ancient civilisations of Egypt, Mesopotamia and India); significant space is devoted to 'minority nationalities' (*shaoshu minzu* 少數民族) such as Tibetans and Uyghurs (controversy over whose 'Chineseness' is nowhere acknowledged in the text); and the glories of Chinese culture are celebrated with reference to philosophy, literature, art and technological prowess in the form of the 'great inventions', such as printing and gunpowder. The modern relevance of the latter is stressed through a linkage between early Chinese rockets and the contemporary National Space Programme (LSEB 2006c: 53).

The representation of Chinese culture and identity supplied here is essentially identical to that found in mainland school textbooks (see Vickers 2009), except that it is not tied to celebration of the Communist Party's role and is stripped of the 'socialist' sloganeering that is still an obligatory, if increasingly tokenistic, feature of mainland texts. As noted above, Hong

108 *Edward Vickers*

Kong people have generally never evinced much uncertainty over their cultural or ethnic identity as 'Chinese', so that this celebratory representation of the national cultural heritage and contemporary national revival – stripped of ideological gloss and references to the party or socialism – is well calculated to chime with a long-established local discourse of 'Chineseness'. Indeed, the shift over recent years in mainland school texts (and state propaganda) away from a revolutionary socialist vision of national identity towards an embrace of 'traditional Chinese values' and a celebration of the legacy of '5,000 years' of glorious Chinese civilisation has undoubtedly rendered the bridging – in school curricula and other fields – of the ideological divide between the mainland and Hong Kong much easier than might have been foreseen in the mid 1980s.

Besides inculcating a sense of local and national identity, the aims of the 'liberal studies' course also encompass the inculcation of a critical awareness of important 'global' issues. A Manhattan Press volume on 'globalisation' purports to offer a balanced range of perspectives on cultural, technological, institutional as well as economic facets of this phenomenon (though not any environmental ones), and the challenges as well as opportunities that these present for the world in general, and Hong Kong and China in particular. The crucial importance for Hong Kong of meeting the challenges posed by globalisation – especially through upgrading the local education system – is emphasised, echoing a common refrain of official pronouncements in recent years (Vickers 2009: 66). However, particularly in its treatment of the 'challenges' that globalisation poses, this volume appears to equate 'globalisation' with 'Westernisation' or Western hegemony, assuming for China and for Hong Kong as part of China) the posture of underdog or victim. Thus, the suffering of Chinese farmers is attributed to the terms agreed (by the West) for China's entry into the World Trade Organisation, without any discussion of the role that domestic policy might have played in exacerbating China's widening urban–rural divide. The cultural 'problems' relating to 'McDonaldisation' or 'Disneyfication' in underdeveloped countries are highlighted, but whether the spread of Han culture in 'backward' regions of China creates similar 'problems' is not discussed. China's increasingly active role as a commercial partner, aid donor and arms exporter in regions such as Africa and South and Southeast Asia is nowhere mentioned. Moreover, the exploitation of Chinese workers in mainland factories is attributed to 'transnational corporations' (Vickers 2009: 62), even though pay and conditions in many such factories are reportedly far better than those in many belonging to Hong Kong-based entrepreneurs, not to mention China's murky network of penal labour camps.

Invitations to exercise the 'critical thinking' that is a defining goal of the 'liberal studies' curriculum thus do not apply to the coverage in local textbooks of issues relating to the Chinese mainland. However, with respect to issues relating purely to Hong Kong itself, it is still a different story. In the Manhattan Press textbook *The government and I*, a number of highly contentious issues in local politics are presented to students for debate (LSEB 2006b). Indeed, such is the state of Hong Kong's post-retrocession political system that it is almost impossible to conceive of any way of covering it while avoiding controversy. The British solution to this sort of problem for almost the entire pre-1997 period was to discourage or ban altogether discussion of political issues in schools (Morris 1992). However, the introduction of elections as an integral feature of Hong Kong's mini-constitution (the 'Basic Law') and the requirement in the 'liberal studies' curriculum that students be familiarised with this constitution licence textbook writers to invite debate not only on issues such as free speech and the freedom to demonstrate, but also on questions of when direct elections for the chief executive should be introduced (Morris 1992: 48), or when the Legislative Council should be entirely constituted by direct elections (Morris 1992: 30, 35). The Manhattan Press book goes so far as to suggest the intriguing classroom activity of staging not just one but two mock elections for chief executive – the first by direct election ('one man, one vote'), and the second involving indirect election by an 'election board' partly appointed by the teacher – and then asking students to compare the results of each.

Nevertheless, what is not highlighted in the text on *The government and I* is the reality that, in the case of Hong Kong, the role of the teacher is performed by the central government in Beijing. Moreover, when students are invited to discuss the timing of Hong Kong's move to direct democracy, the text fails to remind them (although their teacher may not) that, whatever they may think on this issue, it is Beijing that will decide. By implying that students – as future citizens – should have a say in such matters, the school curriculum reflects the contradictions inherent in Hong Kong's hybrid constitution – neither authoritarian nor democratic. The system as it stands can only function smoothly if Hongkongers can be persuaded, after leaving school, to continue to trust in the pedagogical authority of their leaders in Beijing.

Current 'liberal studies' texts, like those for subjects such as history and Chinese history, thus appear designed to persuade pupils to trust in, and identify with, the broader Chinese nation, by avoiding all controversy in discussion of matters relating to the mainland. The politics and society of mainland China are portrayed in an almost unremittingly positive light in Hong Kong textbooks, which offer local students a vision of their 'motherland' largely identical to that found in mainland texts – minus the (increasingly empty) socialist sloganeering. In discussion of local issues by contrast, acknowledgement of controversy seems possible – but any tensions are represented as the product of factors internal to Hong Kong. Whereas China as a whole is portrayed as enjoying stability and rapid developmental progress, Hong Kong's stability and prosperity are represented as rather more fragile – implicitly underlining the need for the protective trusteeship of Beijing. Meanwhile, the existence of tension between Hong Kong and the mainland, or the possibility that some of the region's political controversies may relate to policies originating in Beijing, is nowhere entertained. Instead, students are incessantly reminded that the only proper attitude to the nation and the national authorities is one of enthusiastic and largely uncritical patriotism.

Conclusion

It is possible to overstate the extent of the shift that the post-retrocession 'National Education' project represents in the way in which local pupils are taught to see their identity. Current attempts to promote a sense of state-centred Chinese patriotism have been able to build on foundations of cultural chauvinism long encouraged, in a more depoliticised fashion, by the curricula for school subjects such as Chinese history. Since the 1990s, official strategies of political socialisation in Hong Kong have converged strikingly with those seen on the mainland – with one significant difference: in Hong Kong, the object of patriotic loyalty is presented simply as 'China', rather than the party-state with its 'socialist' ideology. But, when socialism in China has become an increasingly hollow slogan, and the party's claim to legitimacy is based increasingly on its economic performance and trusteeship of 'Chinese culture', the substantive difference in terms of patriotic ideology today is smaller than was envisaged (probably by all sides) when the 'One Country – Two Systems' model was proposed for Hong Kong in the early 1980s. Overall, this convergence owes as much to the mainland abandonment of socialism as it does to the Hong Kong authorities' drive to actively promote a sense of identification with the People's Republic of China.

As the above account has shown, that official drive to socialise Hongkongers as patriotic Chinese citizens has gathered pace over recent years. A 'National Education' programme of the range and scope of that envisaged by the Hong Kong government's Commission on Strategic Development in 2008 would have created huge ructions had it been rolled out immediately following the 1997 retrocession, sparking accusations that the Chinese government was intent on stamping out Hong Kong's autonomy in short order. Fear of such a reaction doubtless partly explains why a more forceful and sweeping scheme of patriotic re-education was not introduced earlier. However, it appears that the massive popular demonstrations of 2003 against attempts to enact 'anti-subversion' legislation within Hong Kong have prompted the local and mainland authorities to step up efforts to strengthen patriotic consciousness. The contrast between local arrangements for commemorating the fiftieth and sixtieth anniversaries of the People's Republic illustrates this strikingly – the former (in 1999) was celebrated in a low-key and tentative manner, whereas the latter (in 2009) was marked with far greater fanfare and accompanied by a plethora of 'National Education' initiatives (see EDB 2009a, b, c, d).

While the shock administered to the local authorities and the Beijing leadership by the 2003 demonstrations seems to have been pivotal in the decision to intensify the 'National Education' campaign, other factors may have contributed to the abandonment of the more 'softly, softly' approach of the early post-handover period. These may include a calculation on the part of the authorities that the Hong Kong media are now sufficiently cowed, and the international community is sufficiently inured to the idea of Hong Kong as just another Chinese city for little risk to be attached to a more forceful programme of nation-building in terms of possible damage to Hong Kong's international image. Any risk that does remain may have been rendered more tolerable by Hong Kong's decreased relative importance to a China that is now far more assured in its direct commercial and financial dealings with the rest of the world, and that is developing stronger direct ties with, and a stronger economic hold over, Taiwan. At the same time, China's increased prosperity enhances its capacity to sugar the patriotic education pill with extensive exchange programmes for students and teachers, promises of mainland investment for businessmen, and opportunities for ambitious Hongkongers in various fields to play a bigger role on the larger national stage.

None of this means that the 'National Education' programme is guaranteed to succeed in its objectives. In their 2008 study, Matthews, Ma and Lui argue – on the basis of survey and interview data – that young Hongkongers evince a far more utilitarian (and arguably cynical) attitude to nationhood than their mainland Chinese or American counterparts (Mathews et al. 2008). They suggest that Hongkongers have come to apply in the sphere of identity a set of market-based values rooted in Hong Kong's capitalist development and its status as an exceptionally globalised metropolis. This leads them to speculate that the Hong Kong approach to nationality may herald the wider rise of a post-national approach to identity – a conclusion that seems to echo the views on nationalism of scholars such as Hobsbawm. However, this vision of Hongkongers pursuing a market-based approach to identity perhaps overlooks the limitations to the freedom of discourse over identity – both now and in the past – in the spheres of schooling and officially sponsored cultural expression. Hong Kong's pupils have always been exposed, through schooling, to a set of highly chauvinist messages regarding Han Chinese culture. To this has now been added a concerted official drive to promote state-centred Chinese nationalism, reinforced by the lure of association with an increasingly prosperous and 'developed' China. If there is a 'market' for identities in Hong Kong, it is therefore increasingly being cornered by the People's Republic. Moreover, so long as the exercise of free choice in the selection of Hong Kong's government remains circumscribed by Beijing-backed structures and procedures, the prospects of official backing for a strong line on local distinctiveness from the Chinese mainland remain vanishingly slight.

In considering the way in which policymakers and curriculum developers have interwoven discourses of local or regional identity, 'Chineseness', and 'internationalism' or 'Asianism', it is instructive to compare the case of Hong Kong with those of Shanghai and Taiwan (discussed in other chapters in the present volume). It will become apparent that, in the period since the mid 1990s, the official discourse on local, national and international identities in Hong Kong has tended to converge with that of Shanghai, while dramatically diverging from Taiwan (particularly during the years of Democratic Progressive Party (DPP) rule between 2000 and 2008). For the authorities in all three places, internationalism has come to be seen as central to local (or national) identity. However, whereas in Shanghai 'internationalist' rhetoric serves primarily to signify openness for global business and is deployed to enhance Chinese pride in the nation's global status, in Taiwan (especially under the DPP regime) international ties both past and present have been highlighted in order to dilute the previous emphasis on the island's unadulterated 'Chineseness', and to assert a distinctive 'Taiwanese' identity. In Hong Kong, the period from the 1970s to the 1990s saw the rise of a strong popular sense of distinctiveness vis-à-vis the Chinese mainland – the principal 'other' in distinction from which Hong Kong's identity came to be defined. However, since the 1990s (or even earlier), the politics of the retrocession have blocked off any possibility for Hong Kong to pursue the Taiwan route, channelling official efforts at political socialisation towards the mainland mainstream (for all Beijing's assurances about preventing the mixture of Hong Kong's 'well water' with mainland 'river water'). Although it remains too early to determine the effects of this project of patriotic re-education, the official intent is clearly to ensure fulfilment of the observation that 'Hong Kong identity came into being in the shadow of its own demise' (Matthews *et al.* 2008: 12).

Notes

1 The author would like to thank Nick O'Connell, Lisa Leung, Paul Morris and Agnes Lam for their generous help and advice in the preparation of this chapter. He would also like to acknowledge the support of the British Academy through a 'Small Research Grant', which funded a 2004 visit to Hong Kong during which the interviews with Ng and Ting were conducted. Finally, thanks go to Gotelind Müller-Saini and to Daniela Schaaf for their patient and meticulous editing of the manuscript.
2 This was not the first such public scandal over attempted official interference in the autonomy of a local institution of higher education. An earlier incident in 2000 had revolved around an attempt by the chief executive's 'special advisor' to pressure the University of Hong Kong to stop one of its professors from conducting polling research that illustrated the unpopularity of the government. This prompted the resignation of the university's vice-chancellor (who was widely accused of having initially failed to mount a sufficiently robust defence of academic freedom).
3 Meanwhile, as Willy Lam points out, throughout the entire period since 1997, London has claimed that post-retrocession Hong Kong has been a success story 'if only to prove that Britain has not "sold out" Hong Kong people' (Lam 2007: 39).
4 In the early 1980s, the sociologist Lau Siu-kai coined the term 'utilitarianistic familism' to describe the Hong Kong ethos (Lau 1981). However, by tying this to an essentialising vision of 'Chinese' culture and values, he was misrepresenting the vestiges of a refugee mentality that has in fact undergone significant shifts over the subsequent thirty years – as witnessed by the high levels of political participation in contemporary Hong Kong.
5 The poster, published by Hubei Fine Art Publishing House, is reproduced (by permission of the publisher) on the cover of Vickers (2005).

6 I participated in one such tour in 1994, after a prolonged struggle to convince CTS staff that, despite my British nationality, I was indeed a 'local' teacher (as I was contracted on local terms). This tour, which took us to 'Silk Road' sites in Xinjiang, was carefully managed to restrict opportunities for contact with Uyghurs, and the tour guides only spoke Mandarin – prompting my Hongkongese colleague, who spoke no Mandarin, to remark to me that he felt as much like a foreigner as I did. A point was made of taking this Hong Kong group to see the statue of Lin Zexu, hero of the Opium War, that adorns the peak of a hill overlooking Urumqi, and every opportunity was taken to remind us of the vandalisation of Xinjiang's archaeological treasures by imperialistic foreign explorers.
7 A plea was also issued to residents of public housing blocks to refrain from hanging washing out of their windows on that day, so as to avoid making Hong Kong appear messy or disorderly in the eyes of the wider world.
8 Military training has been a compulsory component of the university curriculum in mainland China since shortly after the suppression of the 1989 Student Movement.
9 In 1998 a private corporation sponsored an exhibition in Hong Kong on former communist premier Zhou Enlai, but this was not supported or hosted by the Hong Kong Museum of History (Ting 2004, interview).
10 This suggests a pattern of informal contacts between 'advisors' or friends of the chief executive and local public institutions similar to that which was revealed in the scandal of 2000 at the University of Hong Kong (see note above).
11 A convergence greatly assisted by the mainland regime's effective abandonment over the same period of socialism as the state ideology, and its replacement with a brand of nationalism that portrays the Communist Party as the legitimate custodian of the glorious heritage of '5,000 years' of Chinese civilisation.
12 The two examples that the booklet gives of issues that teachers could use as the basis for classroom discussion and project work are 'sports' (this was the year before the Beijing Olympics of 2008) and GM crops.
13 This is exactly the same gloss on the events of 1989 as that adopted by the Hong Kong Museum of History's audio-visual display on the handover – at the end of the 'Hong Kong Story' permanent exhibition (see Vickers 2005: 72).

Interviews

Louis Ng, Director of the Antiquities and Monuments Office, Hong Kong, 2 February 2004.
Joseph Ting, Director of the Hong Kong Museum of History, Hong Kong, 3 February 2004.

Bibliography

Adamson, R. and Morris, P. (2010) *Curriculum, schooling and society in Hong Kong*, Hong Kong: Hong Kong University Press.
Chan, J. and Lee, F. (2007) 'Media and politics in Hong Kong: a decade after the handover', *China Perspectives*, no. 2 (special feature: Hong Kong, ten years later): 49–56.
Chan, K. and Morris, P. (1997) 'The Hong Kong school curriculum and the political transition: politicisation, contextualisation and symbolic action', *Comparative Education*, vol. 33, no. 2: 247–64.

Cheng, H. (2009) 'Hong Kong freedom fight', *Wall Street Journal Asia*, 29 May. Available online at: http://online.wsj.com/article/SB124353956762563681.html (accessed 27 August 2009).

China Daily, Ping Lun (Opinion) (2004) 'Looking to the past to ensure the future', *China Daily* comment piece, 23 February. Available online at: www.chinadaily.com.cn/english/doc/2004–02/23/content_308316.htm (accessed 26 August 2009).

Coey, C. (2008) 'Building international higher education hubs in Singapore and Hong Kong', unpublished MA dissertation, London: Institute of Education.

Crawford, B. and Leung, A. (2009) 'Police foil plot to kill Martin Lee', *South China Morning Post*, 30 May.

EDB [Education Bureau, Hong Kong] (2007a) *Liberal studies: it benefits you for life* (booklet). Also available online at: http://334.edb.hkedcity.net/doc/eng/ls%20booklet%20eng.pdf (accessed 15 September 2009).

—— (2007b) Liberal studies curriculum and assessment guide, Secondary 4–6.

—— (2008a) Zhongguo dai ren hang tian keji zhuanti 中國帶人航天科技專題 [Special topic on the technology of China's manned space programme].

—— (2008b) Wusi Yundong 五四運動 [May Fourth Movement]. Available online at: http://resources.edb.gov.hk/mce1/54movement/intro.htm (accessed 8 December 2009).

—— (2009a) Xianggang lingxiu sheng jiangli jihua: guoqing jiaoyu kechengban 香港領袖生獎勵計劃：國情教育課程班 [Programme for 'National Education': visit to Beijing on 8 April 2009]. Available online at: http://cd1.edb.hkedcity.net/cd/mce/ne_course/14th%20NE%20course/index.htm (accessed 8 December 2009).

—— (2009b) 'The 60th anniversary of the founding of the People's Republic of China' National Education Seminar Series. Available online at: www.edb.gov.hk/FileManager/SC/Content_7178/60_years_seminars_revised_4.pdf (accessed 31 August 2009).

—— (2009c) 'Passing on the torch – National Education Programme series: National Education Exchange Programme on the mainland for junior secondary and upper primary students (2009)', *Education Bureau Circular Memorandum*, no. 91. Available online at: www.edb.gov.hk/FileManager/TC/Content_2428/NEEP_2009E.pdf (accessed 7 September 2009).

—— (2009d) Gaige Kaifang Sanshi Nian 改革開放三十年 [Thirty years of reform and opening]. Available online at: http://cd.edb.gov.hk/ls/ReformOpeningUp/index.asp?cid=1 (accessed 31 August 2009).

Gu W. 古偉豐 (2004) 'Wang bu liao de ... Xianggang saimahui Xianggang lingxiusheng jiangli jihua guoqing jiaoyu kectheng' 忘不了的 ... 香港賽馬會香港領袖生獎勵計劃國情教育課程 [(Unforgettable ...) Memoir of the Hong Kong Jockey Club Hong Kong Leading Students Award Scheme National Education Curriculum]. Available online at: www.bshlmc.edu.hk/2004/osact/act2 (accessed 8 December 2009).

HKG [Hong Kong Government] (2003) 'Ai wo zhonghua he guoqing shuangzhou' peiyang xuesheng guomin shenfen rentong 「愛我中華賀國慶雙周」培養學生國民身份認同 ['Love my China, celebrate the foundation of the nation fortnight.' Cultivating students' sense of national identity]. Government press release, 18 September. Available online at: www.info.gov.hk/gia/general/200309/18/0918182.htm (accessed 7 September 2009).

Hong Kong Museum of History (2009) *Past exhibitions*, Hong Kong Museum of History, Leisure and Cultural Services Department. Available online at: www.lcsd.gov.hk/CE/Museum/History/en/ex_past.php (accessed 12 September 2009).

IFEX [International Freedom of Expression Exchange] (1998) 'Hong Kong media organisations jointly condemn attack on radio journalist Albert Cheng', 1 September. Available online at: www.ifex.org/china/hong_kong/1998/09/01/hong_kong_media_organisations_jointly (accessed 27 August 2009).

Kan, F. *et al.* (2007) 'Keepers of the sacred flame: patriotism, politics and the Chinese history subject community in Hong Kong', *Cambridge Journal of Education,* vol. 37, no. 2: 229–47.

Lam, W. (2007) 'Beijing's policy towards Hong Kong and the prospects for democratisation in the SAR', *China Perspectives,* no. 2: 34–9.

Lau, S. (1981) 'Utilitarianistic familism: the basis of political stability in Hong Kong', in A.Y.C. King and R.P.L. Lee (eds) *Social life and development in Hong Kong,* Hong Kong: Chinese University Press, 195–216.

Law F. (2005) 'Xianggang qingshaonian junshi xialingying' jieye dianli: jiaoyu tongchouju changren mishuzhang Luo Fan Jiaofen zhi ciquanwen 香港青少年軍事夏令營」結業典禮：教育統籌局常任秘書長羅范椒芬致辭全文 [Closing ceremony of military summer camp for Hong Kong youth: complete text of the speech by Permanent Secretary of the Education Bureau, Law Fan Chiu Fan]. Available online at: www.edb.gov.hk/index.aspx?nodeID=134&langno=2&UID=101833 (accessed 7 September 2009).

Leung P. (2007) *Tongshi jiaoyu: shenfen rentong* 通識教育 身分認同 [*Liberal studies: a sense of identity*], Hong Kong: Longman.

Lilley, R. (2000) 'The Hong Kong handover', *Communal/Plural,* vol. 8, no. 2: 161–80.

Loh, C. (2007) 'Alive and well but frustrated: Hong Kong's civil society', *China Perspectives,* no. 2 (special feature: Hong Kong, ten years later): 40–5.

LSEB [Liberal Studies Education Board] (2006a) *Liberal studies in life: globalisation,* Hong Kong: Manhattan Press.

—— (2006b) *Liberal studies in life: the government and I,* Hong Kong: Manhattan Press.

—— (2006c) *Tongshi xin tiandi: Zhonghua wenhua yu xiandai shenghuo* 通識新天地 中華文化與現代生活 [*Liberal studies in life: Chinese culture and modern life*], Hong Kong: Manhattan Press.

Lui, T. and Chiu, S. (2009) *Hong Kong: becoming a Chinese global city,* London and New York: Routledge.

Mathews, G. *et al.* (2008) *Hong Kong, China: learning to belong to a nation,* London and New York: Routledge.

Morris, P. (1992) 'Preparing pupils as citizens of the Special Administrative Region of Hong Kong: an analysis of curriculum change and control during the transition period', in G. Postiglione (ed.) *Education and society in Hong Kong,* Hong Kong: Hong Kong University Press, 117–45.

Morris, P. *et al.* (2000) 'Education, civic participation and identity: continuity and change in Hong Kong', *Cambridge Journal of Education,* vol. 30, no. 2: 243–62.

Morris, P. (2009) 'Education, politics and the state in Hong Kong', in M. Lall and E. Vickers (eds) *Education as a political tool in Asia,* London and New York: Routledge.

Pepper, S. (2006) *Keeping democracy at bay: Hong Kong and the challenge of Chinese political reform,* Cambridge, MA; Lanham, MD: Rowman and Littlefield.

Pun L. (2009) 'Xianggang Wenxueguan de 'di san tiao lu'' 香港文學館的第三條路 [A 'third way' for Hong Kong's Literacy Museum]. Available online at: http//mhkl.wordpress.com/feed/xct2 (accessed 12 September 2009).

Scott, I. (2000) 'The disarticulation of Hong Kong's post-handover political system', *The China Journal*, no. 45: 29–53.

TGNE [Commission on Strategic Development: Task Group on National Education] (2008) *Promotion of National Education in Hong Kong – Current Situation, Challenges and Way Forward*. Available online at: www.cpu.gov.hk/english/documents/csd/csd_2_2008.pdf (accessed 12 September 2009).

The Hong Kong Literary Museum Initiative (2009) Xianggang xuyao wenxueguan 香港需要文學館 [Hong Kong needs a literary museum]. Available online at: http://mhkl.wordpress.com/feed/xct2 (accessed 12 September 2009).

Tsang, D.Y.K. (2008) 2008–9 Policy Address: 'Embracing new challenges', Hong Kong: government of the Hong Kong SAR. Available online at: www.policyaddress.gov.hk/08–09/eng/docs/policy.pdf (accessed 25 August 2009).

Tung, C.H. (1998) Speech to Asia Society (untitled), 7 May. Available online at: www.asiasociety.org/policy-politics/tung-chee-hwa (accessed 25 August 2009).

—— (2001) Keynote Address by Hon. Tung Chee Hwa, Chief Executive, Hong Kong Special Administrative Region of the People's Republic of China, at the Opening Ceremony of the 14th General Meeting of PECC, 28 November 2001. Available online at: www.pecc.org/PECCXIV/papers/Tung-Chee-Hwa.pdf (accessed 25 August 2009).

Veg, S. (2007) 'Cultural heritage in Hong Kong: the rise of activism and the contradictions of identity', *China Perspectives*, no. 2 (special feature: Hong Kong, ten years later): 46–8.

Vickers, E. (2005) *In search of an identity: the politics of history as a school subject in Hong Kong, 1960s–2005*, 2nd edn, Hong Kong: Comparative Education Research Centre.

Vickers, E. (2007a) 'Fight for an outpost of liberty', *Times Higher Education Supplement*, 1 June. Available online at: www.timeshighereducation.co.uk/story.asp?storyCode=209198&sectioncode=26 (accessed 25 August 2009).

—— (2007b) 'Frontiers of memory: conflict, imperialism and official histories in the construction of post-Cold War Taiwan identity', in S. Jager and R. Mitter (eds) *Ruptured histories: war, memory and the post-Cold War in Asia*, Cambridge, MA: Harvard University Press, 209–32.

—— (2007c) 'Museums and nationalism in contemporary China', *Compare*, vol. 37, no. 3: 365–82.

—— (2009) 'The opportunity of China: education, patriotic values and the Chinese state', in M. Lall and E. Vickers (eds) *Education as a political tool in Asia*, Abingdon: Routledge, 53–82.

Vickers, E. and Kan, F. (2005) 'The re-education of Hong Kong', in E. Vickers and A. Jones (eds) *History education and national identity in East Asia*, New York and London: Routledge, 171–202.

Vickers, E. et al. (2003) 'Colonialism and the politics of Chinese history in Hong Kong schools', *Oxford Review of Education*, vol. 29, no. 1: 95–111.

Zhao, S. (1998) 'A state-led nationalism: the patriotic education campaign in post-Tiananmen China', *Communist and Post-Communist Studies*, vol. 31, no. 3: 287–302.

5 Telling histories of an island nation

The academics and politics of history textbooks in contemporary Taiwan

Lung-chih Chang

This chapter contrasts the preceding discussion of attempts to educate Hong Kong citizens into a 'Chinese' identity with moves on Taiwan to promote a sense of identity emphasising the island's distinctiveness vis-à-vis China. It aims to provide a contextual and comparative perspective on the often intense debates over history textbooks in contemporary Taiwan. Using the Knowing Taiwan controversy in the 1990s as an example, it first outlines the historical and institutional backgrounds of post-war history education and textbook reform in Taiwan. Based on case studies of major policymakers, textbook authors and school educators, it points out how the debates over history have reflected important political, social, academic and cultural trends since the lifting of martial law in 1987, including the development of nationalism, the rise of Taiwan Studies and the democratisation of the popular media. Through the textual analysis of the textbook portrayal of major events such as the 1937 Nanking Massacre and the 1947 February 28th incident, it discusses the changing narratives of Taiwan's past and the way in which depiction of the island's most significant 'others', China and Japan, has shifted over time.

Introduction

The revision of history and history textbooks in East Asia has received important scholarly attention in recent years. Historians not only look into the contested, if not contentious, nature of historical revisionism, but further analyse the roles of official policy, academic research and popular media in shaping new historical discourse and collective memory (Richter 2008).

Taiwan underwent a significant transformation in political, social and cultural realms following the lifting of martial law in 1987. On the one hand, the history curriculum reform constitutes one of the major education efforts to rectify the old political orthodoxy of authoritarian rule. On the other hand, the rise of Taiwan studies testifies to the island's new search for post-colonial collective identity in the age of globalisation. The general nativistic, if not

118 *Lung-chih Chang*

nationalist, trend towards Taiwanisation is characterised by scholars as the indigenisation (*bentuhua* 本土化) movement (Makeham and Hsiau 2005).

This chapter aims to offer an overview of the education and research of Taiwan history, with special focus on education reform, academic trends and identity politics in post-martial-law Taiwan. Until now, most of the previous works on Taiwan's textbook controversies tend to emphasise the rifts in political ideology and national identity (Wang F. 2005). Without denying the impact of identity politics and political parties in shaping public opinion, the author argues that it is important to view history textbooks as a special form of knowledge and examine its production, transmission and reception through various state and non-state institutions and agents (Apple 1993). The following discussion will focus on one of the major events concerning senior secondary school history textbooks in Taiwan, namely the controversy of the curriculum 'Knowing Taiwan' in 1997 (Corcuff 2005).

The major argument of this chapter is divided into four sections. The author first traces the historical background of the indigenisation movement to Taiwan's post-war history and the incomplete question of decolonisation. The following sections examine the development and impacts of the indigenisation movement on history education reform, the academic paradigm shift and the identity politics debate through case studies of the *Knowing Taiwan* textbook, the Institute of Taiwan History in Academia Sinica and the history controversy about colonial modernity. The conclusion is a further reflection on the nature and prospects of the education reform and academic research in Taiwan history in the age of globalisation (Chang 2008).

Reforming history education in post-martial-law Taiwan: the *Knowing Taiwan* textbook controversy in 1997

In June 1997, a new set of junior secondary school textbooks entitled *Knowing Taiwan* (*Renshi Taiwan* 認識台灣) became the focus of intense debate in Taiwan. As the first 'Taiwan-centred' textbooks in post-war education history, the contents of *Knowing Taiwan* received mixed reactions from politicians, historians and educators. During the following four months, it was estimated that more than 250 reports, 18 editorials and 100 columns on the textbook issue appeared in major newspapers, along with numerous commentaries and debates on TV and other electronic media (Tu 1998: 158). The new *Knowing Taiwan* textbook series consisted of three separate volumes, namely history, geography and society, each compiled by different committees and authors.[1] To be sure, the compilation of *Knowing Taiwan* textbooks went through the following processes (Huang 1996):

1   In June 1993, the Ministry of Education decided to revise the junior secondary school curriculum and incorporate new courses on Taiwan.
2   After drafting, public hearings and official meetings, the Ministry of Education announced the new curriculum standard in October 1994.

Telling histories of an island nation 119

Figure 5.1 Cover of the *Knowing Taiwan* textbook

3   The Institute of Compilation and Translation (*Guoli Bianyiguan* 國立編譯館) took charge of forming editorial and review committees in May 1995.
4   The editorial committee consisted of twenty-three specialists and educators who met for several meetings to decide new curriculum guidelines.

5 The history section was chaired by Huang Hsiu-cheng, professor of the Department of History at the National Chung-hsing University. Huang invited Wu Wen-hsing, history professor at the National Normal University, and Chang Sheng-yan, from the National Chung-yang University, to co-author the new textbook.
6 The draft copy was completed for editorial committee review in February 1996 and scheduled for the new school year starting September 1997.

Despite the textbook policymaking, compilation and reviewing processes, the history volume of the *Knowing Taiwan* series was fiercely attacked by the New Party Legislator Lee Ching-hua and the historians Wang Hsiao-po and Wang Chung-fu, who held a public hearing on 3 June 1997 that marked the beginning of a four-month controversy. The critics raised the four following academic and political issues during the textbook debates (Wang C. and Wang H. 1997):

1 relations between Taiwan and China;
2 evaluations of Japanese colonial rule in Taiwan;
3 implications of Taiwanese independence;
4 personal attacks on President Lee Teng-hui.

Although the third and fourth issues remained the rhetoric of party politics and political wrangling among politicians, the first two were seriously debated among historians of different ideological camps. Facing the accusations of 'de-Sinicisation' and 'glorification of Japanese colonialism', the textbook authors responded by reiterations of the following principles of writing (Wang F. 2001):

1 adherence to the MOE curriculum standard and guidelines;
2 practical concerns for classroom pedagogy;
3 increase in the ratio of modern and contemporary history;
4 new attention to cultural, social and educational histories;
5 respect for objective historical facts and neutral usage of terms.

In addition to a legal doctrine and a professional ethnic, they further pointed out the major features of the new history textbook:

1 a holistic view of Taiwan's history and society;
2 a balanced view of colonisation and modernisation;
3 an emphasis on multicultural understanding and civil values;
4 hands-on classroom activity and discussion design.

Meanwhile, historian Tu Cheng-sheng and his students were also criticised for their compilation of the society volume of *Knowing Taiwan*. Unlike his counterpart on the history volume, Tu remained adamant in his call for centrality of Taiwan in his concentric view of history pedagogy (Tu 1998).

After nearly eight public hearings and four mass demonstrations, the new, revised curriculum was put into practice in the name of a tentative version in September 1997.[2]

Identity politics, paradigm shift and education reform: recontextualising the *Knowing Taiwan* textbook controversy

What is the nature of the *Knowing Taiwan* history textbook? How should we understand the compilation process and the resultant controversy? As mentioned in the previous discussion, the 1997 history textbook was the product of official policymaking and institutional process: it was based on the new MOE curriculum standard and the NICT curriculum guidelines of junior secondary school education. Meanwhile, as a special form of official knowledge, history textbooks not only carried the function of legitimisation and political socialisation, but also reflected important changes in the social landscape and in cultural thinking. It is the complex interplay between political, academic and educational visions and practices that constitute the context of the *Knowing Taiwan* controversy in 1997 (Liu *et al.* 2005).

The past in the present: divided memories and post-colonial identity politics in contemporary Taiwan

The education reform and academic advancement of Taiwan history began to take shape against the complex history of post-war political economy and social change. Unlike many former colonies in Asia, Africa and Latin America, Taiwan did not become a new nation state after the end of Japanese rule in 1945 (Liao and Wang 2006). To be sure, Taiwan's decolonisation process in the aftermath of World War II was first disrupted by the Chinese Civil War and then by the Cold War (Ching 2001). Owing to the corruptive takeover practices of the Nationalist government [KMT (= GMD)], the island's retrocession to the Republic of China (ROC) resulted in a tragic uprising and suppression in February 1947. And, following the debacle in mainland China, the KMT regime led by Chiang Kai-shek (1887–1975) emigrated to Taiwan in 1949, and decades of authoritarian rule began. The dual political structure under Japanese colonialism persisted with the new Chinese ruling bloc or the so-called mainlanders (*waishengren* 外省人), who took over the major state apparatus and inherited former colonial infrastructure on the island (Wakabayashi 2008; Chu and Lin 2001).

As Taiwan became an anti-communist bastion during the Cold War, the island's economy was rebuilt with US aid in the late 1950s and 1960s and developed into one of the newly industrialised countries in East Asia (NICs) in the 1980s (Harrell and Huang 1994). Meanwhile, the withdrawal of the ROC from the United Nations and a series of diplomatic setbacks had led to the liberalisation of the KMT and the formation of political opposition in the 1970s. With support from the grass-roots and urban middle-class Taiwanese in local and national elections, the first opposition party, the Democratic Progressive Party (DPP), was formed in 1986. In the face of changing domestic and international situations, Chiang Ching-kuo (1910–88), the son of Chiang Kai-shek and the third ROC president, lifted martial law and opened cross-strait family visits in 1987 (Rigger 1999). Taiwan's democratisation process continued under Lee Teng-hui (1923–), the first Taiwanese to become KMT party chairman and ROC president. The new political trend towards Taiwanisation reached its climax in 2000, when oppositional DPP candidate Chen Shui-bian (1950–) won the presidential election.

At the same time, the controversy over national identity was fuelled in the 1990s, with advocates for either Chinese reunification or Taiwanese independence, who split into different political alliances (i.e. Pan-Blue vs. Pan-Green camps). The domestic debate over constitutional reforms and Taiwanese nationalism was complicated by the changing cross-strait relations in the course of the island's growing economic ties with mainland China (Charney and Prescott 2000; Fell 2005). In 2008, Taiwan experienced another regime change with the KMT candidate Ma Ying-jeou (1950–), who defeated the scandal-ridden DPP government and became the new president of the ROC (Rubinstein 2008).

Meanwhile, as the result of democratisation of knowledge in post-martial law Taiwan, the indigenisation movement also led to diversification of historical discourse among official, academic and popular histories on Taiwan. Originating in the unique historical trajectory of politics and culture in post-war Taiwan, the trend towards indigenisation is closely related to the identity politics of ethnicity and nationalism. The various responses and reactions to Taiwan's indigenisation movement do not only exemplify the complexity of national identity and cross-strait relations in contemporary domestic politics and international diplomacy. To be sure, the mingling of nativism, nationalism and globalisation in Taiwan's identity debates testify to the unresolved historical task of decolonisation since the end of World War II (Corcuff 2002; Vickers 2007).

The above examples of contemporary history controversies in Taiwan testify to the politicisation of ethnicity and confrontation between Taiwanese and Chinese nationalisms that have resulted in history controversies regarding Japanese colonialism on the island (Brown 2004). In a real historical sense, the complex interplay between political, academic and educational visions and practices had led to the textbook controversy on *Knowing Taiwan* in 1997 (Chen, W. 2005).

Discovering history in Taiwan: the emergence of a 'Taiwan-centred' history since the 1980s

The rise of Taiwan studies characterises the trend towards indigenisation since the late 1980s. It was not until the political democratisation that Taiwan history gradually transformed from a marginal discourse of opposition politics to a legitimate field of scholarly pursuit (Hsiau 2000). Once considered as

Figure 5.2 Taiwan-centred map

subordinate to orthodox Chinese history, if not seditious to the KMT regime, the research and discussion of Taiwan history have become a legitimate and flourishing academic field in post-martial-law Taiwan (Wang Q. 2002). As an academic undercurrent during the Japanese colonial period and a political taboo under the Chinese Nationalist rule, the study of Taiwan's history witnesses the coexistence, competition and negotiation of various research traditions. The trajectory of Taiwanese historiography is a reflection of the island's tumultuous political history, with discontinuous legacies of Chinese local history, Japanese colonial history and Western area studies since the introduction of modern scholarship in the late nineteenth and early twentieth century (Eskildsen *et al.* 2005). In addition to academic paradigms, another current of Taiwan history can be traced to Taiwanese political discourses, from anti-colonial movements in the Japanese period to post-war overseas independence movements that were censored and banned by the KMT government under martial law (Chang 2009).

Characterised by its emphasis on the land and people of Taiwan, the new academic trend towards indigenisation aims at recovering the experience of the neglected and at repositioning the periphery as centre (Chang 1997). The new generation of historians endeavours to overcome the academic parochialism of orthodox Chinese and Japanese national historiographies (Chang 2004). With the input of new talents and resources, the study of Taiwan history has developed into a vibrant discipline, with a solid archival infrastructure and new research horizons that have received international recognition. These collective efforts not only achieved new academic legitimacy in the mid 1980s but also evolved into a bourgeoning intellectual field with its own momentum and innovations (Peng 2002).

The symbolic event of the paradigm shift was the founding of the Institute of Taiwan History (ITH) in Academia Sinica. The predecessor of ITH can be traced back to the establishment of the Taiwan History Field Research Office in 1986. This project was initiated by the renowned Harvard archaeologist Chang Kwang-chih (1931–2001), who had directed a pioneering interdisciplinary regional research project of central Taiwan in the 1970s. As a joint effort of four major humanities and social science institutes in Academia Sinica, the Taiwan History Field Research Project symbolised the recognition of Taiwan history by mainstream academia in Taiwan. In 1993, the preparatory office of the institute was approved by the board of Academia Sinica as a response to growing public demands and pressure from politicians of both parties. Built on two decades of infrastructure building and scholarship, the ITH became a fully-fledged institute in 2004. Consisting of an interdisciplinary research faculty, the ITH has become the leading institution of research on Taiwan history and differs from its counterparts on mainland China, which engage in a state-sponsored, policy-oriented study of Taiwan.

One of the major empirical achievements of Taiwan-centred history is the extensive collection and compilation of historical sources. The representative projects include the translation of Dutch–East India Company records; the digitalisation of Qing memorials in the Palace Museum; the opening of Japanese–Taiwanese Government General archives; and the official reports and oral histories of the 228 Incident of 1947. The three major archival centres on Taiwan history are the National Taiwan University Library (formerly Taihoku Imperial University), the National Taiwan Library (formerly the Library of the Japanese Government General) and the Taiwan Provincial Historical Commission (now renamed Taiwan Historica). In addition, numerous local agencies and research groups were set up in the 1980s and 1990s and have been active in collecting and compiling written, visual and oral historical records of Taiwan (Tsao 2000).

The founding story of the ITH in Academia Sinica epitomises the new historical trend towards indigenisation in Taiwan. For example, the ITH is currently composed of five research groups on major aspects of Taiwanese history, including colonial-political history, socio-economic history, cultural history, ethno-history and environmental history. Together with promising researchers in major universities, these intellectual efforts have helped to lay the groundwork for an integrated and multifaceted island history that is different from conventional Chinese, Japanese and Western narratives of Taiwan. Deploying interdisciplinary methodologies from the humanities, social sciences and cultural studies, historians endeavour to piece together the historical landscape of Taiwan that has long been fragmented and marginalised in conventional historiographies (Wu and Wakabayashi 2004).

Telling histories of an island nation 125

Another indication of the rise of Taiwan studies is the significant increase in Taiwan history-related college courses and graduate programmes since the late 1980s. As evident in Table 5.1, the rapid increase of Taiwan-related graduate programmes, especially during 2001–7, testifies to the academic and political efforts of indigenisation by the DPP government. Meanwhile, although the first MA thesis on Taiwan history appeared in 1966, the first Ph.D. dissertation was not completed until 1983. Table 5.2 is the synopsis of MA theses on Taiwan history from 1966 to 2001, which shows the changing trends in historical eras and themes by the researchers into Taiwan history.

Table 5.1 Synopsis of new graduate programmes on Taiwan history and literature (1997–2008)

Year	History	Language and Literature	Aboriginal Studies	Hakka Studies	Ph.D. Program	Total
1997	0	1	0	0	0	1
1998	0	0	0	0	0	0
1999	0	0	0	0	0	0
2000	0	1	0	0	0	1
2001	0	0	1	0	0	1
2002	1	2	0	0	1 (Lit)	4
2003	0	4	1	1	1 (Lit)	7
2004	2	3	0	2	0	7
2005	1	2	0	0	0	3
2006	0	0	1	1	0	2
2007	1	0	0	0	1 (Hist)	2
2008	0	1	0	0	0	1
Total	5	14	3	4	3	29

Source: Author's estimate based on information from Ministry of Education, ROC; www.edu-data.info/pages/school_class_list.aspx

Table 5.2 Synopsis of Masters theses on Taiwan history (1966–2001)

Eras	Politics	Economy	Society	Culture	Religion	Other	Total
Dutch era (1624–61)	0	1	0	0	0	0	1
Zheng era (1662–83)	2	0	0	0	0	1	3
Qing era (1684–1895)	2	29	39	0	5	10	95
Japan era (1895–1945)	6	30	47	11	2	7	103
Post-war (1945–)	11	27	23	21	3	11	96
Cross-eras	3	22	10	10	16	4	65
Total	34	109	119	42	26	33	363

Source: Liu Tsui-jung (2003), 'On the study of Taiwan environmental history: new research perspective (Japanese translation)', *Newsletter of Japan Association of Taiwan Studies*, no. 5: 177.

'Bringing Taiwan history back in': the education reform and textbook revision in post-martial law Taiwan

The reform of education is one of the most important efforts of the indigenisation movement in post-martial law Taiwan. Initiated by progressive academics and senior secondary school teachers, thousands of teachers, parents and intellectuals took part in a mass demonstration on 10 April 1994, calling for the deregulation and democratisation of Taiwan's education system. The executive Yuan responded by forming an ad hoc education reform committee chaired by Dr Lee Yuan-tse, a Taiwanese Nobel laureate in chemistry and then president of Academia Sinica. The committee published its recommendation in 1996 and outlined the goals of education reform as follows:

1 holistic education;
2 student-centred education;
3 multicultural education;
4 constructivist teaching;
5 curriculum integration;
6 school-based curriculum;
7 curriculum evaluation;
8 learning assessment (Chen, J. 2002).

In terms of history education, the new efforts in reforming curriculum design and pedagogy can be represented by the publication of a new set of junior secondary school textbooks entitled *Knowing Taiwan* (*Renshi Taiwan* 認識台灣) in 1997. The new textbook consists of three volumes, on Taiwan history, geography and society. The compilation and policy-making process of the new textbooks can be summarised as shown in Table 5.3.

In terms of history education, there were three major changes in curriculum design and history pedagogy:

1 deregulation of textbook policy: from the national standard version of NICT to 'one curriculum and multiple versions' by textbook publishers;
2 democratisation of history education: from indoctrination of 'patriotism and national spirit' to cultivation of 'historical consciousness and core competence';
3 global perspective and civic education: from 'centrism' to 'multiculturalism' that emphasises autonomy, respect for difference and understanding universal values such as human rights and environmental consciousness.

After the initial controversy, the 1997 *Knowing Taiwan* curriculum was formalised with minor revisions in 1998. After five years in practice, the textbooks were replaced by the new grade 1–9 curriculum (*jiunian yiguan* 九年一貫) in autumn 2001 (Hsu 2008).

Telling histories of an island nation 127

Table 5.3 Synopsis of the *Knowing Taiwan* textbook revision project

Time	Event
June 1993	The Ministry of Education decided to revise the junior high school curriculum and incorporate new courses on Taiwan.
October 1994	The Ministry of Education announced new curriculum standard after drafting, public hearings and official meetings.
May 1995	The Institute of Compilation and Translation (*Guoli Bianyiguan*) took charge of forming editorial and review committees.
Summer 1995	The editorial committee consisted of 23 specialists and educators who met for several meetings to decide new curriculum guidelines. The history section was chaired by Huang Hsiu-cheng of National Chung-hsing University.
February 1996	The draft copy was completed for editorial committee review and scheduled for new school year 1997.
Summer 1997	Controversy broke out surrounding the next textbook series.
September 1997	The new textbook put into practice as 'tentative version'.
September 1998	The curriculum was formalised with minor revisions.
September 2001	The *Knowing Taiwan* textbook series was discontinued and replaced by new Grade 1–9 (*jiunian yiguan*) curriculum.

Source: Huang (1996); Hsu (2008).

Managing identity and differences: textual analysis of the *Knowing Taiwan* history textbook

During the *Knowing Taiwan* debates, the authors of the history textbook discussed and revised some of the contents and terms of their narrative in response to various academic and political criticisms.[3] In the following discussion on the narration and revisions of the *Knowing Taiwan* history textbook, the author will focus on the construction of Taiwanese subjectivity and redefinition of its 'others', especially three major sets of 'we–other' relations, namely the changing historical narratives on the Taiwan relationship with China and Japan and the question of Taiwanese indigenes.

Taiwan-centred narrative and historical periodisation

In their revision of curriculum guidelines in 1995, committee members adopted the lecture structure of eleven chapters and twenty-four sections for the teaching period of one academic year (twenty-six lectures).

Compared with its predecessors, there were several major features in the new history textbook outline:

1 Taiwan-centred perspective: the new outline no longer subscribed to the old master narrative that subordinated the island history into fragments of orthodox Chinese history.

128 *Lung-chih Chang*

Table 5.4 Outline of *Knowing Taiwan* history textbook (1995 revision)

Chapters	Titles	Section numbers
1	Introduction	0
2	Pre-history culture and indigenous society	2
3	Period of international competition	2
4	Period of Zheng regime in Taiwan	2
5	Early period of Qing rule in Taiwan	3
6	Later period of Qing rule in Taiwan	3
7	Period of Japanese colonial rule	3
8	Education, scholarship, and society in Japanese colonial period	3
9	Political change after the WWII	3
10	Economics, culture and society after the WWII	3
11	Prospects for the future	0

2 Multicultural perspective: the narrative begins with an introduction of archeological findings and aboriginal society that differed from traditional Sinocentric immigration history.
3 Neutral rendering of different regimes: the authors adopted neutral descriptive terms instead of the old anti-foreign Chinese nationalist rhetoric in the periodisation.
4 Special attention to social and cultural developments: the authors increased descriptions of long-term social change and the island's multiple encounters with modernity.

Taiwan's relations with China and Japan

During the 1997 textbook debates, the committee adopted the following major revisions in response to criticisms of de-Sinicisation and glorification of Japanese colonialism:

1 It is noteworthy that, while the authors of the new history textbook adopted the rhetoric of objectivity and neutrality in the face of ideology-charged criticisms, they maintained their Taiwan-centred perspective throughout the revision debate.
2 The authors maintained important sections on early Taiwan–China interactions but no longer resorted to the rhetoric of irredentism and patriotism of Chinese nationalism.
3 The usage of ROC on Taiwan reflected the departure from the imagined geography of the Chiang Kai-shek regime towards the indigenisation of the KMT government under the leadership of President Lee Teng-hui.

Telling histories of an island nation 129

Table 5.5 Summary of major revisions of *Knowing Taiwan* history textbook (1997)

Issues of debate	Original text	Revised text	Editor's explanation
Glorification of Japanese colonialism	Japanese rule (*Rizhi*)	Japanese colonial rule (*Riben zhimin tongzhi*)	The original abridgement aims to lessen the student's burden for memorisation without any ideological concerns.
		Added sections on Japanese colonial development of Taiwan's economy and education. Added sections on Japanese legal discrimination against Taiwanese people	It is important for students to know the facts and recognise the duality of colonial modernisation.
		No addition of descriptions on comfort women and Taiwanese soldiers in WWII	The compensation issue is still unresolved and the descendents of those people are still alive.
De-Sinicisation and anti-China sentiments	Period of post-World War II	Period of Republic of China on Taiwan	In recognition of current political reality of de facto territory of Taiwan, Penhu, Kinmen and Mazu. ROC on Taiwan is adopted instead of post-war (*zhanhou*) and glorious retrocession (*guangfu*).
		Maintain the usage of Western calendar before 1945	In accordance with historical and neutral facts without adoption of Japanese or Qing era names.
	Taiwanese	Unchanged	Increase in descriptions of Taiwan-China Relations.

Source: Hsu (2008: 122–7).

4   The authors endeavoured to provide a balanced view of the Japanese colonial period by adding new contents on colonial modernisation in Taiwan's education and public health.
5   Previous political taboos such as the 228 Incident of 1947 appeared in senior secondary school history textbooks, along with new sections with the emphasis on Taiwan's post-war experience of economic development and democratisation.
6   The anti-communist rhetoric of old textbooks was replaced by sections on cross-straits military tensions and peace talks. The conclusion calls

for prospects for equal and reciprocal interaction in the twenty-first century (Huang 1996).

Taiwan's ethnic relations and the internal 'others'

As an example, in the introduction of the *Knowing Taiwan* history textbook, the authors outlined four major features of Taiwanese history:

1 plural society and culture;
2 frequent interactions with the outside world;
3 flourishing international trade and commerce;
4 immigrant spirit of adventure and struggle.

From the perspective of multiculturalism, the main text begins with the narration of pre-historical cultures and archaeological sites in Taiwan, followed by a synopsis of different ethnic groups of Taiwanese indigenous people. After descriptions of Han immigration in the Qing dynasty and colonial/modern transformation under Japanese rule, the authors surveyed political, economic, cultural and diplomatic developments in post-war Taiwan. With emphasis on social integration, community building and plural value, the textbook calls for a new identity of a 'life community' (*shengming gongtongti* 生命共同體) of Taiwanese citizens. Despite the criticisms of neglecting the history of the minorities and issues of national identity, the new recognition of various social classes and ethnic groups and their different historical experiences constituted one of the master narratives in the *Knowing Taiwan* history textbook (*Taiwan Lishi xuehui* 2003).

Conclusion

The history textbook is a special form of official knowledge that involves various state and non-state institutions and agents in its production, transmission and reception. The *Knowing Taiwan* history textbook is significant in Taiwan's post-war education history, because for the first time Taiwanese history was featured and narrated in a single volume. Unlike previous studies that had focused solely on the issue of identity politics and individual authors (such as Tu Cheng-sheng), this chapter revisits the textbook controversy from three interrelated perspectives.

First, the chapter recontextualises the textbook controversy as the result of a complex interplay between changing political conditions, academic discourse and education reform in post-martial-law Taiwan. Second, it traces the controversy to the institutional background and policy-making process of textbook production and history education in the 1990s. Last, but not least, it explores the question of authorship and representation and how history narrative was shaped by the debates among politicians, historians and educators in 1997.

Telling histories of an island nation 131

Despite the political fever and media frenzy during the *Knowing Taiwan* controversy, it is important to recognise the very nature of history textbooks as tools of history pedagogy and not as direct reflections of political ideology and academic fashion. In the final analysis, it is the senior secondary school teachers and their students who constitute the subjects of history education. As an important step towards indigenisation and democratisation, the compilation and implementation of the *Knowing Taiwan* textbook signify the transformation of Taiwan's education reform from a 'state-centred' enterprise to a 'society-based' movement.

After two decades of collective efforts, it has become a new consensus in post-martial-law Taiwan that new history textbooks and historical pedagogy should emphasise autonomy, consciousness and competence over indoctrination and ideology. Instead of the indoctrination of patriotism and national spirit, more and more historians and educators in Taiwan currently consider history education as a gateway towards new global visions and civic education on autonomy, respect for difference and understanding of universal values such as human rights and environmental consciousness (Cohen 2003). Although the tensions between nation building, transitional justice and post-colonial differences remain unresolved, the younger generations in Taiwan are now open-minded and better equipped to deal with the past and to work for their future in a world full of diverse memories (Wu J. 2004; Duara 2002).

Postscript

As of July 2010, a new round of textbook controversy arose surrounding the revision of history textbook guidelines by the new Ministry of Education under president Ma Ying-jeou and the KMT government. For ongoing public discussion by concerned scholars, schoolteachers and young students in Taiwan, please refer to the following site: http://98history.blogspot.com/

Notes

1 For the full text in English, see the following webpage of the National Institute of Compilation and Translation: http://dic.nict.gov.tw/~taiwan/history.htm.
2 History, geography and society were combined into one teaching field of social studies in the new curriculum.
3 There were sixty-six revisions in the history volume and ninety-four revisions in the society volume.

Bibliography

Apple, M. (1993) *Official knowledge: democratic education in a conservative age*, New York: Routledge.
Brown, M. (2004) *Is Taiwan Chinese? The impact of culture, power, and migration on changing identities*, Berkeley, CA: University of California Press.
Chang, L. [Zhang Longzhi] 張隆志 (1997) 'Zhuixun shiluo de Fuermosa buluo: Taiwan pingpu zuqunshi yanjiu de fansi' 追尋失落的福爾摩莎部落——臺灣平埔族群史研究的反思 [Search of the lost tribes of Formosa: reflections on the historical study of

Taiwan Plains Aborigines], in F. Huang *et al.* (eds) *Taiwanshi yanjiu yibainian: huigu yu yanjiu* 台灣史研究一百年：回顧與研究 [*A centennial retrospective on the research of Taiwan history*], Taipei: Zhongyang yanjiuyuan Taiwanshi yanjiusuo choubeichu, 257–72.

—— (2004) 'Zhimin xiandaixing fenxi yu Taiwan jindaishi yanjiu: bentu shixueshi yu fangfalun chuyi' 殖民現代性分析與臺灣近代史研究：本土史學史與方法論芻議 [Colonialism and modernity in Taiwan: reflections on recent historical writing], in M. Wakabayashi and M. Wu (eds) *Kuajie de Taiwanshi yanjiu: Yu dongyashi de jiaocuo* 跨界的臺灣史研究──與東亞史的交錯 [*Transcending the boundary of Taiwan history: dialogue with East Asian history*], Taipei: Bozhongzhe wenhua youxian gongsi, 133–60.

—— (2008) 'Re-imagining community from different shores: nationalism, post-colonialism and colonial modernity in Taiwanese historiography', in S. Richter (ed.) *Contested views of a common past: revisions of history in contemporary East Asia*, Frankfurt am Main and New York: Campus Verlag, 139–55.

—— (2009) 'Dangdai Taiwan shixueshi lungang' 當代台灣史學史論綱 [Outline of contemporary Taiwanese historiography], *Taiwan historical research*, vol. 16, no. 4: 161–84.

Charney, J.I. and Prescott, J.R.V. (2000) 'Resolving cross-strait relations between China and Taiwan', *American Journal of International Law*, vol. 94, no. 3: 453–77.

Chen, J. (2002) 'Reforming textbooks, reshaping school knowledge: Taiwan's textbook deregulation in the 1990s', *Pedagogy, Culture and Society*, vol. 10, no. 1: 39–72.

Chen, W. (2005) 'The history of an alien-nation, or the alienation of history? The controversy over history textbook reform in Taiwan in the 90s', *Asia-Pacific Forum*, no. 28: 90–103.

Ching, L. (2001) *Becoming 'Japanese': colonial Taiwan and the politics of identity formation*, Berkeley, CA: University of California Press.

Chu, Y. and Lin, J. (2001) 'Political development in 20th-century Taiwan: state-building, regime transformation and the construction of national identity', *The China Quarterly*, no. 165: 102–29.

Cohen, P. (2003) *China unbound: evolving perspectives on the Chinese past*, New York: Routledge Curzon.

Corcuff, S. (ed.) (2002) *Memories of the future: national identity issues and the search for a new Taiwan*, Armonk, NY: M.E. Sharpe.

—— (2005) 'History textbooks, identity politics, and ethnic introspection in Taiwan: the June 1997 *Knowing Taiwan* textbooks controversy and the questions it raised on the various approaches to "Han" identity', in E. Vickers and A. Jones (eds) *History education and national identity in East Asia*, New York: Routledge, 133–69.

Duara, P. (2002) 'Postcolonial history', in L. Kramer and S. Maza (eds) *A companion to Western historical thought*, Oxford: Blackwell Publishers, 417–31.

Eskildsen, R. *et al.* (2005) 'Special issue on Taiwan', *Journal of Asian Studies*, vol. 64, no. 2: 275–424.

Fell, D. (2005) *Party politics in Taiwan: party change and the democratic evolution of Taiwan, 1991–2004*, New York: Routledge.

Harrell, S. and Huang, C. (eds) (1994) *Cultural change in postwar Taiwan*, Boulder, CO: Westview Press.

Hsiau, A. (2000) *Contemporary Taiwanese cultural nationalism*, London: Routledge.

Hsu Y. [Xu Yuchen] 徐宇辰 (2008) 'Zhanhou Taiwan Guo(chu)zhong Lishi jiaokeshu de yanbian' 戰後臺灣國（初）中歷史教科書的演變 [The development of history textbooks in junior secondary school in post-war Taiwan, 1948–2007], Masters thesis, Taichung: National Chung-hsing University.

Huang H. [Huang Xiuzheng] 黃秀政 (1996) 'Guomin zhongxue *Renshi Taiwan (lishi pian)* ke de kecheng yanding yu jiaocai' 國民中學「認識臺灣(歷史篇)」科的課程研訂與教材 [The curriculum discussion and compilation of junior secondary school *Knowing Taiwan* history textbook], Guoli bianyiguan tongxu 國立編譯館通訊 [Newsletter of the National Institute of Compilation and Translation], vol. 9, no. 2: 11–16.

Liao, P.-H. and Wang, D. D.-W. (eds) (2006) *Taiwan under Japanese colonial rule, 1895–1945: history, culture, memory,* New York: Columbia University Press.

Liu, M. *et al.* (2005) 'Identity issues in Taiwan's history curriculum', in E. Vickers and A. Jones (eds) *History education and national identity in East Asia*, New York: Routledge, 101–31.

Makeham, J. and Hsiau, A. (eds) (2005) *Cultural, ethnic, and political nationalism in contemporary Taiwan: Bentuhua*, New York: Palgrave MacMillan.

Peng M. 彭明輝 (2002) *Taiwan shixue de Zhongguo chanjie* 台灣史學的中國纏結 [*China in Taiwanese historiography*], Taipei: Maitian chuban.

Renshi Taiwan 認識台灣 [*Knowing Taiwan*] (1997), history volume, Taipei: National Institute of Compilation and Translation.

Richter, S. (ed.) (2008) *Contested views of a common past: revisions of history in contemporary East Asia*, Frankfurt am Main and New York: Campus Verlag.

Rigger, S. (1999) *Politics in Taiwan: voting for democracy*, New York: Routledge.

Rubinstein, M.A. (ed.) (2008) *Taiwan: a new history*, Armonk, NY: M.E. Sharpe.

Taiwan Lishi xuehui 台灣歷史學會 [Taiwan Historical Association, THA] (ed.) (2003) Lishi yishi yu lishi jiaokeshu lunwenji 歷史意識與歷史教科書論文集 [Proceedings on historical consciousness and history textbooks], Taipei: Daoxiang chuban.

Tsao Y. [Cao Yonghe] 曹永和 (2000) *Taiwan zaoqi lishi yanjiu xuji* 臺灣早期歷史研究續集 [*The sequel to research on Taiwan's early history*], Taipei: Lianjing chuban gongsi.

Tu C. [Du Zhengsheng] 杜正勝 (1998) *Taiwan xin, Taiwan hun* 台灣心、台灣魂 [*Taiwanese heart, Taiwanese soul*], Kaohsiung: Hepan chuban.

Vickers, E. (2007) 'Frontiers of memory: conflict, imperialism, and official histories in the formation of post-Cold War Taiwan identity', in S. Miyoshi Jager and R. Mitter (eds) *Ruptured histories: war, memory, and the post-Cold War in Asia*, Cambridge: Campus Verlag, 209–32.

Wakabayashi M. 若林正丈 (2008) *Taiwan no seiji: Chūka Minkoku Taiwanka no sengoshi* 台湾の政治―中華民国台湾化の戦後史 [*The politics of Taiwan: the post-war history of Taiwanisation in the Republic of China*], Tokyo: Tōkyō University Press.

Wang C. [Wang Zhongfu] 王仲孚 and Wang H. [Wang Xiaobo] 王曉波 (eds) (1997) *Renshi Taiwan guozhong jiaokeshu cankao wenjian* 認識台灣國中教科書參考文件 [*Reference materials on the Knowing Taiwan junior secondary school textbooks*], Taipei: Taiwanshi yanjiuhui.

Wang F. 王甫昌 (2001) 'Minzu xiangxiang, zuqun yishi yu lishi: *Renshi Taiwan* jiaokeshu zhengyi fengpo de neirong yu mailuo fenxi' 民族想像、族群意識與歷史：「認識台灣」教科書爭議風波的內容與脈絡分析 [National imagination, ethnic consciousness and history: content and context analyses of the getting to *Knowing Taiwan* textbook disputes], *Taiwanshi Yanjiu* 台灣史研究 [Taiwan Historical Research], vol. 8, no. 2: 145–208.

—— (2005) 'Why bother about school textbooks? An analysis of the origin of the disputes over the *Knowing Taiwan* textbooks in 1997', in J. Makeham and A. Hsiau (eds), *Cultural, ethnic, and political nationalism in contemporary Taiwan: Bentuhua*, New York: Palgrave MacMillan, 55–99.

Wang Q. 王晴佳 (2002) *Taiwan Shixue wushi nian (1950–2000): chuancheng, fangfa, quxiang* 臺灣史學五十年 (1950–2000): 傳承、方法、趨向 [*Writing history in Taiwan: tradition and transformation, 1950–2000*], Taipei: Maitian chuban.

Wu, J. (2004) *Reimagining Taiwan: nation, ethnicity, and narrative*, Taipei: Council for Cultural Affairs (Taiwan).

Wu M. 吳密察 and Wakabayashi M. 若林正丈 (eds) (2004) *Kuajie de Taiwanshi yanjiu: Yu dongyashi de jiaocuo* 跨界的臺灣史研究: 與東亞史的交錯 [*Transcending the boundary of Taiwanese history: dialogue with East Asian history*], Taipei: Bozhongzhe wenhua youxian gongsi.

II
History writing in school textbooks
Practical considerations

6 New curriculum reform and history textbook compilation in contemporary China

Li Fan

This chapter discusses practical curriculum considerations. It begins by discussing the latest Chinese curriculum reforms, which have experimented with topical arrangements crossing national borders and integrating Chinese and world history – in contrast to the 'traditional' chronological and regionally divided approach. Difficulties that have arisen in the implementation of these reforms are then described and analysed. A second section examines in greater detail the textbooks for 'History' and 'History and Society' produced in line with the new curriculum guidelines. Finally, in the form of a case study, the chapter discusses the problematic impact of the prescribed goals of 'emotional attitudes and values' on the process of textbook compilation, and the contradictions this has involved, thus linking up with the issues of 'emotional and value-oriented' education (and specifically patriotic education) already touched upon in several earlier chapters.

Introduction

Secondary school history textbook compilation in China has greatly changed from the original 'one syllabus, one version' to 'one syllabus, many editions' and is no longer monopolised by the People's Education Press since the beginning of the twenty-first century. This change is directly rooted in the curriculum reform of basic education in contemporary China. In this new curriculum system, the 'syllabus' is replaced by 'curriculum standards'. Although the textbooks are still compiled in accordance with curriculum standards, they are not confined to one edition any more, and diversity is provided by several coexisting editions. In this context, the secondary school history curriculum has been revised, and new textbooks, such as *History and society*, have been compiled. The new history textbooks stress the importance of cultivating the 'emotions and values' of students, which, however, has entailed some controversies that call for further study and discussion.

This chapter is composed of three parts. Part one introduces the new curriculum reform in contemporary China; part two systematically scrutinises the textbooks of 'history' and 'history and society' under the new curriculum; part three discusses how to embody 'emotion and values' in the textbooks.

The new curriculum reform and the establishment of history curriculum standards

In recent years, China's basic education has been changing from being exam-oriented to being quality-oriented, which lays a solid foundation for the strategy of developing the country through science and education. Therefore, since 2001, China has undertaken a curriculum reform based on the *Compendium of curriculum standards for compulsory education (tentative)* [*Jichu jiaoyu kecheng gaige gangyao (shixing)* 《基础教育课程改革纲要(试行)》] enacted by the Ministry of Education (*Zhonghua Renmin Gongheguo Jiaoyubu* 2001a). The main objectives are: more initiative instead of mere knowledge transfer, which means that the acquisition of basic knowledge and skills is at the same time also a process of nurturing learning ability and correct values; instead of being discipline-centred, focused on categories and disintegrated, curriculum structures should now be more balanced, comprehensive in argumentation and selective in terms of the topic range; instead of being overly complicated, one-sided, outdated and book-oriented, the curriculum content now should be more closely connected with students' life and modern society development, more pertinent to students' learning interest and experience and should carefully select the essential knowledge and skills for lifelong learning; instead of a curriculum management system being overly concentrated, it now should be shared by three levels of agencies (national, local and school), and should be more open to the needs of the local level and the level of schools and students etc.

The curriculum established by this reform is called the 'new curriculum'. According to different situations in elementary schools and senior secondary schools, the new curriculum consists of an integrated curriculum and a divided curriculum. Elementary schools take the integrated curriculum as a guideline and design courses, such as 'ethics and life', 'ethics and society', 'science', 'arts', 'Chinese', 'mathematics', foreign languages, 'sports', without 'history'. Junior secondary schools adopt both the integrated and divided curriculums, which should cover subjects such as 'Chinese', 'mathematics', foreign languages, 'ethics', 'history and society' (or 'history' and 'geography'), 'science' (or 'physics', 'chemistry', 'biology'), 'arts' (or 'music', 'fine arts'), 'experimental practice', 'sports and health' etc. (the choice of courses depends on the individual school). Non-compulsory education in senior secondary schools gives priority to the divided curriculum and offers compulsory courses and a variety of elective courses, both including history courses.

During the curriculum reform, 'curriculum standards', in place of the previously existing 'syllabuses', were established in various courses. 'History' and 'history and society' curriculums have four standards, namely, *History curriculum standards for full-time compulsory education*, *History curriculum standards for normal senior secondary schools* and *History and society curriculum standards for full-time compulsory education I and II* (*Zhonghua Renmin Gongheguo Jiaoyubu* 2001b, 2003, 2001c, 2001d). 'History and society' as a new course in this reform is an interdisciplinary course that integrates history, geography and other humanities and social sciences. It is mainly a combination of original history and geography courses for junior secondary schools, but also incorporates sociology, psychology, education, economics, politics, culture and other relevant content and is equivalent to social studies in Western countries. The course is aimed at civic and humanistic education, cultivating innovation, abilities of social practice and social responsibilities, and is supposed to promote students' social development and further establish a sound foundation for students to become qualified citizens in a modern socialist country. However, under this general principle, there are still differences in its perspective, and therefore two variant editions of *History and society curriculum standards for full-time compulsory education* (*Zhonghua Renmin Gongheguo Jiaoyubu* 2001c, 2001d) have been established, which differ in terms of curriculum content.

Curriculum standards spell out the principles for the character, general idea, objectives, contents and the implementation of the curriculum and are generally divided into preface, course objectives, content criteria – which is the core – and implementation suggestions. Curriculum standards are the basis for both teaching arrangements and textbook compilation. In this, the curriculum standards for 'history' and 'history and society' are the same. They stipulate the character of the courses and the goals that should be achieved in terms of knowledge and skills, processes and methods, emotions and values and, finally, which contents should be selected for the textbooks. For example, the *History curriculum standards for full-time compulsory education* states:

> History (grade seven to nine) is a compulsory course in the stage of compulsory education [...] the history curriculum should focus on the universal, fundamental and developmental characteristics of compulsory education and serve all students; it should lay the foundation for students entering and adapting to society and for further secondary school education.
> (*Zhonghua Renmin Gongheguo Jiaoyubu* 2001b: 1–2)

Such regulations set the guidelines for the compilation of 'history' and 'history and society' textbooks, which in their compilation and writing must fully correspond to the above-mentioned regulations.

'History' and 'history and society' textbooks under the new curriculum

With the implementation of the new curriculum, a series of new, experimental textbooks have been compiled for teaching. 'History' and 'history and society' textbooks came out in various editions, showing a trend towards diversification, e.g. the junior secondary school 'history' textbooks of the People's Education Press, the Beijing Normal University Press, the East China Normal University Press and the Zhonghua Publishing House; the senior secondary school history textbooks of the People's Education Press, People's Press, the Yuelu Publishing House and the Elephant Press; and the 'history and society' textbooks of the People's Education Press and the Shanghai Education Press. There are some differences in text and form, but, as they follow the same curriculum standards, they do not differ much in content.

Although the *History curriculum standards for full-time compulsory education* (*Zhonghua Renmin Gongheguo Jiaoyubu* 2001b) and the *History curriculum standards for normal senior secondary schools* (*Zhonghua Renmin Gongheguo Jiaoyubu* 2003) represent two different levels of schooling, both stress the educational function of history, which is determined by characteristics of the school subject 'history' itself and changing circumstances. The contents in their basic and their individual features are to bridge the gap between reality and social development, and aim at a holistic development of the students. This is declared as the principle of compiling history textbooks. The *History curriculum standards for full-time compulsory education* stipulate that history contents should be divided into six parts, namely ancient Chinese history, modern Chinese history, contemporary Chinese history, ancient world history, modern world history and contemporary world history. Accordingly, junior secondary school history textbooks are composed of three series in six volumes for seventh- to ninth-grade students: two series in four volumes for Chinese history, and one series in two volumes for world history. The *History curriculum standards for normal senior secondary schools* stipulate that history courses should be divided into compulsory and elective courses. The compulsory courses are composed of *History I* (emphasis on politics), *History II* (emphasis on socio-economic and social life) and *History III* (emphasis on thought and culture, science and technology), while elective courses have six parts, including an introduction to 'major reforms in history', 'democratic thoughts and practices in modern society', 'war and peace in the twentieth century', 'comments on Chinese and foreign historical figures', an 'exploration of historical mysteries' and 'a view on world culture heritage'. Consequently, senior secondary school history textbooks are composed of nine volumes, in accordance with these themes.

'Topics to learn' appear as the basic form of content organisation in both junior and senior secondary school history textbooks. Although they are arranged in a chronological order, the primary concern is not sedulously to reproduce a complete historiography. Junior secondary school history textbooks focus more on content integration, which includes different sections of Chinese history and world history, whereas senior secondary school history textbooks focus on the topicality of their contents, mingling Chinese history with world history. These arrangements are reasonable, without doubt, and also show some innovative character. The themes are fixed by reorganising certain content into certain topics, which depend on the curriculum requirements and the authors' perspectives. More importance is attached to selectivity, rather than to rendering a complete historiography, which would easily entail overlaps in learning. Chinese and foreign histories are taught in both junior and senior secondary schools chronologically. However, owing to some defects in the curriculum standards and owing to limitations of the textbook compilers, a lot of problems in current textbooks occur: contents overlap, or some important historical content is not covered anywhere. Because the compulsory senior secondary school history textbooks *History I, II* and *III* are focused on politics, socio-economics, thought and culture, some similar historical issues are covered by all three books. A good example is the Third Plenary Session of the Communist Party. It first appears in theme four, 'Political construction and motherland unification in modern China', of *History I*, stating that 'China has now entered into a new period of reform and opening up and the political construction has now entered into a new era' (Zhu 2005: 67). Then it appears in theme three of *History II*, 'China's socialist construction', with the comment that the

> reform and opening up policy in the Third Plenary Session marked China's historical transformation from 'taking class struggle as the key link' to taking economic construction as the centre, from a rigid or semi-rigid system to a comprehensive reform, from a closed or semi-closed situation to an opening up to the outside world.
> (Ma 2005: 45)

The same issue appears again in theme four in *History III*, 'Major theoretical achievements in twentieth century China', which says that the event signified 'the re-establishment of the guideline of emancipating the mind and seeking truth from facts, and the realisation of setting things right in theory and ideology' (Wang 2005: 68). Thus, similar historical content is scattered over the three books as a result of the curriculum standards and the corresponding textbook compilations and is consequently studied repeatedly within three semesters. Although the narrative perspective and the writing manner of the three books are different, the identical historical content and basic information result in undue repetition. If it were set in the same book and analysed thoroughly from different perspectives, such as political construction, economic construction, ideology and theory, this important historical content could be more fully understood by students, and the teaching objective could be better achieved. Another example is the two world wars, which are only covered in the elective course 'War and peace in the twentieth century', which means that many students will not study this content at all, causing a major deficiency in learning about such significant historical events.

The *History and society curriculum standards for full-time compulsory education* stress the humanistic, comprehensive and practical features of the 'history and society' course, but there are still many aspects of cognitive differences when it comes to the concrete content of this course. Social life and human civilisation are regarded as the core of learning and exploration in the *History and society curriculum standards for full-time compulsory education I*. The three topics of learning about social life are: 'We are growing up in society', 'Economy, politics and culture nearby us' and 'The region and environment we live in'; the two learning topics about human civilisation are: 'Chinese history and culture' and 'World history and culture' (*Zhonghua Renmin Gongheguo Jiaoyubu* 2001c: 3). The subjects of social life and historical changes are also covered in the *History and society curriculum standards for full-time compulsory education II*, but here it is the field of society that is particularly stressed. Based on 'describing society as a dynamic process and understanding today's society within a historical perspective', three topics are set. The first, 'The world we live in', explains the nature of society, focusing on elements of social life; the second one, 'Our inherited civilisation', discusses why society is how it is and integrates historical facts that reflect the development of society; the third one, 'Opportunities and challenges we are facing', explains how a society should be, focusing on contemporary social issues of common concern (*Zhonghua Renmin Gongheguo Jiaoyubu* 2001d: 3).

The history and society curriculum standards for full-time compulsory education I and II are different in terms of curriculum content, and thus textbooks have also been compiled in two separate ways. In accordance with *History I*, the textbooks have six volumes: 'We are growing up in society', 'Economy, politics and culture nearby us', 'The region and environment we live in', 'Chinese history and culture', 'World history and culture' and 'Social explorations: skills and methods'. In accordance with *History II*, the textbooks have three series and five volumes: 'The world we live in' (I and II), 'Our inherited civilisation' (I and II) and 'Opportunities and challenges we are facing' for seventh- to ninth-grade students. Textbook compilers stress that *History and society* is a comprehensive textbook, and therefore disciplinary demarcations should be downgraded, and knowledge and skills pertinent to geography, society, politics and economics are to be covered in the particular topics. Consequently, the published textbooks show a relatively clear demarcation between society and history on the basis of the *Curriculum standards I*, but those in accordance with *Curriculum standards II* integrate knowledge of both. With the objective of providing common social knowledge and a better understanding of society, they connect knowledge of history, geography, society, politics, economics and culture, and so on, more in line with the so-called 'social studies' textbooks. For example, when studying about Shenzhen 深圳, ancient Loulan 楼兰 or Beijing 北京 in 'regional stories' of 'The world we live in', students learn to understand the evolution of history and civilisation, and geographical and environmental changes, and only then go on to study how to measure changes – i.e. chronology and the calendar (Wei and Zhao 2005: 100–6). This way of writing reflects the integration-oriented characteristics in *History and society*. However, as they touch upon various disciplines, cover comprehensive contents and are inconsistent in their logic, they have entailed difficulties, not only for students' comprehension, but also for teachers' class teaching.

One should mention that both course designs, 'history' and 'history and society', focus on innovation in structure and style in history textbooks. In each lesson, apart from the main texts, there are special sections of introductory character, information cards, knowledge links or issues to learn, think about and discuss. Colour printed images accompanying the text are regarded as an important part of today's textbooks. All of these changes cater to the needs of today's students and reflect the characteristics of the time.

Up to the present, different editions of *History* and *History and society* textbooks have been published for experimental use in different places in China. The first round of experimentation was completed in junior secondary schools; the history curriculum standards were consequently revised, and new textbooks have been compiled accordingly. *History* for senior secondary schools served as an experimental version in more than ten provinces and municipalities, but the results are not satisfactory. Therefore, it has been necessary to reformulate the curriculum standards and then compile new textbooks.

Achieving the goal of an 'emotional and value-based' education

In the *History curriculum standards for full-time compulsory education* (*Zhonghua Renmin Gongheguo Jiaoyubu* 2001b) and in the *History curriculum standards for normal senior secondary schools* (*Zhonghua Renmin Gongheguo Jiaoyubu* 2003), the 'course objective' is one of the core contents and consists of three aspects: knowledge and capacity, process and methods and emotion and values. The 'emotion and value-based' aspect in particular has been strongly advocated and has been taken very seriously by textbook compilers.

In accordance with the new curriculum standards, two aspects of emotion and values are highlighted: first, the understanding of Chinese national conditions, an identification with national history and culture, a cultivation of a national spirit and patriotic sentiments; and second, an understanding of the diversities in human history and society, comprehension of and respect for cultural traditions of different regions, countries and nationalities, absorption of the outstanding achievements of human civilisation and the formation of an open world-view. These two aspects are clearly reflected in the history textbooks under the new curriculum. On the one hand, the status of Chinese civilisation is highlighted in the teaching about Chinese history, and the greatness of Chinese history and civilisation is embodied in political, economic and cultural aspects. The necessity of national unity and ethnic integration, and historical and cultural identification are also emphasised. At the same time, the promotion of national patriotic figures in history is also highlighted to nurture students' sense of patriotism. On the other hand, the overall arrangement of textbooks shows that – though Chinese history still outweighs world history[1] – compared with the past, the latter has seen an increase in proportion.[2] This is due to the need to cultivate students' emotion and values. The formation of an open world-view must start with knowing a diverse world history. An understanding of the politics, economies and cultures of different countries and nationalities can foster students' sense of the diversity and differences in human society, and their respect for different cultural traditions.

Through the design of textbooks sketched out above, it does not seem to be difficult to embody the goal of emotion and values, but in practice this is not the case. The decisive reason is that this goal sometimes does not easily go with complex historical facts. China is a multi-ethnic country; the emotion and value-based education calls for identification with national history and culture and the nurturing of national spirit; identification thus should go with the history and culture of the pluralistic whole that is the Chinese nation, and the national spirit should represent the spirit of the entire Chinese nation. In order to meet these requirements, the textbooks tended to highlight contents on ethnic integration and national unity and stressed that peaceful coexistence among ethnic nationalities was the mainstream in China's history. Historical figures that emerged in interethnic wars, such as Yue Fei (岳飞; 1103–42) or Wen Tianxiang (文天祥; 1236–82) are no longer named 'national heroes' (*minzu yingxiong* 民族英雄). Yue Fei thus is retitled 'the famous general of anti-Jin resistance', and Wen Tianxiang as the 'minister of the pro-resistance group' (Qi and Ma 2001: 53–67). In contrast, the heroes who mounted resistance against foreign invaders, such as Qi Jiguang (戚继光; 1528–88), famed for combatting Japanese pirate invaders, or Zheng Chenggong (郑成功; 1624–62), who took Taiwan 台湾 from the Dutch, are now titled 'national heroes' (Qi and Ma 2001: 96–104). Such a definition shows that the textbook identifies itself with the entire Chinese nation. This, of course, contributes to the identification with national history and culture, but it also obscures some issues on ethnic relations, especially the legitimacy of Han 汉, i.e. the main nationality's resistance against the rule by other ethnic nationalities. Therefore, it caused some dissatisfaction and controversy.

Besides that, there are tensions between the two teaching goals of emotion and value-based education: national identification and patriotism on the one hand, globalisation and cosmopolitanism on the other. It is not easy to keep a balance between these two: for example, in the compulsory textbook for senior secondary schools, *History I*, the first topic in Chinese history treats the political system in ancient China, and the first topic in world history is 'Political civilisation in ancient Greece and Rome'. In the introduction to the 'Political system in ancient China', the textbook authors wrote:

> From the beginning of the Warring States Period [*Zhanguo shidai* 战国时代], China had developed a centralised political system. With the establishment of the unified authoritarian empires Qin 秦 and Han 汉, the bureaucracy, with imperial power as core, became the dominant force in society. Despite frequent change of dynasties, the bureaucracy had become increasingly perfect. Both the establishment of the administrative organisation and the adjustment of a management system signify the strengthening of absolute monarchy. In the late Qing 清 period, the highly centralised autocratic dynasty finally trended toward the end. However, the traditional historical inertia continued to affect the political life of modern times.
>
> (Zhu 2005: 3)

In the introduction to the 'Political civilisation in ancient Greece and Rome', the textbook authors stated:

> Democracy in Greece and the legal system in Rome represent the outstanding achievements of political civilisation in the ancient West,

Curriculum reform and textbooks in China 145

a heritage that has been passed on to modern Western countries [...] Understanding the construction of democracy in Greece and the legal system in Rome, as well as their influence on modern society and politics, is helpful for China's building a democracy and a legal system.

(Zhu 2005: 89)

The two above cited paragraphs give readers an impression that China has always been under an autocratic system since ancient times, while democratic and legal traditions have existed in Western countries since the establishment of ancient Greece and Rome. Obviously, there are value judgements entailed in these statements. This kind of self-description approach that regards the West as the 'others' or as a 'model' is quite common in Chinese history textbooks. Whether these two citations accord with historical facts is certainly a different matter. In terms of the emotion and value-based education, this kind of narrative is certainly helpful to foster an open world-view among students, but, at the same time, it contradicts the objective of identifying with national history and culture and cultivating a patriotic spirit to a certain extent. This tension between the two objectives has brought about great controversy. Similar issues exist in the elective course textbook for senior secondary school: *Democratic thoughts and practices in modern society* (*Jindai shehui de minzhu sixiang yu shijian* 《近代社会的民主思想与实践》). How to describe the 'self' and the 'others' and coordinate this with the required emotion and value-based education needs further reflection and discussion of textbook authors as researchers in order to solve such problems.

Conclusion

'History' and 'history and society' textbooks under the new curriculum are still in an experimental process. The experiments in junior secondary schools have endured twists and turns, and those in senior secondary schools have been on the brink of failure. This shows that textbook reform in China is not an easy task. It involves Chinese national conditions and textbook censorship, as well as teachers' qualifications and students' acceptance; a variety of constraints make it difficult to carry out the reform in practice. The implementation of emotion and value-based education is just one of these difficulties, and more issues remain to be explored and resolved.

Notes

1 It might be remembered that, in accordance with the new curriculum, two series in four volumes about *Chinese history* (*Zhongguo lishi* 中国历史) were assigned to grades seven and eight, and one series in two volumes about *World history* (*Shijie lishi* 世界历史) was assigned to grade nine in junior secondary schools. Chinese history and world history are, however, blended in senior secondary schools; each occupies half of the content.
2 Prior to the new curriculum, in junior secondary schools, Chinese history was assigned to the first and second years, and world history to the third year as well; however, in senior secondary schools, there was only a compulsory course on

modern Chinese history assigned to the first year. Modern world history and ancient Chinese history were intended for the second and third years only, as elective courses for some students.

Bibliography

Li W. 李伟科 (ed.) (2007) *Putong gaozhong kecheng biaozhun shiyan jiaokeshu, lishi bixiu* 普通高中课程标准实验教科书·历史必修 [*Experimental textbooks of normal senior secondary school curriculum criteria, compulsory, history*], Beijing: People's Education Press.

Ma S. 马世力 (ed.) (2005) *Putong gaozhong kecheng biaozhun shiyan jiaokeshu (Lishi di er ce)* 普通高中课程标准实验教科书(历史第二册) [*Experimental textbooks of normal senior secondary school curriculum criteria, compulsory, history*, vol. 2], Beijing: People's Press.

Qi J. 齐吉祥 and Ma Z. 马执斌 (ed.) (2001) *Yiwu jiaoyu kecheng biaozhun shiyan jiaokeshu: Zhongguo lishi (qi nianji xia ce)* 义务教育课程标准实验教科书 中国历史 (七年级 下册) [*Experimental textbooks of full-time compulsory education curriculum criteria, Chinese history for grade seven*, vol. 2], Beijing: People's Education Press.

Wang Z. 王子今 (ed.) (2005) *Putong gaozhong kecheng biaozhun shiyan jiaokeshu lishi bixiu (di san ce)* 普通高中课程标准实验教科书历史必修 (第三册) [*Experimental textbooks of normal senior secondary school curriculum criteria, compulsory, history*, vol. 3]. Beijing: People's Press.

Wei Z. 韦志榕 and Zhao S. 赵世瑜 (ed.) (2005) *Yiwu jiaoyu kecheng biaozhun shiyan jiaokeshu lishi yu shehui (Women shenghuo de shijie qi nianji shang ce)* 义务教育课程标准实验教科书历史与社会 (我们生活的世界七年级上册) [*Experimental textbooks of full-time compulsory education curriculum criteria, history and society: 'The world we live in'*, grade seven, vol. 1], Beijing: People's Education Press.

Zhonghua Renmin Gongheguo Jiaoyubu 中华人民共和国教育部 [Ministry of Education of the People's Republic of China] (comp.) (2001a) *Jichu jiaoyu kecheng gaige gangyao (shixing)* 基础教育课程改革纲要(试行) [*Compendium of curriculum standards for compulsory education (tentative)*], Shanghai: Shanghai Education Press.

—— (2001b) *Quanri-zhi yiwu jiaoyu lishi kecheng biaozhun (shiyangao)* 全日制义务教育历史课程标准 (实验稿) [*History curriculum standards for full-time compulsory education (provisional draft)*], Beijing: Beijing Normal University Press.

—— (2001c) *Quanri-zhi yiwu jiaoyu lishi yu shehui kecheng biaozhun (I) (shiyangao)* 全日制义务教育历史与社会课程标准 (I) (实验稿) [*History and society I curriculum standards for full-time compulsory education (provisional draft)*], Beijing: Beijing Normal University Press.

—— (2001d) *Quanri-zhi yiwu jiaoyu lishi yu shehui kecheng biaozhun (II) (shiyangao)* 全日制义务教育历史与社会课程标准 (II) (实验稿) [*History and society II curriculum standards for full-time compulsory education (provisional draft)*], Beijing: Beijing Normal University Press.

—— (2003) *Putong gaozhong lishi kecheng biaozhun (shiyan)* 普通高中历史课程标准 (试验) [*History curriculum standards for normal senior secondary school (provisional)*], Beijing: Renmin jiaoyu.

Zhu H. 朱汉国 (ed.) (2005) *Putong gaozhong kecheng biaozhun shiyan jiaokeshu, lishi bixiu* 普通高中课程标准实验教科书·历史必修 [*Experimental textbooks of normal senior secondary school curriculum criteria, compulsory, history*, vol. 1], Beijing: People's Press.

7 The 'others' in Chinese history textbooks
A focus on the relationship between China and Japan

Su Zhiliang

This chapter maintains the focus on the practical aspects of textbook design, with specific reference to the way Japan is presented in Chinese history textbooks as an 'other'. This discourse on Japan's image is situated in the context of recent political developments and curricular changes. By looking in particular at textbooks developed for use in Shanghai, it also considers the recent pluralisation of the school textbook market in China, and the degree to which this has made possible the expression of regional perspectives on historical issues. The author suggests alternative ways of presenting Japan and briefly reflects on the project, in which he has taken part, to devise a tri-national (China–Korea–Japan) history textbook, and the ways in which this has been informed by European experiences in developing 'common' textbooks.

Introduction

China, Korea and Japan are all major countries in the East Asian region that, in ancient times, sustained a long-lasting, peaceful relationship in the context of the tribute system. However, in modern times, wars broke out in Asia, as Japan grew stronger. The relationship between China and Japan is usually described as '2,000 years of friendship, 50 years of war'. But the '50 years of war' left a deep scar in Chinese society.

Chinese history textbooks mainly lay emphasis on the Japanese invasion of China. However, with the implementation of the 'opening policy', Chinese textbooks have changed. While holding on to their sharp criticism of the invasion, Chinese history books also began to praise Japan's modern reforms, such as the Meiji Restoration, the democratic reforms after World War II, the fast recovery and development of the economy, and the combination of traditional and modern Western culture. The textbooks even speak highly of the Japanese support of other countries, including China, via Official Development Assistance (ODA).

This chapter will discuss how 'others' in national history interpretations are defined and evaluated, based on the changes in historical narratives about Japan in Chinese history textbooks. In doing so, the focus will be on three

148 *Su Zhiliang*

issues: the Chinese self-strengthening movement of the late nineteenth century vis-à-vis the Meiji Restoration, which turned out to be the 'other' for Chinese modernisation endeavours. Second, the chapter addresses the 1894–5 Sino–Japanese War, which caused Chinese intellectuals to consider Japan as a model for modernisation. Finally, during the period of Japanese invasion of China (1931–45), the foundations for the present rise of China were laid.

In 2005, the transnational history book *History that opens the future: the modern and contemporary history of three East Asian countries* (*Dongya sanguo de jin-xiandaishi. Yi shi wei jian; mianxiang weilai* 东亚三国的近现代史。以史为鉴。面向未来) was published thanks to the joint efforts of Chinese, Japanese and Korean history scholars. The editors tried to learn from European experience to conceptualise a 'common history'. However, just as it needed a long time for Europeans to arrive at this point, cooperation and the creation of common concepts in the region of East Asia will still need some time.

The Chinese history textbook system and its reform

The year 1978 was a turning point in modern Chinese history. Chinese society began to experience a total change from isolation or half-isolation to opening up. China had changed dramatically in the preceding thirty years, and Chinese historiography and history textbooks made much progress. The main subject of traditional Chinese historiography was the ruling class's history. The dominating method of class analysis, which meant interpreting history from the point of view of class conflict, implied that the whole history of mankind was to be studied in this framework. A classical example can be seen in the negation of all the activities of the Nationalists (*Guomindang* (GMD) 国民党), even their efforts in fighting the Japanese, or in the many emotional descriptions concerning the atrocities committed by the Japanese Army. For example, one depiction runs:

> Wherever the Japanese invasion army went, it burnt, killed and plundered with extreme brutality. Countless cities and villages turned into ashes; a million Chinese people were cruelly killed. A frenzied massacre was committed after the Japanese Army occupied Nanking. Some of the peaceful Nanking residents became the target of shooting training, some were buried alive, and some were stripped of their organs while alive. No less than 300,000 people were massacred in not much longer than a month, and one third of the houses in Nanking were destroyed. Corpses were scattered and debris piled like mountains in Nanking at that time. With the ghostly wind blowing, the city was a hellish place.
>
> (*Zhongguo lishi* 1979: 51)

Emphasis was also laid on the struggle of the peoples in Asia, Africa and Latin America: for instance, the Korean people's anti-Japanese struggle, the peak of the Indian National Movement (1905–8) and the Korean people's uprising on 1 March 1919 (*Shijie lishi* 1978: 68–74, 142–6). Chinese historiography has experienced a very significant change over the last thirty years regarding its subject, which shifted from the previous 'Emperor focus' to the normal people. Under these conditions, Chinese history textbooks also came to differ substantially from the old ones.

Before 1978, there was basically only one edition of history schoolbook for junior and for senior secondary schools used in China. This textbook was published by the People's Education Press in Beijing. It can be described as an official interpretation of history, forcing the latter as 'the' historical memory into teenagers' minds. This interpretation was very conservative, inflexible and rigid. During the period, when radical 'leftist' ideas dominated China, world history was reduced to the history of the international communist movement, and Chinese history was simplified to a mere history of class conflicts, a history of the struggle between 'Confucianism and Legalism', and a history of the just line (Maoism) against the flawed ones (everybody else's views). This clearly did not reflect historical evidence, but rather that history education had become a tool for political education, regardless of historical authenticity.

After 1978, China gradually entered an era of diversification. For example, Shanghai was designated as an 'educational experimental zone' in 1990 (the only such zone in China). Thus, Shanghai enjoyed some autonomy in editing textbooks and organising its own college entrance examinations. In the 1990s, Chinese education reform was extended to a national scale.

The research field for historians has expanded enormously in time coverage, extent and depth of focus during the last 20 years. The basic trend of Chinese history research, in short, is in a process of widening the perspective of the historical view. This enlargement of perspective means that the traditional top-down approach is now complemented by a bottom-up one, giving due attention to the lower classes as well. Furthermore, a paradigm shift had occurred from political history to economic and cultural history, and then to social history as well. Thus, the *History curriculum standards* (*Lishi kecheng biaozhun*《历史课程标准》), issued by the Ministry of Education, now enhanced content related to social, scientific, educational and cultural history, while keeping its emphasis on political history.

After the reform in the 1990s, the *History curriculum standards for full-time compulsory education* were finally issued by the Ministry of Education in 2001 (*Zhonghua Renmin Gongheguo Jiaoyubu* 2001). The textbook editions available for junior secondary school gradually expanded into ten versions:

- first, the one published by People's Education Press (Renmin jiaoyu chubanshe 人民教育出版社版), which is used in most provinces;
- second, the one published by Beijing Normal University Press (Beijing Shifan Daxue chubanshe 北京师范大学出版社), designed for four-year junior secondary school courses (in places where elementary school is only five years instead of the standard six years);

- third, the one published by Sinomaps Press (Zhongguo ditu chubanshe 中国地图出版社), which is used in some regions;
- fourth, the one edited by Guangdong Province called the *Coastal Version* (*yanhai ban* 沿海版);
- fifth, the one edited by Sichuan Province for inland remote areas, called the *Inland Version* (*neidi ban* 内地版);
- sixth, the one published by Zhejiang Education Press (Zhejiang jiaoyu chubanshe 浙江教育出版社) for use in remote areas;
- seventh, the one edited by Huadong Normal University (Huadong Shifan Daxue 华东师范大学), which is used in some regions;
- eighth, the one edited by Shanghai Normal University (Shanghai Shifan Daxue 上海师范大学), published by Huadong Normal University Press, for use in Shanghai;
- ninth, the one published by Shanghai Education Press (Shanghai jiaoyu chubanshe 上海教育出版社), being an integrated course covering the fields of history and society;
- tenth, the one published by Yuelu Press (Yuelu shushe 岳麓书社), used in some regions.

As far as senior secondary school is concerned – since the Ministry of Education's issuing of the *History curriculum standards for normal senior secondary schools (provisional)* in 2003 – four kinds of senior secondary school history textbook were published, which passed the examination procedures of the National Committee for Elementary, Junior and Senior Secondary School Textbook Approval. They consist of editions of textbooks published by the People's Education Press (Renmin jiaoyu chubanshe 人民教育出版社), the People's Press (Renmin chubanshe 人民出版社), the Yuelu Press (Hunan)(Yuelu shushe 岳麓书社) and the Daxiang Press (Daxiang chubanshe 大象出版社) (Henan). All these versions of senior secondary school history textbooks are edited according to the *History curriculum standards for normal senior secondary schools (provisional)* (*Putong gaozhong lishi kecheng biaozhun* 《普通高中历史课程标准》 (*Zhonghua Renmin Gongheguo Jiaoyubu* 2003)), but each has its own characteristics.[1]

These different versions of textbooks are now competing with each other. As the local governments are permitted to choose among textbook editions autonomously, a new market for schoolbooks has emerged. Some editions are used more, others less. By the introduction of market elements, the choice in textbooks has consequently profited. However, ideological disputes are still rather fierce in China. I edited a senior secondary school history textbook for use in Shanghai, with the idea of writing it from the viewpoint of a history of civilisation. This, however, met with staunch opposition on the part of some conservative historians. They put continuous pressure on the government, which, eventually, was forced to call on the educational board to withdraw my textbook from further use.

Chinese history textbook depictions of Japan

After the foundation of the People's Republic of China (PRC) in 1949, the government held education to be very important. The 1950s Chinese history textbooks stressed the political impact. To the Chinese Communist Party (CCP), which fought a bloody battle to gain its ruling position, 'the other' was its rival: namely the Nationalist Party or *Guomindang* (GMD). Thus, in the depiction of the war of resistance against the Japanese, many paragraphs were used to condemn the GMD for collaborating with, or not resisting, the Japanese Army. On the other hand, the GMD Army's combat at the front was rarely mentioned. Instead, the textbooks pointed out:

> Because the leaders of the GMD followed the line of surrender, the Chinese Army was totally defeated on the battlefield, though the soldiers were eager and determined to fight the Japanese.
> *(Chuzhong lishi* 1956: 62)

In the book for teachers' reference, there are even more condemnations:

> Since the early days of the anti-Japanese movement in the northeastern provinces [Manchuria], the GMD, which is by its nature reactionary, feared the growth of anti-Japanese militia. It sided with the Japanese Army and undermined the anti-Japanese struggle from within.
> *(Chuji zhongxue keben zhongguo lishi di si ce jiaoxue cankaoshu* 1959: 61)

When the Japanese Army invaded Shanghai in 1932,

> no assistance at all was given by the GMD Government to the 19th Route Army, which was fighting the Japanese.
> *(Zhongguo lishi* 1957: 29)[2]

> The reactionary GMD did not support the Shanghai people's anti-Japanese efforts. On the contrary, they even actively undermined these attempts.
> *(Chuji zhongxue keben zhongguo lishi di si ce jiaoxue cankaoshu* 1959: 63)

> The GMD followed a one-sided anti-Japanese line of the big landlords and capitalists, which meant they wanted to fight the Japanese Army only by way of the government but feared and opposed the comprehensive line of a people's war.
> *(Chuji zhongxue keben zhongguo lishi di si ce jiaoxue cankaoshu* 1959: 83)

> The GMD Government never stopped to negotiate with and capitulate to the Japanese ever since the war of resistance started. As the clique around

Wang Jingwei [汪精卫; 1883–1944] surrendered to the enemy, it became more and more likely that the pro-US-clique around Chiang Kai-shek would also capitulate to the enemy. The CCP's insistence on fighting the Japanese Army and its growing strength in leading the anti-Japanese resistance was the biggest obstacle in the GMD's way to surrender.

(Chuji zhongxue keben zhongguo lishi di si ce jiaoxue cankaoshu 1959: 87)

Most of the opinions cited above are not in accordance with the historical facts. As for the depiction of atrocities committed by the Japanese Army, the Nanking Massacre cited above is the most typical example, but is in no way unique:

After the Japanese imperialists had occupied Manchuria, they practised a cruel colonial rule over the people. From the Central Government to local administrations to the most basic administrative levels, the entire political system of so-called Manzhouguo 满洲国 was under Japanese control. The so-called *Baojia* System 保甲制度 of mutual control groups was widely practised there, which meant that ten families were mutually responsible and would be punished all for one person among them who had committed a crime. The Japanese imperialists practised an education of enslavement in this region, suppressing the patriotic mind of the people in Manchuria. They also advocated planting and smoking opium in order to destroy the Manchurian people's health. The Japanese Army committed countless crimes in the Northeast [Manchuria] such as burning, killing, plundering and raping.

(Zhongguo lishi 1957: 38)

Since research on the war of resistance was not yet very advanced, many Japanese atrocities were unknown at that time. There was no mentioning of 'comfort women' (*congjun weianfu/jūgun ianfu* 従軍慰安婦) yet. Recently published textbooks, however, record some facts about 'comfort women': '200,000 Chinese women were captured and enslaved as "comfort women" by the Japanese Army to meet the sexual needs of their soldiers' (Su *et al.* 2006: 206).

Chinese history textbooks usually spent many paragraphs on describing the Japanese invasion of China. With the implementation of the opening-up policy, contents, however, started to change. The amount of descriptions of Japanese atrocities has been reduced remarkably.[3] While keeping their condemnation of the Japanese invasion, Chinese history textbooks also began to praise Japan's modern reforms, such as the Meiji Restoration, the democratic reforms after World War II, the successful economic recovery and the combination of traditional and modern culture. Japan's developmental aid to other countries, including to China, is also appreciated in today's textbooks.[4]

The Shanghai history textbook for senior secondary school, class three (Su et al. 2006), furthermore, comprises a topic called 'The modernisation process of the major developed countries in the world'. Here the history of modernisation of six developed countries is presented, including Japan (the others are Great Britain, France, Germany, the United States and Russia). Three lessons deal with the development of Japanese modernisation. They are entitled: 'Out of Asia into Europe', 'The way into the war' and 'Regeneration and prosperity'. This design was an innovative step in China. I would like to discuss this topic with respect to the aspects mentioned below.

First, I would like to compare the Japanese Meiji Restoration with the self-strengthening movement in China.[5] Thereby, the Meiji Restoration turned out to be the referential 'other' of the Chinese type of modernisation. On the basis of a class conflict view of history, Chinese textbooks of the 1950s put great emphasis on class also in the context of the Meiji Restoration. It was considered as a reform of the landlord and capitalist class. A 1956 textbook asserted:

> The Meiji regime was an alliance of feudal landlords and the bourgeoisie. Therefore, the Meiji Restoration was an incomplete bourgeois revolution. Although, the government took some top-down measures favoring the development of capitalism, many feudal remnants were preserved. The exploitation of rural areas was even stronger than before because after the Meiji Restoration the peasants were under double oppression from both the feudal landlords and the capitalists. Thus, there were more than 160 uprisings in ten years.
>
> (*Shijie lishi* 1956: 26)

The view of history changed after 1978, and, consequently, textbooks took a more positive attitude towards the Meiji Restoration:

> The Meiji Restoration led Japan on to the road of developing capitalism. Along with abolishing unequal treaties, retrieving national rights and casting off the national crisis, Japan became a strong country in Asia.
>
> (*Shijie lishi* 1978: 22)

The Shanghai textbook for senior secondary school, class three students edited by myself states:

> The former centre of Asian civilisation, China, was crushed by Britain in the middle of the nineteenth century. This event shocked Japan profoundly. How should one deal with the challenge of Western civilisation? Japan, which managed successfully to depart from Asia and turn towards Europe by the Meiji Restoration, rose quickly to become an oriental industrialised strong nation. The foundation of the modern Japanese political system was laid by issuing the Japanese Constitution based on the Prussian Constitution at the end of the nineteenth century.
>
> (Su et al. 2006: 135)

The second volume of the textbook on world history, used in Shanghai, which I edited as well, takes 'the expansion of capitalism in Asia and the Asian response' as a lesson heading and praises the Meiji Restoration:

> Following the Western model, Japan developed education, took elementary education as a basis and energetically popularised the education of its citizens. In 1873, the enrollment rate in elementary schools amounted to 28.1 per cent. This increased up to 99 per cent in the following 50 years [...] The Japanese Government also established various scientific institutions to do research, and thus scientific research started to develop. The great leaps in education empowered the development of the Japanese capitalist economy.
> (Su *et al.* 2008: 10)

The textbook also indicates that 'the Meiji Restoration preserved many feudal remnants, which negatively affected the later development of Japan' (Su *et al.* 2008: 10). The textbook for junior secondary school on world history, which Professor Wang Side edited, also devotes many paragraphs to describing the great importance the Japanese attached in modern times to education and science:

> Ever since the beginning of the Meiji Restoration, Japan had made huge efforts to develop educational institutions and trained large amounts of talent for various professional sectors. After the war, the percentage of education expenditure in the GDP rose to over 20 and ranked first among all capitalist countries. Compared to the education expenditure in the year 1960, the figure would increase 3.7 times until 1970. Meanwhile, the government continually readjusted its focus in education to adapt to shifts in the economic structure. E.g., during the period of economic recovery, great attention was paid to improve the general quality of the work force, focusing on the general compulsory elementary education. When the government propped up heavy and chemical industries in the late 50s and 60s of the twentieth century, training technicians became the educational focus. After 1970s, when the Japanese industrial structure underwent a shift towards knowledge-intensive industries, the government gave priority to developing creative-innovative specialists on the highest level, and on the middle level specialised technicians capable of implementing and adapting new technologies. Furthermore, many enterprises offered additional professional education to their employees.
> (Wang *et al.* 2004: 95)

The paragraph following the above one explains, in even more detail, how the Japanese government established scientific research. Also, the textbook for senior secondary school, class three students edited by myself stresses the merits of the Japanese educational system:

The 'others' in Chinese history textbooks 155

In the early phase of the Meiji Restoration, the [Japanese] Government put forward the slogan 'Civilisation and enlightenment!' (*bunmei kaika* 文明開化) which was advocated to introduce Western civilisation. Shortly after, Japanese customs and culture in fact had undergone a change. E.g., the Samurai or *bushi* (侍/武士) were no longer allowed to bear their traditional hairstyle or to wear a *katana* 刀; Western suits replaced Japanese clothing (*wafuku* 和服). With the Tennō taking the lead to have beef and milk, Western meals became more and more popular. Nevertheless, what affected Japan most were the reforms in education. After the establishment of the Japanese Ministry of Education (*Monbushō* 文部省) in 1871, the modern Western education system was systematically introduced into Japan. A three-tier educational system, composed of elementary school, middle school and university, replaced the old type of domain and private schools usually run in temples. Elementary school education was to be compulsory. Tōkyō University was established in 1877, and students with outstanding performance were annually elected and sent by the government to study in Europe or the United States. All these reforms in education generated many excellent people to ensure the rapid development of the Japanese economy and the implementation of other measures taken during the Meiji Restoration.

(Su *et al.* 2006: 141)

What we are trying to convey here with the above sentences is an indirect criticism of China, implying that the Chinese case was far less successful in the field of education compared with the Japanese at that time.

Chinese textbooks, however, also usually analyse the limiting aspects of the Meiji Restoration; for example, 'While the Japanese decided to develop capitalism on their own, they also took the road of external expansion through colonial means. Eventually, Japan became a new threat to peace in Asia' (Zhu *et al.* 2006: 87). And the teachers' reference book states: 'After the Meiji Restoration Japan gradually began to take the road of aggression towards others, launching several waves of military expansion against our country' (*Chuji zhongxue keben shijie lishi, xia ce, jiaoxue cankaoshu* 1956: 160). However, it also makes the point that 'teachers must make it clear that the Japanese militarists are different from the working people. The Japanese and the Chinese people as such traditionally are friendly to each other' (*Chuji zhongxue keben shijie lishi, xia ce, jiaoxue cankaoshu* 1956: 160).

Second, the successful Meiji Restoration became a hot topic in Chinese academia two decades ago, especially in comparison with the failed Chinese 1898 reforms. This issue even made it into the college entrance exams. Since China had been defeated by Japan in the Sino–Japanese War (1894–5), Japan was considered a model of modernisation by Chinese intellectuals. The defeat in the war was an unprecedented shock to China and the Chinese people and obliged people from all walks of life to think about the future of their country. The Shanghai textbook edited by myself compares the different attitudes

156 *Su Zhiliang*

towards learning Western sciences by analysing statements of Li Hongzhang (李鸿章; 1823–1901), an important official in the late Qing government.[6] The textbook also states:

> After signing the Treaty of Shimonoseki, China faced the danger of being carved up by the big powers [. . .] The Chinese people [finally] started to wake up due to this impending disaster of being carved up.
> (Su *et al.* 2007: 27)

> The stinging defeat in the Sino–Japanese War and the ensuing danger of being carved up alarmed the Chinese intellectuals and they, one after another, started to explore various ways to save the country.
> (Su *et al.* 2007: 29)

> In the world wide setting of intense struggle for survival, the Chinese people finally went beyond the limitations of a 'Chinese learning as the essence, western learning for practical use' approach and started to look more openly towards the West, adapting the constitutional systems of Britain and Japan with the Emperor as a public sovereign.
> (Su *et al.* 2007: 31)

Some textbook editions, however, also point out:

> Since the Japanese Tennō Government tended to favor more and more the belligerent road of external expansion and invasion, this meant not only that the modernisation process of Japan's victims was interrupted, but also the modernisation process of Japan itself went down the wrong path.
> (Su *et al.* 2006: 143)

Third, China's modern power arose during the Japanese war against China, which dated from 1937 to 1945. The Shanghai textbook edited by myself uses the words, 'A great wall made of flesh and bones' as the heading of this lesson (Su *et al.* 2007: 92), and, already in the 1950s, this phase was characterised as follows:

> In September 1944 at the People's Political Council in Chongqing, the former representative of the CCP, comrade Lin Boqu [林伯渠; 1885–1960], called the people to arise and abolish the one-party dictatorship of the GMD and to establish a joint government. The slogan of establishing a joint democratic government reflected the democratic demands of the various classes of people and directed the democratic struggle in the GMD-ruled areas towards a clear political goal. All democratic parties, people's organisations and overseas Chinese supported this slogan in unison. This was the climax of the democratic movement in China.
> (*Zhongguo lishi* 1956: 74)

Fourth, I would like to analyse the topic of the peaceful development of post-war Japan and the interpretation of the war. As editor of the Shanghai textbook, I analysed the different attitudes in Japan and Germany concerning war guilt in the 'Exploration and contention' section:

> Both, Germany and Japan, initiated World War II and were defeated. However, their attitudes toward their war guilt differ substantially. Under massive pressure of the international community, Germany exposed and criticised Nazi crimes quite thoroughly. Many Nazi criminals were punished, and those convicted were closely scrutinised. The German people as a whole also reflected upon the period of National Socialism while their leaders made sincere apologies to victims and victimised countries repeatedly. The German Government also offered continuously reparations to the victims. In Japan, on the contrary, under the protection of the Americans, the Shōwa Tennō 昭和天皇 was not prosecuted, and most of the Japanese war criminals were not justly punished. Many war criminals even occupied important positions in the post-war government, e.g., Kishi Nobusuke [岸信介; 1896–1987], who was Japanese Prime Minister from 1957 to 1960. Japan consequently did not reflect on its own history seriously and did not criticise its guilt thoroughly, which resulted in many flawed ideas on imperialism being still current. That the Japanese right wing is more and more rampant day by day and that Japanese leaders glorify the war of invasion are all phenomena closely related to these flawed ideas. With growing economic power, Japan is now actively trying to gain a permanent seat in the United Nations Security Council. However, this meets resistance from the Asian neighbouring countries, which Japan invaded, and from all peace-loving people.
>
> (Su *et al.* 2005: 156)

The following paragraph then raises the question, 'According to you, how can Japan become a "leading country, universally recognised by the international community", when displaying an attitude towards denying its own history?' (Su *et al.* 2005: 156). In the unit 'Review and reflect' of the Shanghai textbook, the students are asked to analyse this question further:

Answer the questions after reading the materials provided!

Material one:
Japan surrendered unconditionally on 15 August 1945. On 16 August, in Japan the cabinet of [Prince] Higashikuni no miya [東久邇宮 resp. Higashikuni Naruhiko 東久邇稔彦; 1887–1990] was formed, which took charge of the surrender procedures. On the second day after the establishment of the cabinet, the new Prime Minister, Higashikuni no miya, talked about the war responsibility by telling the journalists that the reason for defeat did not only lie in the mistake of the government's policy,

but also in the degeneration of national morality. Therefore, all citizens should reflect their behavior completely. A general repentance by all citizens would be the first step to reconstruction.

Material two:
Generally speaking, the Meiji Restoration was the beginning of Japanese modernisation. A modern political system was established, and state and society changed in character. The climax of modern construction, which should have caused a total victory in modernisation, would have appeared during the reign of Emperor Hirohito [裕仁;1901–89], if Japan had followed the objective law of history. However, Japan launched a war of invasion, which caused its defeat and a regression in modernisation. Although Japan's history was influenced by multiple factors, one cannot deny that the Mikado Hirohito bore a historical responsibility – namely a historical responsibility he could not shift away from himself – for the war. This is also an important lesson of Japanese modernisation.

Please answer:
1   In your opinion, do Japanese citizens share a responsibility for the war?
2   Starting with the Sino–Japanese War, continuing with the Russo–Japanese War to the war of aggression in China by Japan, which resulted in the Pacific War: which way did the Japanese modernisation take? What influence did these wars have on Japan?

(Su *et al.* 2005: 151)

As editor, I also expressed my worries about Japanese textbooks in the 'Review and reflect' section:

Before the results of Japanese textbook screening came out in early April 2005, the *New History Textbook* [i.e. Fujioka *et al.* 2005], compiled by the editors of the Japanese Society for History Textbook Reform [*Atarashii rekishi kyōkasho o tsukurukai* 新しい歴史教科書をつくる会; *Tsukurukai* for short], became a hot topic in public opinion again. Since the *New History Textbook* greatly distorts historical facts, some Japanese civil organisations call it 'ferocious book' [*hidoi kyōkasho* 酷い教科書]. The so-called ferocious book is full with ultra-nationalist views, constructing the state around the Mikado. It advocates that Japan should rule Asia because it is superior to other Asian countries. The book is designed with a Japan-centered history view, hiding all facts about the Japanese afflicting damage onto other countries, instead promoting a victimisation consciousness. It praises aggressive behavior, the merits of invasion by citing the Asian Co-Prosperity Sphere slogan and asserts that Japan launched war only out of self-defense. It furthermore praises the spirit of sacrifice of the Japanese people actively supporting the war effort. Thus, what do you think is Japan's attitude towards the war?

(Su *et al.* 2005: 157)

Efforts to construct an East Asian common history

Since 2002, South Korean, Japanese and PRC-Chinese history scholars have been working together. After ten tough consultations, the above-mentioned common book, *History that opens the future: the modern and contemporary history of three East Asian countries* (*Dongya* 2005), was published in the capitals of Korea, China and Japan and appeared in three languages in June 2005. This was a difficult, but meaningful, endeavour because this book is the first 'textbook compiled for various countries' in Asia. It transcends the 'national model' by establishing 'regional channels'.

The writers tried to follow the example of Europe and to construct a 'common history'. This book takes the modern history of China, Japan and Korea as a subject, describing the course these three countries took in an easily accessible style. It stands out in its wholesale, objective presentation of the history of invasion and resistance to invasion between China, Korea and Japan, and it also addresses some of the remaining problems for Japan after the war. Of particular interest is the fact that this book covers topics such as the Yasukuni Shrine (*Yasukuni jinja* 靖国神社), non-governmental compensations, the ODA, 'comfort women' and so on, taking up the key historical facts. By this means, the book exposes the historical reality of Japan's invasion of China and Korea. And, with convincing evidence about Japanese atrocities, it confronts the Japanese right-wing textbook, which has massively distorted this fact.

This common textbook breaks through traditional patterns and considers all problems between the three countries in the framework of an East Asian perspective. The outstanding feature of this book is its preciseness. All figures given are verified with great circumspection. Let us take the sensitive number of the victims during the Nanking Massacre for an example. The book carefully adopts two figures. The first one is the result of the Nanking Military Court's investigation, according to which 119,000 people were collectively slaughtered and another 115,000 people were slaughtered individually and in scattered places. The second figure follows a record used by the Court of the International Military Tribunal for the Far East (IMTFE), according to which more than 200,000 people were killed in the first six weeks, when the Japanese Army occupied Nanking. This leaves the reader room to ponder the issue. In contrast, in the *Tsukurukai* textbook, edited by the Japanese right wing, the Nanking Massacre is barely mentioned. Only an explanatory footnote states that:

> At this time, many Chinese soldiers and civilians were killed or wounded by the Japanese Army (the Nanking Incident). Yet, documentary evidence has raised doubts about the actual number of victims and the truth about the incident. There are various opinions and the debate continues even today.
>
> (Fujioka *et al.* 2005: 199)

The common textbook, instead, analyses the Tokyo Trial's judgement further. Though it fully asserts the international judgement, it also analyses the latter's shortcomings in pointing out issues not addressed by the trial: for example, the court did not put on trial Mikado Hirohito, Japan's colonial rule over Taiwan and Korea, the 'comfort women' system or the country's biological warfare.

The book *History that opens the future* records a weighty historical experience, yet it is also a book that tries to open up the future and criticises Japanese textbooks, which 'whitewash' history. My co-authors and I hope this book may help to overcome engrained differences of view between the countries involved to move towards reconciliation. Through this, we also want to support the progressive forces in Japan, to prevent Japanese rightist textbooks making it into classrooms.

However, just as Europe had a long way to travel, cooperation and a joint work of construction in the region of East Asia will need a long time as well. Owing to today's economic globalisation, the interconnectedness between people has become greater than ever before. At present, almost 100,000 Japanese and South Koreans live, study or work in Shanghai. Therefore, it is very urgent to make the textbooks to be in line with international standards. I sincerely hope that we will expand and continue the cooperation in East Asia to enable new history textbooks to enter the classrooms and increase their impact.

Notes

1 A new version of the national *History curriculum standards* will be completed and issued soon.
2 This is, of course, far from historical reality.
3 Textbooks such as those in Shanghai and those published by Beijing Normal University Press all reduced the space allotted to the anti-Japanese war.
4 In the *Chinese history textbook for grade seven* (vol. 2) (Su *et al.* 2007), a junior secondary school textbook for Shanghai students edited by myself, there is this passage: 'The relationship of friendly cooperation was further improved after the signing of the Sino–Japanese Treaty on Peace and Friendship. Afterwards, the Japanese Government put the plan of Official Development Assistance (ODA) to China into effect' (Su *et al.* 2007: 128). This was the first time a Chinese history textbook mentioned the Japanese ODA to China. Some other textbooks only focused on the establishment of a diplomatic relationship between China and the United States and ignored the same between China and Japan (e.g. the textbook *Lishi* published by Beijing Normal University in 2002).
5 The self-strengthening movement in China was a reform, supported by the Qing government, which advocated learning from the West to make progress. It started during the 1860s and ended in the 1890s. Thus, the reform covered almost the same time-span as the Meiji Restoration (1868–1912).
6 The textbook section 'Review and consider' cites the following letter (written by Li Hongzhang) to the Chinese Office for the Affairs of Foreign Countries (a kind of Chinese pre-foreign ministry):

> Up to now, Britain and France considered Japan as a peripheral country, which can be treated casually. This enraged the Japanese Emperor and his officials

and they sought out brilliant members of the imperial clan and outstanding sons of important officials to visit these two countries [Britain and France, S.Z.] to study all kinds of knowledge. This they implemented later at home and thus they are now able to drive steamers and install canons themselves. When the British thought to intimidate them with some canon shots and troupes last year and assumed to have an easy play, they however resisted skillfully and the British had to give up [. . .] I, Hongzhang, think that if China wants to strengthen herself, she should also learn the foreign countries' advanced techniques.

(Su *et al.* 2005: 198)

Bibliography

Chuji zhongxue keben 'Shijie lishi', xia ce, jiaoxue cankaoshu 初级中学课本《世界历史》, 下册, 教学参考书 [*Teacher's reference book for 'Chinese history' (for junior secondary school)*] (1956) Vol. 4, Beijing: People's Education Press.

Chuji zhongxue keben 'Zhongguo lishi' di si ce jiaoxue cankaoshu 初级中学课本《中国历史》, 第四册, 教学参考书 [*Teacher's reference book for Chinese History (for junior secondary school)*] (1959) Vol. 4, Beijing: People's Education Press.

Chuzhong lishi 初中历史 [*Chinese history (for junior secondary school)*] (1956) Vol. 4, Beijing: People's Education Press.

'Dongya sanguo de jin-xiandaishi' gongtong bianxie weiyuanhui《东亚三国的近现代史》共同编写委员会 [Common editorial commission of the Modern and contemporary history of three East Asian countries] (ed.) (2005) *Dongya sanguo de jin-xiandaishi. Yi shi wei jian; mianxiang weilai* 东亚三国的近现代史。以史为鉴。面向未来 [*History that opens the future: the modern and contemporary history of three East Asian countries*], Beijing: Shehui kexue wenxian.

Fujioka N. 藤岡信勝 *et al.* (eds) (2005) *Atarashii rekishi kyōkasho* 新しい歴史教科書 [*New history textbook*], Tokyo: Fusōsha.

Lishi 《历史》 [*History (for grade eight)*] (2002) Vol. 2, Beijing: Normal University Press.

Shijie lishi 世界历史 [*World history (for junior secondary school)*] (1956) Vol. 2, Beijing: People's Education Press.

Shijie lishi 世界历史 [*World history (for senior secondary school)*] (1978) Vol. 2, Beijing: People's Education Press.

Shijie lishi 世界历史 [*World history (for grade eight)*] (2002) Vol. 5, Beijing: Beijing Normal University Press.

Su Z. 苏智良 *et al.* (eds) (2005) *Lishi* 历史 [*History (for senior secondary school class three, expanded version)*], Shanghai: Shanghai Education Press.

—— (2006) *Lishi* 历史 [*History (for senior secondary school class three, expanded version)*], Shanghai: Shanghai Education Press.

—— (2007) *Shijie lishi* 世界历史 [*Chinese history (for grade seven)*], vol. 2, Shanghai: Huadong Normal University Press.

—— (2008) *Shijie lishi* 世界历史 [*World history (for grade eight)*], vol. 2, Shanghai: Huadong Normal University Press.

Wang S. 王斯德 *et al.*(eds) (2004) *Shijie lishi* 世界历史 [*World history (for grade nine)*], vol. 2, Shanghai: Huadong Normal University Press.

Zhongguo lishi 中国历史 [*Chinese history (for junior secondary school)*] (1956) Vol. 4, Beijing: People's Education Press.

Zhongguo lishi 中国历史 [*Chinese history (for senior secondary school)*] (1957) Vol. 4, Beijing: People's Education Press.

Zhongguo lishi 中国历史 [*Chinese history (for senior secondary school)*] (1979) Vol. 4, Beijing: People's Education Press.

Zhonghua Renmin Gongheguo Jiaoyubu 中华人民共和国教育部 [Ministry of Education of the People's Republic of China] (comp.) (2001) *Quanri-zhi yiwu jiaoyu lishi kecheng biaozhun (shiyangao)* 全日制义务教育历史课程标准 (实验稿) [*History curriculum standards for full-time compulsory education (provisional draft)*], Beijing: Beijing Normal University Press.

—— (2003) *Putong gaozhong lishi kecheng biaozhun (shiyan)* 普通高中历史课程标准 (试验); [*History curriculum standards for normal senior secondary schools (provisional)*], Beijing: People's Education Press.

Zhu H. 朱汉国 *et al.* (eds) (2006) *Lishi* 历史 [*History (for grade nine)*], vol. 1, Beijing: Beijing Normal University Press.

8 Rewriting history in a textbook in contemporary Japan

Miyake Akimasa (Chiba University)

This chapter follows up on the consideration of practical issues in conceptualising textbooks, complementing the two earlier chapters on China with an experience from the Japanese side. The author describes the complexities of the official process of reviewing textbooks, and the challenges this presents to authors and publishers. Finally, he presents his personal experience as a co-author of a widely used textbook on Japanese history for senior secondary school. He discusses the innovative features of this textbook, and argues for a new approach to writing Japanese history from a more transnational perspective, involving collaboration with non-Japanese scholars with the aim of representing multiple viewpoints and voices.

Introduction

This chapter, in which I am going to state my personal views on chosen topics, is divided into three sections. In the first section, I primarily discuss the institutional framework and the actual state of affairs in which history textbooks were composed and authorised in post-war Japan until the 1980s, especially with respect to the question of the coursework's organisation and the authorisation of textbooks. In the 1990s, history textbooks became an issue of social and political debate in Japan and other countries. Thus, the second section addresses the issues that were in question, how they were taken up and what the salient features of the debate were that arose during this period. The last part deals with the special characteristics of the Japanese history textbook for senior secondary school co-authored by myself.

History textbooks in Japan until the 1980s

The philosophy underlying the Japanese school educational system and its institutional framework was fundamentally revamped after World War II. The post-war statutory regulations concerning education – such as the constitution and the Fundamental Law of Education (*Kyōiku kihon hō* 教育基本法) – emphasised the consolidation of the autonomy and independence of the educational system to root out any inappropriate control over the educational administrative system. The centralised governance of the Ministry of Education (*Monbushō* 文部省 (MOE)) was abolished, and school boards were constituted anew to make them fit into the framework of local autonomous bodies, in line with the new principles of decentralisation and democratisation. The School Board (*Kyōiku iinkai* 教育委員会) is one among the various administrative committees, such as the Committee on Labor Affairs (*Rōdō iinkai* 労働委員会) or the National Public Safety Commission (*Kōan iinkai* 公安委員会), and derives its model from the institution of local self-government in the United States of America.

In Japan, textbooks had been placed under severe state control right from the end of the nineteenth century, and it was only after the year 1947 that the system of government-designed textbooks was abolished, shifting to a system of mere authorisation. Although textbook authorisation was intended to be placed under the surveillance of the various regional school boards, a shortage of paper supply immediately after the war forced the decision to shift executive power of textbook authorisation to the office of the Minister of Education as an arrangement for the 'foreseeable future'.

As regards history education, on 31 December 1945 the extant school curricula of 'moral training' (*shūshin* 修身), Japanese history and geography were declared to be abolished by the General Headquarters (GHQ), respectively, the Supreme Commander of the Allied Powers (SCAP), General Douglas MacArthur, and all related textbooks and teaching manuals were retracted. At that time, the GHQ/SCAP expected the Japanese government to set up a new model of history education. However, the draft of the national history textbook the Japanese government worked upon still kept intact a lot of mythological content, and it was upon the directive of the Civil Information and Education Section (CIE) of the GHQ/SCAP that the draft was completely rewritten. Thus, it was in October 1946 that the government-designed common history textbook for primary schools, *The course of the nation* (*Kuni no ayumi* くにのあゆみ), was published, to be followed up by the *History of Japan* (*Nihon no rekishi* 日本の歴史) for secondary schools and *Japanese history* (*Nihon rekishi* 日本歴史) intended for teachers' education. With these textbooks, the teaching of history, which had been temporarily discontinued by the GHQ/SCAP, was resumed. The 'moral training' curriculum, which was discontinued along with the Japanese history and geography curricula, was revised to form a new civics curriculum, and the new social studies coursework was to combine the subjects of civics, history and geography, akin to the US model.

In May 1947, the draft proposal for the *Official school curriculum guidelines: social studies edition, Part I & II* (*Gakushū shidōyōryō shakaika hen I II* 学習指導要領社会科編I, II) was published by the MOE in order to define the basic standard for education and teaching from this year onwards. In the beginning, it was divided into a general edition and individual coursework editions. Furthermore, owing to the fact of being a draft proposal, it was limited to serve as a standard curriculum guideline only. The guideline for the social studies edition was partly amended in October 1948, and, in 1951, completely revised. Now, the policy to make students learn 'Japanese history' (junior secondary school) and 'Japanese history and world history' (senior secondary school) – all as subjects within the social studies curriculum – was outlined in detail.

Starting with the academic year of 1952, the authorisation system of senior secondary school history textbooks took effect. One can say that it was only during this period that history textbooks with individual traits first appeared in public. However, this took place amid a reverse trend in which the educational administration made a big volte-face and modified the educational content of school curricula considerably. This 'became starkly visible in two major movements: first, in the revision of the official school curriculum guidelines, and second, in the tightening of control over textbook authorisation' (Ienaga 1963: 329).

The social studies edition of the official school curriculum guidelines was revised in the years 1955 (primary and junior secondary schools) and 1956 (senior secondary school) and was followed by a further revision in both content and structural format in the years 1958 (primary and junior secondary school curricula) and 1960 (senior secondary school curriculum). For example, in the 1956 high school curriculum's revision, the clause 'to inculcate an attitude that would deal with historical facts with a rational and critical temperament' was deleted and, in its place, the sentence 'to raise the consciousness of being a Japanese' was included. With respect to the structural aspect of the revision, official school curriculum guidelines enacted after the year 1958 were regularly announced via official gazettes as public notifications passed by the MOE (but for schools for the physically/mentally challenged). Furthermore, these directives were enforced with the claim of 'possessing a legally binding power'. Meanwhile, in a partial modification of the School Education Act (*Gakkō kyōiku hō* 学校教育法) in the year 1953, the competency of textbook authorisation that had been hitherto temporarily shifted to the office of the Minister of Education was now permanently set there.

In 1950, a commission for approval of textbooks and other instruction material was set up, and, in 1956, a system of official textbook scrutiny was established. This happened against the backdrop of a charge levelled against textbooks in 1955 by the political parties then in power. In August 1953, a written report submitted by the Liberal Party in the National Diet stated, 'Throughout the whole of education the question of morals is neglected, and this is the fundamental shortcoming of Japanese education today. The bias towards social and economic history even in the field of history education' was declared the cause of the said problem. In August 1955, the Japan Democratic Party (*Nihon Minshutō* 日本民主党; not to be confused with the contemporary Democratic Party of Japan) published a pamphlet entitled *The problem of alarming textbooks* (*Ureubeki kyōkasho no mondai* うれうべき教科書の問題) – which appeared until the third issue – and started a campaign against the alleged partisan character of contemporary textbooks. As a response, the MOE replaced the council members of the commission for textbook approval, and thus a number of textbooks were actually branded as biased and, therefore, disqualified. Eventually, the Liberal and the Democratic Party merged to form the Liberal Democratic Party (LDP) in November of the same year, which then continued to wield power over a long period until the year 2009 (with two interruptions in 1993 and 1994).

The following year, 1956, witnessed a forced passing of a new School Board Act, making for the fact that the previous system to elect members by popular vote was now replaced by a system of nomination by the president of the board. That meant a major setback for the citizens' participation in the administration of educational affairs. Although a legislative bill to tighten control over textbooks and to transfer the power of adoption of textbooks away from schools into the hands of school boards did not succeed, the control of the MOE over textbook authorisation now entered a phase of consolidation. In 1962, in tandem with a policy to provide primary and junior secondary school textbooks free of cost, the power to adopt textbooks, which had rested within the jurisdiction of each school, was finally abolished and placed into the hands of school boards. On the other hand, the official school curriculum guidelines for senior secondary schools were revised subsequently in 1960, 1970, 1978, 1989, 1999 and 2009, almost once in a decade.

In 1965, Ienaga Saburō (家永三郎;1913–2002) filed his first lawsuit to fight against the treatment of his Japanese history textbook draft application for senior secondary school, which had been submitted for authorisation in the academic year of 1962 and which was subsequently only approved on condition of modification. As the modifications were not accepted, his textbook was disapproved in the end, which led to his second lawsuit, filed in 1967. In the 1970s, three court decisions were passed, all of which were technical wins for Ienaga's case (one of them was only a partial win). In fact, the 1970 decision of the Tokyo District Court regarding the second lawsuit filed in 1967 ruled that the disqualification of the draft application was in violation of the Japanese Constitution and the Fundamental Law of Education. It was only owing to this judgement that a certain sense of restraint appeared on the part of the administration for approving textbooks.

However, the LDP kicked off a campaign alleging the spread of 'tendentious' textbooks in 1980, which became an issue of fervent social debate. The LDP set up an in-house committee on textbook issues, and right-wing organisations joined in, aggravating the situation even further. At this juncture, the targets for attack were the curriculum of social studies, especially the subjects of civics and contemporary society, and works of literature included in the coursework of the national language. Even during Japanese history and world history textbook authorisation procedures, the MOE handed on a number of suggestions for corrections and amendments to be carried out. Thus, during the textbook authorisation of the academic year 1981, passages concerning the Japanese invasion and its colonial rule became an issue of controversy, inviting criticism from East and Southeast Asian countries, escalating into the so-called 1982 Textbook Controversy (*1982-nen rekishi kyōkasho mondai* １９８２年歴史教科書問題).[1]

It is significant to take note of the fact that there was a surge of criticism, both at home and abroad, against the blatant high-handedness with which textbook authorisation was being carried out, amid a counter campaign driven by the LDP against what was alleged as 'deviationism' (*henkō* 偏向) on the part of textbook compilers. Ienaga, who had been compiling textbooks since 1952, said to me during an interview, 'I am experienced with textbook compilation for almost 30 years now. But I know no precedent to the horrendous way in which the textbook authorisation procedure in the 1980s was undertaken.'

In August 1982, the then Chief Cabinet Secretary Miyazawa Kiichi (宮澤喜一; 1919–2007) publicly stated that 'the Japanese Government and the Japanese people are deeply aware of the fact that acts by our country in the past caused tremendous suffering and damage to the peoples of Asian countries, including the Republic of Korea (ROK) and China.' Furthermore, he promised that 'Japan will make corrections at the government's responsibility.' In this manner, the controversy surrounding textbooks was resolved. Even the MOE stated it would make partial amendments in its approval policy. However, the proposals for 'corrections' (*teisei* 訂正) in the MOE-approved textbooks submitted by the compilers Ienaga Saburō *et al.* were all turned down by the ministry. In response to this, Ienaga filed his third lawsuit in 1984 against both the non-acceptance of 'corrections of both true and false clauses' (*seigo teisei* 正誤訂正) and the 'conditional qualification' (*jōkentsuki gokaku* 条件付互角) of the textbook draft that had been proposed for authorisation in the academic year 1983.

In total, the court trials starting from the first lawsuit in the year 1965 to 1997, the Supreme Judicial Court verdict related to the third lawsuit; the whole lawsuit ran for a period of altogether 32 years. In the final verdict, Ienaga lost both the first and second lawsuits. As regards the third lawsuit, it was judged that the ministerial approval of the textbook in itself was in accordance with the constitution, but that there was a deviation from a certain issue in the discretionary power of the ministry, and the case was closed with a partial win for Ienaga's petition.

From 1982 onwards, a clause on 'neighbouring countries' (*kinrin shokoku jōkō* 近隣諸国条項) was incorporated into the guideline standards for the authorisation of textbooks and curricula materials [aiming at preventing further diplomatic rifts, G.M.]. In 1986, a textbook draft (initially published by Hara shobō 原書房, later by Kokusho kankōkai 国書刊行会 and currently by Meiseisha 明成社), whose compilation was promoted by the rightist organisation the National Conference to Defend Japan (*Nihon o mamoru kokumin kaigi* 日本を守る国民会議), was approved by the commission for textbook approval. This decision encountered the demand for reconsideration by the Chinese government and also aroused criticism from the South Korean government. In the wake of such protests, the already approved textbook was amended in several places at the special directive of the prime minister. In an extraordinary commission on education that was held before, some argued for the abolishment of scrutiny in the approval procedure, albeit these opinions did not feature in the final report. Against the background of these developments, the MOE eventually revamped the system of textbook authorisation considerably after 1989, and not all results have been made public yet.

Changes in the 1990s

In 1989, the official school curriculum guidelines were completely revised, and the coursework of the subject of history in senior secondary schools, too, was altered in many respects. This very same coursework is being followed to date.[2] The subject of social studies carried out until then was segregated into geography/history and civics. In the subject of geography/history, although world history was made compulsory, Japanese history and geography were only optional subjects. Further, the subjects of world history and Japanese history were subdivided into A and B coursework, in which course A primarily covered modern and contemporary history, holding two credits over a period of one year (whereas, from 1999 onwards, the revised official guidelines sharpened it to exclusively deal with modern and contemporary history). In contrast, course B covered pre-modern, modern and contemporary history, with a total of four annual credits. Course A, of both Japanese history and world history, was offered in vocational and distance education schools, apart from some municipal schools, but course B was introduced in most municipal schools. However, a few senior secondary schools (especially those focused on preparing for entrance into universities) offer both courses. A look at the ratio of opting for course A to course B shows that, in the mid 1990s, the ratio was about 1:2, whereas in 2004 data show that the ratio changed to 2:3. It can also be seen that the number of schools offering course A is on the increase each year. However, if one takes a look at the number of examinees opting for course B in the common entrance examination held at various public and private universities all over the country, their number is of overwhelming magnitude compared with those opting for course A. That has been the trend all these years.

As for the comparative ratio of textbooks published in 1999, six publishing houses brought out seven textbooks following the *Japanese history A* curriculum, and nine publishing houses published nineteen textbooks following *Japanese history B*. Although the number of publishing houses declined compared with the 1980s, the total number of textbooks dealing with Japanese history has grown. This must be seen in the context of the bifurcation into course A and course B.

As has been mentioned earlier on, the system of textbook authorisation underwent some very significant changes by the end of the 1980s, and some relaxation set in in the authorisation of passages related to war experience. Whereas the authorisation procedures until the 1980s were totally behind closed doors, from the academic year 1991 onwards, the drafts of textbooks submitted for authorisation and the suggestions of the authorisation panel were both made public, following changes in the system incorporated in the academic year of 1990. The ministry prided itself for calling it a 'notable achievement' (*kaizen* 改善). Yet, except for the subject of history, authorisation regulations became even stricter, and the number of textbook drafts that were treated as disqualified increased (textbooks relating to home economics etc.). Moreover, the enforcement of amendments grew all the more tricky. For example, the time period allocated for corrections was drastically shortened, and, also, the time for counter-arguments was reduced. Thus, in practice, authors and publishing houses were often put in a position in which they generally could only abide by the suggestions of the authorisation panel.

However, through the 1980s, there was a notable change in the mindset of the people at large and also of the government in regard to the war past. The earlier thoughtless stance of justifying the Fifteen Years War and colonial domination finally faded into the background. It was the steady accumulation of concrete achievements in the field of historical research that formed the backdrop against which relations with foreign countries actually improved in a number of ways. In addition, beginning with South Korea, a democratisation of polity in the various countries and regions of East Asia set in, which facilitated transnational exchange of opinions beyond the official stances of governments.

In 1993, the then prime minister, Hosokawa Morihiro (細川護熙; 1938–), made a general policy speech on taking over office at the opening Diet session, in which he publicly offered an 'apology and a sense of deep regret for Japan's act of invasion and colonial rule'. Eventually, it became a practice for prime ministers, regardless of their political affiliation, to mouth the words of 'regret' (*hansei* 反省) for Japan's 'act of invasion' (*shinryaku kōi* 侵略行為). It is to be noted that the textbook of social studies stipulated for the year 1995 carried a comparatively extensive coverage of the Fifteen Years War.

Furthermore, there was a rise in the awareness related to the issue of history textbooks in the public. There was also a development in the mass media, which not only reported the gist of the results of textbook authorisation, but also featured a host of news items related to this issue. The trend to undertake international comparison and collaboration relating to history textbooks, centring around historians and educationists, grew, and many textbooks of foreign countries were translated into Japanese and published. After the mid 1980s, a number of research publications appeared that dealt with the question of how Japan's war act was covered in the textbooks of different Asian countries. In addition, from the latter half of the 1980s decade onwards, initial efforts were made to seek a mutual understanding and appreciation of the issues concerning textbooks, on a non-official level, between China, South Korea and Japan, or merely between South Korea and Japan.

It was as the result of such efforts that common history textbook material was published simultaneously in China, South Korea and Japan in the year 2005.The Japanese language edition was published by Kōbunken 高文研

publishers and is entitled *Mirai o hiraku rekishi – Higashi Ajia san-goku no kingendaishi* 未来をひらく歴史: 東アジア三国の近現代史 (*History that opens the future: the modern and contemporary history of three East Asian countries*).

Against this background, how did the content of Japanese history textbooks for senior secondary schools actually change during this period? Let us look at the chief characteristics of that change. First, the description of modern/contemporary history in the course A and B textbooks increased in volume. Regarding the authorship, another change took place. Researchers who specialised in modern and contemporary Japanese history began to take part in textbook writing, except one publication I mentioned initially, [the (right-wing, G.M.] one that was released by Hara shobō and later on by Kokusho kankōkai and by Meiseisha respectively). Furthermore, in modern and contemporary history, parts dealing with Korea increased decisively in volume. In nearly all textbooks, the following issues received coverage, namely: the debate on conquering Korea in 1873 (*seikanron* 征韓論); the Ganghwa Island Incident in 1875 (*Kōkatō jiken* 江華島事件) and the ensuing Ganghwa Treaty of 1876 (Korean–Japanese Treaty of Amity; *Nitchō shūkōjōki* 日朝修好条規); the sequence of events from the Imo Mutiny of 1882 (*Jingo jihen* 壬午事変) leading to the Gapsin *coup d'état* in 1884 (*Kōshin seihen* 甲申政変); the Osaka Incident of 1885 (*Ōsaka jiken* 大阪事件) as part of the Freedom and People's Rights Movement (*Jiyū minken undō* 自由民権運動); the First Sino–Japanese War 1894–5 (*Nisshin sensō* 日清戦争); the so-called Righteous Armies (*Gihei* 義兵) and the colonialisation of Korea; the exploitation policy of oriental lands (Korea) and land survey projects; the March First Korean Independence Movement of 1919 (*San-ichi dokuritsu undō* 三・一独立運動) and the Japanese reaction to it; the 1923 Great Kantō earthquake (*Kantō dai-shinsai* 関東大震災 [in the wake of which also many Koreans were lynched, G.M.]); the emergence of new conglomerates (*zaibatsu* 財閥) [and their economic hegemony, G.M.]; the government policy of the Japanisation (*kōminka* 公民化) of Korea and newly conquered territories and forced resettling; the issue of 'comfort women' (*jūgun ianfu* 従軍慰安婦) [forced prostitution for the army, G.M.]; the 1943 Cairo Declaration (*Kairo sengen* カイロ宣言); the independence and partition of Korea; the 1950–3 Korean War; the 1965 Korea-Japan Treaty on Basic Relations (*Nihonkoku to Dai-Kanminkoku to no aida no kihon kankei ni kan suru jōyaku* 日本国と大韓民国との間の基本関係に関する条約) etc.

Second, in connection with the change mentioned above, it became possible to briefly write about aggressive acts committed by Japan during the past wars. It was also at this time that sections related to 'comfort women', who were made to serve the Japanese Army, appeared on the pages of the textbooks, and these descriptions were carried in almost all textbooks. It is popularly assumed that the 'comfort women' issue came to the fore owing to an incident that took place in South Korea in 1991. At that time, a former 'comfort woman' revealed her real name and demanded an apology from the Japanese government. However, it was in the 1980s that the basic work to trace and document the identities of 'comfort women' actually started in South Korea. In Japan, too, historians were piling up rigorous research work on various aspects of this issue. It was amid these developments that the textbook on Japanese history for senior secondary schools entitled *Shōkai Nihonshi* 詳解日本史 (*An introduction to Japanese history*), compiled by Aoki Michio (青木美智夫) *et al.*, carried the following passage, which caught the attention of the public:

> As for the true face of the Greater East Asia Co-Prosperity Sphere [. . .] it was in the year 1940 that the Korean League of National Spiritual Mobilisation [*Kokumin seishin sōdōin chōsen renmei* 国民精神総動員朝鮮連盟, M.A.] was reorganised to form the Korean League for National Concerted Power [*Kokumin sōryoku chōsen renmei* 国民総力朝鮮連盟, M.A.] and thus mobilisation of the Korean people was reinforced. In 1944, the conscription system was introduced to Korea. Around 200,000 Korean women were enlisted into the militant cadre (*teishintai* 挺身隊) and many were roped in to serve as comfort women for the Japanese Army.
>
> (Aoki *et al.* 1990: 299)

As a result of the revelation of an official document in 1992 that proved the Japanese Army's involvement and control in installing 'comfort facilities' and recruiting 'comfort women', the then prime minister, Miyazawa Kiichi, paid a visit to South Korea and apologised to President Roh Tae-Woo. It was also after this revelation that passages describing the issue of 'comfort women' were included even in junior secondary school textbooks on social studies.

In June 1995, the House of Representatives adopted a resolution 'to make a new resolve for peace by learning from history', and a decision was made in August the same year to hold informal talks at cabinet meetings on the occasion of the fiftieth anniversary of the war's end (statement by Prime Minister Murayama Tomiichi (村山富市; 1924–)).

Nevertheless, a number of rebels came to the fore from within the LDP to oppose the cabinet on the occasion of the resolution. It may be recalled that, during the 1990s, the Japanese economy and society entered an acute phase of prolonged stagnation after the collapse of the 'bubble economy'. The unemployment rate rose, and thus concern about employment grew. In such an atmosphere, where the future seemed bleak, a surge of domestic rhetoric emerged targeting people of different nationalities, ethnic backgrounds and minority communities, thereby giving vent to the general frustration and discontent prevalent in society at that time. The issue of 'comfort women made to serve the Japanese Army' that was dealt with in history textbooks was taken up as a further target of attack. The gist of the argument was that, neither this phrasing existed during the said period, nor did any kind of 'forced hauling up' of women, akin to an image of being dragged by ropes tied to their necks, take place. Instead, the lobby argued that it was inappropriate to charge the country's representative organs of irresponsibility for what was alleged to be the actions of private parties. Further, the lobby also made a loud hue and cry about what was branded as 'self-denigrating' or 'masochistic textbooks' (*jigyakuteki kyōkasho* 自虐的教科書), claiming that they perverted the 'pride of Japanese people' (*Nihonjin no hokori* 日本人の誇り) and 'ruined Japan' (*Nihon o dame ni suru* 日本をだめにする). In 1995, the Research Society for a Liberalist View of History (*Jiyūshugi shikan kenkyūkai* 自由主義史観研究会) was formed. It ran a political campaign that primarily aimed at the 'comfort women' issue and received extensive coverage in the history textbooks. Moreover, in the following year of 1996, the *Tsukurukai* was launched by like-minded people from the right wing rallying together.

In the midst of such heavy attack, there appeared a junior secondary school history textbook that did not mention any issue of 'comfort women' in its revised version at all. However, in the case of senior secondary school history textbooks, it became a general practice among all publications to carry descriptions of the issue concerning 'comfort women', except for the one released by Hara shobō (and later by Kokusho kankōkai and Meiseisha), which had never referred to Japanese colonial rule at all.

Third, descriptions of post-World War II history increased. These accounts emphasised a description of Japan in the context of its relationship with East Asia. For example, the textbook *Japanese history B* (*Nihonshi B* 日本史B), compiled by Naoki Kōjirō 直木孝次郎 *et al.*, made specific reference to the 1990 keynote address by President Roh Tae-Woo in the National Diet, the speech by Prime Minister Miyazawa Kiichi in the National Assembly of South Korea in 1992 and the summit meeting of 1993 between Prime Minister Hosokawa and South Korean President Kim Young-sam in the context of the history of Koreans under Japanese colonial rule (Naoki *et al.* 1994: 362–3).

Moreover, there was an increase in the number of textbooks that covered the long-drawn-out diplomatic negotiations between South Korea and Japan, which ultimately culminated in the summit meeting of 1965. Issues such as the making of the post-war Japanese Constitution and the history of the development of human rights for people of foreign nationalities residing in Japan also appeared (Tanaka *et al.* 1997: 121).

The fourth chief aspect of change that needs to be mentioned here concerns the authorisation of textbooks that took shape during the 1990s. As has been noted earlier, it was during this decade that the MOE adopted the practice of making public the drafts of textbooks that had been submitted for authorisation, as well as announcing the gist of the suggestions made by the authorisation panel. Despite the fact that not all details were revealed, I will try to outline the actual state of affairs relating to the way in which textbook drafts were authorised and rectified.

The authorisation panel usually would pick up topics where specified numbers were given in textbooks and raise many objections. For example, a textbook draft that stated, 'young Korean women numbering from around 50,000 to 200,000 were forcefully drafted as comfort women into the service of the Japanese Army by the Japanese Government and military authorities' was, at the behest of the suggestions made by the ministry's authorisation panel, rectified to, 'a number of young women were sent to the frontline as comfort women in the service of the Japanese Army by the Japanese Government and military authorities'. The remarks made by the panel said, 'It is desirable that the draft-writers take into account the current status of research work regarding the numbers of comfort women who served the Japanese Army', and they also made a remark that went, 'It is feared that the use of the term "forceful drafting" related to comfort women would be misinterpreted as being a forceful draft under the National Draft Ordinance issued by the Japanese Government'. Further on, in the case of a different textbook draft, the clause stating the figure of Korean 'comfort women' as 'around 100,000' was rectified to 'a number of comfort women' in the remarks made by the authorisation panel (the above-mentioned cases refer to the textbook authorisation process of the academic year 1992; cf. *Nihon shuppan rōdō kumiai rengōkai* 日本出版労働組合連合会 [The Japan Labor Union Confederation of Publishers] 1994: 36–43). Different suggestive remarks were also made with respect to the number of people who participated in the March First Korean Independence Movement of 1919 and the number of those who were forcefully hauled up during war times.

Moreover, there were a number of remarks made by the authorisation panel that pushed for a positive portrayal of the post-war Japanese government's position on the colonial past. For example, a passage in a textbook draft went, 'But the Japanese Government, while stressing the legitimacy of the Japan–Korea Annexation Treaty, adopted a position wherein it neither acknowledged that Japan had waged a war of invasion into foreign territory, nor did it clearly assume responsibility for the war.' That passage was replaced by, 'In the address made by Prime Minister Murayama in 1995, in the Japan–Republic of Korea Joint Declaration of 1998 as well as in the Japan–China Joint Declaration of the same year, remorse was expressed towards the colonial rule and invasion.' The reason for this change was described in the authorisation panel's remarks as follows: 'The expression [carried in the textbook draft, M.A.] is one that would invite a misunderstanding with regards to the Japanese Government's position on the responsibility for war, etc.' (these cases refer to the academic year 2001; cf. *Nihon shuppan rōdō kumiai rengōkai* 日本出版労働組合連合会 [The Japan Labor Union Confederation of Publishers] 2003: 57–9). Or, there was a request that another textbook passage, which stated, 'there remain many unresolved issues like post-war compensations associated to the issue of the deportation of Korean civilians and comfort women to serve the Japanese Army', be rectified to 'the issue of compensations between the countries has been settled', and it was finally carried only as a line in the annotations (academic year 2002, *Nihon shuppan rōdō kumiai rengōkai* 日本出版労働組合連合会 [The Japan Labor Union Confederation of Publishers] 2004: 62–3). And, in the academic year 2006–7, the authorisation panel suggested changes for a textbook draft passage that described the coercive role of the Japanese Army in the 'collective suicide' of civilians during the Okinawan battle in the war. This topic has also become an issue of fervent debate.

On the other hand, the *Tsukurai* compiled history textbooks for junior secondary schools, which received the authorisation of the ministry in 2001, 2005 and 2009. Although this happened against the backdrop of a wide rallying for support from the right wing, it was met with severe criticism from home and abroad; there was no further increase in the number of approved copies that circulated. However, in 2009, with the powerful support of Yokohama's mayor, the board of education in Yokohama city partially adopted this textbook. On another side, there was even criticism from members associated with the said society, claiming that the protests 'were due to the contents being too rightist', and this resulted in internal conflicts as well as repeated factional splits, alignments and realignments.[3]

However, it needs to be noted that there has been a considerable toning down in the description of Japanese assaults and aggression related to the Fifteen Years War period, especially vis-à-vis the issue of 'comfort women', after the heavy attacks launched against textbooks compiled by organisations such as the *Tsukurukai*.

Towards a new understanding of history through history textbooks

It was in 1990 that I began to write history textbooks for senior secondary schools. Of course, I don't write them all by myself, but I compile them in collaboration with other scholars and editors. The curriculum followed is that of *Japanese history A*, and our publisher is Tōkyō shoseki (東京書籍). The number of copies in circulation has exceeded 70,000 each year, and it occupies a top-three position in terms of circulation numbers among textbooks in the combined group of courses A and B for the school subject 'Japanese history'.

As a result of the policy for 'pressure-free' education in the latter half of the 1990s and its subsequent revision, recent Japanese history textbooks display the following main characteristics: either an increase in the total amount of tightly packed information in order to meet the needs of the university entrance examinations; or oversimplification in a drastically cut written text, with increased use of photographic plates. The Japanese history textbooks that rank first and second in terms of circulation numbers are representative of these two types, respectively. Textbook types such as the one we produced, which seek to infuse novelty in terms of content, individual writing styles and differing points of view (Tanaka *et al.* 1997, 1999, 2001, 2004, 2007), are actually rare in number. In fact, such types only appear as the current rankings three and four on the list.

The textbook co-authored by myself carries seven distinct articles in the form of columns under the heading 'Views from across the world: an open space for dialogue'. The columns are written by scholars who do not hold Japanese citizenship, i.e. they are not Japanese nationals. In the textbooks related to the disciplines of social studies and geography/history, this is the very first attempt to involve the participation of non-Japanese authors. The reasons why we decided to incorporate these columns in the composition of the textbook are explained below.

In general, we wanted to stress the following three aspects: first, to concretise the perspective of 'learning history from the point of view of the present'; second, to examine the history of Japan in the context of its relations to other countries; and, third, to grasp the history of modern Japan by turning our gaze to the diverse facets of local regions and societies at large. In short, we aimed at contemporariness, an international perspective and appreciation of diversity. It is on the lines of such a perspective that the different chapters and sub-chapters, the sections of 'A look out into local regions' and 'A look out into the times', as well as the special articles – one incorporated into each of the five chapters in the form of columns, with the group heading 'Portrait of a 17-year-old'[4] – and the like have been organised.

As a result of such a conceptualisation, this textbook is also composed in such a way that it starts with the chapter 'Our times', referring to the age in which the pupils who use the textbook actually grew up – not with that dealing with the end of the Tokugawa period and the time of the Meiji Restoration – and only then proceeds further on to the next chapter dealing with the period of the Meiji Restoration, coinciding with the beginning of the Japanese modern period. Moreover, the description of the post-war period, i.e. the time after the end of World War II, already starts with the Okinawan War and the occupation of Okinawa under the title 'Defeat and occupation'. The reason for beginning this chapter with the description of the Okinawan War is based upon the fact that the original meaning of the term 'occupation' refers to the occupation of Okinawa, which preceded that of the Japanese mainland. With respect to the content, too, the description related to Okinawa and Hokkaido has increased in volume, following the point of view of emphasising diversity. Owing to the adoption of an international perspective, the content descriptions of various chapters, in principle, begin with the international environment surrounding Japan during the respective historical periods, involving an innovation that facilitates the reader approaching the history of Japan from within a context of world history.

All the writers of this textbook hold the view that the standpoint to grasp the history of Japan from within an international framework should be materialised, not only in the overall composition of the textbook, but also in the respective issues taken up by the individual writers. Furthermore, it is no overstatement to say that Japanologists from all over the world are taking an avid interest in the history textbooks published in Japan. In addition, the public at large, from various regions of the world, have come to know of the Japanese system involving textbooks and their authorisation by way of the court trial cases related to textbooks. Moreover, there is widespread international interest in the 'revisionist' and 'fundamentalist' trend in Japan in recent years as regards Japanese history textbooks. Namely, the moves that are proclaimed to 'recover history with a sense of pride' have negatively impacted on historians and related educationists. In this context, the question of how the history textbooks in Japan should take shape in the future, with respect to both content and the system governing them, has become a matter of great significance, not only to Japan, but also to future relations with the world at large.

Precisely because of this, we wanted to involve non-Japanese in the writing project, and thus the column 'Views from across the world: an open space for dialogue' was born. The seven column articles and their authors are:

1 'Possibilities for an understanding of history that transcends national borders', by Andrew Gordon (Harvard University, US-American);
2 'Multi-cultural and multi-ethnic Japan', by Tessa Morris-Suzuki (Australian National University, British);
3 'The Asianism of Japan and Korea', by Cho Keungdal (Chiba University, Korean, with permanent residence in Japan);
4 'The formation of Japanese ethnicity and national language', by Lee Yeon Suk (Hitotsubashi University, South Korean);
5 'Modern Japan as seen from India', by Brij Tankha (Delhi University, Indian);
6 '"Overcoming the past" in Japan and in Germany', by Wolfgang Seifert (Heidelberg University, German);
7 'Japan and the world after the "Gulf War": views from the "Middle East"', by Mahdi Elmanjdra (Mohammed V University, Moroccan).

The writers of the column articles come from different regions worldwide, and their native languages, too, are diverse. They reflect how research work on modern and contemporary Japanese history, in a wide sense of the term, is being undertaken in different parts of the world today.

In fact, the category of 'foreign researchers' includes two types, namely one that refers to those 'foreign nationals' residing in Japan and actively taking part in Japanese society, using the Japanese language as their chief medium of expression; and another that includes those primarily living in countries or regions outside Japan and doing research either in their respective native tongues or in some other language. Among the first group, i.e. researchers of foreign nationalities residing in Japan, many take up in their work the fundamental issue of various kinds of pressure that historical developments in modern Japan exerted upon minorities living in Japan during the given period. And among the second, i.e. the foreign researchers primarily living outside Japan, there is a lot of research that has critically pursued the question of how modern Japan has actually been mirrored in its relationship with others in the world.

Even in the case of historical research activities on modern and contemporary Japanese history conducted in Japan, it should be noted that it was in the wake of a worldwide growth in research on Japan after the 1970s, especially beginning in the latter half of the 1980s, that many academic journals and encyclopedias actively started to introduce and review research work on modern/contemporary Japan that was being undertaken in different countries and regions of the world. The journals *Annual Bulletin of Contemporary Japanese History* [*Nenpō Nihon gendaishi* 年報日本現代史, published by Azuma shuppan 東出版 and later by Gendai shiryō shuppan 現代史料出版], inaugurated in 1995, and *The Japanese Journal of Contemporary History* [*Dōjidaishi kenkyū* 同時代史研究, published by Nihon keizai hyōronsha 日本経済評論社], starting in the year 2008, are such examples. As for encyclopedias, for example, the *Encyclopedia of post-war history: enlarged new edition* [*Sengoshi daijiten: sōho shinpan* 戦後史大事典—増補新版] (edited by Sasaki Takeshi 佐々木毅 *et al.*; published by Sanseidō 三省堂 2005) includes in its final bibliographic part, 'Explanations to the documents: foreign research', Japanological research works on the post-war history of thirty-eight countries and regions across the world.

Furthermore, the extra volume of the *Iwanami shoten* (岩波書店) course series on Japanese history (published from 1994 to 1995) included John Dower's essay, 'Current portrait of Japanese society', and also another essay by Carol Gluck entitled, 'The metahistory of post-war historiography'. It is noteworthy that this particular edition stands in contrast to the earlier two courses on Japanese history published by *Iwanami shoten* (1962–4 and 1976–7), which had not even taken note of research on Japanese history abroad. Moreover, after the 1980s, collaborative research publications in Japanese involving the participation of foreign researchers were no longer unusual, and there was a trend for collaborative publications on Japanese historical research to be published also in languages other than Japanese. Our textbook, too, reflects this new situation.

Finally, I would like to add a word about the expectations we had for the articles in the column 'Views from across the world: an open space for dialogue' and their writers. First, we expected a portrayal of how the history of modern and contemporary Japan looked from outside Japan and from the peripheral areas within – i.e. away from the core. Though there is a 'generally modern' Japan, there are also specific Japanese characteristics [which should become evident in this perspective, G.M.]. Next, there was the need to address the question of how to convey the points of contention that are unavoidable in the consideration of modern Japanese history to the pupils, as this also belongs to the fast-changing research areas that have been the focus of the international community in recent years.

Owing to its nature as a textbook, the main texts of the chapters are narrated in a chronological order. In contrast, the column articles, which are closely linked to the main text, have been required to delve into specific thematic issues. The writers of the column articles in 'Views from across the world: an open space for dialogue' have adequately understood our purpose and wrote what they deemed necessary for the needs of the respective themes. Though it is difficult to forecast how Japan and the world will take shape in the twenty-first century, there is no doubt that the present senior secondary school students of Japan will come into contact with people from different countries or of different ethnicities and mingle with them in their future lives. For example, as regards occupational life, border fences dividing peoples will invariably be lowered, be it in blue-collar or white-collar jobs. Even in universities and other such institutions, exchange between both students and faculties, transcending national and ethnic boundaries, is bound to increase even further.

What then is the kind of understanding of history and insight that pupils are expected to acquire? The need to address that very question and the expectation that they see themselves in terms of a dialogue with people from all over the world are the greatest aims of the column 'Views from across the world: an open space for dialogue'. And this also is the basic contention we want to put forward with our textbook.

Concluding remarks

There might be a variety of opinions on the question of how one should compose Japanese history textbooks in the future. I have laid stress on the opening up to the world outside Japan in a double sense: One is to rewrite the *contents* of Japanese history in a way that opens it up to the outside. Another is to *write* the Japanese history textbooks *along with scholars from foreign countries*. The former will help grasp the modern and contemporary history of Japan within the framework of Northeast Asia. The latter will facilitate a diverse group of scholars to be associated with the project of composing textbooks right from the initial stage of planning.

Notes

1   There is also the [right-wing, G.M.] opinion that it was only 'misreporting' that initially sparked off the controversy and that this was precisely what led to the 'self-denigration' of Japanese textbooks. The following passage was published in 2001, in the January–March bulletin *Rekishi* 歴史 of the Japanese Society for History Textbook Reform (*Atarashii rekishi kyōkasho o tsukurukai* 新しい歴史教科書をつくる会; *Tsukurukai* for short):

> Why is it that textbooks have become so distorted? Well, there are a number of reasons, but most significant of them all are: the incident of misreporting concerning textbooks in 1982, the approval procedures of *Japanese History: New Edition* in 1986 under foreign pressure and the vicious circle of textbook compilation and election. This clarifies the incident and the system that have contributed to the deterioration of textbooks. The 'textbook misreporting incident' involves a series of events that followed the misreporting in the mass media, which stated, 'The MOE, which was undertaking the approval of history textbooks for senior secondary schools, was instrumental in putting the term *advance* in place of the term *invasion*.' As result of this reportage, both China and South Korea raised strong protests demanding a revision of these descriptions in the textbooks of our country. It was the very first case of foreign pressure in the history of textbook approval in our country.

However, as the government did not deal with it resolutely, this incident has led to severe ramifications by leaving behind unsettled problems for the future.

To be precise, the newspaper report, published in June 1982, which stated that the term 'invasion' of North Central China by the Japanese Army carried in the textbook draft was altered to 'advance' at the behest of official instruction and approval, is not commensurate with fact at that given year. But there were these alterations with regard to Southeast Asia. Further, against suggested corrections related to the description of the massacre of Okinawan people by the Japanese Army, the Okinawa Prefectural Assembly passed a unanimous resolution in September of the same year demanding a restoration of the original description in the proposed draft.

2 Moreover, as part of this revision, the total number of school hours of primary, junior secondary and senior secondary schools, as well as the curriculum content of all levels, too, was drastically reduced. In 1998–9, official guidelines urging for an educational environment free of pressure were introduced, and both school hours and the curriculum content of all subjects were further reduced. This invited criticism of a deterioration in general educational standards in the country, which, in turn, led the Minister of Education, Culture, Sports, Science and Technology to review the new policy of pressure-free education in 2005. Meanwhile, beginning in 2002, the ministry adopted a changed version of its interpretation of the official guidelines and shifted its stance to enhance a 'learning which continually develops' (*hattentekina gakushū* 発展的な学習).

3 Japan, after the war – and especially during the period of rapid economic growth – built a society in which economic and social inequalities were not very pronounced. However, by way of the long-term stagnation of the 1990s and policies of 'structural reform' and of easing various restrictive regulations at the end of the century, Japanese politics took a turn towards a society wherein inequality, both in terms of opportunities and results, became a visible fact also in international comparison. In this situation, some of those who considered this state of affairs as 'being odd' sought its causes in secret manoeuvres of what they alleged to be 'anti-Japanese forces'. This idea was channelled via a host of different media, such as print and visual media, as well as via news reportage, constituting a huge market in the field of culture. It was in this context that the *Tsukurukai* could function as an organ to swamp this market with its products. Thus, there also arose a power dispute over the rights and interests involving this market, and it is believed that that was an aspect that was connected to the said internal conflicts and fights for leadership rights within the *Tsukurukai* as well.

4 When encountering history textbooks, it is not uncommon for senior secondary school students to feel that history is a fact of the past and so far away from their own selves. Thus, to provide a point of contact between history and senior secondary school students in the textbook, we envisaged the column 'Portrait of a 17-year-old'. Its aim is to present accounts of a 17-year-old living in different eras, as 17 is the average age of the students using the textbook. The specific titles of the respective column are:

- 'Life expectancy of a 17-year-old in the past and present time: a statistical point of view';
- 'Living through the closing phase of the Tokugawa regime: the households of a village headman and of a tenant farmer';
- 'The creation of [the concept of] "Youth": the case of a juvenile from the Meiji period';
- 'A young girl who traveled into colonial territory: a historical document as seen through photo albums';
- 'En masse employment: far away from home'.

Bibliography

Aoki M. 青木美智男 et al. (comps) (1990) *Shōkai Nihonshi* 紹介日本史 [*An introduction to Japanese history*], Tokyo: Sanseido.

Ienaga S. 家永三郎 (1963) 'Sengo no rekishi kyōiku' 戦後の歴史教育 [Post-war history education], *Iwanami kōza: Nihon rekishi* 岩波講座。日本歴史 [Iwanami course: Japanese history], vol. 22, Tokyo: Iwanami shoten.

Miyake A. 三宅明正 (2002) 'Hontō ni atarashii rekishi kyōkasho to wa nan darōka' 本当に新しい歴史教科書とは何だろうか [What are the new history textbooks really all about?], *Rekishi hyōron* 歴史評論 [Historical review], vol. 632.

—— (2002) *Sekai no ugoki no naka de yomu Nihon no rekishi kyōkasho mondai* 世界の動きの中で読む日本の歴史教科書問題 [*Reading the issue of Japanese history textbooks within the context of global trends*], Tokyo: Nashinokisha.

—— (2006) 'Kingendai no Kankoku–Chōsen wa dō shirusarete kitaka' 近現代の韓国・朝鮮はどう記されてきたか [How have South and North Korea been described in Japanese high school history textbooks?], in H. Miyajima 宮嶋博史 et al. (eds) *Kindai kōryūshi to sōgo ninshiki III, 1945-nen o zengo shite* 近代交流史と相互認識〈3〉一九四五年を前後して [*History of modern exchange and mutual consciousness III, before and after 1945*], Tokyo: Keiō University Press.

MOE (ed.) (1946) *Kuni no ayumi* くにのあゆみ [*The course of the nation*], Tokyo: MOE.

—— (1946) *Nihon no rekishi* 日本の歴史 [*History of Japan*], Tokyo: MOE.

—— (1946) *Nihon rekishi* 日本歴史 [*Japanese history*], Tokyo: MOE.

—— (1947) *Gakushū shidōyōryō shakaika hen I, II* 学習指導要領社会科編I, II (*Official school curriculum guidelines: social studies edition, Parts I & II*), Tokyo: MOE.

Naoki K. 直木孝次郎 et al. (eds) (1994) *Nihonshi B* 日本史B [*Japanese history B*], Tokyo: Jikkyō shuppan.

Nihon Minshutō kyōkasho mondai tokubetsu iinkai 日本民主党教科書問題特別委員会 [Japan Democratic Party Special Committee on the Textbook Problem] (1955) *Ureubeki kyōkasho no mondai* うれうべき教科書の問題 [*The problem of alarming textbooks*].

Nihon shuppan rōdō kumiai rengōkai 日本出版労働組合連合会 [The Japan Labor Union Confederation of Publishers] (ed.) (1994, 2003, 2004)) *Kyōkasho repōto* 教科書レポート [Report on textbooks].

Nitchūkan san-goku kyōtsū rekishi kyōzai iinkai 日中韓三国共通歴史教材委員会 [Trilateral Joint History Editorial Committee of Japan, China and South Korea] (ed.) (2005) *Mirai o hiraku rekishi: Higashi Ajia san-goku no kingendaishi* 未来をひらく歴史：東アジア三国の近現代史 [*History that opens the future: the modern and contemporary history of three East Asian countries*], Tokyo: Kōbunken.

Tanaka A. 田中彰 et al. (eds) (1997, revised edns 1999, 2001, 2004, 2007) *Nihonshi A. Gendai kara no rekishi* 日本史A。現代からの歴史 [*Japanese history A. History from a contemporary view*], Tokyo: Tōkyō shoseki.

III
Self-assertion, revisionism and historical reconciliation

Conflicts and perspectives

9 The 'Tokyo Trial view of history' and its revision in contemporary Japan/East Asia

Steffi Richter

This chapter sets the whole Japanese textbook debate in the context of the broader difficulties that East Asia has experienced in coming to terms with its World War II past. It focuses on Japanese historical revisionism as expressed not only in textbooks but also in other media. It was precisely the so-called third textbook debate, which revolved around the presentation of Japanese history in school textbooks, that spurred the broader campaign of historical revisionism in contemporary Japan. The very name of the 1996-founded 'Japanese Society for History Textbook Reform' (Atarashii rekishi kyōkasho o tsukurukai, in short: Tsukurukai), which channelled these activities into a movement, exemplifies the importance attributed to the textbook medium. The undertakings of the actors involved, however, have by no means been limited to the sphere of textbooks. The purpose of the chapter, therefore, is to illuminate the complexity of these diverse interacting levels and media by focusing on recent controversies over the 'Tokyo Trial' as presented in two filmic takes on the subject. Thus, the chapter pursues themes alluded to in earlier chapters while considering the broader media and historiographical context in which history education operates.

Introduction

This chapter focuses on a time that heralded the end of the Cold War period in Japan. The radical changes of this time lead to fierce debates on who 'owned' the interpretation of World War II and the subsequent post-war period. Commonly, this time is thought to have started with the symbolic year '1989', which was of enormous impact in Japan – and therefore in East Asia as a whole. The bursting of the highly speculative Bubble Economy in 1989–90 caused a harsh economic crisis that accelerated some crisis phenomena, which were already observable in other social spheres. The death of Tennō Hirohito (裕仁; 1901–89) at age 87 not only represented the gradual demise of the generation that experienced and remembered World War II; what also ended was the Shōwa 昭和 era, a 'period of illustrious peace', that commenced with the enthronement of Hirohito in 1926. During the first third of his reign, he was the head of the state and the military, as well as the high priest of the (then state) Shintō religion. As such, he was involved in the decisions to wage war against China (from 1937) and the USA and other colonial powers in the Pacific region (from 1941; Bix 2008). With the unconditional surrender on 15 August 1945, these wars ended in a disastrous defeat for Japan. Without ever being called to account for his decisions, the Tennō remained on the throne after the war and acted as the 'symbol of the unity of the people'. This situation had paradoxical consequences for processing the past in Japan, especially with regard to 'communicating murder'. Therefore, in the following, it is unavoidable also to take a look back to the post-war period, which coincided with the Cold War period.

In Japan, a debate about Japanese modern history (a *Historikerstreit*) occurred in the mid 1990s and was initiated by conservative-nationalist circles (Richter 2003: 1–26). They declared that the post-war historical consciousness was in fact a 'masochistic view of history' (*jigyaku shikan* 自虐史観). School textbooks and other media constructed and spread an image of Japan and its modern history that made it impossible for young people to be proud of their own country and to develop a healthy national consciousness. One concept of the rhetorical strategy employed by these circles (which counted historians, scholars, writers and journalists among them) was the 'Tokyo Trial view of history' (*Tōkyō saiban shikan* 東京裁判史観)[1] and how it could be overcome. In what follows, I will describe how this concept is used to reinterpret the Tokyo Trial from the perspective of a right-wing conservative neo-nationalism, which attempts to downplay or even deny the 'Nanking Massacre', forced prostitution and labour and other war crimes, and to bring these revisionisms into a dominant position.

It is notable that, for the period under investigation here, i.e. the years after 1989, this struggle for meaning is only to a small extent observable in the debates among scholars (historians) and their scholarly-analytic text production. Rather, it was by the means of the print media (including *manga*), movies, television, video and DVD that history was staged and communicated in the form of 'narrations' (Assmann 2007: 149–54). Thus, to demonstrate the above-mentioned revision of the Tokyo Trial and other historical incidents, the essay will focus on two movies that have been recently discussed in Japan: first, the documentary drama *The seven 'death-row prisoners'* (*Shichinin no 'shikeishū'* 「七人の『死刑囚』」), the first part of a (not yet completed) trilogy entitled *The truth of Nanking* (*Nankin no shinjitsu* 「南京の真実」, director Mizushima Satoru 水島総 2008a);[2] and, second, the movie *Best wishes for tomorrow* (*Ashita e no yuigon* 「明日への遺言」, director Koizumi Takashi 小泉堯史 2008). On the occasion of the sixtieth anniversary of the Tokyo Trial, i.e. its sentences and executions, both movies approach the tribunal in their own way. In fact, this is a continuation of what was already observable on the occasion of the seventieth anniversary of the 'Nanking Massacre' (*Nankin gyakusatsu* 南京虐殺)[3] the year before: round anniversaries of incidents of the recent past become integrated into current debates, and their historical meaning is superimposed by a political meaning.

As a key starting point for the assessment of these developments, it should be emphasised that the growing mobilisation of history in the mass media since the mid 1990s is not an expression of some inability or unwillingness of 'the Japanese' to come to terms with their responsibility in the war, as is often asserted in the West, particularly in the German mass media. Rather, analysing these subjects reveals the ruptures within Japanese society over the ways in which the national and post-colonial history is remembered. An example of these ruptured memories was the debate that ensued around the fiftieth anniversary of the end of the Asian–Pacific War, in the summer of 1995. On that occasion, Prime Minister Murayama Tomiichi 村山富市 initiated a declaration of the Japanese Lower House that was meant to include an apology for the suffering inflicted on the Asian people 'through aggressive acts' in the past.[4] Though already strongly qualified after a ferocious debate, the opponents of this 'Resolution to renew the determination for peace on the basis of lessons learned from history' (*Rekishi o kyōkun ni heiwa e no ketsui o arata ni suru ketsugi* 歴史を教訓に平和への決意を新たにする決議) initiated numerous activities that aimed at a 'general settlement' with post-war Japan (which is, sometimes, also denoted as the 'post-war regime'). In the aftermath arose a whole network of conservative associations that were supported, not only by influential politicians, but also by related financial and mass media circles. This is true, for instance, for the Japanese Society for History Textbook Reform (*Atarashii rekishi kyōkasho o tsukurukai* 新しい歴史教科書をつくる会; *Tsukurukai* for short) founded in 1996, which is a central node of this network (Richter 2001, 2003, 2005). Although the *Tsukurukai* was dissolved in 2006 owing to inner conflicts (Tawara 2008), the historical revisionism it proposed has, through personal contacts with other organisations, developed into a movement that needs to be taken seriously.

A striking characteristic of this movement is its activism: the revisionists founded the *Tsukurukai* society in response to the first ever mention of the dark chapter of forced prostitution (the 'comfort women' system) between 1937 and 1945 in all officially authorised secondary school history textbooks. The aim was to reverse this 'masochistic view of history', of which this incident was, in their view, a prime example. Induced by various current events, one historical subject was brought up after another (this also, by the way, has an effect on the commercialisation and 'entertainmentisation' of history, which should not be underestimated): first, it was the 'comfort women', then the 'Nanking Massacre' and, finally, the 'Tokyo Trial' along with the 'Battle of Okinawa' (March–July 1945), which were also triggered by school textbooks and caused a ferocious debate.[5]

All these activities, however, also show the reactive nature of this movement: it is reactive owing to its conservative undertones, which cast a spell on the whole of crisis-ridden Japanese society during the so-called 'lost decade' of the 1990s; it is accompanied by the populace's anxiety over the ending of an era – an era that, albeit during the Cold War and under the protective 'umbrella' of the USA, had provided so many Japanese with collective and individual wealth, as well as stability and security. Furthermore, the movement can also be called reactive based on its confrontational, defensive stance towards the hitherto rarely discerned voices of memory that, since the 1990s, struggle 'to acquire a place in the publicly recounted war story' and that are an 'assault on the heroic narrative'[6] accepted until now (Gluck 2007: 66). Although it is noteworthy that, in 2005, the subject of 'forced prostitution' was removed from all officially approved secondary school history textbooks, the voices of women from Korea and other Asian countries who had been sexually enslaved by the Japanese military during the war and the activities of national and transnational NGOs or the so-called Asian Americans resulted in a deeper than ever entrenchment of this subject in Japanese public discourse (Gluck 2007: 69). The 'Asian factor', which did not return to the geopolitical agenda and into the collective memory of Japanese society before '1989' (cf. the two events mentioned at the beginning) played, and still plays, a central, if contested, role as a wider and sustainable public commemoration of the other topics as well.

The two aforementioned movies, *The seven 'death-row prisoners'* (*Shichinin no 'shikeishū'*), the first part of *The truth of Nanking* (*Nankin no shinjitsu*) and *Best wishes for tomorrow* (*Ashita e no yuigon*) may serve as evidence for these developments. *The seven 'death-row prisoners'* deals with the seven Class A war criminals who were sentenced to death in the Tokyo Trial and executed in December 1948 (cf. the *Excursus: war crimes trials and Japan*). The director, Mizushima Satoru, claiming again and again that, allegedly, a 'Nanking campaign' was produced by China as part of an anti-Japanese media war, describes his trilogy as a contribution to the preservation of security in his own country (Mizushima 2007: 86). Accordingly, 'Asia' appears here as a threat in the shape of the political, economic and military superpower 'China', against which every Japanese must proudly fight. In the following section, I will first illuminate the context of the production of this movie, and then analyse the movie itself by picking out some topics that are relevant with regard to the aforementioned struggle for meaning.

The truth of Nanking: *the seven 'death-row prisoners'*

Since the beginning of 2007, the Japanese mass media have increasingly reported on activities dedicated to the 'examination of the Nanking Incident'. This was to counter the rising 'anti-Japanese propaganda' inside and outside Japan, which was said to be expected in connection with the upcoming seventieth anniversary of the 'surrender of Nanking' (*Nankin kanraku* 南京陥落) – as the massacre is euphemistically labelled by the so-called 'illusion faction' (*maboroshi-ha* まぼろし派), which consists of people who argue that only a small number of 'incidents' (*jiken* 事件) took place in Nanking and therefore maintain that there can be no talk of a '(great) massacre' (*(dai-) gyakusatsu* (大)虐殺). At a press conference on 24 January 2007, Mizushima announced that, in reaction to various Chinese and American film projects about Nanking, he would shoot a Japanese film entitled *The truth of Nanking* as an answer to such 'propaganda'.[7] This is not the first time that Mizushima has become active in this field. Since 2004, he has been engaged in the production of the web-based cultural channel *Japan Culture Channel Sakura* (*Nippon bunka channeru Sakura* 日本文化チャンネル桜, or *Channeru Sakura*, for short), which is officially supported by members of the *Tsukurukai*, such as one of its founders, Fujioka Nobukatsu (藤岡信勝), who has his own timeslots in the programme. Owing to the programme's themes and the prominent figures that support *Channeru Sakura*, the channel has to be understood as a key node in a network of protagonists, who pursue polarising and often even defamatory historical politics, especially towards China and Korea, which resonates or even coincides with the ambitions of the ruling right-wing political circles in Japan.

With the help of this network, Mizushima was able to mobilise financial and other resources for the production of his movie.[8] On 14 December 2007, a symposium took place that announced the completion of the trilogy's first part. On 25 January 2008, the movie had its first non-public screening at the Yomiuri Hall in Tokyo, which was preceded by a press conference with more than 1,000 people attending.[9] Although the movie has not yet been released in Japanese cinemas, it was shown at nationwide non-public screenings (*shishakai* 試写会) for free and open to everybody who registers in advance by telephone.[10] Occasionally, Mizushima himself travels the country as well, introducing the movie. At these events, he not only verbalises the aforementioned scenario of threat and conspiracy, but also compares himself and his combatants, with their aim to spread the truth about Nanking by affirming, 'And yet there was no Nanking Massacre, never!', to Galileo Galilei's defiance towards the church ('And yet it moves!') after his recantation before the Inquisition (ironically, this myth has been debunked recently; Mizushima 2008: 3). According to Mizushima, China is merely interested in distracting people from its own barbaric past (recent and older) by spreading the lie that 300,000 Chinese people – civilians and soldiers – were killed by Japanese troops in the aftermath of the fall of Nanking. Moreover, it is China's alleged aim – for example through movies, which are part of a 'Nanking Massacre campaign' – to establish an image of 'Japan' as an external enemy, which could then serve as a bogeyman for the Chinese people to unload their hate when the internal contradictions in China become obvious after the Olympic Games (Mizushima 2008: 3).

It is the movie's declared aim to convince the people in Japan and the world[11] that the seven men sentenced and executed at the Tokyo Trial were in fact martyrs (*junnansha* 殉難者), who fell prey to the political will of the victors (here, the term Class A criminals (*A-kyū senpan* A級戦犯) is put in quotation marks):

> This [*The seven 'death-row prisoners'*] is a movie that consequently sticks to the truth and focuses on those people who move us. Accordingly, this

movie will leave an impression on the people and engage the sympathy of the whole world. Moreover, this movie, based on human documents depicting the last hours of the seven war commanders in a frank and honest manner, is a message to the people who will live 50 or 100 years in the future. Despite the fact that these seven men were mistaken in various aspects, we are convinced that it is precisely them, the well-known 'Class A war criminals', who can transmit the true shape and the spirit of the pre-war Japanese to the world.

(Eiga *Nankin no shinjitsu* seisaku iinkai 2008: 5)

Thus, the filmmakers' intention is not only to tell the 'historical truth'; they want to show the seven men as proud, brave and patriotic humans – attributes that, according to them, the present-day Japanese people lack as much as the ability to face death with dignity. (In this respect, Mizushima spoke of a 'splendid death' (*rippana shinikata* 立派な死に方) at one of his various public appearances.)

Next, the content of the movie itself will be analysed in order to demonstrate how its alleged 'historicity' is subordinated, from the very beginning of the film, to the aforementioned propagandistic-ideological aspiration to reconstruct Japanese identity by staging and interpreting historical sources. The way in which this happens is based on a grotesque and banal logic: the 'truth about Nanking' lies simply in the fact that it was impossible for a 'Nanking Massacre' to have taken place, as the Japanese are not able to order – to say nothing of committing! – such an atrocious act. Revisionists admit to the occurrence of single offences against the law of war then in force, but they maintain that such trespasses were always strongly punished if they became known. But, apart from that, it was a time of war, and killing is always part of war; the Japanese military did not act differently from the military of other countries, the revisionists claim. Based on the general assumption that the Tokyo Trial was an act of 'victors' justice' (*shōsha no sabaki* 勝者の裁き),[12] two premises that structure the whole movie can be identified: first, the argument, *tu quoque*!, or 'you, too!' Second, the 'humanisation' or 'glorification' of the seven men sentenced to death at the Tokyo Trial.

The movie starts with footage of the air raids on Tokyo by American B-29 bombers of 10 March 1945. The sequence is accompanied by the following comment: 'For the first time in the history of humanity, 100,000 people were massacred in the course of only one night.' This is followed by a sequence that includes photographs and footage from the atomic bombing of Hiroshima and Nagasaki in August 1945, which 'killed 300,000 people'. All this is accompanied by the assertion that 'it was from this very day, that the preparations for the lie of the 300,000 dead of the "Nanking Massacre" started'. One intention behind this number play is to suggest that it was, in fact, the American military who killed hundreds of thousands of civilians through their 'indiscriminate bombings' (*musabetsu bakudan* 無差別爆弾) (which were never put to trial in accordance to International Law).[13] Another

The 'Tokyo Trial view of history' 189

one is to invert the chronology of the course of war as such. Both 'Pearl Harbor', the starting point of the so-called 'Pacific War', and 'Nanking', a part of the Chinese–Japanese War (breaking out on 7 July 1937), occurred in advance of the American bombings. Furthermore, the past is narrated in a way that juxtaposes the 400,000 'actually' killed Japanese with the 'lie' of 300,000 dead Chinese people. Proof of the former is delivered with the images, whereas the latter have no images and thus are implied to be fictitious. In a sense, the movie develops its subsequent storyline on the basis of this 'lie of a lie'.

Naturally, the Tokyo Trial plays an important role in this movie. In the next sequence, original footage of the trial is used, which fits into the aforementioned narration: Ben B. Blakeney, who defended the accused Tōgō Shigenori (東郷茂徳; 1882–1950) and Umezu Yoshijirō (梅津美治郎; 1882–1949), is used as a principal witness to emphasise that the victor, too, had committed war crimes. In May 1946, Blakeney, in a now well-known speech, argued that it was actually a legal mistake to hold the defendants individually responsible for a war that was actually the act of a state. If killing in times of war or on the battlefield was to be prosecuted as the act of an individual, it was also necessary to mention the names of those who planned, ordered and executed the dropping of the atomic bombs. Since the 1950s, those critics who wanted to relativise or even deny Japan's war guilt have drawn their arguments from this viewpoint. Mizushima instrumentalised Blakeney's pleading, too: on the one hand, he uses it in the sense of the aforementioned logic of *tu quoque* (you, too!) by justifying the actions of his own country with the help of the example of other countries; and, on the other hand, denying the individual guilt of the defendants with regard to all charges lets him meet the second premise of the movie – the idea of denying the term 'war criminal' and turning the executed men into martyrs instead.

At the aforementioned press conference in the spring of 2008, Mizushima called the protagonists of his movie *rippana kata* 立派な方 – 'great men'. At the beginning of the film, Mizushima shows the 'true faces' of the defendants using original footage from 12 November 1948, the day the verdict 'death by hanging' was pronounced seven times. In the following part of the documentary drama, various events, historically provable by written and oral documents, are re-enacted by actors in great detail (*tetteiteki ni chūjitsu ni* 徹底的に忠実に). Particular focus is put here on former Army General Matsui Iwane (松井石根; 1878–1948), who represents both controversies, the 'Nanking Massacre' and the 'Tokyo Trial', as it was under his command that the Central China Expeditionary Force took over Nanking and committed the subsequent atrocities. The final 'judgement of the International Military Tribunal for the Far East' reads as follows: 'Estimates made at a later date indicate that the total number of civilians and prisoners of war murdered in Nanking and its vicinity during the first six weeks of the Japanese occupation was over 200,000' (Hyper War Foundation 2003: 1015).[14]

For the following two and half hours, the movie minutely describes the two days between the announcement of the date of their execution on 21 December

1948 and the execution of Matsui and the other six men on death row at Sugamo Prison (巣鴨プリズン).[15] For that purpose, Mizushima used detailed replications, not only of the prison cells, but also of the execution room. It is shown, again and again, how Allied Forces check the functional efficiency of the execution apparatus, located in this room. Most notably, the movie shows in great detail how Matsui, accompanied by the Buddhist prison chaplain Hanayama Shinshō (花山信勝; 1898–1995), prepares for his death.[16] In the movie, Hanayama talks with Matsui and the other six men, prays for them, makes them recite Sutra, prepares a religious farewell ceremony after their final meal, takes their poems and farewell letters and finally accompanies them to their execution and wishes them a pleasant last journey. The slowness of these deeply religious acts evokes dignity and sympathy. Even the guarding victors pay deference to them. The dramaturgy is interrupted only once to 'prove' the Japanese military's discipline and high level of civilisation. In this sequence, Matsui's thoughts travel to a statue of the Buddhist goddess of mercy (*Kōa kannon* 興亜観音) in Atami, to which he made a donation in 1940 to commemorate the dead soldiers on both sides of the Chinese–Japanese War (this is to prove that he was a proponent of the ideal of *kōa* 興亜 – the idea of a commonly strong Asia). Moreover, there are parts of documentaries that show the apparent peacefulness of the occupied city of Nanking after the battle. They were filmed by Japanese cinematographer Shiroi Shigeru 白井茂, who had followed the Japanese troops to the battlefields in order to capture their glorious victory for Japanese audiences. This sequence is also accompanied by written comments taken directly from the revisionists' rhetorical armory. They pose the following questions: How is it possible to kill 300,000 people in a city whose population had already shrunk to 250,000? Where are the corpses that were allegedly covering the streets? Is it not more likely that the faces of the people presented in Shiroi's movies express relief about the gradual restoration of order under the Japanese military? This rhetoric falls far behind the results of historical research. Nevertheless, the movie claims authenticity that is suggested in two ways:

First, the use of documentary film material suggests reality 'how it really was'. In a conversation reproduced in a programme on Mizushima's movie, revisionist historian Higashinakano Shūdō (東中野修道) claims that Shiroi's documentary footage shows 'Nanking as it really was at that time'. Second, the director attempts to reproduce the scene of the trial and the execution in as detailed a manner as possible. However, according to German historian Hans Mommsen, originally referring to the Hitler movie *Der Untergang* (*Downfall*), employing such cinematographic effects does not mean producing historical evidence (as quoted in Wildt (2005), first paragraph). Authenticity has become an exposed myth, especially when it comes to staged forms of expression such as the 'documentary drama' (therefore also called 'faction'). The producers of *The truth of Nanking* not only insist on being authentic, they also equate this asserted 'naturalism' with historicity and truthfulness. However, this is precisely what is lacking not only in the movie itself, but also in the whole discourse about it (and all other topics that historical revisionism tries to reinterpret). Historicity, as we know after the linguistic/cultural turn, can be understood as awareness of the relativity of one's own perspective, as the insight that historical facts are products of contentions with other perspectives and perceptions. Hence, truthfulness can no longer be reduced to the assertion of 'facts', but has become something that implies the possibility of experiencing (and the readiness to be responsible 'for what we accept as true' – Foucault, as quoted in Daniel (2001: 388)). At the aforementioned press conference, Mizushima announced that 'we want to launch the Nanking International Court (*Nankin kokusai daihōtei* 南京国際大法廷) this summer', which will gather representatives from China, the producers of other movies on Nanking and Japanese scholars who assert that the massacre had actually taken place. This sounds very open and pluralistic, and Mizushima, for his part, is convinced that 'if we can discuss our position fairly, we will never lose! We will necessarily destroy all these lies!' However, he also says that his challenge is unlikely to be accepted. According to a member of the Lower House, Nishimura Shingo 西村慎吾, who supports Mizushima, 'we have to win this war over ideas. Otherwise, the soul of our people will be annihilated.' This is a language that has the same structure as the movie: whatever arguments are exchanged, the only truth that is legitimate in the end is one that serves the preservation of the Japanese identity and the reconstruction of pride and dignity – as it is embodied by the *The seven 'death-row prisoners'*.

Best wishes for tomorrow

The second movie, *Best wishes for tomorrow*, was shown in Japanese cinemas for eight weeks in March and April 2008. The film was directed by Koizumi Takashi (who was born in 1944 and is a disciple of Kurosawa Akira 黒澤明) and produced by Hara Masato (原正人). The movie deals with the trial of a Class B war criminal, former Lieutenant General Okada Tasuku (岡田資; 1890–1948), who was commander of the 13th Area Army in the Tōkai region in 1945. (This event is also known as the 'Okada case' or 'Okada trial' and took place in Yokohama from March to May 1948.)[17] Together with nineteen of his subordinates, he was accused of the summary execution of thirty-eight captured American airmen who participated in the bombing raids on Nagoya (Japan's third largest city) on 14 May 1945, which caused large casualties among the population. Okada regarded the captured airmen, not as POWs, but as war criminals and ordered their beheading. During his trial, he took personal responsibility for the execution order. In his opinion, the air raids on Nagoya were indiscriminate (*musabetsu bakugeki* 無差別爆撃) and therefore a violation of International Law. Not only his defence, but also the prosecutor and the judge came to understand his position. Nevertheless, Okada insisted that the executions were carried out, not as retaliation against military actions – which American Military Law allowed for – but as judicial punishments, which in the case of POWs was not permitted according to

American Military Law. Although Okada was informed about this distinction, he did not change his testimony. So, finally, Okada was found guilty and sentenced to death by hanging. As a consequence, Okada's subordinates evaded the death sentence, because their commander took full responsibility for the executions.

This movie picks up as a topic the debates on the different appraisals of the bombings, the treatment of POWs, as well as an officer of high rank taking responsibility for his actions.[18] The fact that the subordinates owe their lives to their commander endows the movie with a considerably emotionalised dramaturgy: here, Okada is presented as a father figure who – regardless of his own fate – reassures his 'prison sons' and encourages them for their future. Owing to his deeply rooted Buddhist faith, Okada radiates a calmness and dignity in the movie that causes his subordinates to call him 'father'. Another narrative strand of the movie is Okada's 'real' family, which follows the trial sitting in the auditorium. The movie begins with the following words of his wife, Okada Haruko (岡田温子), saying, 'Despite the fact that my husband is standing in the dock, I am still proud to be the wife of Okada Tasuku'. And it concludes with the words of her husband saying, 'Haruko, everyday you take pains to follow this process without us being allowed to talk to each other. Yet still, I can read from your changing facial expressions what you mean. To exchange a smile, that's enough. It tells me that I will win this in any event.' Here, the cohesion and wordless love of a family are presented as ideals that Japanese society has lost, together with the other aforementioned values, namely self-responsibility, pride, dignity and bravery. According to an interview with producer Harada published in the conservative newspaper *Sankei shinbun* 産経新聞 on 29 February 2008, Okada personifies the ideals that the Japanese people once embodied and which they look up to again today. In the same interview, he also estimated, before its premiere, that more than one million people would see this movie.[19]

In this respect, the movie seems to pursue the same goal as *The truth of Nanking*, as it emphasises a Japaneseness, the former common sense and values of which disappeared or became threatened 'from the outside'. To director Koizumi, his movie is therefore not merely a historical drama. To him, the most important thing to be learned from history is the ability to listen to those who grappled with a fate inflicted upon them and who decorously fulfilled their duties. In his opinion, Okada was such a man. Accordingly, the aim of the movie is to display his last months in a 'true and unprejudiced manner' (cf. the homepage of the movie under the link 'comments'). With their explicitly didactic aim to communicate something to contemporary Japanese society – particularly the younger generation – the movies *Best wishes for tomorrow* (as a work of art and as a 'text' that goes beyond it) and *The truth of Nanking* participate in a discourse that mobilises the past in order to refound identities and, thus, revises history.

Finally, I would like to focus on certain important master signifiers ('point de capiton' (Lacan)) and discoursive strategies of argumentation to reflect upon the continuities and discontinuities of 'communicating murder' in the post-war and post-post-war period in Japan. First, it is necessary to mention two important differences between the two movies that also reflect differences in the understanding of history within the conservative–nationalist scene.

The movie *Best wishes for tomorrow* also starts with a sequence of documentary footage to introduce its story: it opens with Picasso's *Guernica*, which is said to remember the first global area bombing of civilians. This is accompanied by a female voice-over saying that, already in 1922–3, a ban on this type of warfare against non-military targets was proposed. Subsequently, documentary footage of the air raids of German bombers in England, the English bombings of Dresden, and the bombings of Nanking and Chunking, as well as of Tokyo and Nagoya, are shown. Thereby, Japan is lined up with other culprits who caused the death of a great number of civilians, too. However, what is not expounded as a problem here is the fact that these bombings were part of different wars: some of them were part of wars of aggression, others were the cruel strategy of a defence war. In his book *The views of war of the Japanese* (*Nihonjin no sensōkan* 日本人の戦争観), Yoshida Yutaka 吉田裕 claims that it was the booming war accounts (*senkimono* 戦記物) of the mid 1950s, being published in the wake of a reappearing political-official nationalism in the popular mass media, that failed to refer to the past war as a whole (Yoshida, Y. 1995: 92). For the most part, these were a peculiarly paradoxical mixture of a fascination with technological and tactical details of particular wars or battles and – against the background of individual losses – a simultaneous repulsion of incapable and irresponsible military officers (especially of the army), accompanied by the general pacifistic atmosphere of post-war Japan: 'No more war!'

It is necessary to see all this in the context of 'victors' justice' – a key element of the aforementioned 'Tokyo Trial view of history'. The movie *Best wishes for tomorrow*, however, which deals with the course of the 'Okada Trial', does not apply this view of history. Moreover, contrary to the movie *The truth of Nanking*, where the Japanese protagonists are heroised while the Americans remain anonymous, the latter are endowed with individual personalities as prosecutor, defence counsel and judge, who are treated with respect and sympathy. It seems as if the 'fate of the process that resulted naturally from the war' hovers above everybody. According to Koizumi, his aforementioned words are not merely addressed to the Japanese, but are universally valid.

Concluding reflections

The following elements of the contemporary representation of the Japanese war and post-war history are part of a discursive field that historian Carol Gluck described as a 'terrain of vernacular memory': the opinions of people who have seen these movies, as published in the print media or on Internet forums. Gluck considers this vast and amorphous terrain of 'vernacular memory' as particularly important in the case of Japan, as the state failed to meet the continual memory challenges it faced [...and] ceded the action to society, which, ironically perhaps, took up the cause of war memory with more force and perseverance than in countries like France, where the government addressed war memory as its own political task.

(Gluck 2007: 55).[20]

Accordingly, the opinions of the cinema-going public are (similar to public opinion polls) an important part of this terrain, because they

> figured on a plane somewhere between the consumption and the production of collective views, [... the opinions people express] occupy a kind of middle ground between what they *ought* to say and what they might *really* be thinking. The former is likely to be publicly conditioned; the latter personal, more for the kitchen table.
>
> (Gluck 2007: 55)

Put differently, what takes place with regard to certain topics is a constant 'roaming' between publicly conditioned articulations and their individual 'appropriation' (interpretation) in the sense of the aforementioned struggle for meaning. This becomes obvious through topics that are brought up in the following statements on the movie *Best wishes for tomorrow*:

> First I thought that this is one of those stupid war movies, but then I was impressed. The scenes of the trial, which make up almost half of the movie, include various messages. What is, for instance, the meaning of leadership? Moreover, questions of organisation, the stupidity of wars, the value of life, family, severe criticism of the current situation that lacks any philosophy, life and death, or how men live.
>
> (Employee, age: 38)

A twenty-year-old student writes that he has learned a lot about the Far Eastern military trials that is not written in school textbooks. On his way home, he asked himself what he would do: 'In my opinion, this movie is not addressed at those people who did experience war themselves, rather, it is a reminder to all the people who do not know the war. Is there really no Samurai in Japan anymore?'

Another 20-year-old student asks himself if this is the Japan his ancestors actually wished for. 'And "responsibility", is this not something that is disrespected nowadays?'

> The way how Lieutenant General Okada cared for his family, his subordinates, and his country made my heart beat faster. He did not only save the lives of his subordinates, but also the 'pride' of the Japanese [...] I would like to become a Japanese female who is able to be fully self-responsible.
>
> (Employee in her thirties)

'Lieutenant General Okada's life reminds me of the Way of the Warrior (*bushidō* 武士道) that today's Japanese have forgotten' (member of the Diet, 59 years old).

> Without having experienced war, I grew up in a time when things were getting better in Japan. The movie reminded me that we owe this normal life to the people who experienced war at the cost of great sacrifices, and who did everything for Japan at the risk of their own lives.
> (Housewife in her fifties)

> I wish that many young people who did not experience the war go and see this movie, foremost those ones who hold high positions, since it makes you reflect on responsibility. I thought of my dead grandfather who was at war. If only I had asked him more about his past.
> (Woman, 22 years old)

> Fujita Makoto [famous actor who plays the role of Okada, S.R.] was fantastic! At the end of the movie an elderly women sitting next to me impressed me by saying: 'If only all of the soldiers would have been like him.'
> (Woman, 22 years old)[21]

These representative comments are neither sensational nor particularly new with regard to their content or rhetoric. The early post-war discourse on martyrdom for a better future that blamed the 'irresponsible'[22] military leaders – except the Tennō – for the lost war has already been studied by historian John Dower, who focused on the question: 'What do you tell the dead when you lose?'. According to Dower, this discourse described the military leaders as having deceived their own people (*damasareta* 騙された), who, consequently, must be considered as victims. It was on this basis that the death of soldiers was given a meaning: 'The sacrifices of the Japanese dead might be made meaningful by sloughing off "old filth" and creating a new society and culture' (Dower 1999: 487). This argumentative strategy is not only equivalent to the assertion that Japan would not be as successful without their deaths,[23] but also to the view of current neo-national critics: corruption, egoism or the decay of the family in the present time conjures up the anger of the dead soldiers who gave their lives for Japan and who therefore return as vengeful spirits (*onryō* 怨霊).

With regard to the usage of the rhetoric involving the 'way of the warrior', I have already referred to Yoshida, who hinted at the booming 'war accounts' (or records) already in the mid 1950s, the dissemination and textual nuances of which have changed considerably over the decades. According to Yoshida, with the rise of Japan as an economic superpower since the end of the 1970s, these popular war records gradually entered the world of business and management as well. They were understood as handbooks for the 'corporate samurai' – the salaryman – to give answers to questions such as: How should managers behave in borderline situations? How should expanding companies be structured in order to survive crises? Moreover, texts on management were written in the style of the *senkimono* (Yoshida, Y. 1995: 148–53). These 'corporate *senkimono*' reached their heyday at the end of the 1980s as didactic writings that can teach businessmen how to avoid mistakes. Here, the defeat of World War II was understood as the defeat of the Japanese military as an organisation; it was the obvious aim of these publications to learn from this defeat and to apply it in a positive manner to the companies of the present. Accordingly, the aforementioned movies similarly display single military officers who are presented as 'great men' (*rippana kata*), in opposition to a Japan that is complacent in its peace-orientation (*heiwa boke no Nihon* 平和ボケの日本), and whose cool-headed and dignified attitude should be exemplary for the young generation.

Finally, there is the topic of 'responsibility', which is included in almost all of the comments. It seems that the fact that Okada is appreciated by most moviegoers as the only military officer (or at least one out of a few) who has admitted his responsibility hints at the negative image of the relationship between military leadership and responsibility, at least in the vernacular memory of the past decades. The current reinterpretation certainly needs to be seen in the context of the neo-liberal scenarios of crisis and attempts to overcome it, which can be perceived in Japan (and elsewhere). In these scenarios, among other topics such as free markets or flexibility, first and foremost, responsibility is emphasised: responsibility for oneself and – with a neo-nationalist undertone – for the community as well. As one example, the new 'Fundamental Law of Education' can be mentioned, enacted in 2006. Here, the ideal of self-responsible and autonomous individuals who are proud of their own country is translated into law as a form of cultural standard (*Leitkultur*). Officially, and with the help of the mass media, these virtues are demanded from employees who were thrown out of their career tracks through processes of deregulation and who should meet a new challenge (*sai-charenji* 最チャレンジ) – a piece of advice Okada gives to his 'boys', too – and from young people who were not given the opportunity to get on to such a track. The moviegoers are apparently 'publicly conditioned' with regard to these topics, but they probably endow 'flexibility' or 'self-responsibility' also with their very own personal imaginations – a 'self-meaning' (*Eigensinn*). The comments analysed here, however, all correspond more or less with the understanding of responsibility, love and dignity communicated in the movie *Best wishes for tomorrow*, which remains paternalistic–patriotic.

According to the director, the movie aims to contribute to the reconciliation between former enemies – Japan and the USA. Where, however, is 'Asia' in these movies? The reason why the two movies do not contribute to this topic lies in their thematic foci. Nevertheless, even in a broader context – namely in the many comments and reviews by the directors, moviegoers or the mass media – Asia does not appear. To Yoshida Yutaka, the 'absence of Asia' was another important continuity of the debates on World War II and war responsibility in the whole post-war period. He explains it with the international situation after 1945, when Japan transformed from a former enemy into the 'junior partner' of the USA and, thus, into a stronghold against communism in Asia. Moreover, by shifting all war responsibility to the military, 'some kind of tacit agreement developed between the Tennō and the people to not thematise war responsibility' (Yoshida, Y. 2005: 96). This is a process in which the USA, too, played a crucial role by decisively contributing to repression of the development of 'perpetrator consciousness' (*Täterbewusstsein*) in Japan, particularly with regard to Asia. Certainly, this is a legacy that still prevails. However, as mentioned in the beginning, with the 'Asian factor' returning to the geo-political agenda since the 1990s, the (collective) memory of Japanese society was set in motion. Within historiography, according to Yoshida, research on war crimes and war responsibility finally became an established field, and, in collaboration with (post-)colonial studies, it is not only (East) Asia, but also Japanese modernity, that is being reconsidered. This new knowledge is also perceived within the public sphere (journalism, civil movements), and mutual impulses were initiated, which finally led to a more complex perception of the relationship between victims and perpetrators (Yoshida, Y. 2005: 114–18). Historical revisionists react to this new situation by trying to reduce this complexity by constructing an apparently new, but in fact old, master narration, consciously neglecting Asia, which functions as the new enemy. One example of this process is the movie *The truth of Nanking*. The movie *Best wishes for tomorrow*, on the other hand, stands in the tradition of an abstract pacifism accompanied by nationalism – an 'arrangement' that promises positive (inclusive) identification and that was so characteristic of post-war Japan. Today, however, this introverted nationalism has become more intolerant and, more often, turns against the 'invasion' of the global world, against a cosmopolitisation of one's own 'lifeworld' (*Lebenswelt*). This was probably not the intention of the director, but that does not make the issue less problematic.

Excursus: war crimes trials and Japan[24]

Trials prosecuting war crimes committed by the Japanese Imperial Army in Asia between 1931 and 1945 took place from October 1945 to April 1951. Most well known is the 'International Military Tribunal for the Far East' (IMTFE, *Kyokutō kokusai gunji saiban* 極東国際軍事裁判), also called the 'Tokyo War Crimes Trial', 'Tokyo Trial' or 'Tokyo Tribunal' (*Tōkyō saiban* 東京裁判).

Between September and December 1945, more than 100 former military, political and intellectual leaders were arrested as 'Class A war crimes' suspects (*A-kyū sensō hanzai* A級戦争犯罪; *A-kyū senpan* A級戦犯, for short) and held in Sugamo Prison in Tokyo. Twenty-eight of the defendants were brought to trial (fifteen from the Army, three from the Navy, seven politicians and one diplomat) and accused of 'crimes against peace' (with the 'conspiracy' (*inbō*

陰謀) charge to wage wars of aggression at the center of the trial), 'crimes against humanity'[25] and 'conventional war crimes'. Inaugurated on 19 January 1946 by the Supreme Commander of the Allied Powers (SCAP), General Douglas MacArthur, the tribunal itself started on 3 May 1946 and ended on 12 November 1948, when the sentences against twenty-five defendants were pronounced (two died before the trial had ended; one was released due to a mental breakdown): seven were sentenced to death by hanging (Doihara Kenji 土肥原賢二, 1883–1948; Hirota Kōki 広田弘毅, 1887–1948; Itagaki Seishirō 板垣征四郎, 1885–1948; Kimura Heitarō 木村兵太郎, 1888–1948; Matsui Iwane 松井石根, 1878–1948; Mutō Akira 武藤章, 1892–1948; Tōjō Hideki 東条英機, 1884–1948); sixteen were sentenced to life imprisonment (three died in prison, the others were released in 1955); one was sentenced to 20 years (dying in 1950), one to 7 years imprisonment (released in 1950, then becoming foreign minister, 1954–6). One day after the death sentences were carried out on 23 December 1948, the remaining nineteen Class A war crime suspects were released from Sugamo Prison, even though it was initially stated that far more would be indicted once the first trial had finished.

Eleven judges presided over the Tokyo Trial – one from each Allied Power: USA, UK, France, the Netherlands, Australia (with William Webb as the president), the Philippines, China, the Soviet Union, Republic of China (today Taiwan), India and New Zealand. Joseph Keenan (USA) was appointed as chief prosecutor.

Besides trials against Class A war criminals, there were also trials against persons accused of 'minor' crimes. 'Conventional war crimes' – called 'Class B war crimes' – were distinguished from 'crimes against humanity' – categorised as 'Class C war crimes' – but in Japan they are usually summarised as 'B/C Class war crimes' (*B/C-kyū sensō hanzai* BC級戦争犯罪): atrocities, committed mostly by lower-ranking soldiers. Altogether, 5,700 B/C Class war criminals (among them 148 Koreans and 173 Taiwanese) were accused in 2,244 local trials, conducted by the respective victorious powers:

- USA: 456 trials, from October 1945 to April 1949, in Manila, Yokohama, Shanghai, Guam, Kwajalein Atoll;
- UK: 330, from January 1946 to December 1948, in Singapore, Hong Kong, Malaysia, Burma;
- France: 39, in 1945, in Saigon;
- Australia: 294, from October 1945 to April 1951, in Australia, Singapore, New Guinea, Hong Kong and five other places in the Pacific area;
- Netherlands: 448 trials, from August 1946 to December 1949, in Batavia, Borneo, Sumatra and other places;
- Philippines: 27 trials, from August 1947 to December 1949, in Manila;
- China/Taiwan: 605 trials, from April 1946 to January 1949, in Taipei and nine places in mainland China;
- PR China: 1956 trials in two places (no death sentences!);
- Soviet Union: December 1949, in Chabarovsk.

Altogether, 984 of the 5,700 prosecuted B/C war criminals (23 Koreans and 21 Taiwanese) were sentenced to death, 475 to life imprisonment, 2,944 to more limited prison terms; 1018 were found not guilty.

The first B/C war crimes trial, conducted by the US Army in Manila, began on 8 October 1945. In this controversial tribunal, the former General Yamashita Tomoyuki (山下奉文; 1885–1946) was accused of the 'Manila Massacre' committed by troops under his command. There was, however, good reason to question his command over these units (i.e. establishment of the concept of negative/vicarious responsibility). Eventually, he was sentenced to death (8 December 1945; executed on 23 February 1946). The B/C war crimes trials (except in PR China and Soviet Union) ended in April 1951 in Australia.

In 1958, all paroled persons in Japan classified as Class A war criminals (1955) were granted amnesty; the last eighteen Class B/C war criminals were released from Sugamo Prison, which was subsequently closed. In the following months, a movement started to enshrine the 'heroic souls' of the Class B/C war criminals – and eventually also of the Class A war criminals – in the Yasukuni Shrine, supported by state institutions (especially the Ministry of Health and Welfare), the shrine itself and conservative circles. Founded in 1869 and dedicated to glorifying the soldiers who fell in the name of the Emperor during all modern colonial wars, the shrine played an important role as a symbol of Japanese militarism. According to the Shintō Directive issued by the occupying Allied Forces in December 1945, it was removed from state control. Between April 1959 and October 1967, altogether 984 executed Class B/C war criminals were enshrined in this 'holy space'. The Class A war criminals followed quietly in 1978, and, since Prime Minister Nakasone Yasuhiro paid the shrine a first official visit in August 1985, Yasukuni worship has been seen as a justification of Japan's wars, in particular by neighbouring Asian countries.

Some problems of the Tokyo Trial

1   The most serious problem of the Tokyo Trial, involving enormous consequences for the whole process of coming to terms with (and remembering) war in post-war Japan, was the decision not to accuse the Emperor/Tennō Hirohito of war crimes (which was announced on 3 April 1946) and to exclude him from the trial. This decision was the result of 'collaboration' between different key players, such as the American-led International Prosecution Section (IPS), Japanese officials, SCAP and the Tennō, as well as the war crimes suspects themselves. The main reasoning was that only the continuation of the Emperor System could prevent Japan from a chaotic breakdown and guarantee its democratic reconstruction; and that it was 'essential to thwart Soviet-led "communisation of the entire world"' (Dower 1999: 323). In the following years, the image (or rather myth) was constructed of an almost saintly, peace-loving Emperor, who

had been deceived by the military leaders, just like his subjects (the 'Japanese people'). Blaming the militarists and 'big capitalists' (*zaibatsu* 財閥) for the war, or more precisely for defeat, the door was opened to present the Emperor and the common people as their victims. 'Even the Emperor gets away without taking responsibility, so there is no need for us to take responsibility, no matter what we did', recorded a 20-year-old ex-serviceman of the Navy in his diary, in February 1946 (Dower 1999: 344).

2 This 'tacit agreement' between the Tennō and 'the people' has contributed to the 'double standard' perception of the Tokyo Trial and has strongly influenced the way the war is remembered in post-war Japan. According to the concept of this 'double standard', as it was developed by Yoshida Yutaka, Japan, on the one hand, unavoidably accepts responsibility for the war in the sense of Article 11 of the San Francisco Treaty.[26] On the other hand, in Japan itself, responsibility for the war has been largely ignored, at least until recently, 'when, from the late 1990s, Koreans and Chinese repeatedly evoked Japan's "history problem" (*rekishi ninshiki mondai* 歴史認識問題)' (Gluck 2007: 54).

3 This point of ignorance refers to another problem: the lack of reflection on, and awareness of, the fact that Japan was a colonial power waging a war of aggression against China and other Asian countries and committing atrocities. There are various reasons for this kind of amnesia, and, again, the specific post-war US–Japan symbiosis plays an important role: from the end of 1945, it was officially forbidden by the occupying forces to name the last war the 'Greater East Asia War' (*Dai Tōa sensō* 大東亜戦争, beginning with the Japanese attack on Pearl Harbor on 8 December 1941 and the invasion in Malaysia, Thailand and Bataan/Philippines). Renaming it the 'Pacific War' (*Taiheiyō sensō* 太平洋戦争), the Civil Information and Education Section (CIE) of the SCAP GHQ started a campaign to inform the Japanese people, via newspaper and radio series, about what happened in the (Japanese–American) Pacific War. Although the invasions of Manchuria (1931) and China (1937) were mentioned, neither the Chinese anti-Japanese resistance nor the problem of colonial rule in Taiwan and Korea gained attention. Consequently, Korea had not been present at the trial, with judges or prosecutors, nor had the many colonised Koreans, as forced labourers or female sex slaves (the so-called comfort women), been represented there. This is certainly the most evident example of blending out topics of colonialism and imperialism from the trial.

This amnesia went along with a certain lack of willingness among the Japanese themselves to acquire knowledge about the wars in Asia in order to overcome the still existing sense of superiority or disdain towards 'Asia'. 'No China war, no Asia, no Empire – [. . .] the imperial territories were suddenly expunged from the official story of the war, leaving the homelands (*naichi* 内地) populated by an allegedly mono-ethnic national people dedicated to peace and democracy' (Gluck 2007: 51).

4   One of the crucial points being debated up to now is how the trials are to be characterised: as 'victors' justice' (*shōsha no sabaki* 勝者の裁き) or as a 'judgement of civilisation' (*bunmei no sabaki* 文明の裁き). According to the Japanese specialist for International Law and History at the Tokyo Trial, Higurashi Yoshinobu 日暮吉延 (2008), the advocates of the latter argue that it was legitimate to investigate the Japanese aggression and atrocities in the form of a 'civilised' tribunal. Insisting on 'law and justice', 'methods of war' such as random bombing and the dropping of nuclear bombs were unavoidable to defeat the aggressors and to diminish the number of victims. In contrast to this view, the exponents of the 'victors' justice' theory refuse the legitimacy of the trials, seeing them as a kind of political revenge of the victors, for various reasons: to accuse and sentence the Japanese leaders for waging the war (and other deeds) individually is a case of *ex post facto* law; not to call on the Allied Powers to account for their own deeds is injustice. Both views, Higurashi continues, are irreconcilable value oppositions, complicated mixtures of nationalism, political ideologies, emotionalism and a moralistic view of war responsibility. Only thorough investigations by historians, legal experts and other specialists over the last decades could reveal that the trials were, of course, both – 'victors' justice' and a 'judgement of civilisation'. The latter perspective expresses a normative aspect – the hope of right and justice as fundamental principles of a new post-war world order, as well as the educational aim to 'warn 100 people by punishing one', i.e. to set a warning example in the name of the future process of demilitarisation and democratisation. Concerning the former perspective, 'victors' justice' represents the aspect of power. The Tokyo Trial (as well as the Nuremberg Trial) was a political institution to leave 'a record of crimes' committed by Japan (and Germany) and to demonstrate the legitimacy and justice of the Allied Powers (Higurashi 2008: 37).

Despite the fact that this position is common sense among the scientific community, historical revisionists in contemporary Japan are using the ideology of 'victors' justice' in order to underpin the so-called 'Tokyo Trial view of history' (*Tōkyō saiban shikan* 東京裁判史観). They not only trivialise the outcomes of the Tokyo Trial as such, but also accuse the whole of post-war historiography as being 'poisoned' by Marxism and/or being enforced from outside. They refuse the idea 'that everything Japan had done between 1928 and 1945 was bad, immoral and malign whereas everything the Allies had done was good, moral and benign' (Takatori 2008: 78) as a 'masochistic view of history' (*jigyaku shikan* 自虐史観). This kind of 'nationalising the good and the bad' can be seen as part of a neo-nationalistic strategy to revise Japan's history in order to render it into a source for pride and patriotism, for a 'healthy nationalism' (*kenzen na nashonarizumu* 健全なナショナリズム).

Notes

1 According to Takatori Yuki, it was Itō Takashi 伊藤隆 who, in 1977, first used the term 'Far East Trial view of history' (*Kyokutō saiban shikan* 極東裁判史観) to attack 'the idea that everything Japan had done between 1928 and 1945 was bad, immoral and malign, whereas everything the Allies had done was good, moral and benign' (Takatori 2008: 80–1; cf. also Awaya 2007: 79). According to Yoshida Yutaka 吉田裕, the term has been widely used since 1983, when political scientist Shimizu Hayao 志水速雄 applied the concept in an article published in the December issue of the monthly journal *Shokun!* 諸君！ entitled, 'Get rid of the magic ban of the Tokyo Trial view of history' (Yoshida Y. 1995: 206–7). It was this journal, 'belonging to the group of hawks among the conservative journals' (Yoshimi 2003: 59), along with other journals such as *Seiron* 正論, *Voice*, or *SAPIO*, that selected this topic as a key instrument in attacking historical revisionism in the 1990s. (In the course of this process, the term was, contrary to Shimizu's use, trivialised and ideologised; cf. Yashiro 2007: 12.)

2 The second part is entitled *Collection of evidence* and is intended to be a documentary featuring footage that allegedly shows that the 'Nanking Massacre' never happened. Part three will be a feature film called *America* (*Amerika hen* 「アメリカ編」).

3 On 13 December 1937, Japanese troops conquered Nanking, which at the time was the capital of China. Since the 1980s, professional historians in Japan, while taking into account the diversity of sources and disciplinary approaches, have come to the conclusion that Japanese troops, for a complex amalgam of historical, military, social and psychological reasons, committed a massacre between mid December 1937 and the end of March 1938, killing approximately 100,000 to 200,000 Chinese civilians and soldiers.

4 Already in 1982, former Education Minister Ogawa Heiji 小川平二 was the first member of the Diet who publicly asserted that the (Second) Chinese–Japanese War was in fact a war of aggression. Yoshida describes this as 'epoch-making', as leading politicians avoided such explicit statements until then. In 1986, former Prime Minister Nakasone Yasuhiro 中曽根康弘 (belonging to the group of 'hawks') was forced to acknowledge the aggressive character of the Asian–Pacific War (Yoshida Y. 1995: 167–9). However, it was also he, who, the year before, officially visited the Yasukuni Shrine as prime minister on 15 August, whereby he paid respect to the seven enshrined war criminals who were sentenced to death at the Tokyo Trial (see below).

5 In this respect, the secondary school textbook acted as a catalyst, too: in March 2007, the Ministry of Education, Culture, Sports, Science and Technology (*Monbukagakushō* 文部科学省; *Monkashō*, MEXT or Ministry of Education, for short) forced the publishers of five high school history textbooks to revise the assertion that the Japanese military ordered (or forced) the people in Okinawa to commit mass suicide (*shūdan jiketsu* 集団自決) in order to avoid being captured by the American troops.

6 Here, Carol Gluck refers to the 'historical one-liners', clearly marking villains and victims

> in strong storylines, which admitted no ambiguity [. . .] The nation-state, which had made the war, was elided into 'the national people', who [. . .] suffered the 'cataclysm of defeat', as in Japan. Total stories of total war, the heroic narratives projected national unity by effacing experiential difference, creating whole nations of partisans, resistants, antifascists – and above all, victims.
>
> (Gluck 2007: 49–50)

7 The *Japan Times*, on 25 January 2007, reported that director Mizushima Satoru (born in 1949) wanted to respond directly to the film *Nanjing* (directed by Bill

Guttentag and Dan Sturman, produced by Ted Leonis), which had won the editing award for documentaries at the Sundance Film Festival just a few days before and which is based on the book *The rape of Nanking. The forgotten holocaust of World War II*, published in 1997 by the American–Chinese author Iris Chang (1968–2004), a much attacked bête noire of Japanese revisionists. At least six more films on the subject are completed or scheduled for completion in the next months; among them is *Nanjing Xmas 1937*, produced by Hong Kong filmmaker Yim Ho, whose film is also influenced by Chang and is supported by the Chinese Ministry of Culture, with a budget said to be around US$35 million; in November 2007, the docudrama *Iris Chang: the rape of Nanking*, directed by Anne Pick and Bill Spahic, premiered in Toronto (McNeill 2007); in February 2009, the motion picture *John Rabe: Der gute Mensch von Nanking*, directed by Florian Gallenberger, was released in German cinemas.

8 According to Mizushima, the production costs amounted to US$2.5 million. The constantly updated balance of the donations account at the movie's homepage mentions a total of 340 million yen (approximately US$3.2 million), donated by more than 7,600 persons (in March 2010).

9 The list of presenters and discussants invited by the director to these two events reads like a 'who's who' of right-conservative history revisionists in Japan.

10 The homepage of the movie offers information on the time and place of screenings (www.nankinnoshinjitsu.com/). These screenings took place, for instance, at civic halls, theatres or exhibition halls, at the facilities of Shintō shrines (including the war museum *Yūshūkan* 遊就館 at the Yasukuni Shrine, where the movie was shown twice a day in April and in August 2008) and at jazz bars – where attendants were only obliged to pay for one 'drink'.

11 English and Chinese versions of the movie should be produced as well. Originally, it was planned that these versions would be released together with the Japanese one – this, however, did not happen.

12 Here, and in other cases, Mizushima ignores the current state of historical research, such as Higurashi (2008) on the two views of 'victors' justice' versus 'judgement of civilisation' (*bunmei no sabaki* 文明の裁き); for more information refer to the appended *Excursus: war crimes trials and Japan*.

13 Serious research on the war crimes trials has already analysed this issue, problematising it in publications that go beyond mere mutual offsetting. In his book, *Embracing defeat*, John Dower mentions explicit numbers: 40 per cent of the 66 most important Japanese cities, 57 per cent of Osaka, 65 per cent of Tokyo and 89 per cent of Nagoya were destroyed by American firebombs. As a result, 9 million people were homeless, and approximately 1 million out of 2.7 million people who died during the war were civilians (Japan had a population of 74 million people at that time; Dower 1999: 45).

14 The Nanking War Crimes Tribunal (1946–7) claimed that 300,000 had died. These estimates:

> set in place the standard understanding of the event in Japanese post-war historiography, and the Supreme Commander of the Allied Powers (SCAP) prohibited any harsh criticism of that judgment during the occupation. But immediately after the occupation was over, those whose voices had been silenced during the occupation began to challenge the established account of Japan's wartime history.
>
> (Yoshida, T. 2006: 51)

15 A former prison in Tokyo, where approximately 4,000 war criminals were detained between November 1945 and May 1958.

16 Hanayama was a Buddhist monk of the Jōdo sect and professor of the history of Buddhism at the University of Tokyo. He was the first monk to be appointed chaplain of the Sugamo Prison in February 1946. During his three years of duty,

he accompanied more than half of the sixty executed war criminals until their execution. His memoires *Discovering peace: records of life and death in Sugamo* (*Heiwa no hakken. Sugamo no sei to shi no kiroku* 平和の発見―巣鴨の生と死の記録), published in 1949, were the most important source for Mizushima's account of the events.

17 The film's storyline is based on *The long journey* (*Nagai tabi* ながい旅), published in 1982 by the author Ōoka Shōhei (大岡昇平; 1909–88), who had experienced the war himself and became well known after 1945 for his war writings, such as the autobiographical short story *Taken captive: a Japanese POW's story* (*Furyoki* 俘虜記, 1948) or the novel *Fires on the plain* (*Nobi* 野火, 1951), on records written by the imprisoned Okada, as well as on the more than 2,000 pages of court records, quoted almost verbatim in the dialogues of the court scenes in the film.

18 Okada considered the trial to be a continuation of the battle and called it 'war of law' (*hōsen* 法戦) in his notes.

19 On the occasion of Koizumi's and Hara's joint visit to Okada's grave to 'tell him about the great success of the movie', the producer announced that, within one month, 500,000 people had already seen the movie.

20 For some aspects of the 'failing of the state', please refer to the appended *Excursus: war crimes trials and Japan*.

21 All comments were taken from the movie's blog (http://ashita.iza.ne.jp/blog/), which has been closed already (last accessed on 24 May 2008).

22 They were 'irresponsible' because they should have been aware of the economic and military inferiority of Japan. Please refer to the comment: 'If only all of the soldiers would have been like him [. . .]'.

23 The official commemoration of Japanese dead soldiers is based on the same rhetoric. On 15 August 1963, the first official 'anniversary of the end of the war' (*shūsen kinenbi* 終戦記念日) was solemnised. Without referring to the character of this war, Prime Minister Ikeda Hayato (池田勇人; 1899–1965) emphasised that the new power of Japan was based on those people who died keeping faith in a prospering of Japan (Yoshida, Y. 1995: 109–10).

24 The following information is mainly based on the *Handbook of the Tokyo Trial* (*Tōkyō saiban handobukku* 東京裁判ハンドブック 1989), published by members of the Tokyo Trial Study Group (*Tōkyō saiban kenkyūkai* 東京裁判研究会), which was founded in 1979 (Sumitani Takeshi 住谷雄幸, Akazawa Shirō 赤澤史朗, Utsumi Aiko 内海愛子, Ubukata Naokichi 幼方直吉, Otabe Yūji 小田部雄次, Satō Takeo 佐藤健生, Shiba Kensuke 芝健介 and others).

25 Both 'crimes against peace' and 'crimes against humanity' were so-called retroactive, i.e. *ex post facto* crimes that had not been established previously and were set up hastily as a legal basis for the purpose of the War Crimes Trial.

26 It was signed on 8 September 1951 and came into effect on 28 April 1952, the day when the occupational era ended. Article 11 reads as follows:

> Japan accepts the judgments of the International Military Tribunal for the Far East and of other Allied War Crimes Courts both within and outside Japan, and will carry out the sentences imposed thereby upon Japanese nationals imprisoned in Japan. The power to grant clemency, to reduce sentences and to parole with respect to such prisoners may not be exercised except on the decision of the Government or Governments which imposed the sentence in each instance, and on recommendation of Japan. In the case of persons sentenced by the International Military Tribunal for the Far East, such power may not be exercised except on the decision of a majority of the Governments represented on the Tribunal, and on the recommendation of Japan.
> (www.international.ucla.edu/eas/documents/peace1951.htm; accessed on 31 May 2008)

Bibliography

Assmann, A. (2006) *Der lange Schatten der Vergangenheit. Erinnerungskultur und Geschichtspolitik*, München: C.H. Beck.

—— (2007) *Geschichte im Gedächtnis. Von der individuellen Erfahrung zur öffentlichen Inszenierung*, München: C.H. Beck.

Awaya K. 粟屋憲太郎 (2007) 'Tōkyō saiban to wa nanika' 東京裁判とわ何か [What does the Tokyo Trial mean?], *Gendai shisō* 現代思想 [Modern thought], no. 8: 71–85.

Bix, H.P. (2008) War responsibility and historical memory: Hirohito's apparition. Available online at: http://japanfocus.org/products/details/2741 (accessed 12 May 2008).

Daniel, U. (2001) *Kompendium Kulturgeschichte. Theorien, Praxis, Schlüsselwörter*, Frankfurt am Main: Suhrkamp Taschenbuch Verlag.

Dower, J.W. (1999) *Embracing defeat. Japan in the wake of World War II*, New York: Norten and The New Press.

Eiga Nankin no shinjitsu seisaku iinkai 映画「南京の真実」製作委員会 [Film Production Committee for the Truth of Nanking] (ed.) (2008) *Nankin no shinjitsu; dai-ichibu: Shichinin no 'shikeishū'* 「南京の真実」、第一部「七人の『死刑囚』」 [*The truth of Nanking, part 1: The seven 'death-row prisoners'*]. Movie, Japan. Available movie homepages: www.nankinnoshinjitsu.com and www.thetruthofnanking.com (accessed 25 September 2009).

Gluck, C. (2007) 'Operations of memory. "Comfort women" and the world', in S.M. Jager and R. Mitter (eds) *Ruptured histories. War, memory, and the post-Cold War in Asia*, Cambridge, MA: Harvard University Press, 47–77.

Higurashi Y. 日暮吉延 (2008) *Tōkyō saiban* 東京裁判 [*The Tokyo Trial*], Tokyo: Kōdansha gendai shinsho.

Hyper War Foundation (2003) *The IMTFE judgement. Chapter VIII: Conventional war crimes (atrocities)*. Available online at: www.ibiblio.org/hyperwar/PTO/IMTFE/IMTFE-8.html (accessed 12 May 2008).

Kittel, M. (2004) *Nach Nürnberg und Tokio. 'Vergangenheitsbewältigung' in Japan und Westdeutschland 1945 bis 1969*, München: Oldenbourg.

Kobayashi H. 小林弘忠 (2007) Sugamo purizun. Kyōkaishi Hanayama Shinshō to shikei senpan no kiroku 巣鴨プリズン—教誨師花山信勝と死刑戦犯の記録 [Sugamo Prison. The chaplain Hanayama Shinshō and the records of the war criminals sentenced to death], Tokyo: Chūkō bunko.

Koizumi T. 小泉堯史 (2008) *Ashita e no yuigon* 明日への遺言 [*Best wishes for tomorrow*], DVD, Japan: Asmik Ace Entertainment, Inc., 110 min.

McNeill, D. (2007) 'Look back in anger. Filming the Nanjing Massacre', *Japan Focus*. Available online at: www.japanfocus.org/-David-McNeill/2599 (accessed 13 July, 2010).

Masaaki, A. (2008) Compulsory mass suicide, the Battle of Okinawa, and Japan's textbook controversy. Available online at: http://japanfocus.org/products/details/2629 (accessed 12 May 2008).

Mizushima S. 水島総 (2007) 'Eiga *Nankin no shinjitsu* seisaku de miete kuru jōhōsen no shinjitsu (1)' 映画「南京の真実」製作で見えてくる情報戦の真実 [The truth about the information war revealed through the making of the movie *Nankin no shinjitsu* (1)], *Seiron* 正論 [sound argument], no. 9: 82–90.

—— (2008) 'Naze, ima, eiga *Nankin no shinjitsu* nanoka' なぜ、いま、映画「南京の真実」なのか [Why the movie *The truth of Nanking* now?], in Eiga Nankin no shinjitsu seisaku iinkai 映画「南京の真実」製作委員会 (ed.) *Nankin no shinjitsu; dai-ichibu: Shichinin no 'shikeishū'* 「南京の真実」、第一部「七人の『死刑囚』」 [*The truth of Nanking, part 1: the seven 'death-row prisoners']. Available online at: www.thetruthofnanking.com/Japanese/MainFrame.html [sublink: kantoku 監督] (accessed 13 July 2010).

Richter, S. (2001) 'Nicht nur ein Sturm im Wasserglas. Japans jüngster Schulbuchstreit', *Internationale Schulbuchforschung*, vol. 23, Hannover: Verlag Hahnsche Buchhandlung, 277–300.

—— (2003) 'Zurichtung von Vergangenheit als Schmerzlinderung in der Gegenwart', in S. Richter and W. Höpken (eds) *Vergangenheit im Gesellschaftskonflikt. Ein Historikerstreit in Japan*, Köln and Weimar: Böhlau, 1–26.

—— (2005) 'Alle vier Jahre wieder und nichts Neues? Das umstrittene "Neue Geschichtslehrbuch" für japanische Mittelschulen', *Internationale Schulbuchforschung*, vol. 27, Hannover: Verlag Hahnsche Buchhandlung, 91–8.

Sakai N. 酒井直行 (ed.) (2008) *Tōkyō saiban wa nani o sabaita ka* 東京裁判は何を裁いたか [*What did the Tokyo Trial judge?*], Tokyo: Shinjinbutsu ōraisha.

Takatori, Y. (2008) 'Remembering the War Crimes Trial', in S. Saaler and W. Schwentker (eds) *The power of memory*, Folkestone: Global Oriental, 78–95.

Tawara Y. 俵義文 (2008) *'Tsukurukai' bunretsu to rekishi gizō no fukusō*「つくる会」分裂と歴史偽造の深層 [*The divison of the 'Tsukurukai' and the deep structure of falsification of history*], Tokyo: Kadensha.

Tōkyō saiban handobukku henshū iinkai 東京裁判ハンドブック編集委員会 (1989) *Tōkyō saiban handobukku* 東京裁判ハンドブック [*Tokyo Trial handbook*], Tokyo: Aoki shoten.

Ushimura K. 牛村圭 (2008) 'B/C-kyū senpan Okada Tasuku chūjō no tatakai – wadai no eiga *Ashita e no yuigon* no shushinkō ga mita mono' BC級戦犯岡田資中将の闘い―話題の映画「明日への遺言」の主人公が見たもの [The fight of the Class B/C war criminal Lieutenant General Okada Tasuku. The *Best wishes for tomorrow* hero's viewpoint], *Bungei shunjū* 文藝春秋 [Literary Times], no. 4: 210–22.

Utsumi A. 内海愛子 et al. (2007) 'Tōkyō saiban ga tsukutta sengo Nihon' 東京裁判が作った戦後日本 [The post-war Japan made by the Tokyo Trial], *Gendai shisō* 現代思想 [Modern thought], no. 8: 44–70.

Wildt, M. (2005) '*Der Untergang*: Ein Film inszeniert sich als Quelle', *Zeithistorische Forschungen/Studies in Contemporary History*, no. 2. Available online at: www.zeithistorische-forschungen.de/16126041-Wildt-1-2005 (accessed 12 May 2008).

Yashiro T. 八代拓 (2007) *Sensō sekinin rongi ni okeru kagai ishiki no hyōshutsu katei* 戦争責任論議における加害意識の表出過程 [*How perpetrator consciousness gradually has been expressed in the discussions about war responsibility*]. Available online at: www.pp.u-tokyo.ac.jp/courses/2007/50020/documents/50020–2.pdf (accessed 27 February 2009).

Yoshida T. (2006) *The making of the Rape of Nanjing. History and memory in Japan, China, and the United States*, Oxford: Oxford University Press.

Yoshida Y. 吉田裕 (1995) *Nihonjin no sensōkan. Sengoshi no naka no henyō* 日本人の戦争観―戦後史のなかの変容 [*The views of war of the Japanese and their changes in the post-war history*], Tokyo: Iwanami shoten.

—— (2005) 'Sensō sekininron no genzai' 戦争責任論の現在 [The current situation of war responsibility studies], in A. Kurasawa 倉沢愛子 et al. (eds) *Naze, ima Ajia Taiheiyō sensō ka* なぜ、いまアジア太平洋戦争か [*The Asia–Pacific War – why now?*], vol. 1, Tokyo: Iwanami shoten, 87–124.

Yoshimi S. (2003) 'Zeitschriftenmedien und der Konsum von Nationalismus', in S. Richter and W. Höpken (eds) *Vergangenheit im Gesellschaftskonflikt. Ein Historikerstreit in Japan*, Köln and Weimar: Böhlau, 55–69.

10 Historical conflict and dialogue between Korea and Japan
A focus on Japanese history textbooks[1]

Chung Jae-jeong

This chapter further discusses the issue of historical revisionism in Japan, focusing on the way in which this has sparked a long-running feud over the interpretation of the past between elements within Korean and Japanese society. Tensions have arisen in particular over statements in the Japanese revisionist textbooks concerning the modern history of Korean–Japanese relations. The authors of the revisionist texts not only portrayed these relations in a manner that was reductionist, but also revealed in their subsequent 'corrections' a disregard for Korean sensitivities, thus fuelling bilateral tensions. It is the severity of these tensions that in turn has spurred recent efforts to overcome these rifts. These have included the emergence of a civil society movement that aims to overcome conflicts over the interpretation of history and contribute to reconciliation between Korea and Japan. In joint work-teams, history researchers and educators have been trying to narrow the gap in historical views and to develop common teaching materials for use in both countries. Thus, the chapter reminds us, tensions at an official level should not obscure the significance of non-governmental contact and initiatives.

Introduction

Korea and Japan have waged a diplomatic tug of war over how to view the past history of, and sovereignty over, Dokdo (Japanese: Takeshima). The ongoing conflict and confrontations that emerged between the governments of the two countries, led at the time by President Roh Moo-hyun of Korea and Prime Minister Koizumi Jun'ichirō 小泉純一郎 of Japan, appear to be more serious than those experienced by any other governments. So much so that the repercussions were expected to last for some time after the terms of the two political leaders had expired. If the strained relations between the two countries do last for a long time, they are likely to affect the friendly and cooperative relations between civilians of the two countries.

It is time to re-establish friendly and cooperative relations between the two governments in their shared goal of enhancing national interests and ensuring peaceful and prosperous lives for their people. To that end, they must seek to settle the matters that have caused friction between them, such as the historical perspective (i.e. the understanding of the history of Korea–Japan relations in modern times, the issue of certain descriptions in Japanese history textbooks, or the acts of homage paid by Japanese leaders at Yasukuni Shrine). Second, the political leaders have to decide how to deal with unresolved matters caused by the past (i.e. Koreans left in Soviet-occupied Sakhalin after World War II; Korean victims of the atomic bombs; Koreans engaged in forced labour or enlisted as Japanese troops during the period of colonial rule and the Pacific War; Korean women forced to serve as sex slaves [i.e. 'comfort women' *jūgun ianfu* 従軍慰安婦, G.M.] for Japanese troops; the return home of Koreans' remains; the return of Korean cultural properties looted by the Japanese during the colonial period; the granting of political rights to Koreans in Japan), and, third, territorial disputes (over Dokdo and the designation of Exclusive Economic Zones (EEZs)). Such historical conflicts have spread beyond the pages of textbooks to politics and diplomatic relations.

Any attempt made by the two countries to solve the historical conflict should deal with the aforesaid three factors. For Koreans, these factors are inextricably related. However, this article intends to focus only on historical perspectives, particularly the issue concerning history textbooks. The author has made many suggestions on desirable ways of overcoming the historical conflict that has arisen between Koreans and Japanese over the past few years.[2] This chapter treats the governments of the two countries as the key actors and focuses on proposing methods of overcoming the historical conflict, while trying to avoid the kind of grandiloquence frequently encountered in recent lectures given by 'famous' scholars.[3] This article will therefore start with an overview of the reasons why the two countries engaged in confrontation over their historical perspectives, the development of the dispute over history textbooks, and the flow of the historical dialogues that have been conducted with a view to overcoming the present situation.

Historical perspectives and conflicts

Historical perspectives: approaches adopted

It appears that, in terms of the historical perspectives adopted by both Koreans and Japanese, there has been some improvement since around 1995, shown by certain changes that have occurred over the past decade with regard to their governments' views on bilateral relations in modern times and imperial Japan's colonial rule over Korea.

In August 1995, the Japanese Prime Minister Murayama Tomiichi 村山富市 issued a statement on the fiftieth anniversary of the end of World War II. He said:

> During a certain period in the not too distant past, Japan, following a mistaken national policy, advanced along the road to war, only to ensnare the Japanese people in a fateful crisis, and, through its colonial rule and

aggression, caused tremendous damage and suffering to the people of many countries, particularly to those of Asian nations. In the hope that no such mistake will be made in the future, I regard, in a spirit of humility, these irrefutable facts of history, and express here once again my feelings of deep remorse and state my heartfelt apology. Allow me also to express my feelings of profound mourning for all victims, both at home and abroad, of that history.

(*Gaimushō* 2010)

Although the statement did not specifically point out Japan's relations with Korea, it did represent a significant step forward, compared with the ambiguous attitude taken by the country's past political leaders. He clearly pointed at the invasion and occupation of neighbouring countries and expressed deep remorse and a heartfelt apology. Factors that brought about such a statement include the Socialist Party's seizure of political power in Japan, which led to a softening of Japanese political views, and the economic development and democratisation of Korea. The statement became the guideline for defining the historical viewsof the Japanese government concerning the wrongs committed by the country in the past.

It was the joint statement for the New Japan–Korea Partnership towards the Twenty-first Century, made in October 1998 by Prime Minister Obuchi Keizō 小渕恵三 and President Kim Dae-jung, that laid the groundwork for advancing a new relationship between the two countries, as well as making great strides in terms of their historical perspectives.

At that session, Obuchi said, 'I humbly recognise the historical fact that Japan inflicted enormous loss and pain on Koreans during its colonial rule over Korea and apologise with painful remorse from the bottom of my heart.' Kim Dae-jung responded by saying, 'I sincerely appreciate Prime Minister Obuchi's expression of his historical view. I think that the current era requires the two countries to make greater efforts to develop future-oriented relations based on reconciliation and friendly cooperation, to overcome the memory of the unhappy past.'[4]

Obuchi's speech was similar to the statement made by Murayama in August 1995, although the former represented a further step forward. It specifically referred to Japan as the perpetrator of colonial oppression and Korea as the victim. With president Kim Dae-jung's 'sincere appreciation' of Obuchi's remarks, the joint statement in October 1998 has given a framework for defining the historical views of the two countries. Thus, even Prime Ministers Koizumi Jun'ichirō 小泉純一郎 and Abe Shinzō 安倍晋三 could not help but assert that they would, at least officially, inherit the historical perspectives contained in the joint statement, although the former caused serious historical conflict by going ahead with his planned acts of homage at Yasukuni Shrine, despite the fierce opposition from Korea's Roh Moo-hyun administration, while the latter was known for holding a stronger rightist stance than the former.

It can be said that, since the mid 1990s, the Japanese government, in terms of its historical views, has basically maintained an apologetic and remorseful stance towards its past colonial rule over Korea. In this respect, one is apt to think that there has been much progress in comparison to 1965, when the Korea–Japan Treaty on Basic Relations was signed. Here, virtually no comment was made on Japan's colonial rule over Korea. However, such historical views have not taken root in Japanese society, as indicated by the fact that Japanese ministers or high-ranking officials often make remarks to the contrary. In fact, even the Japanese government has stuck to the view that it is an undeniable fact that the Japan–Korea Annexation Treaty of 1910 was made through a legal procedure and, hence, valid. Japanese people, including political leaders, frequently display patterns of behaviour or make remarks that impair Koreans' trust in them where their historical perspectives are concerned. Furthermore, the Japanese government is not entirely willing to recognise the illegality and injustice that was perpetrated during the process of bringing the Korean Empire under its control. That is why the Korean governments have kept on asking their Japanese counterparts to show their sincerity regarding historical perspectives with acts rather than words.

A new phase in historical conflict

The international situation surrounding Korea and Japan has changed dramatically over the past few years: the summit between the leaders of the two Koreas; the co-hosting of the World Cup between Korea and Japan; the Japan–North Korea Pyongyang Declaration and the resumption of talks concerning the establishment of diplomatic relations between the two countries; North Korea's admittance of its abduction of Japanese citizens; North Korea's nuclear test; the war in Iraq, and Korea and Japan's dispatch of troops to that country to help the United States; the changes in political power in both Korea and Japan; Japan's adoption of war-contingency laws; summits between the leaders of Korea, Japan and the United States; and so forth. Such a series of events has had a considerable impact on the national interests and historical views of the two countries. Nonetheless, the two countries have basically maintained their stance of holding on to the historical views contained in the New Japan–Korea Partnership towards the Twenty-first Century made in October 1998.

As it happens, however, the governments of Korea and Japan have not held a summit since early 2001 owing to the serious confrontation over historical views. In early 2001, 'new textbooks' for secondary school students compiled by Japanese rightists [i.e. the *Tsukurukai*, G.M.] were approved by the Ministry of Education, Culture, Sports, Science and Technology (MEXT). This rekindled the issue of historical conflict between the two countries. To make the situation worse, Japan started asserting its sovereignty over Dokdo [jap. Takeshima, G. M.] from the end of 2004, and Prime Minister Koizumi Jun'ichirō went ahead with his visit to Yasukuni Shrine despite fierce opposition from the Korean and Chinese governments. In the past, the leaders of the two countries had held semi-annual 'shuttle summits'. The governments of the two countries, led by President Roh Moo-hyun and Prime Minister Koizumi Jun'ichirō, stopped the practice between July 2005 and September 2006. The situation was caused by the Korean government's strong opposition to Koizumi visiting the Yasukuni Shrine on six separate occasions and Shimane Prefecture's designation of a Takeshima Day, which represented an assertion of Japan's sovereignty over Dokdo, in February 2005. In his speech at a ceremony commemorating the March First Independence Movement in March 2005 and a special statement made in April 2006, President Roh Moo-hyun denounced such acts, which he claimed stemmed from Japan's erroneous historical perspectives, and said that he would even consider waging a war of diplomacy against Japan to set the matter straight.[5] In the early days of his term, President Roh Moo-hyun had said that he would not take up the issue of Japan's historical views, but he completely reversed his position in response to the series of steps taken by Japan. This serves as an example of how historical views can play a role in reversing the state of bilateral relations.

Embarrassed by such a reversal of the position by President Roh Moo-hyun, the Japanese government acted as if it did not realise his objective. Some Japanese government officials interpreted the Korean government's recent offensive as a tactic intended to regain domestic popularity by appealing to the people's sense of nationalism, or as a step connected with the Presidential Committee for the Inspection of Collaborations for Japanese Imperialism. The Japanese government displayed virtually no desire to seriously consider the remarks made by the Roh Moo-hyun administration. At times, it also took a hard-line stance in refuting outright the statement made by the Korean government.[6]

The controversy over Prime Minister Koizumi Jun'ichirō's paying homage at Yasukuni Shrine developed as follows: in August 1985, Prime Minister Nakasone Yasuhiro 中曽根康弘 paid homage at the shrine on the fourteeth anniversary of the end of World War II. Neighbouring countries, including Korea, issued a strong protest against his act, and Nakasone stopped the scheduled annual event in response.[7] Koizumi Jun'ichirō paid homage at the shrine on a total of six occasions while in office. His defiant attitude of disregard towards neighbouring countries' strongly worded protests was regarded as a symbolic act that only served to aggravate the historic grievances felt by Koreans. Koizumi Jun'ichirō's explanation for his act of homage at Yasukuni Shrine could be summarised thus: 'I would like to humbly think about the regrettable things perpetrated by Japan during the war and express my condolences to all victims of the war, along with my deep remorse', although it carried a different nuance each time. He continued, 'Japan must never again proceed along a path to war', adding that 'the present peace and prosperity of Japan are founded on the ultimate sacrifices they made'. He also expressed his hope that 'the people of Japan and those of the neighbouring countries would understand my belief if it was fully explained.'[8]

However, his 'hope' did not materialise. The Roh Moo-hyun administration, which had said that it would not regard historical perspectives as a pending diplomatic issue, made a statement of denunciation, and China took similar action. On 1 January 2004, the spokesperson of the Ministry of Foreign Affairs and Trade (MOFAT) made the following statement on Koizumi Jun'ichirō's paying homage at Yasukuni Shrine:

> We believe that if Prime Minister Junichiro Koizumi is to value peace and prosperity of the world, and to develop genuine friendly relations with its neighbors, he should, on the basis of a true recognition of history, respect the national sentiments of neighboring countries. We therefore strongly call for Prime Minister Junichiro Koizumi to stop visiting Yasukuni Shrine.
> (Ministry of Foreign Affairs and Trade, Republic of Korea 2004)

This shows that the Korean government interpreted the repeated act of paying homage at Yasukuni Shrine as an act of whitewashing Japan's invasions and brutal rule over other countries, i.e., in their eyes, it represented a backward step taken in the Japanese government's historical views, rather than taking the trouble to understand the Japanese prime minister's explanation.

Anyone attempting to grasp the historical origins and the nature of Yasukuni Shrine will understand that the concerns expressed by Japan's neighbouring countries, including Korea, are not groundless fears. Prior to Japan's defeat in the war, the shrine, along with State Shintō, played a conspicuous role in instilling militarism and Emperor worship in the minds of the Japanese people, thereby leading them to respond to the state's call to enlist and sacrifice their lives for the Emperor. After Japan's defeat in the war, Yasukuni Shrine was turned into some form of a religious corporation. However, it still remains a place where homage is paid to Japan's war dead in Shintō style. Moreover, even the mortuary tablets of those classified as Class A war criminals by the Tokyo War Crimes Tribunal 1946–8 were placed there by the Japanese government; and also the mortuary tablets of more than 20,000 Koreans who were forcefully mobilised during the colonial period for the Japanese war effort are kept there. The shrine houses the Yūshūkan 遊就館 Military Museum, which is filled with exhibitions that glorify the past war of aggression.[9] Such being the case, it appears not to be easy to alleviate concerns over the possibility of the Japanese government returning to the historical perspectives it had assumed in the pre-war period, even though the Japanese leader tried to defend his act of homage at the shrine with plausible remarks.

Political and diplomatic background of the historical conflict

What is the political and diplomatic background of the confrontational stance taken by Korea and Japan over these historical views? First of all, the system that maintained at a certain pitch the feelings of the two countries about the historical conflict collapsed. The governments of the two countries have been holding fundamentally different views over the need for apology and reparation for the colonial rule of the Japanese empire over Korea. In the process leading up to the signing of the Korea–Japan Treaty on Basic Relations in 1965, the two countries' outright difference of historical perspective was disclosed. Since then, the governments of the two countries have tried not to enter this minefield. Around 1995, the two countries came to share a sense of affinity with each other, as both countries were aiming to establish a free democracy and a market economy, and to promote peace and human rights; they were also coming closer to each other in terms of their historical perspectives. All this culminated in the announcement of the New Japan–Korea Partnership towards the Twenty-first Century by President Kim Dae-jung and Prime Minister Obuchi Keizō.

However, in the ensuing period, Japanese politicians and ministers repeatedly made very inappropriate remarks in an effort to justify Japan's colonial rule over Korea. The MEXT approved the publication of the 'new history textbook' [i.e. the *Tsukurukai's*, G.M.]. Prime Minister Koizumi Jun'ichirō repeated his acts of homage at Yasukuni Shrine, despite strong protests from neighbouring countries. The Japanese government insisted on Japan's sovereignty over Dokdo. Upon witnessing this series of events, the Korean government forcefully asked the Japanese government to take corrective steps, casting doubt on its historical views. Afterwards, in the process of dealing with historical perspectives as a pending diplomatic issue, the two came to have a deeper distrust of each other, rather than enhancing their level of mutual understanding.

In retrospect, 2005 could be considered a major turning point in the historical views held by the two countries. That year marked the 110th anniversary of the Japanese assassination of Empress Myeongseong of Korea, the 100th anniversary of the Eulsa Treaty [i.e. the Japan–Korea Protectorate Treaty of 1905, G.M.] signed between the Korean Empire and imperial Japan, the sixtieth anniversary of the liberation of Korea from Japanese colonial rule that came with Japan's unconditional surrender in the Pacific War, and the fortieth anniversary of the Korea–Japan Treaty on Basic Relations. Sensitive to the history of their relations with Japan, Koreans hoped that the governments of the two countries would jointly present a blueprint for friendly cooperation in the future and constructively reassess their respective historical views of each other in such a significant year. What the governments did was to designate 2005 as the Korea–Japan Friendship Year and hold celebratory events, with the focus only on the fortieth anniversary of the Korea–Japan Treaty on Basic Relations. Korea's historians and mass media felt disappointed and gave such events the cold shoulder. In fact, it was owing to such an atmosphere that the Roh Moo-hyun administration started to place importance on historical views in regard to its relations with the Japanese government.

In the meantime, the Japanese government led by Koizumi Jun'ichirō had a strong desire to allow the country to unburden itself of its past wrongdoings on the occasion of the sixtieth anniversary of the end of the war. Out of such a desire, it often expressed historical views that stimulated people's nationalism and tried to separate the historical issue from pending diplomatic issues in its relations with Korea. Such an attitude struck a chord with ordinary Japanese people who wanted to feel a sense of pride in their country's history and capabilities. In 2005, Japan's historians and mass media concentrated rather on the significance of the Asia–Pacific War and the definition of the relevant responsibility than on the country's colonial rule over Korea and other countries. There was a clear trend to instigate Japanese antipathy against Koreans and to criticise Korean attitudes. Koizumi Jun'ichirō's acts of homage at Yasukuni Shrine were seen as a reflection of his determination to reinforce his political position by taking advantage of public opinion and to re-establish a more positive, Japan-oriented historical view.

The recent instance of historical conflict between Korea and Japan was the result of such discord. Especially, those who had newly risen to power in both countries were not willing to coordinate or heal the conflict through sincere efforts; rather, they appeared to jump on the bandwagon of domestic nationalism. Thus, the situation has started deteriorating in a short time.

Disputes over history textbooks and history-related dialogues

How the history textbook dispute developed

The 'new history textbook' [i.e. the *Tsukurukai's*, G.M.] that was adopted by some Japanese schools after receiving the approval of the MEXT in 2001 and 2005 reignited the spark that had set off the historical conflict between the two countries. The Korean government asked Japan to take remedial steps, pointing out that the Japanese government's historical perspectives were questionable owing to the MEXT's approval of history textbooks that intentionally distorted and belittled Korean history.[10]

The Korean government concluded that the 'new history textbook' approved by the MEXT of Japan in 2001 contained the following views concerning Korean history:

1 Japan had exerted its influence over the Korean peninsula since ancient times.
2 Historically, Korea had long remained a non-independent country subjugated to China, whereas Japan had been a self-reliant independent country outside the influence of the Sinocentric view of the world.
3 Historically, Japan coped wisely with changes in international situations, whereas Korea did not, and thus had failed to jump on the modernisation bandwagon in time.
4 Geographically, the Korean peninsula was a dangerous territory that threatened the security of Japan; as such, Japan had been obliged to keep control of Korea ahead of other powers to protect its security.

5 In terms of bilateral relations, Japan had always been right in the past, while Korea had not. All undesirable situations between the two countries were the fault of Korea.
6 Japan made efforts to help with Korea's modernisation, but Korea was unwilling to accept such help. Inevitably, Japan annexed Korea and provided benevolent rule (Chung 2001a).

In response to the sizzling denunciation (which started in April 2001) by the Koreans and Chinese of MEXT's approval of that 'new history textbook', the chief cabinet secretary and Japan's minister of MEXT made a statement to the following effect: the historical views of the Japanese government and those contained in history textbooks are not always the same. The Japanese government cannot control the historical views contained in history textbooks under the current system of inspection of textbooks and the spirit of the Japanese Constitution, which guarantees academic freedom and freedom of thought. The historical views of the Japanese government were previously disclosed by Prime Minister Murayama Tomiichi's statement (1995) and the New Japan–Korea Partnership towards the Twenty-first Century (1998).[11]

The Korean government rejected the explanation of the Japanese government and asked for the revision of a total of thirty-three controversial items in history textbooks intended for the use in Japanese secondary schools in May 2001. Korean civic organisations condemned the Japanese attempts to distort historical facts and thus carried out active campaigns to dissuade Japanese schools from adopting the 'new history textbook' [i.e. the *Tsukurukai's*, G.M.]. In July 2001, the Japanese government refused to accept the demands for a revision made by their neighbouring countries, and only asked the Korean government to understand the spirit of the constitution and the very system of schoolbook inspection in Japan. For discussion on the textbook issue, it rather proposed to make the effort of setting up a plan for the promotion of joint research on history between the two countries to discuss the textbook issue. At the summit held briefly afterwards, the two countries agreed to launch the Korea–Japan Commission for the Joint Study of History. Members of the commission from both countries met at dozens of sessions and produced more than forty theses in the course of the activities carried out between May 2002 and May 2005. The commission made great strides in the study of the history of bilateral relations; however, the history textbook issue could not be included among the subjects of joint study from the outset, owing to the Japanese side's objection.[12]

In 2005, the conflict between the two countries over Japanese history textbooks was resumed after the 'new history textbook' [i.e. the *Tsukurukai's*, G.M.] was again approved by the Japanese MEXT. The views on history contained in the book that provoked Koreans were as follows:

1 The Japanese emperors belong to *bansei ikkei* 万世一系 (literally meaning 'millions of generations come from a single lineage and an unbroken imperial line') and are greater than their Chinese counterparts.

2   Japan has been the only country in East Asia that has maintained self-reliant independence outside the influence of the Sinocentric view of the world, in contrast to Korea; Japan has adopted cultural features from Korea and China, but retained its originality and uniqueness (which appears to imply that Korea did not keep its originality and uniqueness in adopting Chinese culture).
3   In ancient times, Japan kept a forward base in Mimana in the southern part of Korea and adopted more advanced cultural traits from China by becoming proactively involved in politics in the Korean peninsula.
4   Japan succeeded in transferring power from the Tokugawa *bakufu* 幕府 to the Meiji government amid the need to counter the pressure exerted by the Western powers, whereas Korea failed to meet the need for innovation and modernisation efficiently. During the Joseon Dynasty, the Korean kings remained powerful, attracting talented people to the central government through the state examination system, which left local governments weak. Joseon relied on China for its security and paid tribute to it. It failed to fully recognise the military threat posed by the Western powers. In contrast, Japan, a warrior society, pursued a policy of adopting Western civilisation positively, after seeing the need to cope with the military threat of the Western powers. Japan did not have a state examination system like the one adopted in Joseon. Local lords built up their strength by attracting talented people and were thus able to put an end to the *bakufu* era. Warriors nationwide remained loyal to the emperor. Seeing that the *bakufu* lost strength in the face of pressure from the Western powers, they launched a new era, placing the imperial family at the centre of the entire country.
5   Japan invaded and ruled over Korea as its colony as a means of self-protection and defense. The *seikanron* 征韓論 (the debate on Japan's conquest of Korea) was started in Japan in response to Joseon's arrogant attitude. Being of the opinion that its own security would be jeopardised if Joseon fell into the hands of other countries, Japan occupied Joseon and drove away Qing (China) and Russia in order to help Joseon to build a modernised, independent country. Japan was victorious in the war against Russia, and thus it encouraged Asian hopes for independence from the Western powers.
6   Japan's waging of the Asia–Pacific War was intended to counter China's illegal anti-Japanese movement, and the 'Greater Asia War' was waged for self-protection and the defence of Asians.
7   The 'Greater Asia War' gave Southeast Asians hope and courage for independence. They thought of Japan as the saviour, and the war made it possible for them to regain independence earlier than expected. The United States and the Soviet Union violated international agreements. It is doubtful whether the US bombings of cities in Japan, including the dropping of atomic bombs, the Soviet Union's internment of Japanese in Siberia and the Tōkyō War Crimes Trial, etc. can be justified (Chung 2005).

Unlike in 2001, the Korean government did not ask the Japanese government to take corrective steps for the specified items in the 'new history textbook' [i.e. *Tsukurukai's*, G.M.] edition approved by the Japanese government in 2005. However, Korean civic organisations engaged in violent protest rallies, condemning the approval of the 'new history textbook' and opposing its adoption in schools. Under such circumstances, President Roh Moo-hyun and Prime Minister Koizumi Jun'ichirō agreed to launch the Second Korea–Japan Commission for the Joint Study of History in October 2005 'to deepen the study of history and improve the history textbook issue' as a compromise (see *Kyōdō tsūshin,* 26 December 2006, and *Segye ilbo,* 27 December 2006). The second commission had an improved organisation, including the formation of a history textbook subcommittee, based on the experience of the first commission. However, it only began its activities in June 2007, owing to a delay in the selection of its members on the Japanese side. At the moment, it is hard to say whether the commission will be able to come up with a result that will bring the governments of the two countries closer to resolving the issue of historical views and that of the history textbooks after its two-year-long session. Unless an acceptable solution is found, the cycle of historical conflict may be repeated each time a 'new history textbook' edition obtains approval from MEXT.

How the historical dialogue developed

The historical conflict between the two countries is such that it cannot be settled with an agreement made between the governments. It will require a long and difficult process to effect a change in the historical views held by ordinary people. Accordingly, it would be better to have civic organisations or private research institutes taking charge of the study and education of history, while the governments assume the role of providing them with support, supposing that the two countries took steps to overcome the present rifts by a broader approach.

To be sure, the governments of the two countries have provided support for historical dialogues between historians and history teachers as part of the effort to overcome the ongoing conflict. As agreed by the leaders of the two countries, the Korea–Japan Commission for the Joint Study of History carried out various activities between May 2002 and May 2005, with twelve members from each country taking part in the activities. Each subcommittee held presentation/discussion sessions every other month, alternating between Korea and Japan. Subcommittee 1 was composed of three members from each side and dealt with three subjects in ancient history. Subcommittee 2 was also composed of three members from each side and dealt with three subjects in medieval and early modern history. Subcommittee 3 was composed of five members from each side and dealt with thirteen subjects in modern and contemporary history. A total of six general meetings and forty-five subcommittee sessions were held. The commission published more than forty theses on a total of nineteen subjects. It appears to have accomplished something in terms of the number of theses produced, although there are certainly divided opinions on their quality. It was a great accomplishment that the two sides came to see what had caused the differences of views, although the members often engaged in violent arguments over a particular subject and found themselves unable to bridge the differences of perspective.[13]

The Korea–Japan Meeting of Historians was established in 2001, following the proposal made by the Korea–Japan Joint Commission for the Promotion of the Study of History, which carried out activities for three years from 1997. Aimed at deepening mutual understanding among history researchers of the two countries and widening the opportunities for exchange and cooperation, the meeting held annual sessions, in Korea and Japan alternately. Its major agenda included the trends in historical research in the two countries in the post-war period, the movements for modernisation in world history, and the past and present of nationalism. The results of the discussion were recently published in the form of a booklet, which serves as a handbook for understanding the consciousness of historians of the two countries (*Han-il Yeoksaga Huiui Jojik Wiwonhui* 2002).

In Korea and Japan, the governments still exert considerable influence on ordinary people's historical views. The Ministry of Education and Human Resources of Korea is publishing textbooks on national history, while MEXT of Japan carries out vigorous inspections of national history textbooks, showing that each of the governments has an influence on the formation of people's historical perspectives. This being the case, the current joint study of history supported by the governments of the two countries will continue to work as a way of overcoming historical conflict. In June 2005, the leaders of the two countries agreed to the resumption of the Korea–Japan Commission for the Joint Study of History, apparently because there were few other options to choose from. Under such circumstances, the second commission should carry out its activities in a way that will help the countries to overcome the historical conflict.

Another method worth recommending is that of conducting history dialogues in the private sector. Seeing the deepening historical conflict between the two countries, people in the private sector, including historians, history teachers and students, have started making joint efforts to overcome the problem, and they have ultimately made considerable progress.[14]

The period of history dialogues between Korea and Japan can be divided into two phases. During phase one (1976–2000), the two sides examined each other's historical perspectives and exchanged dialogues for a better understanding of each other. The following achievements were made:

1 A clear definition was made of the difference in views held by people of the two countries on the modern history of bilateral relations, and a careful search for ways of bridging the difference was conducted.
2 A contribution was made to deepening mutual understanding of the textbook-related systems of the two countries.

3 People were led to recognise that a clear knowledge of the history of victimisation and the perpetration of wrongs is required for the establishment of new relations between the two countries.
4 A network of continued joint research was established.
5 Historical perspectives were deepened through discussion.
6 National consensus was formed concerning the need for history dialogue, by making the discussion activities known to the general public.
7 Considerable improvements were made to the contents of the Japanese history textbooks concerning the early modern history of Korea.
8 Relevant know-how concerning joint studies and discussion activities was accumulated.

During phase two (2001–7), the two sides engaged in history dialogues on the need for reconciliation and coexistence. The following achievements were made:

1 Extensive criticism was made of the history education and history textbooks of Korea, and discussion of alternatives took place.
2 A fundamental review of the characteristics of Japan's 'distortion of historical facts' and preparations for a joint stance were carried out, with a view to launching an international network.
3 Efforts were made to develop the historical perspectives of Koreans, Japanese and Chinese in a way that would be conducive to peaceful coexistence, which led to the launch of a people's network for sharing historical perspectives.
4 The three East Asian countries adopted the stance of learning from the Western countries' experience of handling historical views and history textbooks.
5 A movement was launched with the aim of looking at the history textbook issue from a global perspective (this represented a significant attempt by an influential foundation to promote international understanding and peaceful coexistence).
6 Brisk work was carried out to broaden the horizon of the historical views held by each country and to enhance the degree of mutual understanding through the joint development of history textbooks.

Joint compilation of history education materials

There have been five cases of jointly compiled history education materials for use in both Korea and Japan.[15] First of all, there was the result of the joint work carried out by the Association of History Textbook Researchers (of Korea) and the Association of History Education Researchers (of Japan). The associations, comprising twenty professors and graduate students from the University of Seoul and Tōkyō Gakugei University, have held joint symposiums on history study and textbooks twice a year since 1997. Until

2000, the two sides reviewed the contents concerning the history of Korea–Japan relations (from prehistoric to modern times) in national history books for senior secondary students, focusing on the extent to which the results of history studies carried out in each country were reflected in the textbooks in an objective and even fashion.[16] In 2001, the two associations started the joint work to compile history education materials for use in the two countries based on the results. The book adopts the 'chapter–section–item' structure. Each chapter starts with an easy-to-understand statement of the history of each country that the writers would like the students of the other country to know (about two textbook pages). Each section contains six, seven or eight items on no more than six pages, including illustrations or relevant materials. The intention of each section is clearly stated, with the inclusion of three to five pieces of relevant reference literature suitable for students (or ordinary adults). The book targets senior secondary freshmen or juniors. The work process was arranged so as to have a writer taking charge of an entire section and an equal number of Korean and Japanese writers participate in the work. *History education material for joint use in Korea and Japan: the history of exchanges between Korea and Japan – from prehistoric to modern times* (*Yeoksa Gyogwaseo* 2007), which was published simultaneously in both countries in March 2007, covers the entire history of bilateral relations between Korea and Japan, as its title indicates, and contains contents agreed upon by the two sides.

Second came the results of the work carried out by members of the Daegu branch of the Korean Teachers and Education Workers' Union and the Hiroshima Teachers and Education Workers' Union, which together formed a team for the production of joint historic education material to be used in both countries, entitled *History education material for joint use in Korea and Japan/Joseon Official Ambassadors – from Toyotomi Hideyoshi's invasion of Joseon to Joseon Official Ambassadors for Friendly Relations* (*Jyeon-guk* 2005). The book was published simultaneously in both countries in April 2005. The team held a total of seven seminars on the compilation of the book for joint use in both countries between February 2002 and February 2005. The book contains a remark to the effect that it intends to help students learn about the deep historical relations between the two countries and develop a positive attitude towards the reinforcement of the existing peaceful and friendly relations.

The third case concerns the results of the joint work carried out by the Association for Korea–Japan History Education-related Exchanges (of Korea) and the Association of Japan–Korea History Education-related Exchanges (of Japan). They have made joint efforts from 2002 onwards and have published joint history education-related material entitled *Majuboneun Han-ilsa* [*A comparison of Korean and Japanese history*] (*Han-il Yeoksa Gyoyuk Gyoryu Moim* 2006). Targeting teachers, it chiefly covers the history of relations between the two countries from ancient to modern times, in addition to subjects that may help readers to understand the other country's culture better, as well as Korean culture in Japan and Japanese culture in Korea. The part concerning pre-modern times contains eighteen subjects. The textbook-style book assigns eight pages to each subject, including illustrations and relevant materials. It helps readers to determine the essential points on which to focus regarding the other country's history and culture.

The final case concerns the results of the activities of the Forum on History Views and Peace in East Asia. The forum launched an ad hoc Committee on History Education-related Materials for Joint Use in Korea, Japan and China. The committee met on a total of eleven occasions between March 2002 and April 2005. In May 2005, *History that opens the future: the modern and contemporary history of three East Asian countries* (*Dong-asia Yeoksa Insik-gwa Pyeonghwa Forum* 2005) was published. Its major contents include invasion–resistance, cooperation–conflict and war–peace. The book was arranged in such a way as to maintain its readability for secondary students, while containing information that ordinary adults could find interesting as well.[17]

So far, the three East Asian countries have only been interested in embellishing their respective histories and justifying their own historical views. Under such circumstances, it is a positive thing that they have agreed to make joint efforts to form joint historical views for the goal of peace and joint prosperity.

One more book should be added to the four preceding cases of jointly compiled history education materials: namely, an introductory book on Korean history compiled by historians at the request of the Korean–Japanese Bishops' Association. The book, compiled for joint use in the two countries, is expected to provide a stimulus to other organisations engaged in similar efforts. The compilers of the book say that the book is expected to help people of the two countries to become closer neighbours by promoting a spirit of peace and love and sharing historical views (Lee *et al.* 2004).

It takes a lot of courage, patience and sincerity for the two countries, which used to be hostile towards each other, to reach an agreement on the joint compilation of history education materials for joint use. Needless to say, jointly compiled educational materials will go a long way towards promoting mutual understanding on the part of the people of the two countries and bridging the gap in their respective historical views.

Conclusion

Korea and Japan are very closely related in terms of geography, history, culture and ethnicity and will remain so. It goes without saying that it is most desirable for the people of the two countries to come to understand and respect each other and live in peace. This chapter presents a discussion of historical conflict and dialogues in the hope of helping to find ways of achieving this goal.

The people of the two countries cannot expect to overcome this historical conflict if they only ask those of the other side to improve their historical views. They need to take a more flexible and refined attitude. They should bear in mind that they are involved in special reciprocal relations. The writer would like to make a few suggestions as a conclusion to this study:

1. Historians, history teachers and interested others from both countries should make further efforts to discuss the issue of historical views and explore ways of improving them. The issue still remains at the level of being taken care of by the governments whenever a political or diplomatic situation involving the issue arises. In the course of such a process, people of the two countries have seen misunderstanding and distrust accumulating on both sides. The issue should be left to historians and history teachers, while the governments should only act as providers of support.
2. The government authorities of the two countries should always bear in mind that the issue of historical conflict can easily incite nationalist fervor and may easily fall prey to being used in the name of politics or diplomacy for other goals. Those in the private sector who engage in history dialogues should be particularly cautious about this. Essentially, it is necessary to admit that countries, peoples and individuals are likely to have different historical views. Those concerned need to learn to look at the history of relations between the two countries from an objective and relative perspective, rather than trying to stick to their own ethnocentric path.
3. One should focus on the history of peace and exchange between the two countries. In their bilateral relations that have lasted for more than 1,500 years, the two sometimes adopted an antagonistic stance towards each other. However, such outbreaks of hostility account for a very short period of time compared with the long period of relations based on peace and exchange. Think of the solidarity network formed in the private sector in connection with such issues as the 'comfort women', the status of Koreans in Japan and historical views, the 'sister relations' established between schools, civic organisations or local administrative units. Such a network has gone a long way towards improving the situation by leading public opinion and persuading governments to act positively.
4. When discussing bilateral relations, ways should be explored to involve North Korea. Without involving North Korea, one cannot talk about the modern history of the Korean peninsula fully, and so the picture of the relations between Korea and Japan cannot be a complete one. Thus, one should pay full attention to various aspects of the relations between the two Koreas, as well as between North Korea and Japan.
5. It is not a good idea for either Korea or Japan to look at the other party only from the context of bilateral relations. Each of the two has developed diverse relationships with other countries, so the history and culture of each have many aspects that would not be covered by such a narrow, bilateral focus. With some exaggeration, it may be said of Japan and Korea that the parts of their respective histories that involve the other are very

small indeed. For each to be able to deepen its view of the other, the two should adopt an attitude of looking at the other's history and culture as they appear from diverse perspectives. When the two countries are ready to take such a flexible attitude towards each other, the historical conflict between them may subside considerably, if not completely.

Notes

1 An earlier version of this chapter appeared in Korean as Chung J. (2008) '*Han-Il eui yeoksa galdeung gwa yeoksa daehwa*' [Historical conflict and dialogues between Korea and Japan], in *Hanguk gwa Ilbon eui yeoksa insik* [*The historical perceptions of Korea and Japan*], Seoul: Nanam. Permission granted by Nanam Press.
2 The author recently proposed realistic ways of overcoming the historical conflict between Koreans and Japanese, although it appeared to be a somewhat foolhardy thing to do, considering the rigid situation that has arisen between the two countries as a result of the conflict. For these, refer to the following: Chung Jae-jeong, *Yeoksahakjaga Boneun Han-ileui Yeoksa-galdeunggwa Geukbok Banghyang: Gwgeosa mit Yeongto Munje* [The historical conflict arising between Korea and Japan viewed by a historian and his proposal for ways of overcoming it]; *Dokdo, Yasukuni, Geurigo Han-ilgwangyeui Mi-rae* [Dokdo, Yasukuni Shrine and the future of relations between Korea and Japan]; *Hyundae Ilbon Hakhu*i [The Korean Association of Contemporary Japanese Studies] (2006) *Han-ileui Yeoksa-galdeunggwa Geukbok Banghyang* [The historical conflict arising between Korea and Japan], 30 June 2006; *21Segi Dongbuk-aui Gongdong Beonyeongeul Wihan Yeoksa Munjeui Geukbok* [The need to overcome historical problems for the joint prosperity of countries in Northeast Asia in the twenty-first century]; *Dongbuk-a Yeoksa Jaedan* [Northeast Asian History Foundation], 29 November 2006. This article bases its main idea on what is discussed in these studies concerning historical perspectives and dialogues.
3 *Hangukhak Jung-ang Yeongu-won* [Academy of Korean Studies] (2006) 'Dong-asia-eseoui Jinsilgwa Hwahae' [The truth about the past and reconciliation in East Asia], *2006nyeon Gukje Foreum Munmyeonggwa Pyeonghwa* [The 2006 Global Forum on Civilisation and Peace], 6–8 November 2006; *Chin-il Banminjok Hangwi Jinsang-gyumyeong Wiwonhu*i [The Presidential Committee for the Inspection of Collaboration for Japanese Imperialism] (2006) *Gwageo-chungsanui Bopyeonsunggwa Teuksuseong* [Universality and the specificity of settling past wrongs], 16 November 2006; *Asia Pyeonghwa-wa Yeoksa-gyoyuk Yeondai* [Asia Peace and History Education Network] (2006) '*Yeoksa-daehwui Gyeongheom-gongyuwa Dong-asia Hyeopryeok Model Chakgi*' [The need for sharing experience in historical dialogues and the search for examples of cooperation between East Asian countries], *Dong-asia Yeoksa Insik Gongyureul Wihan Gukje Symposium* [International Symposium for Sharing Common Historical Perspectives among East Asians], 25 November 2006.
4 This was the first attempt made by the heads of state of the two countries to include their historical perspectives in a diplomatic document. It is true that the two countries came much closer to each other in their historical views, although observers have made various remarks about their actual significance. Refer to *Oegyo-tongsangbu* (1998). For the coverage by foreign press media, refer to *Haewoe Munhwa Hongbowon* (1998).
5 Refer to the press release, issued by *Daetongryeong Hongbobiseosil* (2006).
6 See editorials of *Yomiuri shinbun* and *Asahi shinbun* (26 April 2006).

7 The statement made by Chief Cabinet Secretary Gotōda Masaharu (後藤田正晴) on official visits to Yasukuni Shrine by the prime minister and other state ministers on 15 August of this year (1986) says:

> The objective was to mourn for the people in general who became the victims of war for the sake of their homeland and their comrades and to renew Japan's determination for peace in Japan and the rest of the world. It was unrelated to any individual deities enshrined at Yasukuni.
>
> (*Gaimushō* 1986)

8 A statement made on 13 August 2001 by Prime Minister Koizumi Jun'ichirō on Korea and China's protests concerning his paying homage at Yasukuni Shrine, went:

> During the war, Japan caused tremendous suffering to many people of the world including its own people. Following a mistaken national policy during a certain period in the past, Japan inflicted, through its colonial rule and aggression, immeasurable ravages and suffering, particularly on the people of the neighbouring countries in Asia. This has left a still incurable scar on many people in the region [. . .] I believe that Japan must never again proceed along a path to war. Every year, before the souls of those who lost their lives in the battlefield while believing in the future of Japan in those difficult days, I have recalled that the present peace and prosperity of Japan are founded on the ultimate sacrifices they made, and renewed my vow for peace. I had thought that the people of Japan and those of the neighbouring countries would understand my belief if it was fully explained, and thus, after my assumption of office as prime minister, I expressed my wish to visit Yasukuni Shrine on 15 August.
>
> (Available online at: www.zephyr.dti.ne.jp/~kj8899/koizumi_danwa.html accessed 14 July 2010)

9 For the history of the development of Yasukuni Shrine, refer to Takahashi (2005). The souls of more than 2.5 million Japanese who sacrificed their lives for the emperor in the period between the Meiji Restoration and World War II are enshrined there. They include sailors killed in the skirmish at Ganghwado island, Korea, in 1875, those killed in clashes with Korean militias protesting against Japan's attempt to rule over the country, Joseon Governor-General Koiso Kuniaki 小磯國昭, who forced Korean youths to enlist in the Japanese Army, fourteen others convicted as Class A war criminals, and even the 20,000-plus Koreans who were mobilised during the colonial period. The shrine is the place where the emperor invokes the souls of the war dead and praises their heroic acts, extolling them as deities and protectors of the country. Thus, it is not just another famous place in Japan for Koreans or other Asians; paying homage at the Yasukuni Shrine can be seen as an act of extolling Japan's rule over Korea and other Asian countries and the war it waged against the world.

10 For more details refer to Lee and Chung (2002).

11 Available online at: www.mofa.go.jp/region/asia-paci/korea/joint9810.html (accessed 14 July 2010).

A comment made by Chief Cabinet Secretary Fukuda Yasuo (福田康夫) on 3 April 2001 reads as follows:

> Japan's textbook authorisation system is founded on the basic principle that a diverse range of textbooks employing the creativity and originality of private sector authors and editors will be published, and without the government defining specific historical perspectives or outlooks. The historical perspectives or outlooks represented in textbooks should not be identified as

those of the Japanese Government [...] The Japanese Government's basic recognition of its history is reflected entirely in the Prime Minister's statement issued on 15 August 1995 commemorating the fiftieth anniversary of the end of World War II. Japan humbly accepts that for a period in the not too distant past, it caused tremendous damage and suffering to the people of many countries, particularly to those of Asian nations, through its colonial rule and aggression, and expresses its deep remorse and heartfelt apology for that. Such recognition has been succeeded by subsequent cabinets and there is no change regarding this point in the present cabinet.

MEXT minister Machimura Nobutaka's (町村信孝) stated, on 3 April 2001:

> It would violate the spirit of the constitution which guarantees the freedom of thought and conscience to attempt to make a judgment on the historical views of the compilers in the process of textbook inspection. The government authorities' inspection of history textbooks is not carried out to support specific historical views and facts. Textbook inspection is carried out basically to check defects based on objective academic achievements and appropriate materials available in accordance with the inspection criteria concerning the specific descriptions contained in a textbook submitted for approval. The inspection made this time was also carried out on the basis of such a principle. The inspection of society textbooks is carried out in the light of all the relevant clauses of the inspection criteria, including the 'neighbouring countries clause', which asks for necessary consideration of the need for international understanding and cooperation in dealing with historical events in modern times involving neighbouring Asian countries, and the inspection made this time was also carried out in full consideration of the 'neighbouring countries clause'.
> (Available online at: www.mofa.go.jp/mofaj/press/danwa/13/dfu_0403.html and www.ne.jp/asahi/tyuukiren/web-site/backnumber/17/tawara_kyokasyo.htm (accessed 14 July 2010))

12 For matters concerning the commission, see *Han-il Yeoksa Gongdong Yeongu Wiwonhui* (2005).
13 For the results of the studies and the details of other activities carried out by the Korea–Japan Commission for the Joint Study of History, refer to the aforesaid report of the commission and to Kim Tae-sik (2007) '*Han-il Yeoksa Gongdong wiwonhoe Hyeonhwang Mit Gwaje*' [The current status and issues of the Organising Committee for the Korea–Japan Historians' Meeting], *Yeoksa Daehwaro Yeol-eoganeun Dong-asia Yeoksa Hwahae* [Historical reconciliation between East Asian countries through historical dialogues], *Dong-asia Yeoksa Hwahae Gukje Forum* [The International Forum on Historical Reconciliation in East Asia], hosted by the Korea National Commission for UNESCO, and *Dongbuk-a Yeoksa Jaedan* [The Northeast Asian History Foundation], 9–10 October 2007, 224–41.
14 For the trend of historical dialogues between the two countries made over the past thirty-plus years, refer to Chung 1998d and 2006a.
15 Jointly compiled historical education materials currently in use include Lee *et al.* (2004); *Jeon-guk Gyowon Nodongjohap Dae-gu Jibu* [Korean Teachers and Education Workers' Union, Daegu Chapter] (2005); *Dong-asia Yeoksa Insik-gwa Pyeonghwa Forum* [East Asians' Historical Perspectives and Peace Forum] (2005); *Han-il Yeoksa Gyoyuk Gyoryu Moim* [Meeting for Korea–Japan Historical Education-related Exchanges] (2006); *Yeoksa Gyogwaseo Yeonguhui (Hanguk) wa Yeoksa Gyoyuk Yeonguhui (Ilbon)* [Association of History Textbook Researchers (of Korea) and the Association of History Education Researchers (of Japan)] (2007).

16 The results of the analysis of history textbooks were published as: *Yeoksa Gyogwaseo Yeonguhui (Hanguk) wa Yeoksa Gyoyuk Yeonguhui (Ilbon)* [Association of History Textbook Researchers (of Korea) and the Association of History Education Researchers (of Japan)] (2000).
17 See *Asia Pyeonghwa-wa Yeoksa Gyoyuk Yeondae* (2004). The compilers set forth the purpose and significance of the book as follows: to promote the spread of joint historical views among East Asians based on cosmopolitanism and opposed to imperialism and hegemony, while advocating peace and humanism; to promote the efforts made by the three countries for the joint compilation of history education-related materials and to have them reflected positively in the education of students, in contrast to past practice that only focused on criticism of Japanese attempts to distort historical facts, and to enhance the efforts jointly made by historians and teachers of the three countries for the compilation of history textbooks from a cosmopolitan perspective. Available online at: www.japantext.net/data/report.php?mode=V&num=6&id=83&SN=&SK=&SW=&page= (accessed 14 July 2010).

Bibliography

Asia Pyeonghwa-wa Yeoksa Gyoyuk Yeondae [Asia Peace and History Education Network] (2004) *2003 Ilbon Gyogwaseo Barojapgi Undong Bonbu Hwaldong Bogoseo [The 2003 report on the activities of the headquarters for setting the contents of Japanese history textbooks straight]*, Seoul: Asia Pyeonghwa-wa Yeoksa Gyoyuk Yeondae (self-publishing).

Chung J. 鄭在貞 (1998a) *Hanguk-eui Nonri – Jeonhwangiui Yeoksa Gyoyukgwa Ilbon Insik [Korea's logic – history education and perspectives concerning Japan in the transition period]*, Seoul: Hyuneumsa.

—— (1998b) *Ilboneui Nonri – Jeonhwangiui Yeoksa Gyoyukgwa Hanguk Insik [Japan's logic – history education and perspectives concerning Korea in the transition period]*, Seoul: Hyuneumsa.

—— (1998c) *Kankoku to Nihon: rekishi kyōiku no shisō* 韓国と日本: 歴史教育の思想 *[Korea and Japan: ideologies contained in history education]*, Tokyo: Suzusawa shoten.

—— (1998d) 'Yeoksa Gyogwaseoreul Wihan Hanguk Ilbon Hyeop-ui Hwaldonggwa Myeot Gaji Gwaje' [Discussion activities carried out by Koreans and Japanese concerning history textbooks], in *Korea National Commission for UNESCO* (ed.) *21segi Yeoksa Gyoyuk-gwa Yeoksa Gyogwaseo: Han-il Yeoksa Gyogwaseo Munje Haegyeo-ui Saeroun Dae-an [History education and textbooks in the twenty-first century – a new alternative solution to the history textbook issue between Korea and Japan]*, Seoul: Doseo chulpan oreum, Ch. 5.

—— (2001a) 'Ilbon Junghakgyo Yeoksa-gyogwaseo-e Natanan Hanguksagwan-ui Teukjing: Fusōsha Ganhaeng Gyogwaseoreul Jungsimeuro' [Characteristics of views of Korean history contained in history books for middle school students in Japan – with the focus on textbooks published by Fusōsha], *Hanguk Dongnipundongsa Yeongu*, vol. 16: 1–34.

—— (2001b) 'Kankokujin no Nihon ninshiki: sono rekishiteki shinten to kadai' 韓国人の日本認識: その歴史的進展と課題 [The Korean awareness of the Japanese: historical development and challenges], *Tōhoku Ajia kenkyū* 東北アジア研究 [Northeast Asian Studies], vol. 5: 47–66.

—— (2004) 'Hirogaru taiwa, fukumaru giron: rekishi kyōkasho o meguru Nikkan taiwa' 広がる対話、深まる議論: 歴史教科書をめぐる日韓対話 [Expanding dialogues and deepening discussions: dialogues between Japan and Korea concerning history textbooks], in *Rekishigaku kenkyūkai* 歴史学研究会 [Historical Science Society of Japan] (ed.) *Rekishi kyōkasho o meguru Nikkan taiwa: Nikkan gōdō rekishi kenkyū shinpojiumu* 歴史教科書をめぐる日韓対話: 日韓合同歴史研究シンポジウム [*The Korea–Japan dialogue concerning history textbooks: the Korea–Japan Symposium for the Joint Study of History*], Tokyo: Ōtsuki shoten.

—— (2005) 'Ilbonui Junahakgyo "Sae Yeoksa-gyogwaseo" ui Yeoksa-gwan' [Historical perspectives contained in the 'new history textbook' for Japanese secondary school students], unfinished manuscript.

—— (2006a) 'Han-ilui Yeoksa Daehwa: Hwahaewa Sangsaeng-eul Wihan Odyssey' [History dialogues between Korea and Japan – an odyssey for reconciliation and coexistence], *Ilbonhak Yeongu*, vol. 19: 15–48.

—— (2006b) 'Han-il Yeoksa Daehwaui Gudo: Yeoksa Gyogwaseowa Yeroksa Insikeul Jungsimeuro' [The structure of history dialogues between Korea and Japan – with the focus on history textbooks and historical perspectives], in Y. Kim (ed.) *Ilboneun Hangukege Mu-eot-in-ga* [*What is Japan to Korea?*], Seoul: Hanul publishing, part 1, Ch. 2.

Daetongryeong Hongbobiseosil [Presidential PR Secretary's Office] (2006) Han-ilgwangte-Daehan Daetongryeong Teukbyul Danhwamun [President's special statement on relations with Japan], 25 April. Available online at: www.mofat.go.kr/help/search/index.jsp (accessed 14 July 2010).

Dong-asia Yeoksa Insik-gwa Pyeonghwa Forum [East Asians' Historical Perspectives and Peace Forum] (2005) *Mirae-reul Yeo-neun Yeoksa* [*History that opens the future*], Seoul: Hankyoreh.

Gaimushō 外務省 [Ministry of Foreign Affairs Japan (MOFA)] (1986) Statement by Chief Cabinet Secretary Masaharu Gotōda on official visits to Yasukuni Shrine by the prime minister and other state ministers on August 15 of this Year. Available online at: www.mofa.go.jp/policy/postwar/state8608.html (accessed 14 July 2010).

—— (2010) Statement by Prime Minister Tomiichi Murayama 'On the occasion of the 50th anniversary of the war's end' (15 August 1995). Available online at: www.mofa.go.jp/announce/press/pm/murayama/9508.html (accessed 14 July 2010).

Gukjeonghongbojeo [Government Information Agency] (2003) *Roh Moo-hyun Daetongryeong Bang-il Oegyo* [*President Roh Moo-hyun's visit to Japan as a diplomatic overture*], Seoul: Governmental publication.

Haewoe Munhwa Hongbowon [Korean Culture and Information Service] (1998) *Kim Dae-jung Daetongryeong Ilbon Gukbin Bangmun oesingisajib* [*A collection of foreign press coverage of President Kim Dae-jung's state visit to Japan*], Seoul: Governmental publication.

Han-il Yeoksaga Huiui Jojik Wiwonhui [Organising Committee for the Korea–Japan Historians' Meeting] (2002) *1945nyeon Ihu Han-il Yangguk-eseoui Yeoksa Yeongu Donghyang* [*The trends in historical research in the post-war period*], Seoul: Kookhak jaryowon.

Han-il Yeoksa Gongdong Yeongu Wiwonhui [Korea–Japan Commission for the Joint Study of History] (2005) *Han-il Yeoksa Gongdong Yeongu Bogo* [*Report on the joint study of history involving Korea and Japan*], vols I–VI, Seoul: Northeast Asian History Foundation Press.

Han-il Yeoksa Gyoyuk Gyoryu Moim [Meeting for Korea–Japan History Education-related Exchanges] (2006) *Majuboneun Han-ilsa* [*A comparison of Korean and Japanese history*], P'aju: Sakyejul publishing.

Jeon-guk Gyowon Nodongjohap Dae-gu Jibu [Korean Teachers and Education Workers' Union, Daegu Chapter] (2005) *Han-il Gongtong Yeoksa Gyojae Joseon Tongsinsa: Toyotomi Hideyoshi-ui Joseon Cimryak-eseo Uhoui Joseon Tongsinsaro* [*History education material for joint use in Korea and Japan/Joseon official ambassadors – from Toyotomi Hideyoshi's invasion of Joseon to Joseon official ambassadors for friendly relations*], Seoul: Hangil chulpansa.

Kim Tae-sik (2007) 'Han-il Yeoksa Gongdong wiwonhoe Hyeonhwang Mit Gwaje' [The current status and issues of the Organising Committee for the Korea–Japan Historians' Meeting], *Yeoksa Daehwaro Yeol-eo-ganeun Dong-asia Yeoksa Hwahae* [Historical reconciliation between East Asian countries through historical dialogues], Dong-asia Yeoksa Hwahae Gukje Forum [The International Forum on Historical Reconciliation in East Asia], hosted by the Korea National Commission for UNESCO and *Dongbuk-a Yeoksa Jaedan* [The Northeast Asian History Foundation], 9–10 October.

Lee W. and Chung J. (eds) (2002) *Ilbon Yeoksa Gyogwaseo Mu-eot-I Munjeinga* [*What are the problems concerning Japanese history textbooks?*], Seoul: Dongbang media.

Lee W. et al. (2004) *Hangukgwa Ilbon-eseo Hamkke Ikneun Yeolrin Hanguksa: Gongdong-ui Yeoksa Insik-eul Hyanghayeo* [*The history of Korea for Korean and Japanese readers: towards the goal of forming joint historical views*], Seoul: Sol chulpansa.

Ministry of Foreign Affairs and Trade (MOFAT), Republic of Korea (ROK) (2004) Statement by MOFAT spokesperson on Japanese Prime Minister Koizumi's visit to Yasukuni Shrine. Available online at: www.mofat.go.kr/english/help/search/index.jsp (accessed 14 July 2010).

Oegyo-tongsangbu (MOFAT) (1998) *Kim Dae-jung Daetongryeong Ilbon Gongsikbangmun Gyeolgwa (gongdongseon-eon, Yeonseolmun deung Juyogirok)* [*Results of President Kim Dae-jung's state visit to Japan (for joint statements and speeches)*], Seoul: Governmental publication.

Rekishi kyōiku kenkyūkai (Nihon) 歴史教育研究会（日本）[Association of History Education Researchers (of Japan)] (ed.) (2003) *Nihon to Kankoku no rekishi kyōtsū kyōzai o tsukuru shiten: senshi jidai kara gendai made no Nikkan kankeishi* 日本と韓国の歴史共通教材をつくる視点―先史時代から現代までの日韓関係史 [*Perspectives adopted in joint history education material to be used in Japan and Korea: the history of the relations of Japan and Korea from prehistoric to contemporary times*], Tokyo: Nashinokisha.

Takahashi T. 高橋哲哉 (2005) *Yasukuni mondai* 靖国問題 [*The Yasukuni issue*], Tokyo: Chikuma shobō.

Yeoksa Gyogwaseo Yeonguhui (Hanguk) wa Yeoksa Gyoyuk Yeonguhui (Ilbon) [Association of History Textbook Researchers (of Korea) and the Association of History Education Researchers (of Japan)] (2000) *Yeoksa Gyogwaseo Sok-ui Hanguk-gwa Ilbon* [*Korea and Japan in history textbooks*], Seoul: Hyean publishing.

—— (2007) *Han-il Yeoksa Gongtong Gyojae Han-il Gyoryu-ui Yeoksa: Seonsa-eseo Hyundaekkaji* [*History education material for joint use in Korea and Japan: the history of mutual exchanges – from prehistoric to modern times*], Seoul: Hyean publishing.

11 Historical reconciliation between Germany and Poland as seen from a Japanese perspective
The thoughts of a Japanese historian and their development

Kawate Keiichi

This chapter further examines the reaction against right-wing historical revisionism and the endeavours for historical reconciliation in East Asia. It discusses the history of the 'textbook problem' in Japan in comparative context, highlighting similarities and differences with the experience of German–Polish dialogue over history textbooks. The Japanese reception and perception of this European dialogue serves as a background to the discussion of the value and limitations of this 'model' for the East Asian case, taking as its starting point the arguments put forward by the very scholar who introduced the German–Polish dialogue to Japan: Nishikawa Masao. The argument here suggests that new ways of writing history, that involve going beyond the 'traditional' division between one's own national history and those of foreign 'others' without sacrificing one's subject position, might in the long run be more pertinent than the German–Polish model of bi-national reconciliation. This suggestion resonates with Sun Ge's problematisation of the 'East Asia perspective' earlier in this volume.

Introduction

The historical relations between Germany and Poland suggest to us many issues that reflect on modern history in East Asia as well. Japanese historians especially have taken German modern history as the object of comparative research. Their interests range from the process of modernisation to the problem of fascism. Above all, the relations between Germany and Poland are considered a serious matter (Itō 1986). Polish–German relations remind us of the Japanese colonial policy or of wars of aggression. For instance, it has been pointed out that the Japanese government and Japanese intellectuals in the Meiji era had already been interested in the 'Germanisation policy' (*Germanisierungspolitik*) of the Poles during the time of the German Second Empire, in order to develop a Japanese colonial policy in Korea (Lee 1996: 228l; Itō 2002: 8–11). If one considers this historical background, the German–Polish dialogue on history textbooks also becomes an important issue.

In this chapter, I would like to analyse how the attempt to conduct a West German–Polish dialogue on history textbooks in the 1970s and the results of this discourse have been introduced to Japan. In addition, I will also show how the international talks in the East Asian countries (especially between Japan and South Korea, or between Japan and China) have developed since the 1980s.

Since many researchers have already introduced the well-known West German–Polish discourse on history textbooks in the 1970s,[1] I do not need to describe once more the dialogue in Europe. In my opinion, it will be probably more interesting to learn how the European attempt was perceived in Japan, and, furthermore, how the improvement of history textbooks has proceeded in Japan according to the European model.

Japanese historians and history teachers have indeed been actively engaged in issues concerning the connection between history studies and history education since the end of World War II. In the 1950s, some historians already took note of the international conferences on history textbooks (Uehara 1954: 35–40; Bandō 1954: 45–7). However, when a great number of Japanese historians and history teachers became acquainted with the West German–Polish dialogue in the 1980s for the first time, they were deeply impressed. This attempt to reconciliate the former invading country and the former invaded country seemed applicable to Japan, which was a former invading nation in East Asia as well. Discussions between both countries about the 'territorial problem' (*Territorialfrage*), the 'expellees' (*Heimatvertriebene*), 'coming to terms with the past' (*Vergangenheitsbewältigung*) and so on, issues that also matter for Japan, have resulted in a deeper reflection on their own modern history and history education.

Of course, we should promote a similar international dialogue on history books in East Asia in order to overcome narrow-minded nationalism. This is the most important objective. I would also like to reconsider here the problem of mere imitation of the European model, as well as giving a prudent analysis of the present mode of preparing common teaching materials for Japan and its neighbouring countries from this perspective. I will examine this issue in the context of the developments among historians and history teachers in Japan.

The structure of this chapter is as follows: first, I will trace the trend of international dialogues between Japan and its neighbouring countries since the 1980s, which began under the influence of the West German–Polish dialogue. This effort can be divided into two periods: the first period is from the first half of the 1980s to the first half of the 1990s, and the second period is from the second half of the 1990s to the present. Then, I will investigate how the European dialogues were introduced to Japan and which influences they exerted on Japanese history textbooks. After that, I refer to Nishikawa Masao (西川正雄; 1933–2008), a Japanese historian of European modern history (especially German modern history), who played the leading role in the academic circles of historians. He was the one who initially introduced the international dialogue between West Germany and Poland into Japan.

It is important to analyse here his thoughts and their development, and, especially, to examine why he criticised the attempt to prepare a common history textbook, even though he had advanced the international dialogues between Japan and its neighbouring countries. At the same time, I would like to take a closer look at Nishikawa Masao's notions of 'one's own country's history' (*jikokushi* 自国史) and 'world history' (as the history of foreign countries, *sekaishi* 世界史) within the frame of Japanese history education, as this perspective was crucial to him in his attempt to overcome the present problem of history education in Japan.

The 'textbook problem' in 1982 and the beginning of international cooperation for the improvement of history textbooks

In Japan, the Ministry of Education is in charge of approving textbooks. The system of authorised textbooks began under the control of General Headquarters (GHQ) in 1948. After this, authority was delegated from the GHQ to the Japanese government in 1952; the political control of textbooks became tighter after 1958. The struggle against this system began actively, after the beginning of the 'Ienaga Trial' (*Ienaga saiban* 家永裁判) in 1965 – a protest against the history textbook authorised by the Ministry of Education (Kimijima 1996: 170; *Shakaika kyōkasho shippitsusha kondankai* 1984: 350–6). In fact, this movement, which was promoted by many Japanese historians and history teachers in order to improve the history textbooks, was very significant. However, the textbook problem (*kyōkasho mondai* 教科書問題) in 1982 made Japanese historians and history teachers realise anew the necessity to reflect on Japanese modern history from the standpoint of 'the other'. In other words, until then, the effort to improve history textbooks via the struggle against the system of authorised textbooks or trials was advanced by Japanese people themselves, and there was no international effort to improve the history textbooks. In this sense, the 'textbook problem' was a new experience (Ijūin and Nishikawa 1985: 107–8).

The problem occurred when the Japanese government tried to deny Japanese aggression in East Asia through the system of authorised textbooks. As a matter of course, the Japanese government was criticised by their neighbouring countries (*Shakaika kyōkasho shippitsusha kondankai* 1984: 367–70). Japanese historians and history teachers realised the necessity of an East Asian discourse about the possible improvement of history textbooks (Nishikawa 1985a: 25). And, at this point, the international dialogues between West Germany and Poland since 1972 offered a model and an impetus for modification.

Nishikawa was one of those who first introduced the European experience into Japan and emphasised its significance. He wrote:

> The relationship between West Germany and Poland is similar to the relationship between Japan and Korea. Poland and Korea were each for

a long time ruled by the neighbouring country, and both especially suffered national loss during World War II [. . .] In both of these cases dealing with the relations between former colonial ruling country and ruled country, there can be no progress toward mutual understanding on an equal footing without coming to terms with the past [. . .] In the case of Japan and Korea, a long time has passed without dialogue on history textbooks. In contrast, West Germany and Poland have developed such dialogue and conference on history textbooks. Does this experience have anything to teach us?

(Nishikawa 1985b: 305–6)

Nishikawa made a long-term endeavour to foster the international exchange of the walled-off historian academic circles in Japan. With his colleagues (e.g. Yoshida Gorō 吉田悟郎; 1921–) he also founded the Study Group for Comparative History and Comparative History Education (*Hikakushi, hikaku rekishi kyōiku kenkyūkai* 比較史・比較歴史教育研究会 (SGCHCHE)) in December 1982. This SGCHCHE initially advanced an international dialogue between Japan and its neighbouring countries according to the model of the dialogue between West Germany and Poland.

The SGCHCHE invited guest speakers from China and South Korea in August 1984 and organised a symposium entitled *History education in East Asia – one's own country's history and world history*.[2] In 1989, the SGCHCHE organised the *Second symposium of history education in East Asia*, with participants from China, South Korea and North Korea.[3] In July 1991, a seminar on history education in Japan and South Korea was held by the SGCHCHE. In this process, international dialogues between West Germany and Poland were consistently of interest to those who organised these symposia, because the relationship between West Germany and Poland was similar to the relationship between Japan and its neighbouring countries. Nevertheless, as a matter of fact, Japan did not make any effort to reach mutual understanding, as West Germany and Poland had. Instead, the Japanese thought that they had to reflect on their own history.

The points under discussion at every symposium were manifold. The main topic, however, was always how one should describe the relationship between 'one's own country's history' and 'world history'. When one describes history, there is always the question of subjectivity. On the other hand, one must describe one's native history objectively and universally in order to overcome ethnocentrism. Moreover, these two issues should be reconciled within the frame of 'one's own country's history' and 'world history'. From this standpoint, when the SGCHCHE was organised on the occasion of discussing the textbook problem in 1982, the SGCHCHE did not deal with the simple description of a textbook. During the discussion on the textbook problem in 1982, a certain term was claimed to be diplomatically precarious: the word 'aggression' or 'invasion' (*shinryaku* 侵略) in history textbooks was replaced, on official sanction by the Ministry of Education, with the term 'advance' (*shinshutsu* 進出). This was extremely problematic in itself, but a more important issue for the SGCHCHE was a historical awareness as a premise of description in textbooks. In particular, the division of Japanese history education into 'national (Japanese) history' (*Nihonshi* 日本史) and 'world hisory' (*sekaishi* 世界史), i.e. the history of foreign countries, is regarded as a big problem. The fact that 'national (Japanese) history' and 'world history' are taught as two separate school subjects in Japanese high schools reveals this particular point of view. In this case, Japanese history is isolated from 'world history', which only consists of the simple conglomeration of former Western history and Oriental history since the Meiji period. The SGCHCHE thought – against the background of this strict compartmentalisation in schools – that Japanese students are unable to understand the position of Japan in the world; thus it is very likely that mutual understanding between the neighbouring countries was disturbed by these problems. This framework was recognised by the SGCHCHE as a main problem in understanding history (Yoshida 1985: 26–29).

Ten years after the first SGCHCHE symposium on history education in East Asia took place, they held the third symposium in August 1994. On this occasion, the participants not only came from South Korea and China, but also from Taiwan and Vietnam. The topics of this symposium were: 'How to teach American history' and 'The war between Japan and China in 1894/5 in world history – East Asia at the end of the nineteenth century and its modernisation'. According to the report of this symposium, the reason why these topics were chosen is as follows: at the first and second symposia, the participants exchanged their general views about the era when Japan was the assailant. Building on these results, they wanted to advance 'the attempt to approach universal values' through discussing concrete subjects in the frame of 'one's own country's history and world history' (*Hikakushi, hikaku rekishi kyōiku kenkyūkai* 1996: 2–3).

What follows is an overview of Nishikawa's ideas that he has developed on the basis of the West German–Polish dialogue over the past ten years:

1 In this matter, the subject is not only the description of history textbooks.
2 It is also important that one debate the different interpretations by different nations, and deepen one's understanding about the history of others.
3 One should not aim at common history textbooks in Asia.
4 The international dialogue should be carried on by private groups, because history education should be free from any form of political exertion of influence, regardless of the government involved.
5 The frame of such a critical mind is 'one's own country's history' and 'world history' (*Hikakushi, hikaku rekishi kyōiku kenkyūkai* 1996: 2).

As a matter of fact, the West German participants in the West German–Polish dialogue emphasised their own non-official position. Therefore, even though this dialogue began with Brandt's diplomacy in the 1970s – and in this sense was bound by political issues – those involved in the dialogue were able to assert their own ideas. It may indeed be the case that the participants from the Polish side represented the official position, but Nishikawa highly praised the fact that the recommendation was realised beyond the political systems of the two countries. In respect of the results of the third symposium, Nishikawa emphasised the following aspects:

> On the assumption that Japan has its own responsibility as an assailant, it was revealed that there are various additional complications. For instance, China was a former suzerain state of Korea and Vietnam and therefore sent troops to Vietnam during the Sino–French War and troops to Korea during the Sino–Japanese War. Taiwan had been occupied by Japan during the Sino–Japanese War, but Taiwan was returned to China after World War II and the Chinese Revolution. The independence of Taiwan is the present issue. Another example: Vietnam stood against France and Japan, and at last achieved independence during the war against the USA. However, at present, Vietnam cannot disregard the economic power of the USA [. . .] In the third symposium, such complex situation was reported upon. It meant that the symposium reached a new stage where the participants deepen their historical awareness of one another. Not only Japanese participants but also other participants could learn a different view on history from the perspective of the others.
> (*Hikakushi, hikaku rekishi kyōiku kenkyūkai* 1996: 3)

Although the SGCHCHE had promoted such a discourse on history between Japan and its neighbouring countries for ten years, new serious problems about history education and history textbooks have occurred in Japan since 1982. Since the 'problem of history textbooks' developed into a diplomatic problem, the Japanese government and the Ministry of Education have always been sensitive to the fact that the descriptions in Japanese history textbooks were under very close scrutiny by its neighbouring countries. Finally, the Ministry of Education had to reconsider the descriptions. In December 1991, three former Korean 'comfort women' (*ianfu* 慰安婦) filed a lawsuit against the Japanese government. The latter did not accept that the government and the army had a share in this crime against humanity, and the apology was postponed by the Japanese government for fifty years or more. Nevertheless, in early 1992, the Japanese historian Yoshimi Yoshiaki (吉見義明; 1946–) found hitherto undisclosed government documents. The newly found evidence made it clear that the Japanese military had played a direct role in setting up the 'comfort stations' (*ianjo* 慰安所). After that, the Japanese government reversed the official position and admitted that the government had played a crucial role in the system of 'comfort women'. As a consequence, the description of 'comfort women' could not be denied and eliminated by the Ministry of Education any longer and appeared in the history textbook.

Not only did the rise of 'revisionists' from the right wing, who agitate for a 'neoliberal interpretation of history' (*shinjiyūshugi shikan* 新自由主義史観), depend on the conservative tendency of Japanese society, but also, in connection with history textbooks, their emergence stood in connection with their irritation with such an actual revision of the depiction by the Ministry of Education. These 'revisionists' soon organised the so-called Japanese Society for History Textbook Reform (*Atarashii rekishi kyōkasho o tsukurukai* 新しい歴史教科書をつくる会; *Tsukurukai* for short) and wrote their own textbook from their perspective. The Ministry of Education corrected over one hundred factual errors and ultimately approved this textbook for possible classroom use. In the summer of 2001, some schools actually adopted the textbook – less than 1 per cent of all schools, however. Afterwards, the Ministry of Education also accepted the second edition in 2004. In 2005, 4 per cent of all schools chose this second edition.[4] Moreover, since that time, the other textbooks have become conservative. For instance, there is increasingly less information on 'comfort women'.

International dialogues on history textbooks since the mid 1990s: the development of the creation of joint teaching materials between Japan and its neighbouring countries

In such a period of rising nationalistic revisionism from the right wing, the international dialogue between Japan and its neighbouring countries (especially China and South Korea) had reached a new stage. This new stage advanced in the direction of producing common teaching materials or textbooks, for example the attempt to develop common teaching materials between Japan and South Korea.

One of the achievements is the creation of *History education material for joint use in Korea and Japan: the history of mutual exchanges* (*Nikkan rekishi kyōtsū kyōzai: Nikkan kōryū no rekishi* 日韓歴史共通教材—日韓交流の歴史), which was published in Japan as well as in South Korea in 2007.[5] This was one result of the ten-year-long ongoing exchange between Japan and South Korea since 1997.

If one follows the background events, it becomes clear that the former stage was the Japanese and South Korean Joint Study Group on History Textbooks (*Nikkan gōdō rekishi kyōkasho kenkyūkai* 日韓合同歴史教科書研究会 (JSG)). The JSG was also founded under the influence of the international dialogue between West Germany and Poland, which seemed to have a history similar to that of Japan and South Korea. The joint group held many meetings and symposia. According to the report published in 1993, the consensus by the participants was that they wanted to depict Japanese history in such a way that Japan was unequivocally the assailant; this harsh judgement was to be handed down to the younger generation (*Nikkan rekishi kyōkasho kenkyūkai* 1993: 4). Fujisawa Hōei (藤沢法暎; 1936–), who wrote the preface of this report as a representative, also introduced the international dialogue between West

Germany and Poland in detail in the 1980s (Fujisawa 1986). He was interested in the international improvement of history textbooks from the perspective of pedagogy and proposed to transfer such European attempts to East Asia (*Nikkan rekishi kyōkasho kenkyūkai* 1993: 12–19).

The JSG held their meetings and symposia during a limited period of three years. Their main characteristic was that they would not discuss 'historical viewpoints that seemed abstract to them', such as the 'historical viewpoint of East Asia', but they would limit their research object to history textbooks (*Nikkan rekishi kyōkasho kenkyūkai* 1993: 60). The object of this research was not the textbook of world history, but the textbook of national history (the Japanese side used the textbook of Japanese history at high school). At the fourth symposium (the last symposium), the possibility of making common textbooks between Japan and South Korea was also discussed (*Nikkan rekishi kyōkasho kenkyūkai* 1993: 142–3). After they had reported and exchanged their opinions about the analysis of each textbook, they broke up the JSG in 1993.

Based on its results and reflections, the symposium on history textbooks between Japan and South Korea has been newly held since 1997. In this case, historians and graduate students of Tōkyō Gakugei University actually played the main role on the side of Japan, and, on the side of South Korea, the researchers were from Seoul City University. The focus of this common project was also the analysis of each history textbook, but, in this particular case, the concrete aim was to make common teaching materials. According to their assertion, the outcome was not supposed to be a common textbook but common teaching materials. Among the participants, however, there were various opinions. If one reads the interim report, *The viewpoint of producing history education material for joint use in Korea and Japan* (*Nihon to Kankoku no rekishi kyōtsū kyōzai o tsukuru shiten* 日本と韓国の歴史共通教材をつくる視点), which consists of many articles, one can find that the common teaching materials are identical to a common textbook (*Rekishi kyōiku kenkyūkai* 2003: 54, 60–74). Even though it was emphasised that their aim was not to produce a common textbook but common teaching materials, it was important in the first place to believe that it is indeed possible to make common textbooks within the frame of the different systems in both countries in order to produce common teaching materials. Several members of this group thus had no doubt about the idea of making a common textbook. When they indicated the significance of their attempt as well as its difficulties, they always referred to preceding European experiences such as the international dialogues between West Germany and Poland, or the common history book entitled *European history* that was written by authors of twelve European countries and published in France in 1992 (*Rekishi kyōiku kenkyūkai* 2003: 68–9).[6] However, it is to be noted that the latter publication, *European history*, was introduced in Japan as *the* common European textbook, which, in reality, it was not. Even though the Japanese version is subtitled *The common European textbook*, this subheading cannot even be found in the original. As a result, many Japanese people misunderstood the book as *the* common European history textbook.[7]

If one finds any differences between the JSG and the SGCHCHE, they lie in the two groups' focus: the JSG concentrated on analysing senior secondary textbooks of national history, so that the book *History education material for joint use in Korea and Japan* was mainly written about the history between those two countries. On the other hand, the SGCHCHE focused on the relation between 'one's own country's history' and 'world history' throughout.

There were also other attempts to make common teaching materials. For example, the book *History that opens the future: the modern and contemporary history of three East Asian countries* (*Mirai o hiraku rekishi: Higashi Ajia san-goku no kingendaishi* 未来をひらく歴史―東アジア三国の近現代史) was published by the Trilateral Joint History Editorial Committee of Japan, China and South Korea (*Nitchūkan san-goku kyōtsū rekishi kyōzai iinkai* 日中韓三国共通歴史教材委員会) in 2005. In this case, the emergence of the revisionist *Tsukurukai* triggered that attempt. They thought that it was necessary to foster common historical knowledge if they wanted to establish a peaceful community in East Asia against the ethnocentric nationalism that tried to distort historical facts as well as justify the former Japanese war of aggression and colonialism. The scholars, teachers and citizens who share such ideas have embarked on international dialogues since March 2002 and established the Trilateral Joint History Editorial Committee of Japan, China and South Korea (*Nitchūkan san-goku kyōtsū rekishi kyōzai iinkai* 2005). The result led to the above-mentioned book entitled *History that opens the future*. Whereas *History education material for joint use in Korea and Japan* treats general history from prehistory to the present age, the three countries' common textbook is limited to the modern age. At the same time, the most notable feature of this book is that Japanese, Chinese and Korean scholars wrote the units of the content in parallel. This is, in a sense, a compromise between mutual understanding and subjectivity.

Besides these examples, the movement to creating common teaching materials has spread in East Asia in various directions. Also in Europe, a common German–French history textbook was published. In this respect, the attempt to make common textbooks seems to have become a mainstream tendency both in East Asia and in Europe.

Reconsidering the international dialogues on history and the making of common teaching materials

In the previous sections, I have outlined the history of the dialogue on history textbooks, which has been divided into two stages since the 1980s. One of the most recent books on this subject in Japan was published in 2008 and is entitled *History politics in East Asia: Japan–China–South Korea: dialogue and historical cognition* (*Higashi Ajia no rekishi seisaku: Nitchūkan: taiwa to rekishi ninshiki* 東アジアの歴史政策―日中韓―対話と歴史認識), edited by

Kondō Takahiro (近藤孝弘; 1963–). Kondō researched the international dialogue between West Germany and Poland and published the following book: *German modern history and the international improvement of textbooks* (*Doitsu gendaishi to kokusai kyōkasho kaizen* ドイツ現代史と国際教科書改善 (Kondō 1993)). Besides this work, he introduced the idea of international improvement of history textbooks in Europe to Japan from various standpoints and is thus known as a leading expert in this special field. He also reckons that the attempt to make a common history textbook across the borders is possible today, despite actual difficulties (Kondō 2008: 248).

In that case, why did Nishikawa – who had taken the initiative in the international dialogue between Japan and its neighbours – consistently take a prudent attitude against producing common textbooks among countries after 1982? This happened while he was advancing the international dialogue, always referring to the dialogue between West Germany and Poland. Until Nishikawa died in 2008, he persisted in this opinion. In my view, his insistence must be understood in various dimensions. It seems to depend on his standpoint as a historian, as well as being related to the history of the movement against the system of authorised textbooks in Japan. In the following part, I will reconsider the issue Nishikawa pointed out in referring to his work as a historian of European modern history, especially German modern history.

Nishikawa interpreted the lesson of the report called *Recommendations on history textbooks in West Germany and Poland* as being a proposal from a private standpoint. The Japanese system of authorised textbooks showed the danger of state intervention into history or history education from an official standpoint. Nishikawa feared that, whatever viewpoint on history was taken, once the state intervened, it would be the new criterion for official sanction. All movements that I have traced here support this point, and so it was emphasised that their movement was non-official.

On the other hand, a new official movement also began. The first committee of common history research between Japan and South Korea was established by mutual agreement at a summit meeting between Japan and South Korea in 2001. A second committee has been working since 2007. However, even though an official dialogue is promoted, problems have still remained, which Nishikawa pointed out as follows: once such an interpretation of history is built on the official dialogue between the governments, there is always the potentiality that one perspective would be authorised as the only 'right' history, and other standpoints on history would not be accepted. However, taking into consideration the long history of alterations of history textbook content by the system of authorised textbooks in Japan, one can understand that his scepticism is not groundless (Nishikawa 1997: 144).

The second problem is as follows: if one considers the problem of subjectivity in respect of the description of history, it is questionable whether it is possible to create common textbooks between two countries. For example, Nishikawa referred to Fukuzawa Yukichi (福沢諭吉; 1835–1901), a political theorist and thinker of the Meiji era. Fukuzawa advocated that Japan should 'leave Asia and join Europe' (*Datsu-A – Nyū-Ō* 脱亜入欧). In South Korea, on the contrary, Fukuzawa is described as a proponent of Japanese aggression against Korea, or even of Japanese colonial policy. Nishikawa thought that, if the Japanese denied him totally on the basis of such ideas alone, it would mean the total denial of Japanese modern thoughts. Even though he understood such criticism against Fukuzawa, Nishikawa went on to say that he himself was unable to hold the same position. He emphasised the difficulty that – even though he reflects on the Japanese past – he cannot describe history the same way a Korean would do (Nishikawa 1997: 172). He also emphasised that, in the course of promoting an international dialogue and deepening a mutual understanding, much effort should be put on ameliorating each country's national textbooks from its national perspective, rather than creating a common textbook for Asia or the whole world. One should not compromise or avoid disputes and controversial issues in order to achieve a consensus (Nishikawa 1997: 145).

I think that such an assertion is connected to his attitude as a historian. As I have mentioned, Nishikawa left behind a large number of works as a historian of European modern history as well as of German modern history, and he played an important role in developing European modern history in Japan. Two of his works, *World War I and the Socialists* (*Daiichiji sekai taisen to shakaishugishatachi* 第一次世界大戦と社会主義者たち), published in 1989, and his last one, *A group of Socialism International 1914–1923* (*Shakaishugi intānashonaru no gunzō 1914–1923* 社会主義インターナショナルの群像1914〜1923), from 2007, are of special importance here: in these studies, he particularly followed the trend of the socialists who came together in the Second International and constituted the Antiwar and Peace Movement before World War I. It was a hard process of solidarity of people who pursued the same ideal beyond the boundaries of state or nationalism. Through such works, Nishikawa kept the possibility of solidarity firmly in mind, yet, at the same time, he had an acute feeling that it encountered many difficulties.

Nishikawa often emphasised that it was dangerous for Japanese historians if their works depended on borrowed arguments from Europe while they advanced their own works at the same time. This attitude seems to apply to the case of the dialogue on history textbooks as well. It was more important to him what we should learn from European experience and how we should receive this experience.

Modern Japan proceeded along the path of modernisation by receiving many things from Europe. This also applies to history studies and history education. For instance, Japanese history studies and the history education system were built in a framework that divided history into Western history, Oriental history and national history since the Meiji era. In this process, Western history was always a model, and Oriental history was left behind. Even though this division, which especially affected history education, vanished after World War II, the subject of 'world history' at high school, which was born after

World War II, was simply the combination of former Western and Oriental history. This meant that the contents remained unchanged (Yoshida 1985: 25).

This is the reason why the SGCHCHE basically established the theme of 'one's own country's history' and 'world history': it was an attempt to overcome such a view of history that has evolved from the old frame of the three categories. They thought that, if such a historical consciousness remains, one cannot understand one's own national history very well (Nishikawa 1997: 106).

With regard to history studies, Japanese historians, especially scholars of Western history, tended to import the achievements of European historians as well, and regarded this undertaking as sufficient. Nishikawa was always sceptical towards such tendencies and insisted that Japanese historians had better investigate historical materials of various incidents by themselves and develop their own arguments.

This case is applicable to the relationship between German modern history and Japanese. What does it mean for the Japanese to learn from Germany? In Japanese universities, many scholars did research on German history, literature, philosophy and so on. I also tried to do research on German modern history in order to analyse Japanese modern history comparatively. It is true that there are many aspects of German modern history that are worthwhile studying for Japanese. This applies as well to the issue of 'coming to terms with the past' in the Federal Republic of Germany. Compared with the German efforts, Japan has been far from dealing with this delicate issue since World War II. Given the fact that there is such a Japanese problem, is it possible to have such a different perspective?

Although 'coming to terms with the past' in Germany is praised in the world, and Japan should learn many things from Germany's experience, it has not been an easy road for Germany (Nishikawa 1997: 260–86). It also took many years of twists and turns. For instance, the compensation for the Jews began shortly after World War II. In contrast, the compensation for Sinti and Romani, handicapped persons and homosexuals who were persecuted by the Nazis has taken much longer. And, since 1945, there have been several discussions about how to interpret the Nazi period, such as the 'historians' quarrel' (*Historikerstreit*) in 1986–7 or the discussion about Daniel Goldhagen's book (*Hitler's willing executioners* 1996), as well as the debate over the German Army Exhibition (*Wehrmachtsausstellung* 1995–9 and 2001–4). Such aspects are generally unknown in Japan.

I would like to refer to Nishikawa's standpoint once more: he questioned the attitude of the Japanese idealising European experiences and also criticised their arguments, which depended on European arguments even when there was no reason. He was critical of such an idealisation and blind reliance on European experiences, as other countries' problems could also be extended to Japan.

At the end, let me return to the German–Polish dialogue on history textbooks. After the West German–Polish dialogue on history textbooks had been introduced into Japan, information about it spread within Japan. However, sometimes it appeared as a kind of stereotype to many people who do not know how difficult it was to develop such a dialogue. In 1972, the UNESCO Textbook Committee was established in both countries with the goal of making recommendations on history and geography textbooks. After many conferences, these recommendations were edited in 1976 and published in both countries in 1977. The recommendations regarding history textbooks amounted to twenty-six (Gemeinsame Deutsch–Polnische Schulbuchkommission 1995). The dialogue had already had a long history going back to the time before World War II. After the war, the intensity of this dialogue depended mainly on individual efforts such as Enno Meyer's attempts (Meyer 1988: 19–63). Such constant endeavour was seen not only before the publication of the above-mentioned recommendations but also after that. After 1977, the conferences continued, and the text of the recommendation was subjected to scholarly analysis, and many educational influences were considered as well (cf. Jacobmeyer 1988, 1989; Becher *et al.* 2001). Compared with such a long history and many continuous efforts made in Europe, such attempts are relatively new in East Asia, and many tasks of international dialogue are still to be fulfilled in East Asia.

Currently, the German–French common history textbook is being watched with keen interest in Japan as a new trial in Europe. A similar experiment has recently begun between Germany and Poland (cf. Strobel 2008: 26–8). This attempt can also be understood in the context of EU policy. However, is there any possibility that the effort to produce a common history textbook between two countries could alienate other histories, both within and outside the two countries?

As I mentioned, there are already some attempts at producing common teaching materials between Japan and its neighbouring countries. With reference to German political education after World War II (Kondō 2008: 230–50), it is suggested that a possible common history textbook as a method of political education should be considered in Japan as well. Indeed, if one refers to 'coming to terms with the past' in Germany, it seems that a political education in a broad sense should be positively perceived in Japan. Nevertheless, we are still facing the main question about a common history textbook and the reality that the description of history textbooks has been distorted by the Japanese government. As Nishikawa has pointed out, it is not an end in itself to describe the common history textbook itself. Compared with the international dialogues in Europe, we have more problems to tackle. At the least, we should further continue such dialogue and analyse various disputed points in East Asia, in order to understand 'the others'.

Notes

1 Besides Nishikawa's books, articles and essays that I refer to here, one should note the following: Bandō (1982: 58–70) and Fujisawa (1986). The most important work is that of Kondō (1993).
2 The report of this symposium was published in *Hikakushi, hikaku rekishi kyōiku kenkyūkai* (1985a, b).

3 This report appeared in *Hikakushi, hikaku rekishi kyōiku kenkyūkai* (1991).
4 For further explanation of today's Japanese situation see Gordon (2003: 332).
5 Please see *Rekishi kyōiku kenkyūkai (Nihon) and Rekishi kyōkasho kenkyūkai (Kankoku)* (2007).
6 The French title reads as follows: Delouche, F. (1992) *Histoire de l'Europe* [*History of Europe*], Paris: Hachette. In 1994, a Japanese version appeared under the title: *Yōroppa no rekishi: Ōshū kyōtsū kyōkasho* ヨーロッパの歴史―欧州共通教科書 [*The history of Europe: common European textbooks*], published by Tōkyō shoseki.
7 Nishikawa also pointed out this problem (cf. *Hikakushi, hikaku rekishi kyōiku kenkyūkai* (1996: 4)).

Bibliography

Bandō H. 阪東宏 (1954) 'Rekishi kyōiku ni tsuite no Bei–Doku rekishika kaigi ni tsuite' 歴史教育についての米＝獨歴史家会議について [About the American–German Conference on History Education], *Rekishigaku kenkyū* 歴史学研究 [*Journal of Historical Studies*], no. 10: 45–7.

—— (1982) 'Rekishi kyōkasho no kokusaiteki kentō ni tsuite: Nishi Doitsu, Pōrando "Rengō kyōkasho iinkai" no shigoto ni terashite' 歴史教科書の国際的検討について―西ドイツ・ポーランド「連合教科書委員会」の仕事に照らして [The international analyses of history textbooks: the work of the Joint Textbook Committee between West Germany and Poland], *Rekishi hyōron* 歴史評論 [*Historical Review*], vol. 391, no. 11: 58–70.

Becher, U. *et al.* (eds) (2001) 'Deutschland und Polen im 20. Jahrhundert: Analysen – Quellen – Didaktische Hinweise' [Germany and Poland in the twentieth century: analysis – sources – didactic advices], *Schriftenreihe der Bundeszentrale für Politische Bildung*, vol. 456, Hannover: Hahn.

Delouche, F. (1992) *Histoire de l'Europe* [*History of Europe*], Paris: Hachette. (The Japanese title appeared in 1994 and reads as follows: *Yōroppa no rekishi: Ōshū kyōtsū kyōkasho* ヨーロッパの歴史―欧州共通教科書 [*The history of Europe: common European textbooks*], Tokyo: Tōkyō shoseki.)

Fujisawa H. 藤沢法暎 (1986) *Doitsujin no rekishi ishiki: Kyōkasho ni miru sensō sekininron* ドイツ人の歴史意識―教科書にみる戦争責任論 [*The historical consciousness of the Germans: the theory of war responsibility through textbooks*], Tokyo: Akishobō.

Gemeinsame Deutsch–Polnische Schulbuchkommission [Joint German–Polish Commission on Schoolbooks] (ed.) (1995; enlarged edn) 'Empfehlungen für die Schulbücher der Geschichte und Geographie in der Bundesrepublik Deutschland und in der Volksrepublik Polen' [Recommendations on history and geography schoolbooks in Germany and Poland], *Studien zur internationalen Schulbuchforschung*, vol. 22, no. 15, Frankfurt am Main: Diesterweg.

Goldhagen, D.J. (1996) *Hitler's willing executioners. Ordinary Germans and the Holocaust.* New York: Knopf.

Gordon, A. (2003) *A modern history of Japan: from Tokugawa times to the present*, New York and Oxford: Oxford University Press.

Hikakushi, hikaku rekishi kyōiku kenkyūkai 比較史・比較歴史教育研究会 [Study Group for Comparative History and Comparative History Education] (ed.) (1985a) *Jikokushi to sekaishi: Rekishi kyōiku no kokusaika o motomete* 自国史と世界史―歴史教育の国際化を求めて [*One's own country's history and world history: looking for the internationalisation of history education*], Tokyo: Miraisha.

—— (ed.) (1985b) *Kyōdō tōgi: Nihon, Chūgoku, Kankoku* 共同討議―日本・中国・韓国 [*Collaborative discussion: Japan–China–South Korea*], Tokyo: Horupu shuppan.

—— (ed.) (1991) *Ajia no 'kindai' to rekishi kyōiku* アジアの「近代」と歴史教育 [*Asia's 'modernity' and history education*],Tokyo: Miraisha.

—— (ed.) (1996) *'Kurofune' to Nisshin sensō: rekishi ninshiki o meguru taiwa* 「黒船」と日清戦争―歴史認識をめぐる対話 [*The 'black ships' and the war between Japan and China: a dialogue of historical cognition*], Tokyo: Miraisha.

Ijūin R. 伊集院立 and Nishikawa M. 西川正雄 (1985) *'Nishi Doitsu, Pōrando kyōkasho kankoku' to Nishi Doitsu no rekishi kyōiku (jō)* 「西ドイツ・ポーランド教科書勧告」と西ドイツの歴史教育（上）[The *German–Polish recommendations on history textbooks* and history education in West Germany (1)], *Kyōiku* 教育 [Education], vol. 449, no. 2: 94–111.

Itō S. 伊藤定良 (1986) *Ikyō to kokyō: Doitsu teikokushugi to Rūru Pōrandojin* 異郷と故郷―ドイツ帝国主義とルール・ポーランド人 [*Foreign place and home place: German imperialism and the Ruhr Poles*], Tokyo: Tōkyō daigaku shuppankai.

—— (2002) *Doitsu no nagai 19-seiki: Doitsujin – Pōrandojin – Yudayajin* ドイツの長い19世紀―ドイツ人・ポーランド人・ユダヤ人 [*Germany's long nineteenth century: Germans – Poles – Jews*], Tokyo: Aoki shoten.

Jacobmeyer, W. (ed.) (1988) *Zum wissenschaftlichen Ertrag der deutsch–polnischen Schulbuchkonferenzen der Historiker 1972–1987* [*The scientific return of the German–Polish textbook conferences on history 1972–87*], Braunschweig: Georg-Eckert-Institut für internationale Schulbuchforschung.

—— (ed.) (1989) *Zum pädagogischen Ertrag der deutsch–polnischen Schulbuchkonferenzen der Historiker 1972–1987* [*The pedagogical return of the German–Polish textbook conferences on history 1972–87*], Braunschweig: Georg-Eckert-Institut für internationale Schulbuchforschung.

Kimijima K. 君島和彦 (1996) *Kyōkasho no shisō* 教科書の思想 [*The idea of textbooks*], Tokyo: Suzusawa shoten.

Kondō T. 近藤孝弘 (1993) *Doitsu gendaishi to kokusai kyōkasho kaizen: posuto kokumin kokka no rekishi ishiki* ドイツ現代史と国際教科書改善―ポスト国民国家の歴史意識 [*German modern history and the international improvement of textbooks: historical consciousness of a post-nation state*], Nagoya: Nagoya daigaku shuppankai.

—— (2008) 'Higashi Ajia no rekishi mondai to Yōroppa no rekishi seisaku' 東アジアの歴史問題とヨーロッパの歴史政策 [The history problem in East Asia and the history politics in Europe], in T. Kondō (ed.) *Higashi Ajia no rekishi seisaku: Nitchūkan: taiwa to rekishi ninshiki* 東アジアの歴史政策―日中韓―対話と歴史認識 [*History politics in East Asia: Japan–China–South Korea: dialogue and historical cognition*], Tokyo: Akashi shoten, 230–52.

Lee Y. (1996) *'Kokugo' to iu shisō: kindai Nihon no gengo ninshiki* 「国語」という思想-近代日本の言語認識 [*The concept of 'mother tongue': the cognition of language in modern Japan*], Tokyo: Iwanami shoten.

Meyer, E. (1988) 'Wie ich dazu gekommen bin: die Vorgeschichte der deutsch–polnischen Schulbuchgespräche 1948–1971' [What made me to do that: the prologue of the talks on German–Polish schoolbooks], *Studien zur internationalen Schulbuchforschung*, vol. 56, Frankfurt am Main: Diesterweg.

Nikkan rekishi kyōkasho kenkyūkai 日韓歴史教科書研究会 [Japanese–South Korean History Textbook Research Group] (ed.) (1993) *Kyōkasho o Nikkan kyōryoku de kangaeru* 教科書を日韓協力で考える [*Reconsidering textbooks by Japanese–South Korean cooperation*], Tokyo: Ōtsuki shoten.

Nishikawa M. 西川正雄 (1985a) 'Jikokushi to sekaishi' 自国史と世界史 [One's own country's history and world history], *Sekai* 世界 [World], no. 2: 23–6.

—— (1985b) 'Kyōkasho kaizen no kokusai kyōryoku: Nishi Doitsu–Pōrando kyōkasho kaigi' 教科書改善の国際協力—西ドイツ＝ポーランド教科書会議 [International Cooperation for the Improvement of Textbooks: the West German–Polish Textbook Conference], in Hikakushi, hikaku rekishi kyōiku kenkyūkai 比較史・比較歴史教育研究会 [Study Group for Comparative History and Comparative History Education] (ed.) *Jikokushi to sekaishi: Rekishi kyōiku no kokusaika o motomete* 自国史と世界史—歴史教育の国際化を求めて [*One's own country's history and world history: looking for the internationalisation of history education*], Tokyo: Miraisha, 305–30.

—— (1989) *Daiichiji sekai taisen to shakaishugishatachi* 第一次世界大戦と社会主義者たち [*World War I and the socialists*], Tokyo: Iwanami shoten.

—— (1997) *Gendaishi no yomikata* 現代史の読みかた [*The reading of modern history*], Tokyo: Heibonsha.

—— (2007) *Shakaishugi intānashonaru no gunzō 1914–1923* 社会主義インターナショナルの群像—1914～1923 [*A group of socialism international 1914–1923*], Tokyo: Iwanami shoten.

Nitchūkan san-goku kyōtsū rekishi kyōzai iinkai 日中韓三国共通歴史教材委員会 [Trilateral Joint History Editorial Committee of Japan, China and South Korea] (ed.) (2005) *Mirai o hiraku rekishi: Higashi Ajia san-goku no kingendaishi* 未来をひらく歴史—東アジア三国の近現代史 [*History that opens the future: the modern and contemporary history of three East Asian countries*], Tokyo: Kōbunken.

Rekishi kyōiku kenkyūkai 歴史教育研究会 [Study Group for History Education] (2003) *Nihon to Kankoku no rekishi kyōtsū kyōzai o tsukuru shiten* 日本と韓国の歴史共通教材をつくる視点 [*The viewpoint of producing history education material for joint use in South Korea and Japan*], Tokyo: Nashinokisha.

Rekishi kyōiku kenkyūkai (Nihon) and Rekishi kyōkasho kenkyūkai (Kankoku) 歴史教育研究会（日本）と歴史教科書研究会（韓国） [Study Group for History Education (Japan) and Study Group for History Textbooks (Korea)](eds) (2007) '*Nikkan rekishi kyōtsū kyōzai*': *Nikkan kōryū no rekishi: senshi kara gendai made* 「日韓歴史共通教材」—日韓協力の歴史—先史から現代まで [*History education material for joint use in Korea and Japan: the history of mutual exchanges – from prehistoric to modern times*], Tokyo: Akashi shoten.

Shakaika kyōkasho shippitsusha kondankai 社会科教科書執筆者懇談会 [Authors' Round-Table Conference on Social Studies Textbooks] (ed.) (1984) *Kyōkasho mondai to wa nanika* 教科書問題とは何か [*What is the textbook problem?*], Tokyo: Miraisha.

Strobel, T. (2008) 'Startschuss für ein gemeinsames deutsch–polnisches Geschichtsbuch' [Starting point for a joint German–Polish history textbook], *Eckert – das Bulletin*, no. 3: 26–8.

Uehara S. 上原専祿 (1954) 'Rekishi kenkyū to rekishi kyōiku' 歴史研究と歴史教育 [History study and history education], *Rekishigaku kenkyū* 歴史学研究 [*Journal of Historical Studies*], 1: 35–40.

Yoshida G. 吉田悟郎 (1985) 'Jikokushi to sekaishi' 自国史と世界史 [One's own country's history and world history], in Hikakushi, hikaku rekishi kyōiku kenkyūkai 比較史・比較歴史教育研究会 [Study Group for Comparative History and Comparative History Education] (ed.) *Jikokushi to sekaishi: Rekishi kyōiku no kokusaika o motomete* 自国史と世界史—歴史教育の国際化を求めて [*One's own country's history and world history: the pursuit of the internationalisation of history education*], Tokyo: Miraisha, 17–32.

12 Mediating textbook conflicts

Falk Pingel

This final chapter goes further in proposing a more general framework for approaches to textbook conflict mediation. It focuses on the transfer of knowledge through history education from one generation to the next, which is controlled not only by scholarly quality criteria and pedagogical standards, but also influenced by political or ideological agendas. To overcome narrow national/nationalistic approaches to the teaching of history, and the dangers that these entail, international collaborative textbook projects are underway in East Asia, even if these have undergone various changes since the 1990s in terms of structure and methods. This chapter discusses the attractions and limitations of various approaches to textbook projects and tries to identify factors that contributed to the success or failure of past projects. It examines the extent to which the rich experience gained in international textbook consultations in Europe after the Second World War might be applied to the East Asian context, while also considering the alternative of concentrating on and investing in larger projects, as Sun and Kawate propose in their chapters. This may help to inform the search for a truly multilateral, constructive approach to understanding crucial moments of Asian history in the twentieth century, while transcending the post-war European paradigm of reconciliation.

A new focus on education in conflict situation

In the last two decades, 'textbook and conflict' has become a major topic in the debate about long-term, sustainable conflict resolution measures. Two findings, at first glance contradictory, directed the attention of international aid organisations to school textbooks: on the one hand, textbooks have often been misused as transmitters of hate speech and disparaging stereotypes of other nations or cultural and religious communities, and they have contributed to the sharpening of clashes and deepening of emotionally loaded differences between groups; on the other hand, they have also served as tools to combat stereotypes, to bridge gaps between adversary groups and to lay foundations for an advancement of intercultural and international understanding. Klaus Seitz has called this the 'two faces of education' (cf. Seitz 2004).

It is well known that textbooks become a topic of research in the dissemination of peace- or war-oriented values, and that international organisations give them a prominent place in peace-building measures. Scholarly comparative examination of textbooks and their subsequent revision in order to make societies ready for reconciliation and to promote awareness for intercultural and international cooperation were firmly institutionalised in the agenda of the League of Nations after World War I, revitalised by UNESCO after World War II and gained new momentum after the re-shifting of international relations at the end of colonialism and the breakdown of the socialist system since the late 1980s/early 1990s (cf. Pingel 2009a). The latter developments not only brought independence and full sovereignty to formerly suppressed, or Soviet-dominated, societies and states, but also led to cruel infighting, civil war, social unrest and, in some cases, even to interstate wars that should have been a thing of the past, at least in seemingly pacified regions such as Europe. Some of these battlefields became a never-ending story. Protracted conflict not only destroyed the material infrastructure for quality education, it also affected the content of teaching by turning it into a tool for ideological warfare. Confronted with the damaging effect of protracted conflict on school education in general, and on the minds of pupils in particular, international organisations under the leading role of UNESCO came to the conclusion that they should pay more attention to the role of education in shattered societies, in order to give young people a viable perspective that keeps them away from the temptation and pressure of war lords and their activities. Studies commissioned by the World Bank and other organisations critically reviewed the function of primary and secondary education in emergencies in general, and the failures and achievements of international peace education programmes in particular (cf. Smith and Vaux 2002; Bush and Saltarelli 2000). The research results found their way into UNESCO's campaign on 'Quality education for all', in which the textbook issue is of primary importance because, in most emergency and post-conflict areas, nothing can be achieved without appropriate teaching materials. This focus generated further case studies on the revision and renewal of teaching material and curricula in conflict-shattered societies and post-conflict situations (cf. Cole 2007; Tawil and Harley 2004); in addition, more general studies delivered background material for an overall assessment of textbook research and textbook policy (cf. Braslavsky 2006); first stock-taking efforts tried to establish criteria for the success or failure of textbook projects (cf. Höpken 2008).

Since the rearrangement of international relations in the 1990s, new forms of textbook project emerged that were developed by NGOs, teacher organisations or engaged individual university researchers, in addition to traditional bi- and multilateral textbook projects conducted within the framework of UNESCO's engagement in textbook revision. Currently, we find a wide array of agents, methods, objectives and results that influence each other and make the structure of comparative textbook work more complicated and sometimes less transparent than before; however, in the long run, it is hoped that further comparative research will help define a state-of-the-art methodology that will raise the quality of future projects. Until now, textbook revision mostly drew on experience and well-minded pragmatism, rather than on theoretical models of arbitration and peace education. This article tries to systematise the many factors that influence the make-up and results of international textbook projects; it also deals with the particular impact projects may have on curricula and textbooks. Although the main approach is a general one, the article occasionally refers to the East Asian textbook debate. This debate is an interesting testing ground insofar as it deals with the traditional form of multilateral interstate textbook controversies, applying, however, methods and procedures that came to the fore only in recent decades.

If controversies about the presentation of each other's history between nations or states dominated textbook revision from its beginnings until well into the post-World War II period, the shift of the international system from the bipolar world to multilayered globalisation gave textbook revision a new direction: the need to reconcile clashes between the narratives of different ethnic, cultural or religious groups within a state or society created new forms of internal negotiations and external intervention that considerably widened the tools and methods of textbook projects: those in East Asia, for example, show features of both tracks of textbook revision and present a link between acknowledged tradition and future-oriented procedures that have yet to stand the test of practice.

Linking both lines of development is all the more important because the notion of homogenous nation states is increasingly cast into doubt; current concepts of collective identities have to pay tribute to the internal differentiation of modern societies. Partners involved in textbook commissions or research groups can no longer legitimately represent just 'the nation', but have to reflect different identity concepts within society, even if this may weaken its position towards an external 'other'. External representation and internal identity patterns are closely interrelated. In the past, the internal divisions or the 'internal others' of the national self rarely surfaced in international textbook consultations. Today, participants in textbook projects often no longer present 'the nation', but just speak for themselves and represent one of the many strata of a concerned, already well-established or emerging civil society. This is all the more true as projects deal with intrastate affairs in order to reconcile former adversaries after civil war.

The methods of textbook research and the procedures of textbook revision did not develop systematically but historically, answering to varying challenges of violence between and within societies. Nevertheless, this chapter is structured according to systematic aspects. The new patterns of textbook revision have mixed with traditional structures; one form has not replaced the other; they now exist side by side, complement each other or compete with each other. Against this background, different forms of textbook project will be examined according to varying aims, procedures and outcomes. Achievements, problems and shortcomings will also be discussed. However, before dealing

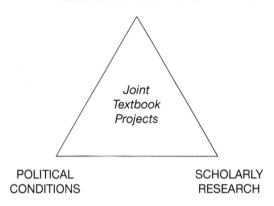

Figure 12.1

with textbook revision, the textbook has to be characterised as a medium with particular features that should be taken into account when making it an objective of revision.

The textbook as a transmitter of consensual knowledge

To understand better the different dimensions of international textbook projects, one has to bear in mind basic characteristics of the school textbook as a particular tool of communication. It does not just transmit knowledge and methods of learning. Being embedded in a structure of state-controlled schooling, it invests this knowledge and methodology with the legitimacy to be transmitted from the older generation to the younger in order to furnish society with competitive intellectual and practical capabilities that guarantee its economic well-being and social cohesion. This is the reason why schooling still is, in general, compulsory and regulated by official guidelines that refer also to textbooks and other teaching material. As the author does not want to go too much into detail for the purpose of this article, he reduces the factors that influence the development of textbooks to three cluster dimensions that represent the 'didactical triangle' by which textbook projects are framed: first, the pedagogical context; second, the political framework; and, third, the scholarly conditions. In short: pedagogy, politics and research.

1   Textbook authors have to adjust the representation of knowledge to the learning capacities of their young readers. This demands restriction on the quantity and detail of information to an amount digestible by a certain age group.
2   The political frame is mainly expressed in the curriculum and other related guidelines that teachers and textbook authors have to abide by.

Normally, the Ministry of Education is the main agent of curriculum construction; however, parents and teachers associations, other interest groups and the public media may have a say as well.

The political framework and the pedagogical context define the criteria of selection for content and methods. They reduce the wealth of possible topics and learning strategies to what is pedagogically feasible and politically wanted, but they should not distort the teaching content.

3   What is taught must be in accordance with the findings of scholarly research.

These three dimensions are hardly ever taken into account in a balanced way in textbook projects. Because distortions are mainly grounded in biased political views, whether they are articulated expressly or integrated as underlying assumptions in guidelines and educational media, the political dimension is predominantly addressed. Research is seen as the most important corrective of biased presentations; this is why textbook commissions are mostly made up of academics. Teachers, not to speak of pupils, are, as a rule, underrepresented. The weight given to the different cluster dimensions has consequences for the procedures and the results of a project, and the impact it has on textbook development and learning processes.

Until well into the 1990s, textbook analysis concentrated on the author's text, which was regarded as the main variable of either a correct or distorted presentation. The broader pedagogical environment, students' attitudes, teachers' beliefs and different styles of teaching and learning were hardly taken into account. Only the professionalisation of teacher education, which, since the 1980s, has become a worldwide trend, contributed to the development of a more research-centred approach to the 'didactics'[1] of history and other subjects. To know the context, however, is important for defining successful implementation strategies. Therefore, recent projects also take into account the results of opinion polls, the role of out-of-school activities and other media used by students, in particular the Internet. The variegated design of many modern schoolbooks is also considered, as is the methodological structure, with particular reference to pictures and tasks that students are expected to solve. These methodological considerations have given rise to theoretical work on the textbook as a tool of communication, the findings of which are applicable to textbook revision projects (cf. Höhne 2003).

The international debate on Japanese history schoolbooks in particular focused almost exclusively on the author's text in a small number of books; these few texts served as a paradigm that characterised, not only the opinion of a relatively small number of authors, but also the population's general attitude towards an evaluation of Japan's role in World War II. Neither the variety of textbook presentations, nor different opinions on the textbook issue as expressed in the Japanese public debate were taken into account. The strong

250 *Falk Pingel*

and narrow textbook approval mechanisms in Japan, which forced authors to use or cancel particular terms (cf. Nishino 2008), have contributed to researchers concentrating almost exclusively on the text; but such a narrowly focused lens no longer provides correct insight into the politics of remembrance and the teaching of the past in the country. Opinion polls conducted regularly since the 1990s show that more people – particularly in younger generations – have become critical of interpretations that whitewash the Japanese government and army; a majority favours compensation and accepts the statement that Japan waged a war of aggression (cf. Sugitani 1998; Saaler 2005). Teachers' unions have taken strong stands against the government's interference in textbook issues and are open to reconciliatory efforts. Highlighting the controversial debate in Japanese academia and the media will help to break away from one-sided accusations and to develop a more differentiated approach. This applies also to the other two countries involved in this debate, Korea and China. The free, critical, public and academic debate on Korea's textbooks is a relatively recent development for the country; any similar experience is still unthinkable in China. In the long run, joint projects should also examine teaching styles and learning objectives and interpret textbooks against the background of official policies of remembrance and out-of-school activities such as museum visits. Korean museums dedicated to the Japanese occupation are designed to stir up negative emotions against the Japanese people and are inappropriate to support a rational approach to the topic (cf. Park, K. 2010 (forthcoming); Kal 2007). If any country has the possibility to question its own position, it is Japan, as it has a variety of textbooks available. Dealing with state-committed crimes is still off-limits to Chinese teachers; they are obliged to uphold their 'nation's spirit [. . .] first'; only the adversaries' interpretations can be critically questioned in order to find 'objective truth' (cf. Li 2010 (forthcoming)). In practice – and this not only applies to classroom debate, but also shaped the communication structures of joint textbook projects until well into the twenty-first century – coping with the other's interpretation does not include critical self-questioning. It is the 'other' who is expected to question the position of the respective project partners. Even in NGO-based or academic groups, national representation and self-assertion have shaped the structure of communication and brought about results that always deal with the juxtaposition and possible harmonisation of different national histories. Transitive communication structures prevail over self-reflexive approaches.

In search for objectivity as intersubjective truth

Given the political background against which comparative textbook projects emerged after World War I, it is obvious that they pursued practice-oriented aims: to free textbooks as the then most important educational medium from obvious stereotypes and biased presentations and, in doing so, make them more *objective*. However, the intended revision should not only be based on political will and moral principles, but should also be grounded on a truth-finding process. Therefore, textbook revision projects need twofold *legitimacy*:

1   a *political* legitimacy offering reputation and acknowledgement for the intervention in a sector of society that is under the supervision of the Ministry of Education;
2   a *procedural* legitimacy that safeguards the objectivity of the process.

The aim of objectivity brought academia into the business of international textbook comparison and revision.

Traditionally, *political* legitimacy was secured through the direct or indirect participation of political authorities in the process. As textbooks from two or more different states were at stake, state agencies – as a rule the ministries of education or pedagogical institutes, depending on state guidelines – established and financed the project group; being an organ of sovereign political entities, each ministry felt free to select its members without necessarily counselling the other partner(s). If the governments were not yet ready to cooperate, international organisations could be asked to act as mediators or serve as an organisational and expert umbrella to facilitate joint work. This instrument, for example, was used for German–Polish textbook consultations as they were planned during the Cold War; diplomatic relations had only been established shortly before the textbook commission took up its work.

Increasingly since the 1990s, projects worked on textbook revision in areas of protracted conflict where official authorities could not find a solution. Here, the issue of legitimacy must be addressed in a different way. These projects cannot derive legitimacy from dysfunctional governments. Instead, they must first develop trust in their work, and then seek reputation and acknowledgement within (parts of) their society.

Political legitimacy is grounded in a balanced *representation* of the partners involved. It goes without saying that in bi- or multilateral international projects, all sides send members in approximately the same number. The question of numerical balance becomes more complicated if the partners represent majority and minority groups; if they are represented according to their (uneven) ratio in the overall population, the communication is politically weighted from the outset, and thus it is likely that the members speak foremost as representatives of their own community; consequently, the majority representation in the final results will probably outweigh the minority; in this case, the political dimension permeates the whole communication, which appears to be a dialogue about claims and rights rather than about truth.

Even if political balance is established, an even-handed representation of qualification is difficult to achieve. To establish balance of qualifications does not pose a problem in projects between partners from countries with well-developed (higher) education systems. Even during the Cold War, Poland, as well as Germany, was equipped with high-level institutions doing research

252 *Falk Pingel*

on the other's country, in disciplines such as history, geography and economics. A rather different matter is the distribution of research qualifications in, for example, Israel–Palestinian project groups. Whereas internationally reputed Israeli experts in Arab studies can easily be recruited, Palestinian scholars doing research in Jewish studies and the history/geography of Israel are hard to find at Palestinian universities. In such cases, partners must seek to establish a nevertheless symmetrical communication. The more advanced partner has to show consideration for the less privileged and may even help develop his or her argument. In any case, discriminatory attitudes are counterproductive and have to be avoided at all cost.

Procedural legitimacy was reached by organising the process of finding results as an academic exercise based on scientifically approved methods. Scientific objectivity became the guarantor for producing unbiased results. From the very beginning, textbook revision and textbook research, politics and science, were interrelated. To come back to the German–Polish Commission: under the organisational umbrella of UNESCO, of which both countries were members, the main responsibility for setting the agenda and organising the meetings rested with two national academic, practice-oriented (or, as we would say today, service-oriented) institutions: the German International Textbook Institute and the Polish Pedagogical Institute. The role of academia becomes even clearer when looking at the regular members and temporary experts of the German–Polish Commission: with a few exceptions, it consisted on both sides of reputed professors from universities and pedagogical academies. The respective ministries functioned only as 'guests' whenever they sent representatives.

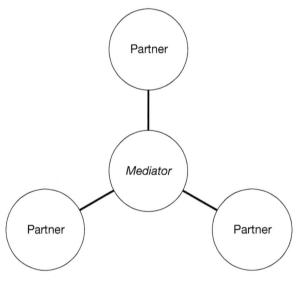

Figure 12.2

Symmetry of communication is of the essence if a project team is not based on an agreement between official authorities, but consists of members of NGOs and civil society groups. Here, the partners cannot draw on any authority, but have to reach an agreement on membership and working procedures themselves. If the conflict in question is still fresh, and a power balance has not yet been reached – which is often the case in post-civil war situations – an external mediator may help to set up a representative group and see that communication lines, roles and procedures are symmetrical, meaning that all partners have an equal share in them. Non-professionals may participate in civil society groups, and symmetrical communication may be at risk because of different educational backgrounds and abilities to express themselves on identity-sensitive topics in a larger group. Here, too, mediators and facilitators can help ease communication; the group can be divided into smaller units to encourage the less gifted speakers to present their comments. In most of the groups working on the Japanese textbook issue, procedural symmetry was never a goal, because only the Japanese textbook policy was under scrutiny, whereas the schoolbooks and education policy of the Chinese or Korean partners were not questioned at all. These asymmetrical objectives led to asymmetrical communication. The one side had wittingly taken over the role of prosecutor, whereas the other had to accept being accused. Accusations have a political or moral undertone that interferes with the scholarly argument.

Textbook research in its own right

International textbook revision follows a political or moral agenda of reconciliation. To reach this aim, it needs a solid research basis on which to base its findings and recommendations. Therefore, in parallel to the unfolding of textbook revision projects after World War I, pure scientific research on textbooks also developed beyond any practice-related framework or political support of the country whose textbooks were examined. Researchers became interested in textbooks as transmitters of knowledge and ideology (cf. Walworth 1938). After World War II, ground-breaking studies appeared that predominantly researched domestic textbooks; only since the 1990s have important comparative studies been published. Although not directly related to the purpose of revising the textbooks, a hidden moral agenda stands nevertheless behind most of these academic works. The studies aim at uncovering stereotypes and systematising the strategies of argumentation that characterise biased presentation. They aim to deliver research-based knowledge of how stereotypes are being developed, and derive strategies of how to avoid them (cf. Nicholls 2006; Foster and Crawford 2006; Schissler and Soysal 2005). Recently, first studies have appeared that also offer evaluations of textbook revision activities (cf. Dimou 2009; Richter 2008). With all these works, textbook revision projects can now draw on a more solid research basis for the practical recommendations they intend to implement.

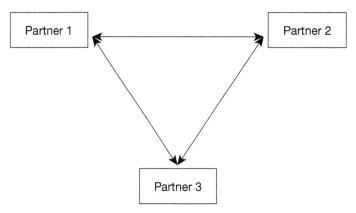

Figure 12.3

Only a few of these research publications result from international cooperation; most of them are written by individual researchers, not by international teams. However, pure research projects on textbooks, too, can be framed as a cooperation model. In this case, scholars from the countries whose textbooks are to be examined take part in the research; the researchers develop a common grid of questions and criteria; pre-tests are supposed to prove that they all use the grid in the same way. Findings need to be discussed in order to identify issues of common relevance. To better understand the specific national or cultural characteristics of textbook representations and guarantee full reciprocity, the analysis can be performed crosswise, meaning that researchers not only analyse books of their own national/cultural background, but also those of others. Crosswise analysis is more time consuming, and the researchers have to know the different languages in which the textbooks are written. Because of these obstacles, crosswise analysis is only rarely applied, although it delivers the most interesting findings for intercultural studies. However, it continues to attract more attention, because it shows that transnational or intercultural cooperation between researchers from estranged societies is possible.[2]

Joint textbook commissions have set a paradigm even for international cooperation within academia. Where contacts between scholars were previously impossible because of political frictions or because certain topics were taboo, joint academic commissions have been installed to break the ice and work on a fact-finding mission to establish a common ground for further and more detailed research. They can precede the work of textbook commissions, or both can work in parallel. As the revision of textbooks is always seen as the more complicated and politically contentious task, parallel work may facilitate progress at both levels. Synergies, however, can only be created if both types of commission communicate and exchange their results and try to develop a common policy towards governments and the public.

In East Asia, textbook research has almost exclusively and narrowly been linked to the debate on the Japanese textbook issue. In fact, it has been politicised or suspected of serving political interests from its very beginnings, so that it could not gain widespread recognition as sincere, objective, 'pure' scholarly work. The moral obligation to engage in reconciliation has made academic work on textbooks just as contentious as the textbooks already were. In particular, Japanese scholars, who have to work against official national politics, are challenged by internal criticism that their scholarly work is politically biased; they have been regarded as belonging to small, left-wing-oriented circles, which do not represent mainstream academia. The increasing, and in principle positive, cooperation between NGOs and scholars from Japan and Korea corroborates, unfortunately, rather than dissolves this close association of political/moral ends and scientific research in the minds of the general public. Therefore, the academic reputation of international textbook revision in East Asia could benefit from the establishment of textbook research units at some universities that engage in pure research which is not directly related to the East Asian textbook debate.

Procedures: balancing the political and scholarly dimensions

The German–Polish Commission opted to keep the political and scholarly dimensions apart and developed a strong self-image as an academic expert group. Consequently, the meetings of the commission resembled academic conferences rather than pedagogical seminars or political negotiations (cf. Borodziej 2003, 2008; Maier 2008). After five years of intensive textbook analysis and in-depth academic debate, they delivered their results to the public and political authorities. However, commissions sometimes do not want, or are unable, to separate politics from textbook deliberations. When politicians or representatives of the ministries regularly participate in the meetings and play an active role, the political dimension is likely to be always present, even if political arguments are not openly expressed. Politicians think of acceptance in the political arena and of implementation in the classroom; power play and pedagogical concerns may suppress the formulation of scientifically grounded arguments that will not stand the test of practice. This may have its advantages as well; if, during its deliberations, the commission can already agree upon a concept that includes politically approved strategies of practical implementation, the results may be introduced into textbook writing and teaching practice within a short time period.

The German–Polish Commission reached its limits when issues of scholarly debate appeared to be so much interwoven with politics that scientific truth was jeopardised. At the time, the Soviet Union ignored the erstwhile existence of the Hitler–Stalin Pact; therefore, the Polish academics were not allowed to make any reference to it – contrary to their own knowledge and conviction; this seemed to be unacceptable to their German colleagues. Insisting on fully revealing the historical truth, or publicising the Soviet ban on mentioning the pact, would have brought the textbook consultations to an end. As both sides strove hard to avoid the failure of the whole undertaking due to obvious political stubbornness, the committee agreed to circumvent the issue. It was agreed to sideline all official meetings and not to touch upon the pact at all; the reason given was that such a discussion would refer mostly to German–Russian relations, which are not topical in German–Polish textbook talks. Omitting this decisive event for the outbreak of World War II gave rise to harsh criticism later on, but it was apparently the only means to protect the work of the commission from open political intervention and potential failure. The commission paid a high price, but the product was delivered.

Any group – as focused on a purely scientific approach as it may be – can reach a point where politics can no longer be ignored, because in the social sciences the researchers themselves base their leading questions of enquiry and the evaluation of their findings on basic moral and/or political principles, which cannot be questioned, even if they are not shared by the whole group. Otherwise, textbook consultations crossing ideological fault lines – for example, between capitalists and socialists, or democratic and authoritarian states – would be impossible; however, in spite of fundamental politico-ideological differences, this sort of textbook consultation can be useful to pave the way for a policy of rapprochement. In the past, differences of opinion going back to basic political or moral convictions have, as a rule, not been addressed in recommendations or in the course of the consultations, but instead were taken for granted. If fostering international understanding and peaceful ways of conflict resolution is both desirable and possible, then a common denominator has to be searched for, in spite of different political, economic, cultural etc. systems. Focusing on shared views and excluding difference may, in fact, be a first step to rapprochement and may have a value in itself: it strengthens the awareness of, and readiness for, cooperation where the memories and wounds of violent clashes are still fresh, and ideological discrepancies seem to be insurmountable.

A process of depoliticisation could be observed during the deliberations of textbook revision committees in Bosnia and Herzegovina. They were set up some years after the war of 1992–5, when the international community initiated a textbook revision process. In their first meetings, the members – mostly senior teachers – acted as representatives of the three ethnic communities: Bosnians, Serbs and Croats. The ministers of education were obliged to secure each community's appropriate representation when selecting the textbook experts. The members felt that they were delegated by, and dependent on, their respective ministers and therefore not in a position to intervene in issues of national pride. The opposition of 'Croat', 'Serb' and 'Bosnian'

Mediating textbook conflicts 257

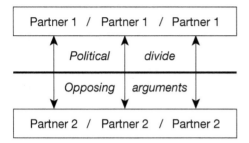

Figure 12.4

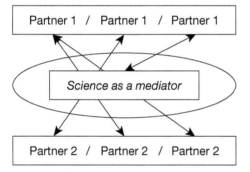

Figure 12.5

arguments could only be overcome by a long process of consultations; step by step, expert opinion overrode political leanings, while controversial arguments developed also within the ethnic groups; coalitions were built to transcend political boundaries. At the beginning of the consultation process, political legitimacy was dominant in the member's self-perception; in the end, expertise in subject matter and professional pride prevailed and lent the members legitimacy when they presented their ministers with a result that would be politically contested (cf. Pingel 2009b; Karge and Batarilo 2009). Although the political mission was never cast into doubt, the weight bestowed upon it shifted in the course of the deliberations towards the self-esteem of being a professional expert. At the beginning, the communication space was structured by the disputing parties; in the course of the consultations, the political communication lines grew fainter, and a cross-cultural academic communication space emerged.[3]

In situations of protracted, violent conflict, governments do not see themselves in a position to engage in consultations with the adversary. This is currently the case in the Israeli–Palestinian relationship. Official contacts between educational institutions and their representatives are either forbidden or not wanted. Both sides, in particular the Palestinians, are under fierce criticism of relating to the 'other' almost exclusively as an 'enemy' (cf. Brown 2003). The Palestinian National Authority regards the border question as unsettled; therefore, neither history nor civics textbooks give a clear account of the country's territory; instead, they mix the cultural, natural and historical boundaries of the region 'Palestine' and associate them with the current political entity of the Palestinian National Authority; such an approach creates obvious misunderstandings. Also in Israel, the concept of a Jewish state receiving legitimacy from ancient Israel leads to distortions of the current political borders. Under these circumstances, it cannot be expected that a harmonised interpretation of the two countries' and peoples' history or present could be formulated. Pedagogical concepts fostering willingness for peaceful conflict resolution have to include experimental approaches that can avoid the deadlocks of official policy. The 'dual narrative' model, which a group of Palestinian and Israeli teachers and scholars developed, has already attracted the attention of international agencies active in the field of peace education.[4] The basic understanding within the group is that a peaceful solution must be found, and that both peoples have a legitimate right to their own state, which implies that the Israeli occupation of Palestinian territory is illegitimate. Nevertheless, the historical roots of the conflict and the chance to come to a peaceful solution are interpreted in different ways. Therefore, the group does not try to elaborate a joint version that can be agreed upon by both sides. In contrast, each side presents its own version of the complicated Israeli–Palestinian relationship in the twentieth century; they then discuss the two narratives together to make them understandable to the respective other side. They deal with contested topics, terms, interpretations and omissions until the text seems to avoid clear bias and disparaging stereotyping, so that it can be regarded as a fair, albeit controversial, juxtaposition of two divergent presentations of the same topic. In the printed version, blank space appears in between the two narratives, which is supposed to be filled by teachers and pupils with questions, proposals or a possible third version resulting from the comparative teaching process.

The aim lies expressly not in a mutual acceptance of one or the other version, but in both sides learning that 'the other side' has developed an alternative narrative that is equally legitimate. As the regular textbooks of either side usually ignore the view of the 'other' entirely (with only a few exceptions on the Israeli side, which resulted in a textbook scandal in parliament and the media), the Peace Research Institute in the Middle East (PRIME) project's 'dual narrative' approach can already be regarded as a great achievement. During the experimental teaching process, drama and role-play help pupils 'to slip into the shoes of the other' and to try out the 'other's' arguments. Trial lessons are videotaped so that problems can be identified and the narratives improved step by step.

Under these conditions, the question of legitimacy has to be considered very seriously: the project members have not been appointed by any official authority – on the contrary, they work against the official lines of politics; they cannot even rely on support from their professional organisations, which take a rather critical stand towards the project; even their families sometimes dispute whether and why they should deal with the 'enemy' and bring its story to the children at home. Formal support is given by the above-mentioned NGO, PRIME, which provides organisation and expertise in communication and seeks funding. Nevertheless, PRIME cannot lend the project much legitimacy, because the project is the organisation's main activity, and the NGO's reputation depends considerably on its success. Under these circumstances, legitimacy must come from within the group and cannot be borrowed from an external agent.

The group agrees on rules of communication that should ensure members can express themselves regardless of their qualifications. Neither deeper subject knowledge, nor a better ability to develop complicated arguments is to be used to suppress the opinion of the 'weaker' partner; the project chairs have to implement in-built positive feedback rules;[5] instead of the members' qualifications, their personality counts, as well as their readiness to further the project and to implement its results. The method of biographical storytelling has been applied to strengthen this personality-oriented approach, which probably marks the most striking difference from groups who rely on legitimacy derived from political representation or academic reputation. Representation was, therefore, not an issue for the group, as the members represented just themselves, and not their profession or nation. In a metaphorical sense, one could say that the group members developed a certain pride in belonging to a consequently peace-oriented minority within their society; they cannot act on behalf of the state, but for the sake of their nation. The more a group has to build on its inner strength and not draw on authority and legitimacy furnished by external agencies, the more it must begin its work with trust-building measures. The group also has to reassure itself of mutual trust whenever it has to cope with external threats, be they impediments or criticism from the government or interest groups such as parents' or teachers' organisations. While the project was going on, the Israeli–Palestinian conflict escalated into open violence and warfare (for example, during the recent Lebanon War and the Gaza Intervention); this situation made it extremely difficult for the group members to stick to the accepted principles of communication and not to lose trust in a peaceful solution or the seriousness of the participants if they belong to the 'other', the 'enemy' side.

The group divides their meetings into joint plenary sessions and separate 'national' gatherings. This helps define the participants' position, but should not be misused to 'nationalise' and harmonise the argumentation of one side vis-à-vis the other, something that occurs often in groups dominated by a political agenda. The different meetings also help overcome language problems: the project's working language is English, because only a few members can communicate in both languages; however, the members' command of English varies, and, hence, clarifying certain issues within the national groups supports keeping symmetry. The language issue is tricky: terms that relate to sensitive issues of collective identities are often associated with moral concepts and behavioural attitudes that can hardly be expressed in translation. A third language can contribute to symmetry insofar as all partners are forced to translate their emotions and associations into a language neutral to the conflict at hand.

In sum – and in contrast to official and/or research-oriented groups – the PRIME project's work can be described as a communication-driven process, whereby the envisioned result is used as the tool for communication; whatever the final result may be, the most important issue is to create a communication space that crosses borders and may set an example for others to follow. In research-oriented groups, it is usually the other way around: communication controlled by rules of scientific objectivity is the tool for producing a result that is the final objective of the group's work.

Different aims, divergent results: a focus on agreement or controversy?

Until the end of the Cold War, the basic principle that textbook-revision projects should aim at joint interpretations shared by all partners remained, for the most part, unchallenged. Accordingly, reaching agreement on controversial issues was considered impossible; their details were to be avoided, or at least to be described in a manner eschewing discriminatory language and stereotypes. Projects that did not achieve this aim failed.[6] The political obligation to produce a harmonised result was in line with a didactical model according to which the schoolbook represents one authoritative, truthful interpretation of the nations' history, geography and society. Such joint official textbook projects are mostly critcised for hiding differences in opinion and conjuring up too harmonious an image of mutual relations; textbook recommendations based on this principle can lead to neutralising the presentation of controversial issues and thus circumvent pressing questions of moral and political education, instead of addressing them directly.

As controversial, multiperspective and comparative approaches have entered the schoolbooks of many countries, dissenting opinions found expression and documentation in the final results of official commissions without the project being declared a failure. Recommendations now state that certain issues cannot be agreed upon and are interpreted in different ways. In practice, however, this has not yet been applied.

Traditionally, the assumption to create new knowledge on the practitioner's side through textbook revision has followed a mechanical model of communication. The ministry of education (or other relevant authorities), the commission working under its umbrella, textbook authors and teachers are understood as elements in a chain of transmitters that transport value-loaded knowledge to the receiver, i.e. the pupil who learns the message and translates it into a behavioural attitude. In practice, however, one has to cope with interferences. The educational authorities are often less willing to implement results elaborated by scholars, who developed them free from political considerations and often without considering the pedagogical environment of the classroom. Sometimes, the official authorities remain the only receivers of the written/printed final document, and further dissemination depends on their willingness to distribute the results. In addition, not all countries have a firm system of textbook approval and admittance, so that market factors can be more influential than political guidelines. Furthermore, teachers read textbooks in different ways, and students have quite different capacities to digest what is fed into them.

Interference in the chain of transmitters may occur on purpose or accidentally, because implementation simply does not receive due attention from those who organise the joint consultations. As a rule, the commissions are dissolved after having presented their results, and mechanisms of monitoring are not taken into account. Responsibilities within governments are often divided; the foreign offices are, as a rule, the leading agencies for setting up the framework for the joint commission. The implementation, however, usually falls into the domain of the ministries of education. As a result, there are very few checks to see whether recommendations have any impact on textbooks, let alone teaching practice. However, without any follow-up activities, even official commissions have only a short-lived, or almost no, impact. The German–French and German–Polish textbook consultations may be unique in that they have been convening fairly regularly for decades and have continuously included the analysis of new textbooks in their meetings.[7] The implementation process associated with these cases has been documented, too.[8] A strong, result-oriented group needs appropriate steering power and coordination of work. This is mainly done by the chairpersons or steering committees in which all partners are represented. They have to identify contentious issues and propose strategies of how to handle them.

Differences in project aims and procedures lead to different results. Most NGO-based projects cannot draw on official support; the government's silent support or at least tolerance is often the only advantage they have. Even if the projects are not in line with the official educational policy, the government may use them as proof of, or pretext for, its alleged openness, or as a guinea pig to try out the 'other's' reaction and explore the room for manoeuvre in cooperation without becoming officially involved. In general, projects that do not fall under the umbrella of state organisations are less reliant on the state when it comes to implementation. If they do not work for the sake of 'pure' research either, they must consider the political and pedagogical implications as soon as they formulate their results. Such projects consequently often avoid abstract recommendations, and instead produce practical material that can be used by textbook authors and teachers alike. The resulting textbook rarely finds its way into the classroom as an obligatory teaching tool, but it may be disseminated as additional, complementary or experimental material, offering new sources for, and methods of, teaching sensitive and neglected topics. Pupils should be acquainted with the 'other's' argument to develop a more profound understanding of it, without necessarily sharing it. However, this requires that a controversial approach is possible in practical teaching, so that pupils can exchange and evaluate controversial arguments in order to form their own opinion. Such an approach is, in particular in East Asian schools, still in its infancy.

If sufficient resources are available, the publication of the material should be accompanied by teacher-training seminars. If sponsored by larger institutions working on an international level, the media can be addressed, and contact with educational authorities can be established. Sometimes, the merit of a project may well be restricted to simply showing that alternatives are feasible. In the end, successful trans-border cooperation may become in itself the most important project result and value.

Contentious pedagogical arguments (such as a certain topic being taboo, because students are too young and not mature enough to understand it) are most often avoided and go unmentioned in research-oriented projects' final documents, because the results do not address a particular age group or school type and leave the translation into any specific pedagogical context to the authorities or practitioners. On the other hand, projects that develop teaching material have to cope with the challenge to adjust their material to the learning abilities of the students, i.e. to reduce content load and complexity, even if it opens their results to political criticism. Particularly NGO-related projects, therefore, tend to prefer producing teaching guides, rather than workbooks for students with ready-made teaching units.

With the emergence of new forms of projects, procedures and results of textbook revision, the communication model has changed accordingly. Many agents from different spheres of influence, such as academia, politics, the media, civil society and interest groups, are involved; they no longer form a chain of command in communication lines, but rather an interrelated communication space where contacts can be established at a variety of nexuses. Consequently, their work is more likely to affect individual textbook authors, teacher trainers and classroom teachers, who take the first steps towards innovation, than the ministries. The implementation of innovations in education, however, can be risky, if it is not protected by an officially established, multilateral reform process; it can trigger so-called textbook scandals; authors can be accused of betraying national interests by giving up national claims without getting any compensation from the 'other' side.[9] In order to cope with such challenges, it is helpful for authors to be linked to

Mediating textbook conflicts 263

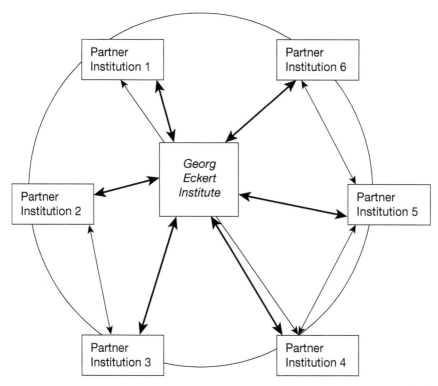

Figure 12.6

a network of NGOs or professional institutes that are active in the field of peace education and textbook revision. Particularly in regions where textbook research is not yet firmly established, networks can help to develop a research-based approach to textbook revision, which may render innovative textbook authors less vulnerable to political criticism. Since 2006, the Georg Eckert Institute has collaborated with textbook authors, researchers and curriculum experts to achieve research-based comparative textbook activities within the Arab world.

Working within the framework of Euro–Arab cultural dialogue, its main aims are to:

- establish an information exchange about aims and methods of international textbook research;
- foster comparative approaches to educational reform in the Arab Middle East and in Europe;
- compare and revise images of 'self' and 'other' through textbook research;
- initiate joint research projects.

A group supported by NGOs and based on the representation of individuals – such as the PRIME project – and official commissions based on the representation of collectives – such as the German–Polish Textbook Commission – may stand for two extreme poles in the spectrum of potential objectives, working methods, criteria for membership and outcomes. Although, under extreme political circumstances, extreme project structures might also be applied to reach the intended aims, today's projects often mix structures and utilise all the different methodological components that textbook projects have developed. Projects with clearly distinct structures may work in parallel on the same topic at the same time; projects may also work with mixed structures, giving each component different weight and functions over the course of the collaboration. Official projects with a long-term perspective, such as the German–Polish or German–French Textbook Commission, already capitalise on the full breadth of this variety. They are involved in, or conduct, teacher- and textbook author-training activities, invite stakeholders to their consultations and organise public meetings; in addition to their recommendations, they also publish teaching materials on topics that resist easy implementation. Projects such as these show that components should not exclude, but complement, each other. In communication-driven projects, a scholarly debate on a purely academic level can help by revealing hidden concepts that underlie the respective other's narratives. In such research-oriented projects, it can be useful to interrupt the academic debate whenever a consensus cannot be reached. Despite the fact that most academics, who consider scholarly argumentation to be the only path to objective truth, still find alternative means of communication, such as role-playing or storytelling, to be peculiar, such approaches can help clarify the divergent points of view.

Since the beginning of the twenty-first century, the East Asian region saw probably the most international textbook revision activities in the world. A variety of structures, ranging from official commissions to NGO-based projects, from the development of joint material to public-awareness campaigns, from research to youth exchange, were applied in these processes. Nevertheless, these undertakings neither fundamentally changed the image of a region that cannot come to grips with its past, nor invalidated the notion that the contested past is still the most serious stumbling block to closer economic, political and cultural cooperation. There is an astonishingly weak potential in the region for acknowledgement of the accomplishments, let alone a readiness actively to propagate them to the outside world. In reverse, self-accusation regarding the respective party's inherent incapability openly to discuss the past prevails, along with continuing criticism from outside. The whole debate still focuses too much on the political level, where even less progress has been made. Politics is seen as the most important dimension of the conflict, and as long as no fundamental changes are visible in this arena, the practical academic and pedagogical work will remain unconsidered. If a topic is mostly interpreted as a political issue, pedagogy and science do not enjoy an independent status; instead, they are seen as subordinate to politics, and even the pressure that pedagogues and scholars sometimes exert on politicians to implement their findings is seen as proof of their dependence on politics.

At this point, it seems to be important to stress what teachers and scholars from China, Japan and Korea have already jointly elaborated, and to invest their results with a positive image that is derived from the quality of their work alone, disregarding whether the result is politically welcomed or not. All three cluster dimensions of textbook revision projects, as they were mentioned at the beginning of this essay, are interrelated, and it is to the disadvantage of the whole undertaking if one is subordinated to the others. The pedagogues' and scholars' points of view in this debate ought to be evaluated in their own right, before they are measured against the criteria of political acceptance. The fixation on a political agreement at some higher administrative level devalues the work of the pedagogues and scholars on the ground; on the other hand, directing public attention to the development of complementary teaching materials, teacher exchange programmes and joint research projects can increase self-esteem and professional pride; it can also contribute to the development of a hidden curriculum, even in highly state-controlled education systems, thus fostering a reconciliatory mood in which the relations between the three countries can be addressed. Besides all these activities, not much concrete research has been devoted to the changes that East Asian curricula and textbooks have actually undergone in recent decades. Even if China, Korea and Japan did not alter the overarching aims of teaching history or related disciplines such as geography and civics, all three countries responded with changes in contents and methods to challenges coming mostly from outside: worldwide testing and standardisation of outcomes, which are supposed to enhance professional mobility and answer the need to produce qualifications with which pupils can compete in a globalised economy. China diversified its textbook system and placed more weight on the international dimension in its history curriculum. Korea has deployed a far-reaching plan of curricular reforms in several steps, so as to educate pupils. The explicit aim is for these students to contribute to the demands of economic growth, political stability and cultural significance that Korea envisions in the years to come. Japan is already an international player in educational research and reform. Analysis of the relationship between societal demands and adjustments in the education system shows that curricula and textbooks are neither fixed, nor are they inalterable, nor part of a national heritage and thus immune to international influences. To include the findings of international comparative educational studies opens up the narrow national horizons in which textbook consultations are often embedded. Furthermore, an in-depth theoretical and methodological debate may help increase the academic reputation of textbook studies and free them from serving political ends in an open or masked manner. Future conferences and publications could refer more systematically to this wider frame of textbook research.[10]

Sequencing the political, pedagogical and research dimensions

Hardly any project is able simultaneously to deal with the scholarly, political and didactical dimensions of its work and to produce results that meet the criteria for scholarly acknowledgement, political approval and didactical implementation. In practice, the procedures of projects are sequenced, and different weight is given to different dimensions at different times:

1. preparation:
   - through political institutions (ministries, international organisations);
   - through NGOs, civil society groups/engaged individual persons;
2. consultation:
   - mixed groups (politicians/scholars/practitioners);
   - separated groups;
3. dissemination of results:
   - report to the political authorities;
   - publication (printed/Internet);
4. implementation at political level:
   - official approval/rejection of results;
   - financial/organisational support for dissemination;
5. implementation at pedagogical level:
   - teacher/author training;
   - development of supplementary material/joint textbooks.

For a concrete example, the author refers again to the German–Polish Commission, because in this case almost all phases have been activated and clearly sequenced:

1. Before the commission was officially established, government statements signalled support for, and a favourable disposition towards, reconciliatory efforts by means of textbook revision. Furthermore, non-political organisations, particularly the Christian churches, made statements to the same effect and organised mutual visits.
2. The broad preparatory phase was an important prerequisite for the consequent period of intensive and, in general, uncontested work of the commission, led by reputed scholars (1972–6).
3. The commission's 'recommendations' were published in both languages in 1976 and made publicly available in both countries. The commission decided to continue with joint consultation after the publication of these recommendations.
4. The publication of the recommendations was followed by a fierce and controversial political debate in both countries. Owing to the federal structure of the education system in Germany, it was left to the *Länder* (federal states) to accept or reject them; only some made their observation conditional for textbook approval (cf. Jacobmeyer 1979). The Polish

government, on the other hand, was hesitant to enforce statements from the recommendations that were politically controversial within the country, such as the Polish policy towards the German minority after World War I.
5   Partly in parallel to the political debate, but with particular emphasis in the 1980s and 1990s, the Georg Eckert Institute was active in teacher-training seminars to ease implementation at classroom level. Didactical material has been published only since the 1990s. In 2008, it was decided to support the development of a regular German–Polish history textbook for the junior secondary level. In contrast to the procedures chosen for the development of a German–French history textbook, the textbook commission is actively involved in steering the process and defining the methodological and content framework for the book.

Sequencing allows the project group to concentrate their activities on one dimension in a certain time period and avoid being overloaded with political, pedagogical and scientific claims all at once. However, sequencing prolongs the project; nevertheless, experience shows that only project groups that work continuously over a longer period of time bring about viable changes in textbooks and classrooms. NGO-driven groups, who tend to have fewer resources at their disposal than official projects, cannot afford to conduct projects over decades, and therefore have to concentrate on one or two dimensions only, or try to work on all three dimensions at the same time. The Center for Democracy and Reconciliation in Southeastern Europe developed a long-term project that, at each phase, produced remarkable results of independent value:[11]

1   The project was planned within the centre, making use of its network and committees.
2   It started with extensive stock-taking and in-depth analysis of history textbooks in the Balkans after the breakdown of Socialist Yugoslavia (cf. Koulouri 2002).
3   Based on these findings, an international group of teachers and researchers, many of whom were recruited from the region, was divided into smaller working groups to develop commentated source material. The intention was to stimulate innovative teaching approaches specifically for the Balkan countries.
4   As a next step, the centre started negotiations with educational authorities in the region to win their support for teacher-training activities. This was a necessary measure, considering the hesitation of some governments to support the centre's activities. There was widespread suspicion that the new teaching materials could replace the state-approved textbooks, or at least undermine their authority.
5   Since then, teacher-training seminars are under way to familiarise teachers with the sources and new teaching methods.

Against a regional curriculum?

For the longest time, writing textbooks was regarded as an exclusively national domain that any bi- or multilateral textbook commission respected, regardless of any recommendations for change and delivery of exemplary material that shows how this change could be achieved. Still, commissions never engaged in the writing of regular textbook series. In recent years, however, projects started to go beyond these limits. The *German–French history textbook* (*Histoire/Deutsch–französisches Geschichtsbuch*, 2006–8) is the first binational regular textbook available, and covers the senior secondary school curriculum for history in both countries. It was written by a mixed team of German and French authors and published – albeit in the two different languages – in identical versions by a French and a German private educational publishing house.[12] Although it is not the direct result of the German–French Textbook Commission's work, it emerged as a result of long-lasting textbook consultations, close bilateral cultural and academic cooperation and the German–French Youth Exchange Programme (*Deutsch–Französisches Jugendaustauschprogramm*). The development of this schoolbook series is of great interest, as it combines state-level expert guidance and management support with civil society initiative and private marketing. It goes back to an idea developed at a German–French youth meeting that took place within the framework of the publicly funded Franco–German Youth Office (*Deutsch–Französisches Jugendwerk*). Delegates of this meeting forwarded the idea to the heads of their governments, who took it up and requested their respective administrations to seek means of realisation. An advisory board was set up representing history experts from academia, the field of education and textbook research. The board checked the current curricula on both sides and defined common denominators that could form the backbone of content issues and competencies to be learned. A tender competition was opened, and binational teams of publishing houses were invited to submit proposals on strategies to best realise the broad framework developed by the board. In the end, only one team took the risk of producing such a book and was accepted by the board. As the economic risk lies totally with the two private publishing companies, the board did not officially commission the company, but could only offer to provide governmental support for making the book known to teachers and the general public, to facilitate classroom use (for example, through easing the somewhat complicated federalised approval procedures on the German side) and to support the author's team with expert advice. The appearance of the first volume, which deals with contemporary history, created a considerable stir in the media and sold well (approximately 40,000 copies on either side by the end of 2008); however, the reason for this success was not only that teachers were eager to use the material, but that the issue of a binational curricular textbook attracted widespread general interest in the public and the education professions. As the forthcoming volumes on the more remote periods of history were no longer supported by a similar media effect, selling figures dropped; whether the series will hold a share in the market that pays off in the longer term remains to be seen. Nevertheless, the most important achievement of the book is that it has proved that transnational cooperation in history teaching is possible and no longer hampered by conflicts of the past. Sometimes, the book is misunderstood as dealing predominantly with German–French relations. This is, however, not the case, as the book covers syllabi that focus not only on national history but also extensively deal with European and world history. The book shows that the national histories are embedded in a wider context, which deserves to be studied in its own right. As such, it hardly reflects typical 'German' or 'French' academic tendencies; rather, the book shows that controversies are linked to different theoretical approaches, which can be discussed and presented without being politicised or 'nationalised'. Only the selection of some topics and the whole didactical design of the book may show a somewhat national colour, as the centralised French curriculum may have exerted a stronger influence on the selection criteria than the diversified German system.

This was not the first nor the only textbook written by an international team of authors and published in almost identical versions in various countries:

- The *European history textbook* paved the way in the 1990s. It goes back to the initiative of an engaged European intellectual and businessman, Frédéric Delouche, and is meant to foster the European dimension in the teaching of history. Developed by a team of authors from a number of European countries, it has, by now, appeared in a second revised edition and was translated into almost all national European languages (cf. Delouche 1998).
- The *Baltic history textbook* was written by authors from the three Baltic countries (Lithuania, Latvia and Estonia); its development was supported by the Council of Europe in order to overcome stereotypes, to strengthen regional awareness and encourage cooperation between the three neighbouring countries, who all regained sovereignty with the collapse of the Soviet Union. This history-writing project was one of the first steps of cross-border cooperation after more than fifty years of foreign domination. The group of authors concentrated on agreeing upon a joint narrative that was likely to find academic approval in the three countries; however, pupils can hardly work with the book; instead, it can best serve as a guide for teachers to communicate to their students the interrelatedness of the three countries' history (cf. Klaupa *et al.* 1999).
- The prize-winning Euroclio project started just the opposite way. It assembled teachers from post-conflict societies in the Balkans, whose education systems were still marked by ethnic and cultural divisions. Focusing on social and micro-history, rather than on political history, the author's team collected source material and prepared it for use in the classroom. The results aim to show that separatism and ethnic clashes were often induced by political power play and nationalism, but were not grounded in differences of life style, religious convictions or cultural

traditions (cf. Euroclio 2008). Most of the region's curricula support a source-based teaching approach; however, the regular textbooks offer little help for pupils with interpreting sources. As a consequence, teachers have to rely on their own professional capacities to introduce innovative teaching methods.
- Over the last decade, various projects in East Asia, producing joint textbooks, share the many characteristics of their European counterparts. Most often, they do not address pupils directly, but instead are intended for teachers' use. Engaged scholars, teachers and NGOs started with this work, before state-official commissions took up the issue and developed multinational textbooks.

None of these products, however, is meant to replace regular, national schoolbooks. Like the German–French curricular history book, the trinational East Asian history book sold relatively well,[13] mainly because it caught the attention of professionals and the general public; so far, we do not know to what an extent it is actually used in classrooms (Iwasaki and Narita 2008).

Not all projects achieve a successful result. The regional approach failed in the conflict-ridden Caucasus. Although a project group supported by the Council of Europe produced a joint book, governments did not agree to its publication, because they did not find their own policy of remembrance appropriately reflected in the result of the project's work.[14]

All the above examples show that agreement can best be reached at an academic level; however, particularly when projects deal with highly contentious topics, due attention should be paid to political approval and the didactical implementation of results. Project groups set up by political authorities or international organisations should not dissolve as long as approval and implementation are not secured. They could raise their voice, exert a certain influence on political agents as well as the public and mould their results later according to didactical requirements that were not sufficiently taken into account during the consultations.

The projects conducted in Europe are embedded in the larger context of European integration. Centralisation and regionalisation go hand in hand in the process of European integration, as large, supranational units such as the Council of Europe or the EU need smaller subunits to develop inner cohesion, a concrete sense of belonging and geographical/cultural identification. Despite a shallow similarity in procedures, European and Asian projects of textbook revision and joint schoolbook production differ in their emphasis on a regional and a multinational level. The Asian projects stress the cooperation between nations in education, not least in order to free inherent national feelings from aggressive nationalism, to transform them into cooperative patriotism and make them compatible with their neighbours' national beliefs and concepts of identity. As yet, however, they are not seen as an intermediary step that opens the door to a larger political or cultural unity embracing all the individual nations. This state of affairs can be compared to the situation in Europe during

Mediating textbook conflicts 271

the post-war decades, when European integration played only a minor role in textbook consultations; its foremost aim was taming nationalism in order to give national feelings a new direction and legitimacy. Germany engaged the most in international textbook talks, as the country had to re-establish a trustful and internationally acknowledged German historical consciousness; European cooperation served, therefore, more as a tool for re-establishing the nation states than as an end in itself. These priorities have definitely changed since the 1990s. Getting access to the emerging European educational space is a driving force for reforming national educational systems and for making the values they transmit compatible with each other. So far, the official textbook projects in Asia lack this broader regional context. They tend to assert the domestic, national version of historical, cultural and political identity and only mould it in so far as it is acceptable to the partners as well; they do not intend to embed the national perspectives into a larger, supranational context that 'neutralises' different national interpretations. Therefore, the examples of joint East Asian textbooks represent a harmonised collection of two or three interwoven national histories, rather than the integrated story of a region broken down into different nation states. Two reasons may be given for this:

1 Asia is not yet a concept that is backed by strong political/military and economic cooperation. Furthermore, textbook projects involving participants from East and Southeast Asia are still in their infancy.
2 The concept of East Asia is still burdened by the discriminating 'prosperity sphere' (*kyōeiken* 共栄圏) of Japan's past. This may be the reason why Korea's efforts to create a Northeast Asian regional awareness and to promote the inclusion of units on Northeast Asian history into the region's history and geography education met with such scepticism in neighbouring countries and is still not positively reflected in their curricula or textbooks.[15]

To this day, the three national histories (of Japan, Korea and China) more compete with each other than look towards a common future. Both the Dokdo (jap. Takeshima) issue between Japan and Korea and the debate on the Koguryŏ Kingdom between China and Korea link historical controversies to current national politics: the second issue is related to China's minority policy, whereas the first concerns a border conflict. Issues such as these brought Daqing Yang to the conclusion that 'the rise of historical revisionism in East Asia' is not only about the past 'but it is also about present-day politics'. As a result, efforts for a dialogue on history and the promotion of Northeast Asian regionalism still have to cope with the effects of national political rivalry in the region (Yang 2008: 43).

There is still a long way to overcome the focus on opposing histories and develop a notion of 'Asianness', as suggested by Jŭngmin Seo: an area of 'knowledge production' for which authors of joint teaching materials have prepared the ground; an area that is inhabited by 'regional civil societies based not on nationality and citizenship but on the location in the web of global production – both material and symbolic' (Seo 2007: 55–6).

Notes

1 This term is a neologism in English, derived from the German *Didaktik*, which German-speaking researchers have preferred to *Methodik* from the 1970s onwards ('methodology of teaching' was the common English term). The new term should not only refer to the way history is taught at school (dealing with the tools the teacher uses, such as textbooks etc.), but also take into account the wider context, such as the influence of public interest in history, the role of museums and commemoration practices and policies, of family stories etc.
2 In this regard, the study by Firer and Adwan (2004) on Israeli and Palestinian textbooks stands out, as the authors – one Israeli, one Palestinian scholar – could present the first and until now only 'inter-subjective' study on the highly contested Israeli–Palestinian textbook issue, which has been dealt with so far only from one side or by external experts.
3 Concerning the opposition of political and scientific communication space, see Luhmann (1993); Habermas (1985) offers a less dichotomised model.
4 See the website of the Peace Research Institute in the Middle East (PRIME): www.vispo.com/PRIME.
5 The rules set up at the beginning of the work follow the trust-building communication model developed by the Israeli head of PRIME, the late Professor Dan Bar-On; his supervising role gave the group stability; this, in turn, invested him with great authority, which he used to also bring about external legitimacy for the project, as proved by successful fund-raising and invitations to universities abroad to report on the project (Adwan and Bar-On 2007).
6 See note 14 concerning the failed production of a Caucasus textbook; also, the US–USSR textbook study of 1977–89 was never implemented because of political objections (Mehlinger 1992; 1985).
7 The German–Polish Commission included a proposal to have subsequent follow-up meetings every two years in their recommendations published in 1976; this has become the rule up to now. Other bilateral commissions, where Germany represents one side, come together at least over a time span of several years to detail recommendations and receive feedback from textbook writers and teachers. With the Georg Eckert Institute for International Textbook Research (and its forerunner, the International Textbook Institute; Becher and Riemenschneider 2000; see also the following website: www.gei.de), German educational authorities have established a unique academic institution that engages continuously in textbook research as well as textbook consultation activities.
8 The German–Polish Commission systematically evaluated the recommendations' effects on academia and on textbooks (Jacobmeyer 1988; 1989). In addition, the Georg Eckert Institute published voluminous documentation of the political debate triggered by the publication of the joint recommendations in Germany (Jacobmeyer 1979). Also, the recommendations were widely disseminated and reprinted several times.
9 The Croatian history textbook author Snježana Koren reports her own case in Koren and Baranović (2009); see also the Georg Eckert Institute's website on textbook revision in Southeastern Europe: www.gei.de/en/research/textbooks-and-conflict.html; Maria Repoussi puts her own case as a 'forbidden' Greek history textbook author into the broader context of textbook approval policy (Repoussi 2008); the case of Ienaga, in Japan, is already legendary (Ienaga 2001).

10 Soon-Won Park signals, through the mere diction of her report, that the production of the trinational history textbook was meant as a counter-measure against the nationalistic textbook developed by the Japanese Society for History Textbook Reform (*Atarashii rekishi kyōkasho o tsukurukai*; *Tsukurukai* for short) of Japan. As legitimate as this may be, it puts the project into a political context, with the consequence that foes or friends will most probably integrate it into their political struggle without changing positions (Park, S. 2010 forthcoming).
11 For further information, please visit the Joint History Project (JHP) website: www.cdsee.org/jhp/index.html.
12 The idea of developing an international history textbook had already been conceived by the International Institute for Intellectual Cooperation in the early 1920s, but after some preliminary work the project was halted because it was 'premature' (Schröder 1961: 71).
13 At the end of 2007: 80,000 copies in Japan, 70,000 in Korea and 130,000 in China (Park, S. 2010 forthcoming).
14 So far, no results have been published; the project was carried out within the framework of the 'Tbilisi Initiative'. (Please see the following website: https://wcd.coe.int/viewDoc.jsp?id=5587&Site=COE.)
15 For a discussion of current concepts of 'East Asia', as opposed to 'Europe', see Lee (2008).

Bibliography

Adwan, S. and Bar-On, D. (2007) 'Leading forward: the experiences of Palestinians and Israelis in the Learning Each Other's Historical Narratives Project', in L. Cajani (ed.) *History teaching, identities and citizenship*, London: Trentham Books, 143–57.

Becher, U. and Riemenschneider, R. (eds) (2000) *Internationale Verständigung. 25 Jahre Georg-Eckert-Institut für internationale Schulbuchforschung in Braunschweig* [*Fostering international understanding. On the occasion of the 25th anniversary of Georg Eckert Institute for International Textbook Research Braunschweig*], Hannover: Verlag Hahnsche Buchhandlung.

Borodziej, W. (2003) 'The German–Polish textbook dialogue', in A. Horvat and G. Hielscher (eds) *Sharing the burden of the past: legacies of war in Europe, America and Asia*, Tokyo: Asia Foundation/Friedrich-Ebert-Stiftung, 35–8.

—— (2008) 'Die Gemeinsame Deutsch–Polnische Schulbuchkommission 1972–2007' [The Joint German–Polish Textbook Commission 1972–2007], *Bulletin of the Institute of Human Rights Studies, Kansai University*, special issue: *Geschichtsbewußtsein und Geschichtserziehung* [*Historical consciousness and history education*], no. 56: 137–52 (German and Japanese).

Braslavsky, C. (ed.) (2006) *Textbooks and quality learning for all: some lessons learned from international experiences*, Geneva: UNESCO, International Bureau of Education.

Brown, N.J. (2003) 'Democracy, history, and the contest over the Palestinian curriculum', in F. Pingel (ed.) *Contested past, disputed present. Curricula and teaching in Israeli and Palestinian schools*, Hannover: Hahnsche Buchhandlung, 99–125.

Bush, K.D. and Saltarelli, D. (2000) *The two faces of education in ethnic conflict*, Florence: UNICEF Innocenti Research Centre.

Cole, E. (ed.) (2007) *Teaching the violent past. History education and reconciliation*, London: Rowman & Littlefield Publishers.

Delouche, F.(ed.) (2nd revised edn 1998) *The illustrated history of Europe*, Quezon City: Phoenix [*Das europäische Geschichtsbuch von den Anfängen bis heute*, Stuttgart: Klett-Cotta]. A Japanese version of the first edition appeared with English summaries: Center for the Education of Children Overseas (ed.) (1997) *History of Europe. An anatomy*, Tokyo: Gakugei University.

Dimou, A. (ed.) (2009) *'Transition' and the politics of history education in Southeastern Europe*, Göttingen: V&R Unipress.

Euroclio (ed.) (2008) *Ordinary people in an extraordinary country. Everyday life in Bosnia and Herzegovina, Croatia and Serbia between East and West 1945–1990* (available also in Bosniak, Croatian and Serbian language).

Firer, R. and Adwan, S. (2004) *The Israeli–Palestinian conflict in history and civics textbooks of both nations*, ed. by F. Pingel, Hannover: Verlag Hahnsche Buchhandlung.

Foster, S.J. and Crawford, K. (eds) (2006) *What shall we tell the children? International perspectives on school history textbooks*, Greenwich, CT: IAP-Information Age.

Geiss, P. and Le Quintrec, G. (eds) (2008) *Histoire/Deutsch–Französisches Geschichtsbuch*, vol. 2: *Europa und die Welt vom Wiener Kongress bis 1945* [*History/ A German–French history textbook*, vol. 2: *Europe and the world from the Congress of Vienna until 1945*], Stuttgart: Klett [*L'Europe et le monde du congrès de Vienne á 1945*, Paris: Nathan].

Habermas, J. (1985) *Theory of communicative actions*, 2 vols, Boston, MA: Beacon Press.

Han, U. et al. (eds) (2010 forthcoming) *History education and reconciliation – comparative perspectives on East Asia*, Frankfurt am Main: Lang.

Höhne, T. (2003) *Schulbuchwissen. Umrisse einer Wissens- und Medientheorie des Schulbuches* [*Schoolbook knowledge. A synopsis of science- and media-based theory*], Frankfurt am Main: Verlag Goethe-Universität.

Höpken, W. (2008) 'History textbooks in post-war and post-conflict societies: preconditions and experiences in comparative perspective', in S. Richter (ed.) *Contested views of a common past. Revisions of history in contemporary East Asia*, Frankfurt am Main and New York: Campus, 373–95.

Ienaga, S. (2001) *Japan's past, Japan's future: one historian's odyssey*, London: Rowman and Littlefield Publishers.

Iwasaki, M. and Narita, R. (2008) 'Writing history textbooks in East Asia', in S. Richter (ed.) *Contested views of a common past. Revisions of history in contemporary East Asia*, Frankfurt am Main and New York: Campus, 271–83.

Jacobmeyer, W. (ed.) (1979) *Die deutsch–polnischen Schulbuchempfehlungen in der öffentlichen Diskussion der Bundesrepublik Deutschland* [*The German–Polish textbook recommendations in the focus of public debate in Germany*], Braunschweig: Georg-Eckert-Institut für internationale Schulbuchforschung.

—— (ed.) (1988) *Zum wissenschaftlichen Ertrag der deutsch–polnischen Schulbuchkonferenzen der Historiker 1972–1987* [*The scientific return of the German–Polish textbook conferences on history 1972–87*], Braunschweig: Georg-Eckert-Institut für internationale Schulbuchforschung.

—— (ed.) (1989) *Zum pädagogischen Ertrag der deutsch–polnischen Schulbuchkonferenzen der Historiker 1972–1987* [*The pedagogical return of the German–Polish textbook conferences on history 1972–87*], Braunschweig: Georg-Eckert-Institut für internationale Schulbuchforschung.

Kal, H. (2007) 'The aesthetic construction of ethnic nationalism: war memorial museums in Korea and Japan', in G. Sin *et al.* (eds) *Rethinking historical justice and reconciliation in Northern Asia. The Korean experience*, London: Routledge, 133–53.

Karge, H. and Batarilo, K. (2009) 'Guidelines guiding history textbook production? Norms and practices of history textbook policy in Bosnia and Herzegovina', in A. Dimou (ed.) *'Transition' and the politics of history education in Southeastern Europe*, Göttingen: V&R Unipress, 307–56.

Klaupa, Z. *et al.* (eds) (1999) *The history of the Baltic countries*, Tallinn: Avita (also available in the languages of the Baltic countries and in German).

Koren, S. and Baranoviū, B. (2009) 'What kind of history education do we have after eighteen years of democracy in Croatia?', in A. Dimou (ed.) *'Transition' and the politics of history education in Southeastern Europe*, Göttingen: V&R Unipress, 91–140.

Koulouri, C. (ed.) (2002) *Clio in the Balkans: the politics of history education*, Thessaloniki: Center for Democracy and Reconciliation.

Lee, E. (2008) 'East Asia discourses in contemporary Korea', in S. Richter (ed.) *Contested views of a common past. Revisions of history in contemporary East Asia*, Frankfurt am Main and New York: Campus, 181–201.

Le Quintrec, G. *et al.* (eds) (2006) *Histoire/Deutsch–Französisches Geschichtsbuch, vol. 3: Europa und die Welt seit 1945* [*History/a German-French history textbook, vol. 3: Europe and the world since 1945*], Stuttgart: Klett[*L'Europe et le monde depuis 1945*, Paris: Nathan] (a Korean edition is already published, a Japanese translation is in preparation).

Li, Y. (2010 forthcoming) 'Sino–Japanese relations in China's history teaching', in U. Han *et al.* (eds) *History education and reconciliation – comparative perspectives on East Asia*, Frankfurt am Main: Lang.

Luhmann, N. (1993) *Risk: a sociological theory*, Berlin and New York: de Gruyter.

Maier, R. (2008) 'Finding a way out of the deadlock in the German–Polish dialogue on history textbooks', in Asia Peace & History Education Institute (ed.) *Crossing the border of historical understanding in East Asia*, Seoul: Sunin Publishing, 231–43 (Korean).

Mehlinger, H.D. (1985) 'International textbook revision: examples from the United States', *Internationale Schulbuchforschung*, no. 4: 287–98.

—— (1992) *School textbooks: weapons for the Cold War, a report of the US/USSR Textbook Study Project (1977–1989)*, US/USSR Textbook Study Project.

Nicholls, J. (ed.) (2006) *School textbooks across cultures. International debates and perspectives*, Oxford: Symposium Books.

Nishino, R. (2008) 'The political economy of the textbook in Japan, with particular focus on middle school history textbooks', *Internationale Schulbuchforschung*, no. 1: 487–514.

Park, K. (2010 forthcoming) 'Remembering wars: war memorial halls and historical disputes in Northeast Asia', in U. Han *et al.* (eds) *History education and reconciliation – comparative perspectives on East Asia*, Frankfurt am Main: Lang.

Park, S. (2010 forthcoming) '*A History that opens the future*: the first common East Asian history teaching guide', in U. Han *et al.* (eds) *History education and reconciliation – comparative perspectives on East Asia*, Frankfurt am Main: Lang.

Pingel, F. (2nd revised edn 2009a) *UNESCO guidebook on textbook research and textbook revision*, Braunschweig and Paris: Georg-Eckert-Institut für internationale Schulbuchforschung/UNESCO.

—— (2009b) 'From ownership to intervention – or vice versa? Textbook revision in Bosnia and Herzegovina', in A. Dimou (ed.) *'Transition' and the politics of history education in Southeastern Europe*, Göttingen: V&R Unipress, 251–305.

Repoussi, M. (2008) 'Politics questions history education. Debates on Greek history textbooks', *Yearbook 2006/07. International Society for History Didactics*, Frankfurt am Main: Wochenschau Verlag, 99–110.

Richter, S. (ed.) (2008) *Contested views of a common past. Revisions of history in contemporary East Asia*, Frankfurt am Main and New York: Campus.

Saaler, S. (2005) *Politics, memory and public opinion. The history textbook controversy and Japanese society*, Munich: Juridicum.

Schissler, H. and Soysal, Y.N. (eds) (2005) *The nation, Europe, and the world. Textbooks and curricula in transition*, New York: Berghahn Books.

Schröder, C.A. (1961) *Die Schulbuchverbesserung durch internationale geistige Zusammenarbeit [Improvement of schoolbook content through international intellectual cooperation]*, Braunschweig: Westermann.

Seitz, K. (2004) *Education and conflict. The role of education in the creation, prevention and resolution of social crises – consequences for development cooperation*, Deutsche Gesellschaft für Technische Zusammenarbeit. Available online at: www.gtz.de/de/dokumente/en-bildung-konflikt-studie-2004.pdf (accessed 1 October 2009).

Seo, J. (2007) 'Multiple layers of "East Asia" as an area', Center for Asia Pacific Partnership: *The 60th anniversary of the end of World War II. World order in the 20th century and reconciliation and co-existence in the Asia–Pacific (Report of the Symposium Center for Asia Pacific Partnership)*, Ōsaka: University of Economy and Law, 43–56.

Smith, A. and Vaux, T. (2002) *Education, conflict and international development*, London: UK Department for International Development (DFID).

Sugitani, M. (1998) 'Interkulturelle Kommunikation als Herausforderung für die Deutschlehrerausbildung im Bereich DaF in Japan. Soziokulturelle Aspekte in der Fremdsprachenausbildung am Beispiel "Vergangenheitsbewältigung"' [Cross-cultural communication as a challenge for German teachers' training in Japan: Socio-cultural aspects of foreign language training by examining the term "Vergangenheitsbewältigung" ("coming to terms with the past")], *Literatur im multimedialen Zeitalter – neue Perspektiven der Germanistik in Asien (Asiatische Germanistentagung 1997) [Literature in the multi-media age – new prospects for German studies researchers in Asia]*, Seoul: Koreanische Gesellschaft für Germanistik, 96–109.

Tawil, S. and Harley, A. (eds) (2004) *Education, conflict and social cohesion*, Geneva: UNESCO International Bureau of Education.

Walworth, A. (1938) *School histories at war. A study of the treatment of our wars in the secondary school history books of the United States and in those of its former enemies*, Cambridge, MA: Harvard University Press.

Yang, D. (2008) 'Historical revisionism in East Asia', in S. Richter (ed.) *Contested views of a common past. Revisions of history in contemporary East Asia*, Frankfurt am Main and New York: Campus, 25–46.

Concluding remarks

Gotelind Müller

This volume, having grown out of a conference, is itself part of an ongoing discussion between academic analysts and scholars involved in history and textbook issues on the ground. This context entails various aspects: on the one hand, this volume adds to existing scholarship on East Asian textbook problems (which has grown over recent years)[1] in the practical dimension, by bringing together textbook authors and academics involved in curriculum development. Together with East Asian historians and scholars involved in transnational endeavours to come to mutual historical understanding and – in some cases – 'common' textbook initiatives, they offer their respective experiences as a background to their reflections and suggestions. On the other hand, this also means there is no uniform 'message' or simple 'lesson' on how to move ahead, though various suggestions are raised. In this context, the comparative framework provided by a look beyond East Asia is helpful to sketch out the possible directions into which developments might be carried.

As the chapter by Sun has shown, the concept of 'East Asia' is not self-evident. Rather, it is highly contested in the 'East Asian' region, with unclear boundaries, and various subject positions influence the way this 'invented' category is dealt with. These dealings, Sun demonstrated as well, are also historically and politically contingent, shift over time and space and should not be dealt with in a purely abstract manner without such broader contexts being taken into consideration. Furthermore, she reminds us that there can well be other 'categories' and reasons to opt for them; this, for example, explains Chinese hesitancy in front of the 'East Asia paradigm', which has become one of the challenges in historical exchanges in 'East Asia' in recent years. As she explains, it is only natural that Japan and South Korea differ in their attitude towards the 'East Asia paradigm', owing to their respective subject positions that comprise their specific historical experiences as future agendas. For the writing of history in general and that in the normative setting of schools, in textbooks, this means that it is embedded in, and depends on, precisely the options chosen of how to draw a line between the 'self' and the 'other'.

As for China, such an 'other' was reflected and defined mainly in her textbooks about foreign or world history. In the curricula, the state defined the limits and contents of 'self' and 'other'. As the chapter by Müller demonstrates, this shifted considerably over the course of time, closely linked to the changing political agendas. The image of 'Europe' as an 'other' is used here as a prism to Chinese self-reflections, which in recent times have also touched upon the desirability and feasibility of constructing a regional identity à la European Union, the economic potential advantages, political risks and historical stumbling blocks. These issues are far from being agreed upon, the chapter demonstrates, as can be gleaned from the way 'Europe' is treated in various world history textbooks of today.

Much of this delineation of the 'self' vis-à-vis the 'other' is done in history textbooks, but, as the chapter by Vollmer convincingly argues, is present as well in other school subjects, namely in civics and ethics, and this not only in particular topics, but in the interpretative framework itself. Taking Japan as an example, he shows how Western (and Asian) 'others' are taken as models or as cases of radical alterity, depending on whether the aim is to argue for imitation (in the sense of 'others' as representing one's own 'past' or 'future') or for cultural relativism. Thus, quite strikingly, this argumentative structure leads even 'liberal' textbooks to ironically take up Nihonron-like arguments of cultural uniqueness. By analysing also the visual representations in textbooks and the implicit categorisations, he concludes that textbooks that transcend the 'us' and 'them' approach, integrating, for example, Japanese thinkers or developments in regional or worldwide ones in their narratives, are still rare.

The awareness of other important factors interplaying with history textbooks in defining a 'self' is also shared in Vickers' chapter on Hong Kong. In this case, the state's agency in constructing a new identity for Hongkongers after retrocession via 'patriotic education' is paramount. This education campaign plays on various levels, in school (in various subjects in addition to 'history') and outside, to guarantee a 'successful' redefinition of the Hongkongers as 'Chinese', as understood by Beijing. For this enterprise it is essential to also nurture some 'patriotic feeling', thus linking cognitive and emotional aspects in education.

Whereas, in Hong Kong, the drive for 'patriotic education' is clearly a primarily top-down process to assimilate Hongkongers into the 'Chinese nation', the case of Taiwan discussed by Chang shows how textbooks become contested grounds for constructing a 'Taiwanese' 'self' apart from the 'Chinese' one, which had been mandatory under the Nationalists. Chang positions these 'textbook wars' in Taiwan, spurred by the *Knowing Taiwan* textbook, in the context of politics, academic explorations in hitherto taboo areas and institutional changes. For this construction of a 'Taiwanese identity', he demonstrates, China and Japan serve as the most important 'others'.

In view of the above reflections on the historical contingencies of the contested issues of 'East Asia', identities and education, the following chapters zoom into the practical dimension of textbook writing, contributed by authors personally involved in curriculum development and textbook writing in the realm of history.

As Li Fan demonstrates in his chapter, national curriculum reform in China ran up against various problems in practice. Although 'new' approaches were tried to overcome the traditional focus on chronology, disciplinary borderlines and the 'us' and 'them' divide, the new curricula often did not stand the test in practice. In fact, though minor 'modernisation' in terms of layout or teaching styles was well received, these more ambitious redesigns came about with too many practical problems to succeed with teachers and pupils. Furthermore, the chapter demonstrates how conflicting goals in the curricula almost naturally lead to unconvincing textbook narrations, which risk running up either against scholarly findings or against politically mandatory 'values'.

The chapter by Su Zhiliang complements this national perspective by the regional one from Shanghai and experiments with local textbooks there. Taking the portrayal of the Japanese 'other' as an example, he not only shows how evaluations of the 'other' changed over time according to the needs of the 'self', but also proposes his own solutions in the textbooks he edited. However, as he makes clear, the 'political factor' is always in the back of the scholar's mind, not the least because he himself had one of his textbooks banned.[2] Thus, in practice, scholarly ambition is circumscribed by considerations of the textbook admission system. However, as he makes also clear from his experience with the trinational 'East Asian' textbook, only an active confrontation with the different aspects of the 'common' past may open up further space to achieve something similar to the German–French common textbook model and bring East Asian textbooks in line with the requirements of today's globalised society.

These issues are taken up from the Japanese side by Miyake in his chapter. He demonstrates how the Japanese textbook admission system influences textbook narratives for the description of the 'self' as well as that of the 'other'. Referring to his own experiences with textbook writing, he argues for a new way to configure the national 'self', i.e. the way to narrate 'Japanese history' by paying due attention to the fractions in this 'self', giving voices to social, ethnic or local specifics, and by positioning the 'self' not as something apart from all 'others' but as interrelated. He suggests that this should be done, not only in the narrative as such, but also by inclusion of non-Japanese scholars in the writing process right from the start. Thus, the complexities of the 'self' as well as the way 'others' see Japan would open up a more diversified picture of what could meaningfully be called Japanese history.

All these practical considerations do, however, operate in the general setting of the societies in which textbooks are situated. And these larger societal contexts decide and frame the possibilities; i. e. which kinds of attitude dominate in textbooks not only depend on the particular authors but also have to be seen in the context of society.

Given the fact that the 'textbook problem' in 'East Asia' started to become an international issue after attempts to revise history textbook narratives that touched upon the descriptions of World War II, Richter's chapter takes up the issue of revisionism and the so-called Tokyo Trial view of history raised as an accusation by those who see themselves misrepresented as 'culprits' by a 'victor's history'. She demonstrates how the Japanese 'self' is remoulded as 'heroic', precisely presenting the so-called A Class war criminals as 'martyrs' on whose sacrifice modern Japan builds. This is presented as a necessary 'reaction' to the East Asian 'others' and their accusing Japan of having simply been an aggressor. Richter details the psychological complexities involved between a 'you too' (by tacitly removing Asia and reconfiguring World War II in a Japan–US framework) and an outright defiant reaction, which tries to emotionally tie the current generation to the 'sacrifices' of their forebears. This, she shows, is transported on various media channels into society, complementing the influence of textbooks, not the least by people affiliated to the group that stood behind the revisionist textbooks from which all started, and in some ways linking up with the post-war tradition of an abstract pacifism combined with nationalism.

These attempts at revising the historical image of the Japanese 'self', however, were precisely the starting point to trigger the 'textbook wars' in 'East Asia'. Chung details the implications in his chapter with a view to Korean reactions. Given the fact of the strong diplomatic repercussions the textbook problem provoked over decades between Korea and Japan, he looks into the attempts to overcome these frictions. Even though such attempts were undertaken on the official level as well, Chung, judging from experience, argues for non-official actors to steer clear of political interference and for the building-up of a more sustained effort that does not depend on particular governments or temporary 'scandals' to keep going. In this context, he discusses the binational attempts to design common history education materials and the trinational textbook initiative, reminding us that one way to ease textbook conflicts would be to broaden the perspective beyond the bi- or trinational relationships.

From the Japanese perspective and with a comparative view of German–Polish reconciliation efforts, Kawate takes up the problem of reconciliation and how textbooks could convey such an idea. As Chung did as well, he argues for a non-official effort to 'take history in hand' and thus away from the prerogative of the state into society or academia. Kawate discusses the way the German–Polish history dialogues were perceived in Japan and uses the case of Nishikawa Masao, who was instrumental in making them known there, to throw into profile the question of an adaptation of this model to East Asia. With Nishikawa, Kawate raises the issue of whether it would not be more pertinent to aim at a more comprehensive framework than the existing bi- or trinational common textbook initiatives. As Sun Ge did in her chapter, he suggests that the subjective position will be always present and in fact indispensable in history writing. Thus, rather than trying to write a 'common' history within one of the many possible geographical ranges, one should try to understand each other's subjective position, consider the viewpoints of 'others' when writing about the 'self' to avoid antagonisms, and accordingly write national history books anew with a view to situating 'one's own history' in a global context.

In his final chapter, Pingel takes up the various arguments proposed in the mediation of textbook conflicts around the globe, but also present in this volume, and builds them into a structured model of mediation processes. Referring to a host of examples, ranging from bi- or trinational textbook endeavours such as the Polish–German, French–German, Israeli–Palestinian, the Baltic or the East Asian ones to post-civil war/inter-ethnic ones as in the Balkans, he presents a model of how such endeavours evolve and which kinds of actor may be involved, discussing the pros and cons of official vs. private initiatives and what the frequent problems encountered are. With a view to the UNESCO initiatives on new textbook writing and quality education, he demonstrates the crucial and multifaceted influence of politics that not only comes into play with nationalist agendas (still fairly prominent in 'East Asia') but also, on the other hand, is necessary to guarantee that projects are not only goodwill enterprises but actually make it into the classroom. Furthermore, he argues that most of the failed projects worldwide suffered from institutional instability and neglect of the follow-up problems, which prevented many projects gaining sustainability.

Thus, this volume intends to open up new lines of inquiry that should be pursued in the future: how should depictions of 'self' and 'other' in textbooks be framed to neither ignore the subjective position nor raise antagonisms? What does this imply for the writing process and authorship? How 'homogenous' may the 'self' be conceptualised as being, when societies are getting ever more complex and mixed? As Miyake and Pingel remind us, there are in fact various perspectives already present in Benedict Anderson's 'imagined' 'national' community. Still, politics in practice tend to the homogenising view of 'the self', and this is unlikely to disappear in the near future. Is it possible to write just 'history' without any national qualification, giving up the 'us' and 'them' divide, as Kawate implies as a question? In the end, textbooks do operate in national education systems. Or is the 'smaller' aim to design bi- or trinational history textbooks, instead of a global transnational history writing, at least practicable, given the fact that they themselves seem to be today the 'new wave' and already encounter much opposition, not only from revisionists? Looking at the many practical aspects involved, one may well argue that the higher the goals, the less likely they will be realised. In fact, as Li, for example, has shown, even experiments with topical arrangement and disciplinary border-crossing run into problems of implementation and acceptance. And the trinational, East Asian textbook in most cases has not yet made it into class. Thus, one is left with the impression that all these potentials, as well as the contingencies addressed in this volume, have to be taken together to make some progress, not only in theory, but also in practice.

Notes

1 Some titles have been referred to already in the introduction. Further pertaining Western references include: Rose, C. (2005) *Sino-Japanese relations: facing the past, looking to the future?*, London and New York: Routledge; Saaler, S. and Schwentker, W. (eds) (2008) *The power of memory in modern Japan*, Kent: Global Oriental; and several works authored or co-edited by Paul Morris since the 1990s.

2 This was mainly due to a news report of Joseph Kahn in the *New York Times* (1 September 2006), which transported the criticism of Su's textbook into the international arena under the flashy header 'Where is Mao? Chinese revise history books' and thus triggered officials to ban it (available online at www.nytimes.com/2006/09/01/world/asia/01china.html?_r=1&ref=world&pagewanted=all; accessed 10 July 2010).

Index

Note: Page entries in **bold** indicate entries of particular importance in large entries.

Abe Shinzō 209
Afghanistan 69
Africa 18–19, 23, 39, 49, 108, 121, 148; South 69
AIDS 78
Allied Forces/Powers (Allies) 41, 48–9, 164, 190, 198–9, 201
America *see* United States of America (USA)
Anderson, Benedict 281
Antiwar and Peace Movement 239
Aoki Michio: *An introduction to Japanese history* 171
APEC 50
Arab 46, 80, 252, 263
ASEAN 49–50
Asian Games 97
'Asianness' (East) 9–31, 271
Atami 190
atomic bombs 188–9, 208, 216
Australia 176, 198–9
axis powers 38

Bacon 74
Balkans 267, 269, 281
Bandung Conference 18, 23, 39
Bataan 200
Batavia 198
Beethoven: *Ode to Joy* 48
Beijing 48, 50, 85–90, **92–100**, 102, 109–12, 142, 149, 278; Normal University Press 139, 149
Belgium 49
Beograd 49
Best wishes for tomorrow (Koizumi) 184, 186, 191–4, 196–7
Blakeney, Ben B. 189
Borneo 198
Bosnia and Herzegovina 256
Brandt 233

Britain 23, 47, 71, 153, 156, 176; and Hong Kong 90, 92, 95, 97, 107, 109; and India 47; political system 71, 73 *see also* England; United Kingdom (UK)
Buddha 74–5
Buddhism 51, 74–8, 190, 192
Burke, Edmund 71
Burma 198

Cairo Declaration 170
calendars and chronology 3, 12, 35, 40, 137, 140, 142, 177, 189, 279; Chinese 34–5, 39; Maoist 40; Marxist 40, 45; Taiwan 127–8; Western 38, 129
Cantonese 92, 102
capitalism 11, 36, 39, 45–48, 51, 153–5
capitalist 39–40, 47, 151, 153, 200, 256; bloc 17, 22; class 153; countries 44, 48, 154; development 111; economy 154; invasion 47; revolution 40–1, 45; system 27; world 22
Caucasus 270
Center for Democracy and Reconciliation 267
Chabarovsk 198
Chan, Margaret 97
Chang Kwang-chih 124
Chang Sheng-yan 120
Charlemagne 41
chauvinism 16, 42, 52, 65, 70, 101, 110–11
Chen Shui-bian (Shuibian) 122
Cheng, Albert 89
Chiang Ching-kuo 122
Chiang Kai-shek 121–2, 128, 152
China: Anti-Rightist Movement 41; 'Citizenship Education' 94, 101 *see also* Hong Kong: 'National/ patriotic Education'; Civil War 92, 104, 121; Communist Party (CCP) 23, 38, **45–6**, 87–8, 94, 98, 101, 106–7, 141, 151–2, 156; (Cultural)

284   Index

Revolution 39, 41–5, 104, 234; Deng era 40; Early Republic 34, 51; 'Gang of Four' 43; Great Leap (Forward) 41, 104; Great Wall 98; Han 43, 107–8, 111, 130, 144; (history) textbooks 2–3, 32–7, 39–51, 137–45, 147–60; June Fourth Incident *see* Tiananmen (Square Massacre); Language Movement 104; mainland 9, 12, 14, 20–1, 86–99, 101–12, 121–2, 124, 198; Manchu Dynasty 34; May Fourth Movement (demonstrations) 36, 95; Ministry of Education 42, 138, 149–50; Nanjing regime 36; National Space Programme 85, 94–5, 107; Nationalist Party (GMD/KMT) **36–9**, 46, 98, 101, 104, **121–3**, 128, 148, **151–2**, 156, 278; opening-up policy 10, 12, 18, 26, 86, 92, 95, **141**, 147–8, 152; Patriotic Education Campaign 87, 98; Qin empire 144; Qing dynasty 34, 51, 98, 124–5, 128–30, 144, 156, 216 *see also* China: Manchu Dynasty; reform 10, 12, 18, 24, 26, 41, 47, 86–8, 90, 95, **137–45**, 148–50, 155, 279; self-strengthening movement 148, 153; Student Movement 86, 92, 104; Taiping (Rebellion) 42; Warring States Period 144 *see also* People's Republic of China (PRC)
'Chineseness' 85, 93, 101, 104–5, 107–8, 111–12
Cho Keungdal 176
Chongqing (Chunking) 156, 193
Christianity 38, 75–6, 78, 266
Churchill 22
Civil Information and Education Section (CIE) 164, 200
Clive, Robert 47
Cold War 10, 14, 17–18, **20–7**, 43, 121, 183–5, 251, 260; fall of the Berlin Wall 17–18, 22, 26; ideology 14, 22, 25–7; 'Iron Curtain' 17, 20, 22, 39; post- 5, 26–7, 45; trade blockade 22
Columbus 42
'comfort': 'stations' 234; 'women' 13, 129, 152, 159–60, **170–4**, 185, 200, 208, 222, 234–5 *see also* forced prostitution
common (history school) textbooks *see* multinational education materials
communism 38, 40, 45, 47, 197
communist 48, 88, 92–4, 101; countries 22, 27; movement 149; regime 87; state 86; world view 39
Confucianism 11–12, 14, 27, 43, 51, 74, 76, 149
Confucius 74
Croats 256
Cromwell 40
cultural relativism 64, 69–71, 79, 278

Democratic People's Republic of Korea 21 *see also* North Korea
Deng Xiaoping 87, 106
Departure from Asia (Fukuzawa) 19
Descartes 74
Diaoyutai islands 88, 104–5 *see also* Senkakuji islands
Diaz 42
Doihara Kenji 198
Dokdo 207–8, 210–11, 213, 271 *see also* Takeshima
Dower, John 177, 195
Dresden 193
Duara, Prasenjit 61
Dutch 42, 144; East India Company 124; era 125

East Asia: community 15, 17, 237; as an entity 10, 12, 27; identity 1–2, 5, 9, 11, 15, 26, 271; narrative 1–2, 5, 10–12, **15–21**, 24–8, 60, 63, 76; perspective 11–12, 14–15, 17, 19, 21, 23, **25–6**, 28, 229; regional integration 27, 51–2
East China Normal University Press: textbook 48, 139 *see also* Shanghai textbook
education: compulsory 39, 44, 102–3, 138–44, 149, 154, 168, 248; emotional and value-based 47, 137, 139, 143–5, 278; higher 91, 102, 105, 251; ideological 45; 'National' 85–6, 94–6, 99–100, 103–4, 110–11; peace 246–7, 258, 263; political 149, 241, 260; reform 118, 121–7, 130–1, 149, 155, 263
Egypt 107
Elmanjdra, Mahdi 176
Engels 39, 43
England 23, 35, 40, 67, 94, 102, 193, 260; Bill of Rights 47; (Glorious) revolution 40, 45–7 *see also* Britain; United Kingdom (UK)
Estonia 269
ethnocentrism 222, 232, 237
Eulsa Treaty 213 *see also* Japan–Korea Protectorate Treaty
Eurocentrism 36, 42
Europe: anthem 48; identity 15, 278; image 2, 16, 32, 45–51, 60, 278; as model 33, 36, 49, 51–2, 60, 62, 229–30; as term 35, 46
European: Community 48; Council 269–70; Union (EU) 16, 26, 48, 50–2, 241, 270, 278
'Europeanness' 51
Exclusive Economic Zones (EEZs) 208

'Far East' 16, 18, 21, 24
Far Eastern Affairs (Far Eastern Institute of the Soviet Academy of Sciences) 23–5
fascism 37, 41, 48, 229
Federation of Trade Unions 88

feudalism 35, 38–9, 42, 46
First International 39
First Sino–Japanese War 148, 155–6, 158,170, 233–4
First World War *see* World War I
forced prostitution 170, 184–6, 208 *see also* 'comfort women'
Formosa *see* Taiwan
Foucault, Michel 74, 77, 191
France 35, 40, 48–50, 52, 67, 73, 153, 194, 198, 269, 281; Declaration of Human Rights (the Rights of Man) 47, 65–6, 69; Paris Commune 40, 45; Revolution 35–6, 40, 45, 47, 71
Freud, Siegmund 77
Fujioka Nobukatsu 187
Fujisawa Hōei 235
Fujita Makoto 195
Fukuzawa Yukichi 77, 238–9; *Departure from Asia* 19

Galilei, Galileo 187
Gama, da 42
Gandhi 74
Ganghwa Treaty 170 *see also* Korean–Japanese Treaty of Amity
Gapsin *coup d'état* 170
Gaya *see* Mimana
Gaza Intervention 259
General Headquarters (GHQ) 164, 200, 231
German Army Exhibition 240
German Second Empire 229
Germany (West) 23, 37, 40, 48–9, 52, 73, 153, 157, 176, 201, **229–32**, 235–6, 238, 240–1, 251, 266, 271
globalisation 28, 49–50, 64, 86, **108**, 117–18, 122, 144, 160, 247
Gluck, Carol 177, 193
Goguryeo *see* Koguryŏ
Goldhagen, Daniel: *Hitler's willing executioners* 240
Gorbachev 24
Gordon, Andrew 176
'Greater Asianism' *see* Japan; Sun Zhongshan (Sun Yat-sen)
Greece 38, 74–6, 144–5
group of Socialism International 1914–1923, A (Nishikawa) 239
Guam 198
Guangdong 96, 150
Guernica (Picasso) 193

Han City (Han Cheng) 20 *see also* Seoul
Han Wudi 41
Hanayama Shinshō 190
Hara Masato 191

Hara shobō 167, 170, 172
Higashikuni no miya, Prince (Higashikuni Naruhiko) 157
Higashinakano Shūdō 190
Higurashi Yoshinobu 201
Hiratsuka Raichō 77
Hirohito, Emperor (Tennō) 157–8, 160, 183–4, 195, 197, 199–200
Hiroshima 188; Teachers and Education Workers' Union 220
Hirota Kōki 198
historiography 36, 44–5, 62, 123, 140, 148–9, 177, 197, 201
history: ancient 39, 42, 44, 140, 217, 220; Chinese 17–18, 34, **36–9, 41–4**, 52, 85, 98–99, 101–2, 107, 109–10, 123, 127, 137, **140–5**, 148–9; class 34, 45, 48, 52; contemporary 26, 120, 122, 140, 168, 170, 176, 178, 217, 268; cultural 36, 120, 124, 149; early modern 35, 47, 217, 219; European 5, 33, 39, 45, 60, 62, 230, 238–9, 269; foreign 33–4, 36–8, 140, 277; German 4, 229–30, 238–40; Japanese **163–6**, 168, 170–1, 172, 174, **176–8**, 183, 220, 233, 235–6, 239, 279; Korean 172, 207–8, 214, 219–22; modern 15, 40, 47, 52, 101, 140, 159, 184, 207, 218, 222, **229–31, 238–40**; national 1, 5, **143–5**, 147, 164, 218, 220, 229, 233, 236–7, 239–40, 269, 281; Oriental 233, 239–40; political 123–4, 149, 269; socio-economic 124, 149, 165; 'victimisation' 34, 219; Western 34, 51, 233, 239–40
Hitler, Adolf 41, 68, 190
Hitler-Stalin Pact 256 *see also* non-aggression pact
Hitler's willing executioners (Goldhagen) 240
Ho Chi Minh City *see* Saigon
Hobsbawm 111
Hokkaido 175
Holocaust 68
Hong Kong 2, 6, 49–50, 85–112, 117, 198, 278; 'Basic Law' 86, 88, 109; Commission on Strategic Development 100, 110; cultural policy 86–7, 92, 96, 100; democratisation 86–8, 90; 'liberal studies' 87, 97, 100, 102–3, 107–9; 'National/patriotic Education' 2, 85–7, 94–96, 98–101, 103–4, 110–12, 278 (*see also* China: 'Citizenship Education'); 'One Country – Two Systems' 87–8, 94, 110; Patten governorship 87; Permanent Secretary for Education 90–1, 95; (post-) retrocession 2, 85, 87, 90, 93–5, **97–100**, 102–3, 105, 109–10, 112, 278; reunification 97, 100; textbooks 85, 89, 97, 100–1, 103, 106–9

'Hongkongeseness' 92, 105
Hosokawa Morihiro 169, 172
Hu Jintao 100
Huang Hsiu-cheng 120, 127
humanism 35, 139, 141

Ienaga Saburō 166–7, 231
Imo Mutiny 170
imperialism 36, 38–9, 43–4, 51, 152, 157, 200, 211
India 10, 23, 38, 40, 47, 75, 77, 107, 124, 148, 176, 198
Indonesia 42, 50, 107, 200
International Law 188, 191, 201
International Military Tribunal for the Far East (IMTFE) 159, 189, 197 *see also* Tokyo Trial *and* Tokyo Tribunal
International Prosecution Section (IPS) 199
Internet 64, 193, 249, 266
Introduction to Japanese History, An (Aoki) 171
Iraq War 50, 210
Islam 38, 69, 75–6
Israel 252, 258–9, 281
Itagaki Seishirō 198
Italy 35, 37, 39, 42, 49–50, 73

Jakarta *see* Batavia
Japan: aggression **40**, 155, 158, 174, 193, 198, 200–1, 209, 212, 229, 231–2, 237, 239, 250; Army/military (Imperial) 60, 148, 151–2, 159, **170–4**, 183, 186, 188, 190–1, 193, 195–7, 200, 234, 250; 'Asianism' 16, 27, 111, 176; atrocities 48, 60, 148, 152, 159, 189, 198, 200–1; 'bubble economy' 171, 183; civics and ethics textbooks 2, 60–81, 278; colonial rule 12, **120–3**, 128–30, 152, 155, 160, 166, 169–70, **172–3**, 199–200, 208–10, 212–14, 229, 232, 237, 239; constitution 67, 70, 72, 153, 156, 163, 166–7, 172, 215; debate on conquering Korea 170, 216; democratic reforms 147, 152; discourses on 79–81, 278; Freedom and People's Rights Movement 70, 170; Fundamental Law of Education 163, 166, 196; 'Greater (East) Asia War' 200, 216; 'Greater Asianism' 19; 'Greater East Asian co-Prosperity Sphere' 16, 19, 158, 171, 271; history textbooks 3, 60–2, 71, 79, 158, **163–78**, 185–6, **207–23**, **230–41**, 278; invasion 14, 104, 147–8, 152, **156–9**, 166, 169, 173, 200, 209, 212, 232; Meiji Restoration 12, 47, 147–8, 152–5, 158, 175; Ministry of Education (MOE, MEXT) 63–4, 155, **164–8**, 172, 210, 213–15, 217–18, 231–2, 234–5; 'moral training' 164; national learning 74; 'neighbouring countries clause' 167; Samurai 155, 194–6; San Francisco Treaty 200; school board 164, 166; School Education Act 165; Shintō 184, 199, 212; Shōwa 157, 183; '(history) textbook problem' 165, 167, 200, 229, 231–2, 280; Tokugawa era 175, 216; unconditional surrender 157, 184, 213; Yasukuni Shrine issue 13, 159, 199, 208–14; Yūshūkan 212; *zaibatsu* 170, 200
Japan–China Joint Declaration 173
Japan–Korea Annexation Treaty 173, 210
Japan–Korea Protectorate Treaty 213 *see also* Eulsa Treaty
Japan–North Korea Pyongyang Declaration 210
Japan–Republic of Korea Joint Declaration 173
Japan–Republic of Korea Treaty on Basic Relations 170 *see also* Korea–Japan Treaty on Basic Relations
Japanese Society for History Textbook Reform 61, 158, 178, 183, 185, 235 *see also Tsukurukai*
Japanese and South Korean Joint Study Group on History Textbooks (JSG) 235 *see also* joint international committees and initiatives: Association of History Education Researchers (of Japan) and Association of History Textbook Researchers (of Korea)
'Japaneseness' 81, 192
Japanisation 170
Jews 68, 240, 252, 258
Jiang Zemin 44
Jiang Zhongzheng *see* Chiang Kai-shek
Jin 33, 144
joint international committees and initiatives: Association of History Education Researchers (of Japan) and Association of History Textbook Researchers (of Korea) 219 *see also* Japanese and South Korean Joint Study Group on History Textbooks (JSG); Association of Japan–Korea History Education-related Exchanges (of Japan) and Association for Korea–Japan History Education-related Exchanges (of Korea) 220; Baltic 269, 281; Bosnia and Herzegovina 256; Committee on History Education-related Materials for Joint Use in Korea, Japan and China 221 (*see also* Trilateral Joint History Editorial Committee of Japan, China and South Korea); Euroclio project 269; first committee of common history research between Japan and South Korea 238; Franco–German Youth Office 268; German–French Textbook Commission

261, 264, 268, 281; German–French Youth Exchange Programme 268; German International Textbook Institute 252; German–Polish Commission 252, 255, 261, 264, 266, 281; Georg Eckert Institute 263, 267; Israel–Palestine 252, 258–9, 281; Korea–Japan Commission for the Joint Study of History 215, 217–18; Korea–Japan Joint Commission for the Promotion of the Study of History 218; Study Group for Comparative History and Comparative History Education (SGCHCHE) 232–4, 237, 240; Trilateral Joint History Editorial Committee of Japan, China and South Korea 237
Judaism 76

Kalimantan *see* Borneo
Kangxi 41
Kant 74
Keenan, Joseph 198
Khabarovsk *see* Chabarovsk
Kim Dae-jung 209, 213
Kim Young-sam 172
Kimura Heitarō 198
King, Martin Luther 74
Kishi Nobusuke 157
Kōbunken 169
Koguryŏ 20, 271
Koizumi Jun'ichirō 207, 209–14, 217
Koizumi Takashi: *Best wishes for tomorrow* 184, 191–3
Kokusho kankōkai 167, 170, 172
Kondō Takahiro 238
Korea: Joseon 216, 220; March First Independence Movement 149, 170, 173, 211; peninsula 11–12, 15, 17, 19–20, 26, 76, 214, 216, 222; Righteous Armies 170; War 17, 20, 22–3, 38, 40, 170 *see also* North Korea; South Korea
Korea–Japan Friendship Year 213
Korea–Japan Treaty on Basic Relations 210, 213 *see also* Japan–Republic of Korea Treaty on Basic Relations
Korean–Japanese Bishops' Association 221
Korean–Japanese Treaty of Amity 170 *see also* Ganghwa Treaty
Kosovo 49–50
Kroran *see* Loulan
Kurosawa Akira 191
Kwajalein Atoll 198
Kyōiku shuppan 73–4, 76, 78

Lacan 192
Lai, Jimmy 89
Latin America 18–19, 23, 49, 121, 148

Latvia 269
Law (Fan Chiu Fan), Fanny 91, 95
League of Nations 246
Lee, Bruce (Li Xiaolong) 99, 104
Lee Ching-hua 120
Lee Chu-ming, Martin 89–90
Lee Teng-hui 120, 122, 128
Lee Yeon Suk 176
Lee Yuan-tse 126
Legalism 43, 149
Lenin 39, 43
Li Hongzhang 156
Liancourt Rocks *see* Dokdo *and* Takeshima
Liao 33
Liberal International 97
lifelong learning 138
Lin Biao 43
Lin Boqu 156
Lin Zexu 113
Lincoln 41
Lithuania 269
Liu Shaoqi 43
Locke, John 65, 68
Louis XIV 40
Loulan 142
Luther 74
Luxembourg 49

Ma Ying-jeou 122
MacArthur, Douglas 164, 198 *see also* Supreme Commander of the Allied Powers (SCAP)
Magellan 42
Malaysia 50, 198, 200
Manchu State *see* Manzhouguo
Manchukuo *see* Manzhouguo
Manchuria 151–2, 200
Manchus 33–4
Mandarin *see* Putonghua
manga 184
Manila 198–9
Manzhouguo 152
Mao Zedong 43, 92; era 19, 45, 92, 104; 'Leaning to one side' 18
Maoism 41, 43–4, 149
Maruyama Masao 77
Marx, Karl 39, 43
Marxism 43–7, 51, 201
Matsui Iwane 189–90, 198
Meiseisha 167, 170, 172
memory 60–1, 121, 131, 185–6, 194, 209, 256; collective 117, 186, 197; folk 86; historical 13, 149; national 1; vernacular 193, 196; war 12–15, 194
Mesopotamia 107
Meyer, Enno 241

Middle East 176, 259, 263
Mimana 216
Miyazawa Kiichi 167, 171–2
Mizushima Satoru 184, 186–91; *The truth of Nanking* 184, 186–93, 197
Mommsen, Hans 190
Mongolia/Mongolian People's Republic 17, 21
Mongols 33, 35, 37–8 *see also* 'Yuan'
Montesquieu, Baron de 40, 65, 68
Morris-Suzuki, Tessa 176
multinational education materials: *Baltic history textbook* 269; *A comparison of Korean and Japanese history* 220; German–French history textbook 52, 236–7, 241, 267–9, 270, 279; German–Polish history textbook 4, 229–41, 251, 256, 261, 267, 280; *History that opens the future* 9, 13, 148, 159–60, 169–70, 221, 237, 270, 279–81; *History education material for joint use in Korea and Japan* 220, 235–7
Murayama Tomiichi 171, 173, 185, 208–9, 215
Mutō Akira 198
Myanmar *see* Burma
Myeongseong, Empress of Korea 213

Nagoya 191, 193
Nakae Chōmin 77
Nakasone Yasuhiro 199, 211
Nanking: 'campaign' 186–7; Incident 159, 186; Massacre 14, 148, 152, 159, 184–93, 197; International Court 191; Military Court 159
Napoleon 40, 47
National Socialism 157
NATO 49
Natsume Sōseki 74, 77
Nazi 157, 240
Nehru 23
neo-nationalism 2, 62, 184, 195–6, 201 *see also* revisionism
Netherlands 49, 198
New Guinea 198
New Japan–Korea Partnership towards the Twenty-first Century 209–10, 213, 215
New Zealand 198
newly industrialised countries (NICs) 121
NGOs 186, 246, 250, 253, 255, 259, 261–4, 266–7, 270
NICT 121, 126
Nishida Kitarō 74
Nishikawa Masao 229–34, 238–41, 280; *World War I and the Socialists* 239; *A group of Socialism International 1914–1923* 239

Nishimura Shingo 191
non-aggression pact 40–1 *see also* Hitler-Stalin Pact
Non-Aligned Movement (NAM) 18
Northeast Asian History Association 3
North Korea 9, 15, 17, 25, 27, 38, 210, 222, 232 *see also* Democratic People's Republic of Korea; Korea
Nuremberg Trial 201

Obuchi Keizō 209, 213
Ode to Joy (Beethoven) 48
Official Development Assistance (ODA) 147, 159
Okada Haruko 192
Okada Tasuku 191–6
Okakura Kakuzō (alias Okakura Tenshin) 19
Okinawa 174–5, 185
Olympic Games 85, 89, 94–7, 100, 104, 187
Ōsaka: Incident 170; shoseki 65

Palestine 252, 258–9, 281; National Authority 258
Pascal 74
Peace Research Institute in the Middle East (PRIME) 259–60, 264
Pearl Harbor 189, 200
Peking *see* Beijing
People's Education Press (PEP): textbooks 48–51, 137, 139–40, 149–50
People's Press 139, 150
People's Republic of China (PRC) 3, **38**, 40–1, 43, 46–7, 51–2, 73, 86, 95, 98, 110–11, 151, 159, 198–9 *see also* China
Persia 40, 46
Peter the Great 40–1
Philippines 50, 198
Picasso: *Guernica* 193
Plato 74
Poland 4, **229–44**, 251–2, 255–6, 261, 264, 266–7, 280–1; Pedagogical Institute 252
political socialisation 1–2, 4, 100, 110, 112, 121
Polo, Marco 46
POWs 191–2
Prussian Constitution 153
Pugachev 40
Putonghua 94, 102, 105

Qi Jiguang 144
Qin Shihuangdi 41
'Queen of Jhansi' 47, 55

Rani Lakshmibai *see* 'Queen of Jhansi'
Renaissance 35, 38, 47, 76

Republic of China (ROC) 121–2, 128–9, 198 see also Taiwan
Republic of Korea (ROK) 167, 170, 173 see also South Korea
revisionism: historical 117, 183, 185, 191, 197, 201, 207, 229, 271 see also neo-nationalism
Roh Moo-hyun 207, 209, 211–13, 217
Roh Tae-Woo 171–2
Rome 38, 144–5
Rousseau, Jean-Jacques 40, 65, 68
Russia 10, 20, 25, 27, 40, 47, 49, 51, 153, 158, 216, 256; (October) Revolution 36

Said, Edward 15
Saigon 198
Sakhalin 208
Sankei shinbun 192
SARS 88
Sartre 74
Second: International 239; Sino–Japanese War 156, 158, 184, 189–90; World War 67, 245 see also World War II
Seifert, Wolfgang 176
Seitz, Klaus 245
Senkakuji islands 88 see also Diaoyutai islands
Seo Jŭngmin 271
Seoul 20, 219; City University 236 see also Han City (Han Cheng)
Serbs 256
Shanghai 3, 86, 98, 111–12, 151, 160, 198, 279; Cooperation Organisation (SCO) 25; Education Press 140, 150; 'educational experimental zone' 149; textbook 48–51, 147, 150, 153–7
Shenzhen 142
Shimizu shoin 65, 67–8, 75
Shimonoseki: Treaty 156
Shiroi Shigeru 190
Shiu Shin-poor 87
Shoah see Holocaust
Siberia 216
Sichuan Education Press: textbook 48, 50–1
Silk Road 76
Singapore 14, 49–50, 107, 198
'Sinocentrism' 17–18, 42, 128, 214, 216
Sinti and Romani 240
'Six-Party Talks' 25
social Darwinism 33
socialism 11, 24, 39, 41, 45, 108, 110
socialist 38, 40–1, 43, **107–10**, 141, 239, 246, 256, 267; bloc 17, 22, 24–5; countries 22, 44, 139
Socrates 74
Solon 41

South Korea 9–10, **12–15**, 17, 19–20, 26–7, 49–50, 52, 62, 159–60, 167, **169–72**, 176, 230, 232–3, **235–9**, 277; Ministry of Foreign Affairs and Trade (MOFAT) 212 see also Republic of Korea (ROK)
Soviet Union (SU) 18, 23–4, 33, **38–45**, 47–8, 51, 198–9, 208, 216, 246, 256, 269; New Economic Policy (NEP) 40 see also Union of Soviet Socialist Republics (USSR)
Spain 23, 35
Stalin 40, 256
Sugamo Prison 190, 197–9
Sumatra 198
Sun Zhongshan (Sun Yat-sen) 98–9; 'Greater Asianism' 16–17
Supreme Commander of the Allied Powers (SCAP) 164, 198–200 see also MacArthur, Douglas
Switzerland 73

Taipei 198
Taiwan 228 Incident 117, 124, 129; Academia Sinica 118, 124, 126; decolonisation 118, 121–2; democratisation 117, 122, 126, 129, 131; 'de-Sinicisation' 120, 128–9; education reform 117–18, 121, 126, 130–1; history textbooks 117–131; identity 117–18, 121–2, 127, 130; independence 21, 93, 120, 122–3, 234; indigenisation movement 118, 122, 126; Institute of Compilation and Translation 119, 127; Institute of Taiwan History (ITH) 118, 124; *Knowing Taiwan* 117–22, 126–31, 278; (post-) martial law 117–18, 122–3, 126, 130–1; Ministry of Education 118, 127; reunification 21, 122; Zheng era 125, 128 see also Republic of China (ROC)
Takeshima 207, 210–11, 271 see also Dokdo
Tang Taizong 41
Tankha, Brij 176
teacher: education and training 100, 103, 164, 249, 262, 264, 266–7
Teikoku shoin 65
Ten Commandments 66
Thailand 50, 200
'Third World' 18–19, 23, 39, 43, 50
Tiananmen (Square Massacre) 87, 95, 106
Tibetans 107
Tōgō Shigenori 189
Tōjō Hideki 198
Tokyo: District Court 166; shoseki 65, 67, 70, 73, 75–6, 80–1, 174; Trial 3, 160, 183–5, 186–7, 188–9, 193, **197–201**, 280; Tribunal 197, 212 see also International Military Tribunal for the Far East (IMTFE)

truth of Nanking, The (Mizushima) 184, 186–93, 197
Tsukurukai **60–3**, **65**, **69–71**, 79, 158–9, 172, 174, 183, **185**, 187, 210, 213–15, 217, 235, 237 *see also* Japanese Society for History Textbook Reform
Tu Cheng-sheng 120, 130
Tung, Chee –Hwa 86, 99
Turkey 40

Uchimura Kanzō 74
Umezu Yoshijirō 189
UNESCO 4, 246, 252, 281; Textbook Committee 241
Union of Soviet Socialist Republics (USSR) 15, 17–18, 22–6; Communist Party 23 *see also* Soviet Union (SU)
United Kingdom (UK) 73, 198 *see also* Britain; England
United Nations 23, 121: Human Rights Committee 49; Security Council 157
United States of America (USA): 9/11 issue 50; Army 199; hegemony 45, 49–51; human rights reports 49, imperialism 43; (Declaration of) independence 47, 66, 69; military bases 15, 20, 25; Military Law 191–2; revolution 35
Uyghurs 107

Versailles Conference 36
Vietnam 14, 21, 40, 233–4
views of war of the Japanese, The (Yoshida Yutaka) 193
Voltaire 40

Wang Chung-fu 120
Wang Hsiao-po 120
Wang Jingwei 151
Wang Side 154
war: accounts 193, 195; Asia(n)–Pacific 60, 185, 214, 216; civil 92, 104, 121, 246–7, 253, 281; crimes 60, 184, 189, 197–9; criminals 3, 157, 186, 188–9, 191, **198–9**, 212, 280; Fifteen Years 169, 174; Greco–Persian 46; guilt 157, 189; Gulf 50, 176; of ideologies 22; interstate 246; Iraq 50, 210; Kosovo 49–50; Lebanon 259; lords 246; Okinawan 174–5, 185; Pacific 158, 189, 200, 208, 213; responsibility 12, 14, 157–8, 171, 173, 185, 189, **191–7**, 199–201, 214, 234; Russo–Japanese 158, 216; Sino–France 234; textbook 278, 280
warfare 193, 259; biological 13, 160; ideological 246
Washington 47
Watsuji Tetsurō 74, 80
Webb, William 198
Wen Tianxiang 144
Western: civilisation 153, 155, 216; countries 41, 139, 145, 219; culture 147; Europe 1, 15–16, 20, 28, 35, 39, 46, 48–50, 70; history 34, 51, 233, 239–40; learning 27–8, 156; science 44, 156; thought 77
world: Bank 246; Cup 97, 210; Health Organization (WHO) 97; 'Third' 18–19, 23, 39, 43, 50; Trade Organization (WTO) 49–51, 97, 108
World War I 35–6, 239, 246, 250, 253, 267
World War I and the Socialists (Nishikawa) 239
World War II 14, 17, 19–20, 22–**3**, 26, 40–1, 43–4, 48, 52, 68, 121–2, 129, 147, 152, 157, 163, 172, 175, 183, 196–7, 208, 211, 230, 232, 234, **239–41**, 246–7, 249, 253, 256, 279–80 *see also* Second World War
Wu Wen-hsing 120

Yamakawa shuppan 73, 77–8
Yamashita Tomoyuki 199
Yanagita Kunio 77
Yang Daqing 271
Yang Liwei 94–5, 97
Yokohama 174, 191, 198
Yoshida Gorō 232
Yoshida Yutaka 193, 195–7, 200: *The views of war of the Japanese* 193
Yoshimi Yoshiaki 234
Yoshino Sakuzō 77
'Yuan' 37–8 *see also* Mongols
Yuanmingyuan 95
Yue Fei 144
Yuelu Press/Publishing House 140, 150
Yugoslavia: Federation 49; Socialist 267

Zheng Chenggong 144
Zheng He 42, 98
Zhonghua Publishing House 139
Zhou Enlai 18

CPSIA information can be obtained
at www.ICGtesting.com
Printed in the USA
JSHW011319201219
3107JS00002B/36